Sacred H[umanity]
Arising W[ithin]

Ascension Through Integrating Your Emotional Body
With Your Spirituality

Jelelle Awen

Copyright © 2017 Jelelle Awen
First Edition
   The author hopes the information in this book will be shared with everyone. Therefore parts of this book may be reproduced and shared without the permission of the author, so long as the information is freely given and the source is acknowledged. No parts of this book may be reproduced for profit without the prior written permission of the author. Send any such requests for permission to soulfullhearts@gmail.com.

   www.soulfullheartwayoflife.com

ISBN: 9781521284346

About The Author:

Jelelle Awen is an Emoto-Spiritual Teacher, Sacred Feminine and Sacred Union Facilitator, Soul Scribe, WaySHOWer, Galactic Love Ambassador, and co-creator/teacher/facilitator/community leader of the SoulFullHeart Way Of Life. She has been on a personal soul awakening and emotional body healing journey for 15+ years, as she has been called to hold space for others and serve love.

She is author of *Keep Waking Up!*, available on amazon.com. Visit soulfullheartwayoflife.com for more information about space holding sessions, group calls, videos, community, writings, and much more. Visit soulfullheartblog.com for daily writings from Jelelle about ascension, awakening, spirituality, parts work, sacred feminine, sacred union, becoming the 5D sacred human, and more. Contact her at soulfullhearts@gmail.com and follow her on Facebook at facebook.com/jelelleawen.

Appreciations

I feel such gratitude for my soul mate, beloved counterpart, co-creator of SoulFullHeart - our healing offering and community, and truly a LIFE partner Raphael Awen for his continual support and reflection of my Higher Self back to me. I do believe he has read every word that I have written in the last nine years... quite a feat! SO many of these writings flowed out of meaningful, vulnerable, often meaty metaphysical conversations with him for which these words were the digestion of all that yumminess and stimulation on ALL levels. And, yes, some of these words WERE written in afterglow... I leave it to you to figure out which ones!

And, so many thank yous to my DEEP soul friend and supporter Gabriel Heartman, who I have had so many chapters of life with! A phase as mates, a phase as friends, a phase as co-parents, a phase as his teacher, a phase now as peers and deep soul friends offering a beloved path and community together... and each phase such a blessed and sacred experience!

Kalayna Colibri has been the feminine 'YES!' in my life, offering the female resonance I've needed in moments of self doubt or question about what I was writing or putting out there. Her courage to go within and to SHOW UP in relationship with me as it shifts between teacher-student and friends has been so inspiring.

Beyond 'daughter' as any kind of role, Shai Tydeman is a reflection of light and how love between souls arises beyond any roles or definitions. I have to say that making her cry from being touched by my writing is one of my favorite things!

Thank you to all of the souls who have taken in and resonated with my writing since I began sharing it on my blog, Soulfullheartblog.com, in 2012. I have been especially touched and inspired by the support of those on Facebook and YouTube (on the recorded writings) since July, 2016 and those who have given so many 'hearts' and 'thumbs' and comments to these words over the months. ALL of this support fuelled my creative inspiration, motivated my muse to write and share more, and helped to heal many years of NOT being seen or read by hardly anyone other than my closest beloveds.

Also thank you to the beautiful and courageous women whom I am blessed to serve love with and co-create with in session space and during group calls! I learn so much from every session that I am honored to lead and participate in, much of which then flowed into the writings in this book!

I also feel such appreciation for Gregg Prescott, editor of in5D.com, who published many of the writings in this book on his popular website. His openness and desire to share writers and Spiritual Teachers with a larger audience has drawn much goodness and resonance to me and to my offering of SoulFullHeart. I also appreciate the other places on the web such as lovehaswon.org for which some of these writings have been shared, often without me even submitting them!

AND TO YOU… who are reading this NOW, in this moment of NOWness… thank you for taking these words into your heart and soul… finding resonance, finding your 'Yes!' which expands and grows mine! Many thank yous and appreciation to you from my heart to YOURS.

Contents

Prologue: Nonlinear Process And This Book	11
The Big Picture: Ascension Of The 5D Sacred Human	17
Emotional Area Of Life	91
Spiritual Area Of Life	155
Mental Area Of Life	243
Social Area Of Life	263
Physical Area Of Life	313
Financial Area Of Life	341
Environmental Area Of Life	357
Sacred Feminine	379
This And That About Love	401

You'll find me rooted in Gaia...
Riding the waves of Her sea, floating in Her waters, walking on Her soil, resting near Her trees.
You'll find me shining in the Sun...
Illuminating the shadows that are hidden, activating codes Of suppressed magic, warming limbs and hearts and minds.
You'll find me drifting in the Stars.....
Floating by the Moon, riding the rings of Saturn, visiting the stars Of my soul's origins.
You'll find me soaring in the Heavens....
Vibrating in the highest frequencies, climbing the greatest Heights, resting on the clouds.
You'll find me in the blending of both....
Reaching up and extending down, creating a column of LOVE, Moving the stardust LIGHT through the deepest inner caverns of Gaia.
You'll find me in conscious duality....
Becoming Sacred Human, merging with ALL while in Celebration of the edges of polarity's dance.
You'll find me in the Love.....
Letting in, receiving, serving love WITH you, becoming One yet Not the same.
You'll find me in your heart......
Remembering that we were never lost, never separated, And awakening once again… re-emerging
AS THE LOVE THAT WE ARE….

~ Jelelle Awen

Prologue: Nonlinear Process And This 'Book'

This is a nonlinear process, this awakening and remembering and ascending. It is a spiral, deepening, going ever deeper into the places inside that are sleepy and numb and buried and layered over. There isn't a straight line to follow, a step-by-step protocol that can be undertaken to reach the end. Because there is no end, only infinite possibilities opening up and up and up.

Linear time and tracking of it is the 3D Self, conditioned to measure in seconds, then minutes, then hours, then days, and so on. This tracking of each moment in this way dulls it down in terms of how you can actually experience it. True experience of the moment, especially through our emotional body and our heart, expands out and then contracts too. It is not a tick in time like a clock offers; it is an invitation to experience and to be in simultaneous frequencies of NOWness.

This writing here in what is called a 'book' is nonlinear. It is written and offered in passages and in moments of creative inspiration that moved through me. The ones that most call you may be 50 pages from now and NOT right now or the one that is 'after' this one. You'll find what you need to most take in, in the moment. Or rather, it will find YOU. Maybe you will pick places at 'random' and see what you are guided to take in that would be most relevant to you in the moment. Maybe you will start from the 'end' and work your way back to the 'beginning.' Allow yourself to dip into what comes in the moment, not because I have offered it one after the other, but because it is where you are called to go.

There are larger themes that I've gathered together to create some chapters and some structure. The main form of this is through the seven key areas of life that we look at through the awakening and healing process that I offer called the SoulFullHeart Way Of Life and they are: emotional, spiritual, mental, social, physical, financial, and environmental. It was challenging at times to delineate this writing into just one area of life, yet the main theme is usually clear. Plus, I've included at the end a section that is about sacred femininity and 'this and that about love' writings, mostly poetry.

You may experience this book as similar to a spiral, a curve and a turn bringing you to one place... another one bringing you somewhere deeper. Many concepts are introduced more than once, yet usually from a new angle or direction or expanded place. I have practiced this kind of writing, sharing these bursts of words during inspired moments, through my blog and posting on social media, especially through Facebook, which I didn't feel resonant with for a long time. The resistance to be on Facebook was a hesitancy to dip my frequency down and for a long time I was impacted so much by energy from what felt like 'outside' that I allowed myself to be influenced in this way.

Now, I see that I can offer from where I am at in MY vibrational frequency and invite others into it through my sharings in written form. Those who are resonant with me will find the writings and those who are not, will not. I discovered that sharing these writings right after they came through me really encouraged and inspired my Divinely gifted inspiration or 'Awen' (hence, the last name that choose me and my beloved Raphael) to move through me to create more and more. Most of these writings were written between January 1, 2017 and May 1, 2017...a very prolifically creative time for me during which I wrote every day and then posted and shared it publically.

Many of the writings in this 'book' were originally shared on Facebook, on my blog, and gratefully on in5D.com, lovehaswon.org and other 'watering holes for awakening souls on the Internet'. I have edited the writings and expanded many of them for this book. Gathering these writings together here allows them space to be unified and not scattered everywhere. It is like creating a pool for you to swim in by gathering the flows and streams into one container.

Because the writings are created in the moment from where I am at in that moment, there is not one voice or perspective but rather many perspectives. Sometimes there is a strong teacher energy that comes through and sometimes there is a student. Sometimes there is the voice and energy of an Archangel aspect, such as Metatron, and sometimes there is my Higher Self speaking of what it remembers and is integrating as soul wisdom. Sometimes there is writing from a 'you' voice and sometimes it is 'we' and sometimes it is 'I.'

This is a new way of experiencing a 'book', yes, and it invites you into a nonlinear place of movement and flow. This is the way I find that creativity most comes, from the right side of the brain, through the heart, more like how energy flows through our bodies in surges and waves. Things being plotted out is limiting, chapters are limiting, even one word after another is limiting yet until we are all awakened to remember nonlinear language, it is what we have to use to share and communicate together.

See if you can feel beyond the one word after another and the structure of a 'book.' There are meditations here to bring you into feeling spaces and to facilitate inner journeys. You'll come across them when they fit with where you are at and where they are needed. There is no right or wrong way to do them as they are only a launching place of self permission that is coming seemingly from me but is actually what you are needing to see about YOU in the moment from your Higher Self.

If we could create every word together in collaboration, that would be a more fifth dimensional experience of exchange through this medium of words. In the energetic sense, felt through energy exchange, we ARE collaborating together. Your taking in of these words and the energy for which they are offered is a form of collaboration with me, even if it is not in the same moment. These words are already past for me even as they are present for you, in this moment, as you take them in. Although, because there is no time and no past or future in fifth dimensional consciousness, we are in the moment together exchanging energy through sharing and receiving.

When I get comments and appreciations of my writing, I almost always thank the person for taking in the energy expressed through my words into their hearts and souls. The taking in of the energy is what allows my own remembering and waking up process to continue and grow. Their resonance or 'reSOULnance' as I like to call it, is what CREATES the reality of whatever I am expressing and sharing about, both for them AND for me. Sharing what I feel in the moment, whatever the arising truth of my experience is, and feeling it being received, also allows me to expand more into my Higher Self and my essence expression as both teacher AND student.

I can thank you already for taking these words and the energy for which I offer them into your heart and your soul. I do not need to thank you only 'after' you have read this whole 'book' as you might never need to go that far or that deep. I can thank you for the moment and feel the exchange of collaboration that is happening between us. From my inner flow of creativity reaches out a desire to connect with yours and to ignite an alchemy between us that may just stay in this form or may move into a form of deeper connection and relationship.

I teach many times in this book about the way of life and process that I personally follow and offer to others in session space holding called the SoulFullHeart Way Of Life. SoulFullHeart is another word for 'service of love' and a process for the embodiment of the 'new Sacred Human' who is full with love in both expressions of the heart and of the soul. I have been co-creating SoulFullHeart as an emotional, spiritual, and physical healing path, way of life, and community in one form or another since 2010 with Raphael, holding space for others to experience this process mostly through sessions and group circles.

If you are drawn to experience a space holding session with me (for women) or another SoulFullHeart facilitator, join me and my beloved Raphael Awen for our group calls, or to come visit us here in Puerto Vallarta, Mexico for an immersion retreat, please visit soulfullheartwayoflife.com for more information.

With much love and blessings on your sacred journey of becoming a Sacred Human,

Jelelle

May, 2017 Puerto Vallarta, Mexico

~

THE BIG PICTURE: ASCENSION OF THE 5D SACRED HUMAN

You ARE a Sacred Human. You ARE an arising wonder. You ARE Infinite Possibilities. You ARE Infinite Awareness. You ARE Infinite Love.

You are invited to remember that you ARE infinite love and to go on a journey to remember this. It is an inner journey of awakening, feeling, healing, ascending, and loving. It is an inner journey of exploration and discovery. It is an inner journey to embody your Sacred Humanity.

It is a journey of reunion with aspects of yourself that you may have forgotten, buried, or suppressed in your psyche or emotional pain body. Aspects that live in the stars. Aspects that live in other dimensions and parallel universes. Aspects that live in the higher, angelic realms.

It is a journey of remembering lifetimes in which aspects of your soul still live, are still being energized, and can be connected with in the moment. Aspects that are part of your Metasoul origination energy, fractals from your soul genesis group.

It is a journey of remembering that which you *are* and letting go of that which you are *not*. It is remembering that you are Infinite Love and anything LESS in your expression is something else for which you are NOT.

It is a journey of loving even that which is NOT love inside of your heart and inside of your soul and, even, inside of the Universe that is within you. Responding with love to anything that is not love invites the possibility that it can become love. Responding to fear WITH love is what heals the fear.

This is the journey for which you are here in this moment in this lifetime on this planetary consciousness known as Gaia. You have chosen as a soul to undergo this journey and it was held with great sacredness and opportunity by your Higher Self and the Divine Source for which ALL originates from and eventually returns.

It is a journey of remembering that as YOU are Infinite Love, so is EVERYONE ELSE. Every soul. Not just some special, awakening souls, but EVERYONE. And, that as everyone is Infinite Love so is every soul connected to the other.

It is a journey of remembering that you are not just connected to every soul as Infinite Love, you are ONE with every soul. It is remembering that you originated from Divine Source along with everyone else.

It is a journey of loving even that which is *not* love within your connections with others. Responding with love to anything that is not love in your connections with others allows you to feel the mirror that these others offer to you of yourself. Learning to set boundaries with others while still holding love in your heart becomes another opportunity to experience your true essence coming forward in Sacred Human expression.

It is a journey of remembering that you are powerful, that your thoughts are powerful, that your energy shapes the Universe within you and extends then to what you experience outside of you.

It is a journey of remembering your heart-based power, your soul-expressed power, your gifted power as offered to you by the Divine Source of All That Is. No soul can take away this power as it is connected to the Infinite Love essence that you ARE. Remembering that no soul can take away your power and to respond with love even when it feels to you as if this is happening is an opportunity for self healing.

It is a journey of remembering that your self, your self love, your self care, your self knowing, are the most important aspects of determining how much you experience yourself AND others as Infinite Love.

Your sense of self AS love grows as you create a container space to experience it and to discover and feel the places inside of you that need your love. As you remember the parts of you that need your love and give them this love, your heart begins to overflow to others. It is from this place of self-loving overflow for which the most nourishing frequencies are available to others.

It is a journey of remembering that the love and care of self is the most important thing you can be, do, and ARE. Responding to parts of you that resist this self love and care with more love. Feeling their resistance as fear, unworthiness, disconnect, while loving that which has created these feelings inside of you. Remembering that you ARE worth, connection, and love in your essence.

It is a journey of ascending, raising your consciousness frequency UP from what you have been conditioned in most of your life within third dimensional (3D) reality. Ascension is remembering your higher consciousness, connecting with your Higher Self, and eventually becoming the version of yourself that vibrates at a high vibrational dimension and frequency, your Higher Self BECOMES you.

It is a journey of embodying your Higher Self in more and more frequencies of expression and experience. Ascension happens as you feel where your consciousness currently is, locating yourself with love, and opening up new possibilities for raising your awareness. Responding with love to that which is dense inside of you, not of your higher frequency, or not coming from your Higher Self, allowing for more ascension and embodiment.

It is a journey of identifying with love what your conditioning has been, both in this life and from other lifetimes, and what continues to lower your consciousness and vibrational frequency. Identifying and becoming aware allows you to engage in a process of deconditioning, healing layers and layers of programmed self to remember your authentic self as a fractal of the Divine.

It is a journey of seeking validation, from within and from sources of love outside of yourself. It is seeking support and templating for the new consciousness that you want to expand in yourself, the consciousness of your Higher Self, in order to water what feels like a seed in the beginning or a spark of the heart. Validation outside of yourself can come in many forms and as you connect more with your Higher Self, you can trust the forms that you draw and are drawn to as mirrors.

It is a journey of realizing that all resonant and nourishing outside sources of validation and support are mirrors of your bigness and of your essence. None of them are bigger, higher, or better than you. They represent who you ARE in your essence and who you will become more and more as you remember and embody your Higher Self.

It is a journey of letting go of that which does not validate and support your essence as Infinite Love as this new consciousness and awareness and awakening inside of yourself.

Letting go with love is an alchemical process with ups and downs, openings and closing downs and can be navigated with a sense of connection to ALL. Letting go with love allows for new space inside of you where love can come to you in new forms, new ways, and new connections. Responding with love to the parts of you that resist letting go allows for more trust as loving self-negotiation deepens and flows from your opening heart and awakening soul.

It is a journey of awakening to an expanded truth about the world, about the frequencies that influence and shape it, and a bigger context much beyond the Human perspective. Awakening to feel how you are made from star dust DNA and beings from the stars. Remembering how you are made from powerful lineages that offer so much support and validation of your galactic nature the more that you connect with and let them in. Responding with love to the parts of you that have fear in response to these star origins allows for more multi-dimensional openings and embracement of the light BEing that you ARE.

It is the journey that you have signed up for as a soul. You wouldn't be reading these words in this moment, taking in this energy of this invitation to you, unless you resonated on some level with this invitation. This invitation is from your Higher Self, who is waiting for you to raise your vibrational frequency so that it can eventually come into and merge with your consciousness.

This invitation is also from the Divine Source of Infinite Love and All That Is that both desire to be reunited with you and is getting great joy from your individual spark of consciousness and your adventures. This is 'conscious duality' where you experience both the wonderful aspects of duality's dance in difference and uniqueness, as well as that of merging into Oneness, feeling that there is only one, without any difference. Both are magically true at the same time!

This journey to become your Higher Self is a challenging one, made both more challenging and less challenging by the times that we are living in now. More and more others are feeling the same invitation to awaken, ascend, and remember. As each individual soul spark embraces this journey, the ALL is impacted by it. The ALL feels that you are remembering and remembers themselves to that much degree with you and as you become more of what you ARE as Infinite Love, then so they can too.

It is a sacred journey. It is a blessed journey, whatever the experiences may be, however challenging or difficult or painful. It is a guided journey with much support, even if you experience being lonely, isolated, or disconnected from others, your Higher Self, and Ethereal BEings as Guides.

This is a journey, yes, and, also, you already ARE all of this. There is nothing to be fixed or that is wrong with you as you ARE this already in your essence. This is the truth that your Higher Self knows as it remembers, as it already IS this. And so it IS.

~

Ascension Invitation

Ascension invites the stretching upward, the blooming and growing, the awakening and expanding. It is the remembering of what has been forgotten. It is the reclaiming of what has been disowned. It is the loving of what has been judged, both inside and toward others. It is the wanting of MORE from your soul and Higher Self, shifting away from the desire center of your 3D Self who wants comfort and safety and to keep life small and to fit in with others. It is the letting go and mourning and releasing of what no longer serves love and the expression of your Higher Self. It is holding space for all of the reactions that come up in the emotional body in response to this process of letting go.

Ascension invites the rising UP of your consciousness, your awareness, your perception of reality as it shifts from inside you. It is the "Ds" of both dimensions and density with the levels of third to fourth to fifth (and beyond) offering shifts and expansions in your experience of your inner world. Each dimensional shift in consciousness offers a new level of claim. It invites in change and transformation at both the practical and the transcendent levels, as what shifts inside starts to shift what you experience AS life on the outside.

Ascension is an invitation from the Universe and Divine Source to claim and embody what is your birthright as a Sacred Human expression in bodily form. It is to feel this birthright without expectation or entitlement, yet to understand that it is a GIFT from Divine Source offered to be experienced WITH you. It is the crystallizing of the physical body to vibrate higher and higher to become more and more your Merkabah, your vehicle of light and multidimensional travel. Holding space for this transition of the physical body is to trust the symptoms that move through are for the reason of this embodiment of your Merkabah.

Ascension invites you to feel what your heart most wants and cries for. What your MORE is that is flushed up and out through desires that come in through your soul. This invitation can press on you, yes, but it never forces. The press comes from your awakening soul and your healing heart. The press comes from your increasing desires for MORE… more intimacy, more connection, more joy, more bliss, more goodness, more service, more empowerment, more inner explorations, more LOVE.

Ascension invites you to feel how the MORE-ness arising inside you can be tamped down and dampened by aspects of you that are afraid for you to desire, want you to remain safe, try to keep you comfortable. These aspects of you, led by your most loyal Protector, are ever vigilant to keep the MORE at bay in whatever ways and means they can. They are like dams trying to block the flood of love that wants to surge through your life. These aspects of you can relax their efforts at blocking through connection with the arising soul-infused and authentic YOU.

Ascension is the more and more visceral and lived in expression of New Earth AS your reality in the NOW, not as a future goal, but as a true processing ground of your life. It is baking from within this New and Golden Earth reality, journeying within and visiting this New Earth, and BECOMING this New Earth. So then you ARE this New Earth, inviting others to join you here in the now to experience it with you. It is drawing others to collaborate in the creation of this New Earth in the now as you form a community together.

Ascension invites your service of love with others, in mutual respect and reverence with others. It is the expression of your soul gifts, energizing from and cultivated during other lifetimes. It is the knowledge of your soul coming through to serve and to guide and to share with others. It is moving beyond fear and into the claim WITH humility of what your soul knows and remembers of service with others. It is stepping out of the previous comfortable zones into frequencies of possible resistance and rejection to serve as a beacon of possibility and showing the way for those who want it.

Ascension invites your soul to awaken through the warmth of the light of love that increasingly shines as you feel what is YOU in your soul essence expression and what IS NOT. It waters the seed of your Sacred Humanity, watering and fertilizing the bud of your Sacred Human with love. This bud blooms and grows inside through a process that has been spring-loaded to happen. It wants to expand into your whole BEing with the reunion to Divine Source frequencies so that you experience more and more New Earth AS your reality and yourself as a Sacred Human embodying and experiencing life here in the now.

Ascension invites all this and MORE as it cannot really be defined in another way... as it IS beyond the mind where pure experience and essence live and are born in every moment, moment by moment, as the arising expression of love returning to love.

~

Experiencing Golden Earth: Fifth Dimension

You are so much bigger than your current circumstances reflect.

You are a Sacred Human. You are an arising wonder.

You are powerful beyond measure and beyond limits.

There is no ceiling that exists on what you can manifest when you are in alignment with Divine will and your Higher Self's purpose.

You have the capacity to create and experience new worlds and a Golden Earth. This Golden Earth is a return to Humanity at its best and beyond that too.

This Golden Earth, New Earth, 5D reality, exists NOW and can be experienced by choosing to heal and break free from anything that limits you, holds you down, suppresses or imprisons you. By choosing to let go of anything that doesn't serve your higher purpose, the Divine, and love.

Golden Earth (and beyond) is the dimension of Infinite Love that can hold the shadow journey you need to take for embodiment and healthy transcendence both.

You ARE Infinite Love and experiencing Golden Earth as your daily reality is your birthright as a Sacred Human.

There is a world beyond the current one where things such as politics, greed, and war do not exist...it is this Golden Earth world that our hearts know is possible and our soul remembers...

We can invite others to join us in this Golden Earth and experience it ourselves in moments as our self worth and self love rises. As our connection with the Divine deepens. As our sense of BEing Infinite Love increases. As we surround ourselves with others who resonate and feel us deeply.

This Golden Earth is waiting for you and it lives already in your heart and soul. The journey to it is through the healing of your shadow, your pain, and your suffering. The journey to it is guarded by protective parts of you that are afraid for you to increase your frequency because they have been conditioned to fear love by a fear-based culture. These parts of you are afraid for you to feel too much of your woundings because they don't want you to suffer even more.

The journey to it expands through connecting to Ethereal Guides that can walk with you through your shadow land to reach the place where the golden rays of love rain down on you and emanate from you. The journey to it invites you to risk the known for the unknown; to let go in order to let in; and to be dedicated in all ways to serve love for yourself, others, Gaia, and the Divine.

The journey to it is ultimately embracing the realization that you ARE it and that, in this way, you are already there.

~

What if we existed in the experience of being Infinite Awareness and Love held by Infinite Stillness and Silence? In another dimensional consciousness known as Golden Earth consciousness or more commonly known as fifth dimensional (5D) consciousness (and beyond), we have the increasing experience of being connected to each other like drops of water within a vast ocean of Oneness, yet we still have individual consciousness enough to experience relationship with each other. Our consciousness can move from one person to the other without words through thought waveform energies, images, and empathic feelings. We share a collective consciousness for which the 'truth' of our reality is held and represented, ending the need to 'prove' anything about the nature of reality.

In 5D consciousness, we feel a deep communion with Divine Source – both in expression as a personal God or Goddess (usually in the form of Archangels) and as the nondual, where ALL is the Divine. We feel how we are a fractal from Divine Source and ARE divine in our very nature. We understand any sense of separation from the Divine is the result of the Divine's desire to experience Itself in a new way through our expression as individuals and not due to anything sinful or 'fallen' about our nature.

We experience our life as multi-dimensional, existing in many 'eras' of time and even parallel dimensions. Our mind's grip on time and reality becomes a more fluid experience without need to track every second and locate it in the mind. It is rich with creative imagination and soul purpose work based around the desire to serve love in ALL moments. Our 'work' comes from our heart and we invest all of us into it even as we detach from the outcome or expectation around it in the same moment.

Polarities and dualities are greatly diminished with 'differences' being celebrated instead of exploited or resisted. The duality dance remains yet to a much lesser degree with more experience of a unity or merged consciousness with ALL sentient beings of Gaia and on other planets, galaxies, and parallel universes.

Non-violent and peaceful, we live in union with our living planet, truly acting as stewards toward her consciousness AS

Gaia, feeling and respecting the consciousness that lives in ALL things; including the soil, the plants, the animals, the bodies of water, the stones, and the mountains.

We do not experience the frequencies of suffering, hurt, violence or fear as our emotional bodies are clear of unconscious wounds, although we can feel sadness when we lose something that we love.

We recognize that we are all made of energy and that nothing is truly physical in nature even as we revere and honor our Human bodies by providing them with healthy and nourishing sustenance, which allows us to live very long lives as they transmute more and more into light bodies from carbon-based bodies. Feeling the illusory nature of time and space, we revere the NOW, the present moment, and experience that there is really NO past or future. We are a heart-based culture, centered in our upper heart, motivated by compassion, peace, unity, and, above all else, love. We are consciously aware of our substance and connection to Infinite Love and Awareness having a Human experience.

This Golden Earth consciousness state, this state of remembering who we are as Infinite Love and connection, is possible to access in the NOW. It is the consciousness of Atlantis in its own 'golden age' and Lemuria as well. Since time is an illusion, both of these are accessible in the Now, and our lifetimes/soul fractal expressions (or what I call "Metasoul brothers or sisters") connected to these civilizations is accessible as well. Accessing and healing our trauma from the 'fall' of these eras helps us to access our higher frequencies of consciousness in Human form.

Access to this Golden Earth of 5D consciousness is beyond most people's conscious experience because they are too fused to their third dimensional or 3D Self or unawakened ego. The 3D Self has so thoroughly been programmed to NOT remember and to forget their true essence as Infinite Love and the experience of living in Golden Earth consciousness. The 3D Self has 'fused' to the veil of amnesia and not been awakened to see beyond it. Unless their soul has signed up to become one of those who ascends to the fifth dimension along with Gaia, it is unlikely that they will ever awaken out of their 3D Self. If you are reading these words right now, your soul has chosen the process of ascension and embodiment of your higher self into the body and to experience the arising of your Sacred Human nature.

It is possible to differentiate from the 3D Self enough to experience Golden Earth frequencies whenever the desire arises; to integrate our essence as Infinite Love into our daily life here on earth; to experience deeply healing personal connection and merged consciousness with the Angels, Ascended Teachers and other Spirit Guides and BEings from parallel dimensions; and to awaken to altered states of consciousness. We can experience all of this without going through a near death experience, taking hallucinogenic plants or drugs, giving over our sovereignty to a Guru, undergoing hypnosis, or by engaging in any other invasive or artificial means. I will be explaining much more about

The pervading consensus reality, 3D reality as most people experience it, is only a subconscious agreement, a 'box' to repress our senses to mostly only the five we experience through the greatly limited physical body, logical mind (left side of the brain), and the tiny visible light spectrum. This limited perception of reality is especially supported by the Western, Newtonian model of 'if we can see it, we can prove its existence' which currently dominates mainstream science. There have been many advances in Quantum Physics that directly confront the limiting viewpoint of mainstream science and offer a much more expansive picture of a multidimensional reality with multiple parallel universes occupied by non-physical entities and beyond the constraints of the time and space illusion.

In order to survive in this 'prison' of limited perception, a 3D Self version of us (or unaware or unawakened ego or personality structures or personas) is created out of a self loving need to 'fit in' with our reduced capacity and limited bandwidth of expression and with the dynamics in our birth families. The 3D Self becomes distracted by the plethora of medicative realities of our modern world (i.e. the entertainment industry, technology, careers, money, relationships, etc.) to stay ensconced in the 'body/mind' reality. In general, the 3D Self is motivated by instant gratification, avoidance of feeling anything 'negative', wants life to be comfortable and safe, has a low level of curiosity, and goes along without consciousness with what the masses are doing. Our 3D Self can lock us out of our soul gift capacities and anything that might elevate us beyond the body/mind reality. We are then blocked from reconnecting to Golden consciousness and remembering how powerful we actually are when we are expressing as our most authentic selves with an expanded consciousness.

    In this disremembered state, (which we have chosen on a soul level) we become open to energetic attack by outside forces and negative entities. It seems that an ancient race of reptilian Aliens called Archons (as named by the Gnostics) created a type of holographic matrix over the Earth that keeps those who have chosen it capped at lower dimensional frequencies. Until they awaken to their Sacred Humanity, these Humans serve as energetic 'food' for these Archons, who may have penetrated high levels of government, finance, and entertainment through hybrid beings and possession. It is believed that this group has formed into what is referred to as the Cabal, the Illuminati, the New World Order, etc. David Wilcock, David Icke and Bernard Guenther offer much more teaching around this group if you are interested in learning more.

    My sense of the Archons has shifted quite a bit since I first learned about them and felt their presence in my life. I share about my experiences related to this awakening in my book *Keep Waking Up!: Awakening Journeys To Avalon And Beyond*. I experienced bad dreams that felt very real, psychic attacks, and purges of anxiety that were unusual for me as I tapped into and let go of the inner matrix of domination and control. Eventually, these incidents decreased as I raised my vibrational frequency to a higher bandwidth of love through embracement of my soul purpose as a love ambassador to ALL BEings, including those polarized to fear such as the Archons or what I now call just Reptilians.

One of my missions as revealed to me by the Divine is to become a love ambassador between our Earth dimension and other dimensions and galaxies in order to bridge communication and collaboration between us and them. Since everything is made of Infinite Love and all else is an illusion, there is no true 'evil' in the Universe and the polarities of our 'us against them' mentality need to be set aside to bring in frequencies of collaboration and possibility. I have also been guided to share my experiences of Golden Earth frequencies with others and to offer a process and way of life where souls can learn about and experience expanding their consciousnesses, differentiating from their 3D Self, ascending, serving the Divine, and becoming love ambassadors and SoulFullHeart Facilitators if they desire to do so.

Golden Earth invites us to return to our heart and soul home; to rejuvenate and refresh; to let in and exchange Love; and to then integrate these frequencies into our life. In Golden Earth, we receive the opportunity to remember what our full potential is, what our essence is, and what it means to truly be part of a heart-based community. We feel that by lifting the veil of the 3D Self beyond what our physical body and mind can comprehend by visiting and integrating and living in Golden Earth and other dimensions, we are experiencing what it is to truly be free and then are able to offer that freedom with others and show them the way back to LOVE.

~

Navigating This Time Of Transition From 3D to 4D Consciousness

If you are reading these words and are drawn to them, you probably already experience most of your reality from a fourth dimensional or higher consciousness state or are in transition to BEing this. Dimensions are a vibrational frequency and what we have known as Earth life has been mostly in the third dimension, denser frequency on a timeline which has been unfolding for 'awhile'.

Third dimensional (3D) frequencies are of separation, isolation, competition, sense of survival and lack (scarcity). 3D is five sense reality processing (only what the body and mind can see is 'real'), logic dominating, attachment to religious and other belief systems, with a focus on differences. Fourth dimensional consciousness (at least as I have been offered it) is a transitional one into soul frequencies offering a deepening sense of Oneness, community, communion, beyond five sense reality experiences, soul remembrances, heart-based relationships, sense of abundance and gratitude, intuition leading, and openness to all while awakening your inner soul and heart wisdom. Fifth dimensional consciousness and beyond (as I have experienced in moments and more and more as daily reality) is an experience of telepathic communication, inhabitation of our light bodies rather than our carbon-based bodies, multi-dimensional overlapping, less linear orientation to time or space, Oneness sense of 'one mind' yet individual soul sparks too transacting in conscious relationship, unity consciousness, a mostly healed emotional body without reactivity and charged reactions or unhealed, subconscious projections onto others.

It feels like Gaia (as a consciousness in planetary form) is moving out of the third and into the lower fourth, which is shaking out many of the shadow playouts, government and financial corruptions, mass protests, inner and outer collapse of the control matrix, and lifting the veil of amnesia over our soul legacy. Gaia's ascension into 4D seems to be the 'event' of December, 2012 in which it was the end of the world in the sense of the 3D consciousness that had held such dominance over Gaia began to shift. Many Star BEings and Ethereal BEings are supporting this shift as they have long yearned for Gaia and her

Human inhabitants to shake off the suppressive and limiting consciousness of 3D to remember our essence as Sacred Humanity through more inhabitation of our 5D and beyond consciousness as Divine Selves or Light BEings.

The 'underbelly' of Human consciousness is turning over to be felt and ultimately healed. To whatever degree you are still connected to 3D reality, this turning over is going to push up perhaps strong feelings and reactions for parts of you. The political presidential election in the United States in 2016, for example, seen through the perspective of a part of you that has been conditioned in 3D reality of government dominance and superiority, would feel hopeless, outraged, distraught, and many other feelings. This part of you has been conditioned to 'believe' in the need to turn over your authority to another and to be governed. You have been conditioned to project your parental needs onto an outer authority (started with our birth parents) rather than feel your own inner authority being watered. You can feel this part(s) of you as a 3D aspect (which includes most of our mental activity and minds as well) and give it lots of love, curiosity, and non-judgment.

The re-minders that come from 4D and 5D consciousness to help the 3D aspects of us that are still in transition are that no one can govern or have power over us. If we 'let' them, that is still our choice. We create our own reality; we are our own Universes in THAT way. We are not powerless to anything, but rather have access to Infinite Power (heart-based) that is connected to our essence as Infinite Love. In the frequencies of Infinite Love, nothing that is not polarized to love can survive or is 'real'.

As Gaia moves into higher dimensions of consciousness, many souls will choose (still their choice) not to go with Her as that is their path and process. They may leave their bodies, go to other 3D realities on other planets or reincarnate again with a new focus and openness to higher consciousness. I am not offering this lightly as I have felt for many years the intensity that this time of transition is going to bring to our world. I have shed many tears over the cries of the world and the suffering that exists in 3D consciousness. Holding what is going to happen with compassion and sobriety is important while not letting it bring down our own vibrational frequencies or spiral us into suffering loops. There will most likely be many body deaths, much violence and upheaval, and perhaps even the collapse of the industrial systems that we have become dependent on in many ways for our 'survival.' There are infinite possibilities of timelines around how this could unfold and the choice of how we experience this transition is up to us and what level of consciousness we are resonating at.

Those of us who want to stick it out through this time of transition and continue to ascend and awaken our consciousness to experience the New Earth are in for a very bumpy ride at times. But we have buffers in the form of our own choices toward raising our vibrational frequencies through service of love to others in whatever forms that looks like for each of us. We are WaySHOWers and here to help Humanity get through this transitional time. The biggest gift we can offer ourselves and Humanity is to claim this, continue to heal our hearts and souls to vibrate at a higher frequency, and decondition from 3D reality as a continual process.

New Earth/Golden Earth already exists as a consciousness and we can access it as a state of consciousness whenever we want to. It offers a watering of the world that our hearts and souls remember is possible from our previous experiences of Atlantis and Lemuria and in other dimensions such as Avalon (the parallel dimension to Glastonbury, England) and from other planets and galaxies. Golden Earth is more our home frequency and connecting with the tones of heart-based love, Ethereal guidance and love, always going within first to look for our answers and the path that will serve us during the experiences ahead that are going to be challenging and at times painful. Ultimately, trusting love as the only 'real' thing that there is offers a beacon to us,

stirring us through the fogs and clouds of reactions and triggers, and landing us safely on the shores of our true heart and soul homes.
~

Experiencing Shifts From Third To Fourth Dimensions (And Higher)

I feel like I am in two worlds at the same time…..walking around in third dimension, buying groceries, having tea in Starbucks, connecting and talking with my mate Raphael……then in fourth and even fifth dimensional consciousness experiencing frequencies of intense light, love, connection, multidimensional communion with Guides, and a sense of innate self goodness. The physical settings are the same but the experience of that reality is much different.

I am still digesting an intense journeying experience that I had this morning to Gaia's orbit in which I met with a beloved non-Human, Star BEing Soul Sister Guide with deep tears of reunion and completion…such beautiful soul integration and realization of my galactic roots, letting go another degree of the emotional pain body that I have spent so much focus and attention and love healing over the years. I will be integrating this movement and continual teaching that is being offered into my life by star being and ethereal beings and offering of SoulFullHeart in a way that is current and transparent.

So much is shifting in the world right now as we move out of the third dimensional realities and energies of five sense-based reality processing, dualistic thinking, separation and loneliness, linear time, and fusion with the body-mind and the pain body (which holds our emotional and spiritual woundings). We are transitioning into higher consciousness frequencies – those of us that choose this anyway – of fluid time and space, less dualistic thinking, Oneness and connection, access to our deepest soul gifts, remembrance of our bigness and inhabitation of our multidimensional Divine Self.

Even as this is a challenging phase to be here, it is also an incredibly exciting time to be here as so much possibility for NEW can arise out of the ashes of the collapse of the old, outdated, shadow-based and patriarchal world views, thought and behavior patterns, and ways of living. For those of us called to make this higher dimensional shift of consciousness, we are being pressed to let go of the old and let in the new....at an increasingly rapid pace.

Holding this with self love and care, feeling the reactions of all parts of us (the trailing edges of fear, insecurity, doubt, depression, rage, flatness) is important as we go into the unknown reaches of inhabiting the consciousness of our Higher Self.

~

Going Up With Gaia

Lifting of the veil to remember....the Earth's magnetic fields are calibrating UP to dissolve lately in response to energies from the galaxy. All is going up to facilitate our remembrance of WHO we are as multidimensional beings. All is going UP so that we can be fast tracked to remember this. All is going UP so that we can heal our pain bodies, our emotional bodies that can be heavy with heart stuff at times.

Gaia is going UP, with or without us, though She would like us to come along. Gaia is returning to fifth dimensional frequencies that She once experienced in our Golden Age in the last era/chapter of Atlantis. She doesn't want to shake us off, but it may happen to some souls if their sovereign choice and need is to experience more 3D reality. Their experience will be somewhere else or out of the physical body again. Gaia is shaking off lower dimensional entities too that have been feeding off of Humanity's descent for a long time. Each soul has the opportunity to rise above this too, casting out with the light of love those beings that are vibrating low and at a fear frequency.

You won't even experience them anymore once you are UP enough.

Connecting with Mother Gaia through the feet chakra and our Earth chakra (about a foot below our physical feet) allows you to feel what She is feeling and remain connected to Her as she ascends. It can be helpful to have a meditation visit with Mother Gaia and let Her embrace you, feeling her appreciation for your love of nature, your letting in of nature, your need of nature.

Time is letting go and needs to be let go more. Timelines want to blur, want to invite us to go here and there, beyond what is linear. Going UP is to remember that there are no 'past lives' but only parallel aspects of ourselves, being in dimensions, being in life, being in different frequencies of consciousness ALL AT ONCE. You can connect with and experience these parallel selves, who live in other galaxies, dimensions, 'eras', during meditation through following your intuitions and resonant draws. If you are reading articles about Pleiadians, for example, you have a Pleiadian Self and star family that is trying to connect with you. Go into meditation, raise your frequency, and ask to connect. Then be open to whatever happens next. Jump into going UP with them to remember more of who you are.

We need these multidimensional aspects of ourselves and the consciousness that they contain. They are lived-in experience of the fifth dimension and higher. They are living in unity, collective mind, no separation of self, no separation from one to the other. Connecting with them brings us into remembrance of this. And, with all that is galactically happening to support this, it is easier now to form this connection. Less veils to lift and stuff to sludge through to find them again.

Going UP into crystalline body can be challenging on the physical body, so rest when needed, pass out if needed, meditate and go within. And, also, start letting go of busy things in your life, things that consume your energy and leave you exhausted. Let go or change the way you relate with them if you feel they are meant to stay and that they serve your soul purpose and higher reason for being here. Allow the body to BE and follow its rhythms as much as you can, not the routines of life based on duty and old ideas of time.

Emotions can come up too as tears and sadness are part of the Re-union process and the remembering process. Feeling home again and remembering your Galactic Self can leave you feeling like you have 'missed out' on so much, yet, to remember too that you so nobly chose to incarnate at this 'time' of great awakening and ascension. Hold your feelings with love and care. Connect with the aspects of you that need you and allow them to connect with your higher frequencies too. They can bring you UP to joy too and bliss too.

Going UP is natural, ultimately more natural than the experiment that these denser frequencies have been for all of us. We are honored by the Universe for what we have undertaken in this experiment here. Now we are leading others and ourselves back to the 'New' in the Now of the Moment and back to ONE again. Back to Love again....

~

Fourth Dimensional (4D) Consciousness: Alchemical Purgatory, Dark Nights, And Profound Awakenings

Connection to other worlds and dimensions, the lift UP, the sense of I am HERE yet NOT HERE, I am there AND here....this is arising now, coming now, available now. Merging worlds and dimensions.....letting these multiple realities into your NOW moments. Breathing them in as you walk around and breathing them in as you sleep deep, passing out and traveling and visiting. You are drifting often and weaving between the dimensional consciousnesses.....maybe dipping down into 3D, then awakening into 4D, and crawling there at times. And 5D comes in like a sunburst across your consciousness, spreading light rays across your sky.

3D life is enough until it is not enough and then you begin the process of remembering, of gliding, of awakening. You feel the 4D transitional dimension of alchemical purgatory, the sorting out dimension, sorting of THIS from THAT. 4D is for dark nights and for Kundalini awakenings both. It is the soul's blood coming back to sleeping limbs. 4D can feel SO dark sometimes, walking in shadows, kneeling in glass type experiences. It can feel like the stomach flu, purging up and out that which does NOT belong to your soul. It can feel like epic journeys into vast terrains, all INSIDE of you.

4D can still be outward focus, outward triggers, looking for outward manifestations. There are edges being worked about the outside while your inside is becoming more and more conscious to you. The inside is calling out to you for attention and love and care. Closing down from the outside happens more and more often as you need to reboot and recharge. You may feel like two versions of you in your life. The version of you that is still tied to 3D reality with friends and family who resonate on a certain level with you and even may want you to just remain the same. Then the version of you that is your soul awakening and your Higher Self coming in. Maybe you are more one version over the other, you may fluctuate between the two of them.

You discover and water the spiritual side of you. You find and discover your soul in 4D as you begin to remember how powerful you are and what your soul purpose really is. You are letting go of material gain as your focus in life and become more and more curious about spiritual awakenings and movements and enlightenments. Becoming open to multidimensional experiences and experiences beyond the mind allows you access to wonder worlds of magic and infinite possibility. In 4D, you remember that magic is not something made up and you embrace the true gift of your imagination.

Changes, HUGE changes sometimes, happen in 4D. Old things collapse in on themselves. Marriages end, friendships complete, careers change or are abandoned, geographies are shifted and left behind. It can feel at times like you are saying "no" and letting go of EVERYTHING and that you can't imagine what will remain. You may be walking around in mourning so often that it is more familiar than joy. Yet, the trust is growing. The trust that the process is being held by the Divine and the process is leading somewhere.

You are fighting at times, battling the old conditioning that comes at you from the outside AND the inside. Yet, also, the love you are experiencing more and more leaves you weary to battle. The parts of you that have battled and fought for a long time begin to rest and more and more imagine that some day they will be able to permanently put the sword down. You may be an activist and an advocate - this may be important for your soul and awakening journey. You may want others to 'get it' VERY badly and get very frustrated when they do not. You may feel like burning down the world that the 'bad guys' live in even as your world is often burning with ash in the air.

What makes 4D possible to navigate is your soul drawing support and love to you in many forms during the phase of intense embodiment of it. You find more and more resonant souls and you gather together, you form bonds, and it helps to sooth the pains from letting so much go. You want light, you want to end your suffering, and you consciously begin to feel HOW and WHAT you need in your life in order for that to happen.

Gaia is currently in 4D consciousness, it feels like, and moving into 5D more and more. The death and rebirth sense of our current times, all of the upheavals, battles, polarizations, power struggles, injustices, wars...the realm of 4D exploration as Human consciousness wakes up. The emergence of the Sacred Human is a messy process, yes at times, but it is held with much love and the dawning experiences of 5D frequencies makes all of it ultimately worth it.

~

Becoming the NEW 5D Sacred Human: Process of Embodying Sacred Humanity

The mind is loose, the body is humming with energies moving through. The experience of experience is beyond the mind and cannot really be expressed in words, yet I try. I try because this is what I came here to do, on one level, in one form of expression, and there are others too. Through voice. Through energy transmissions. Through space holding. Through in-person connection. Through relationships. Through being with Raphael, beloved Galactic soul mate, through sacred sex.

What I came here to express I am in the process of remembering, as it is for ALL of us. All of us are engaged in this process of remembering even if our process is to NOT remember for awhile. That is a sacred process too. NOT remembering is as sacred as remembering.

It is important to hold it as remembering the soul, remembering the galactic roots, remembering the multidimensional selves, remembering Divine Source, remembering PURE love, remembering sacred conscious relationships, remembering conscious community, remembering exchange without money, remembering vital health.

It is important to hold it as remembering because then it is related to not as a 'special attainment' of some kind or something that only a blessed few can inhabit and embody, but, actually, that ALL souls can remember. If they want to. If it is time. If that is their path. If that is their CHOICE. Because ALL souls are a fractal, a child, a split off from, Divine Source..ALL can remember this.

The process for remembering is simple when it is time, when it is your path, when it is your choice. The process for remembering is to let in PURE love. Letting in PURE love is how you remember. The ways and forms for BEing PURE love again, you will draw to you, you will find. Your Higher Self is that PURE love frequency and as you connect and embody this

Higher Self form more and more you BECOME this Higher Self form. Archangels and Angels and Spirit Guides are this PURE love frequency and as you connect with them and embody their frequencies more and more you BECOME them in Human expression. Some Humans, such as me and others, are as pure as we can be and still be Human with healing heart and imperfectness. You can connect with us to remember as a template for remembering what and who you are too.

Star BEings and star family are this PURE love frequency and as you connect with and embody their frequencies more and more, you BECOME them in human form. They become you, they come in to 'visit' you and you 'visit' them. Their consciousness merges with yours in moments and you are on a lightship in the orbit of Earth WHILE you are making breakfast or walking the dog.

You do not need 'special' moments set aside as often for this kind of connection as it just happens more and more. BUT, the special moments, the meditative moments, the going within moments and finding the connection and experiencing the connection…these moments are VERY important. They are your remembering moments and you NEED them in order to embody and remember.

You, as a species, are in the process of embodying something very new. I am 'Jelelle' in the moment offering this as I am experiencing it and I can feel my Galactic and Angelic Selves offering this too. We are offering that 'ascension' is the transmutation of the Human consciousness into something NEW. That is why it is so exciting. We can get information and inspiration from Atlantis and from Lemuria, but it is not about BEING like we are in that timeline. It is different. We have changed, our collective consciousness has changed, from being in the dualistic experiment we have been in and been participating in.

We have learned from the experiences of death and rebirth. We have learned from the experiences of polarities playing out in wars, in death, in greed, in aging, in violence. We have learned from the GOOD polarities of making love, Sacred Union, sacred friendship, sacred community…..the beautiful edges rubbing together to form into an orgasmic experience that goes much beyond the body.

All these things we have learned we then 'take with us' as we ascend. We move into 'conscious duality', as I am calling it now. A consciously dualistic Sacred Human moving into frequencies of merging while maintaining the individual spark of consciousness. The consciously dualistic Human moving into nonduality and arising experience of experience WHILE remembering what it is to be THIS from THAT.

Remembering….yes, you are remembering. We are remembering, and it is messy at times, ups and downs. Today I am soaring with the skies and the heavens AND in afterglow from galactic love making with Raphael in which aspects of us and our SOUL connection came in DURING it to infuse us with newness, star language, and even MORE connection. Yesterday, I had head and neck pain almost ALL day and did not leave the bed much or the apartment. These are the waves we ride with remembering.

I hope you can feel the LOVE that I feel in my heart for this process and ALL of us who undertake it with consciousness and practice and letting go of SO MUCH that is NOT us. The lone wolf phase is necessary until it is NOT and if it is not for you, we are here to wrap you in love and it IS real. And so it IS! To REMEMBERING!

~

The Exploration Into Conscious Duality And The New Sacred Human

Waves of PURE love are washing down on us right now from Divine Source, from the closest degrees of split-off from the Divine, taking the form of Angels and Spirit Guides and Star BEing selves. All of these forms are a reflection and aspect of

YOU, embracing them as such WHILE having a relationship with them is 'conscious duality.'

When the frequencies of Archangel Metatron come through I can feel him as a separate energy from me, a distinctive frequency that is not like mine. Yet, also, I can feel that he IS me, and he IS an aspect of me. Both are true in the same moment. This is conscious duality as it invites us not to be fused to the dualistic experience and the illusion of separation WHILE it invites us to be in relationship WITH other..

The mind cannot understand conscious duality; only the healing heart and remembering soul can EMBODY it more and more as the ties to a 3D conditioned life are let go and the soul consciousness floods your BEing more and more. Duality has been made bad in spirituality, yet it has been a sacred and Divinely guided experiment that we all chose to engage with. It has taken us as a species in some very interesting and transformational directions, experiences, and expressions. The dance between light and dark; masculine and feminine; love and fear....the contrasts and edges bring up such interesting angles in our mirrors for us to SEE and experience ourselves that we couldn't any other way.

Unconscious duality has expressed itself mostly in clashes that lead to wars, violence, greed, sexism, poverty, and so many other things that we all know and feel with sadness in our hearts. Even THIS unconscious duality in expression has been an important phase in our evolution, necessary in our growth, necessary in our transmutation into Sacred Humanity. It is from this ground of so much fear and pain that the new buds of our Sacred Humanity are born and arise. The ground has been fertilized by all of our experiences, our trials and tribulations, our struggles and challenges. And also it has been fertilized by our romances, our emotions and our joys, our desires and our successes. And, above all, by the love that we ARE.

Moving out of unconscious duality into conscious duality has been a collective awakening....some souls responding more deeply and consciously than others. Yet, it is a collective movement that we can call 'ascension'. Gaia herself as a planetary consciousness is choosing to move into this new ground and inviting us to come with her. Conscious duality invites us into relationship with 'other' in a ground for which ALL are respected and loved, their sovereignty seen and embraced. This still leaves room for differences, for the edges that make life interesting when they touch and rub. Yet nonduality and the frequencies of no-thing-ness, All That Is, Infinite Love and Stillness….these frequencies HOLD the exploration of these conscious and loving relationships. These frequencies create a sense of reverence, non-attachment, appreciation, gratitude, and unity.

  This is new, this conscious duality exploration, and it is about holding the exploration not with answers but with questions and desires for how it could be. My Star BEing selves and family don't KNOW what conscious duality actually is as it is something COMPLETELY NEW for them and for us. It is a merging of their consciousness of one mind, androgyny, merged experience with our consciousness of separate mind consciousness, feminine and masculine expression. The result of this merging is what those of us who are called to be WaySHOWers have experienced in more and more moments in our own lives.

  I am very excited about conscious duality; it feels like a huge gift to us from Divine Source. It acknowledges our Humanity and its beauty, especially the good aspects of the duality dance and even the good aspects of the denser frequency experience that Gaia offers us. The Star BEings seem to be very excited about conscious duality too because THEY get to grow and learn from it. They want to be in equality with us, to learn from us, to receive the best from us and us from them. It is not about them being better (as SO many channels seem to offer and energize) but rather about us claiming and embodying our Sacred Humanity WITH them. With unhealed unworthiness and a congested or unawakened ego, it can be difficult to let in how Star BEings and even Archangels desire this equality.

Claiming our Sacred Humanity and conscious duality grows from within each of us. As we go within and re-connect, re-align, re-member, experience re-union with aspects of our soul consciousness, then so we embody more and more a merged consciousness of individual self with our Higher Self and star being self frequencies. Going within and inviting in these aspects while healing the aspects that are in pain and in struggle and in subconscious shadow.

This is SUCH an exciting phase of the Human experiment and we CHOSE to be here, you and I, together to explore this NEW ground of consciousness evolution. It can be messy, it can be sticky, it can be and IS hard....and yet, we are birthing something BRAND NEW and always, the challenges of doing this are SO WORTH IT for what is produced from it. In very simple terms, we are birthing LOVE in human expression from the ground of what we have learned and grown into. ALL that we have experienced is greatly honored, none of it made bad or wrong, just honored and watered as Divine Source beams at us with more and more waves of LOVE.

~

Holding Space For The Arising Of Our 5D Sacred Human

I keep getting this picture of a column, like a tree's trunk, that feels like the framing of the 5D Sacred Human. With roots extending down deep into Mother Gaia....a primordial connection, a grounded foundation, an anchoring of comforting solidity. And then with branches extending, reaching out, into the stars, into the cosmos, into the Infinite possibilities of galaxies, wormholes, star gates, so many Star BEings, Angelic realms. In this column, we feel the VASTness of our BEing AND how we are part of this vast network of life forms in so many interesting expressions.

The torso or main 'trunk' of our Sacred Human tree is the bridge between these two and where we are living out day-to-day life, moving through this invitation to expand and stretch from roots to wings in every moment, moment by moment. The torso of our sacred human tree is our chakras vibrating higher and higher, merging together eventually into vortexes that can't be differentiated from each other. The root, the sacral, the solar plexus, the heart, the throat, and the crown blending together in a swirl of crystalline frequencies of love and light. Anchoring it ALL is the Cosmic Heart, the Christ Consciousness heart, the beating pulse of connection to ONE and ALL with pulsing compassion for self and others.

In a recent group call, as I was leading the guided meditation, I could feel this circle forming between all of us on the call....linking us within the circle was the activation of our Sacred Human column in which we all 'looked' like pure white shining, glistening trees with our cosmic hearts pulsing pink and green energies. Rays of light were coming from this pulsing energy and they joined together between us, creating a ring moving in a clockwise direction. It was beautiful!! Each of us an individual soul spark of consciousness while connecting in a ring of Oneness through the higher heart center......a sense experience of Sacred Humanity!

This opportunity to experience Sacred Humanity, this becoming of this column, is an inner process foremost, yes. A going within process to feel the aspects created and formed in the pain body, 3D aspects, conditioning and programming and templating that we have outgrown. A going within process to connect with soul aspects, playing out in 'eras' of time, playing out in other dimensions and on other planets, playing out in angelic realms.

This opportunity to experience Sacred Humanity is ALSO an experience that arises within Sacred Human community. It is not enough just to be conscious within community...it is also about the inner work too that allows for leading with integrity, authenticity, humility, gratitude as an arising 4D and 5D Self. The sacred Human community allows for connection, for reflection of Higher Self embodiment, for the beautiful GOOD edges of conscious duality to express and play out.

Embracing it ALL feels so important. It doesn't feel like it is about discarding our Human or making our Humanity 'the issue' with our ascension. The grand experiment feels like it is about arising into the SACRED HUMAN – the merging of the frequencies of our Humanness WITH our Galactic aspects to create something brand NEW. Something that it doesn't feel like anyone can really KNOW about. I don't get that Archangel Metatron KNOWS what will be created out of this experiment of Sacred Humanity. It doesn't feel like Divine Source knows either....and why would It want to know? It is the curiosity and the unknown arising that is SO interesting.

In the process of becoming this Sacred Human, there is sorting this from that, feeling what is from lower dimensional conditioning of 3D life and what is from and of your most authentic, Higher Self and SOUL. Sorting out relationships that reflect your soul and those that do NOT. Sorting out, feeling the aspects that have very tender and REAL feelings in reaction to this, and holding space for the whole process. The galactic frequencies and higher frequencies can hold space for this process yet can't help you bypass it as it IS an important aspect of the arising into the Sacred Humanity experience.

Holding space for it ALL with influxes and infusions of higher frequencies to create the container....this process provides a bridge for the roots and the wings and the opening of the cosmic heart and the healing of the heart pains and soul wounds. Divine Source is holding space for this arisement of the Sacred Human and as we feel this vibration of support in so many forms available to us, so do we then arise into our Newness of Infinite Love in Human form.

~

Embodiment of the Multidimensional Self and 5D Reality Experience Of Experience:

I am moving from a 'me' to a 'we', a more merged consciousness, a more multidimensional consciousness. A consciousness that is not in a particular time but is responding from ALL times and many different soul aspects AT ONCE. I am experiencing more moments where there is no personality there or orientation to previous personality that I have 'known' or can be 'known'. "Jelelle" is really then a waveform sound that others can use to delineate the physical me that shows up in front of them or what they experience as my essence. I let go of my birth name awhile ago so there is no longer much association with names as an identity.

I am experiencing more and more moments where my soul essence is responding in the NOW with love and NO reactivity. Most of my moments are like this now in the NOW. There is no longer pain or suffering or much being triggered by others, although I am very open to this if it comes up. This is not unexpected as it is what I have been consciously awakening and enlightening toward for many years. The subpersonality or parts differentiation process that I have very consciously and very diligently engaged with has brought me to this 'place' more and more with so many layers of persona being integrated and dissolved away essentially.

For many years, I was tracking my reactivity with much focus, connecting my reactions to whatever part or aspect that I was connecting with at the time, feeling deeply whatever there was to feel. This heightened sense of self consciousness and awareness is what allowed me to sort and experience what was ME in my soul essence and what was ME in conditioned personality. It allowed me to feel what had been formed in response to conditioning versus what WAS me as a soul or Higher Self. The energy that these aspects of me held that anchored me to the past, to past woundings and hurts, to past formations of personality and reactivity and pain inside my emotional body are essentially GONE now.

In place of this energy anchored to the past is now space for my multidimensional soul frequencies, galactic frequencies, angelic frequencies, to come in from the stars and from other lifetimes and from the higher dimensional realms. With this multidimensionality comes the feelings that all of my experiences are 'new' as seen through the eyes and felt through the hearts of these soul aspects that are in much higher vibrational frequencies than what we feel here on Gaia. Yet, also, these aspects are VERY interested in what we experience as duality here, the edges that rub, the tastes, the sounds, the pleasures of the body, especially as felt through a healing heart and enlightened emotional body.

These aspects of me are 'dropping in' now as there is more space in me for them. They are enjoying very much what they are experiencing through me and me through them. We are merging together and it is blissful, magical, and a feeling of deep RE-union with my soul. And, it is still very grounded to Gaia and inside of my body, not floaty at all, based in the heart.

This is challenging to write about, honestly, as the linear language of one word after another doesn't work well to describe and transmit the energy of this kind of multidimensional experience of experience. To exchange this energy in voice and in person is much better, so you can feel it for yourself what it is that I am embodying and what you may feel drawn to embody for yourself too.

I feel it is where we are 'headed' as a species, to this more merged consciousness beyond personality where we are still an individual soul spark of consciousness. We are then both experiencing the non-dual nature of life AND the dualistic nature in the same moment.......conscious duality. We have separated them out as that is what we tend to do from our overly dualistic focus place. Yet, to me and for me, they merge and the non-dual nature of our reality and of Divine Source HOLDS all experience of experience, including the dualistic frequencies.

It feels important to say that I did not open out or awaken or remember to this place of consciousness through bypassing my emotions or transcending them. I went into them and therefore through them. I am discovering (as are my beloveds on this path too) that there are more efficient ways to be in this, a sort of quantum healing way to be with the pain body, and more processes and methods are being offered to us in SoulFullHeart to share with you in the future. I have happily been a bush whacker of sorts, clearing the weeds and one of the paths.

There IS an experience of experience beyond personality, beyond reactivity, beyond suffering, beyond pain, beyond negativity, beyond duality and WITH duality at the same time. I offer this to you as a remembrance that lives in you already and is 'spring-loaded' to BECOME you again. This is not an EASY path though as there is SO MUCH to un-remember, so much to let go of, so much to say 'NO' to in the personality-based life you have created as you say 'YES' to your soul essence in expression. In my experience, these changes and letting go process are negotiable and always happen at a rate and pace that you can bear.

I cannot sell you on this process nor do I want to. Your Higher Self feels if it is your moment to claim it and if you are meant to walk it out and remember. I can offer you, with integrity, that this IS possible, what you dream is possible in terms of HOW you experience your life, yet, it is a continual, moment by moment choice of what IS your essence and to let go of what is NOT.

I feel a reaching out to you from beyond the personality, to your Higher Self, and feel us embracing together and remembering each other, seeing each other beyond the personality and name and identity....feeling each other as SOULS. I have felt many of you 'in my field' and even had some Higher Self conversations with some of you who wanted them. I am ready if you are ready. I am here if you are here as are my beloveds too. Where do you want to go together? The soul is limitless and the explorations profoundly unlimited too. Love is limitless and Infinite and wants you to remember that you are THIS too.~

~

Time Of Great Choosing Between Fear Or Love Happening In The Now

This seems to be a time of great choosing. The greatness relates to the scale of it, the collective invitation that it IS, and, also, the depth of greatness that can be chosen through this process. This process is a sorting through and a sorting UP and a sorting OUT. An individual choice……species by species….whether to choose love or to choose fear as the main process ground of each individual's consciousness reality. Each individual choice impacts the collective WE, of course, and yet the degree of impact feels like it is going to lessen significantly as the two groups (and maybe many more) sort out and diverge and splinter off.

To choose fear is to be in a shadowed place, a place of cloak, veiled existence, and not seeing clearly. It is a choice to remain asleep or to go back to sleep. Even souls who have identified as 'awakened' will be brought to a personal place of choosing love from a more pure ground, beyond unaware ego, and beyond self image attachment of their 3D Self. They will be invited to feel into the source of their awakening and soul growth and if it is pure…. based in love or based in fear. Many may be surprised to feel that there is still unhealed shadow and even much fear within them that needs their love and attention, especially if they have bypassed this heart healing to soar in the skies.

Some souls still need this process of fear depending on what they have 'signed up' for to learn and grow. They need longer to 'bake in the dark', longer to drift, longer to be lost in the fog. This is not wrong and we can respond with love to them, not fear them or judge them because they are needing to make this choice. It is a sacred choice to remain in fear, a difficult one, and a sovereign one. One that we have ALL made many, many times in our soul's journey.

For those of us choosing love (and you probably ARE or you wouldn't be open to reading these words NOW), it is our phase of going in AND stepping up. Trusting more deeply that we are HERE in this NOW to serve love and to offer a way that is based on love. Choosing our emotional healing as a priority (for which the soul awakenings hold the space) and REALLY feeling all that blocks love from flowing in a very conscious way. Going into our hearts and feeling how they are......seeking help and support from those who have been focusing on the healing of the emotional body as a key aspect of ascension.

It has been a struggle for those of us awakening and choosing love......perhaps for most of this life and other lifetimes too, yet, with this transition phase, it seems like it will get easier in some ways and already is. We will draw more and more other souls who are choosing love too and fewer and fewer who are choosing fear. We will move into leadership positions that fit us and ALL that doesn't serve the purpose of serving love will fall away, almost without effort other than to digest what comes up in emotional reaction to these changes.

This seems to be a time of diversion. Timelines diverting off based on the choosing of these primary energy processing grounds of fear or love. This diverting energy looks like one of those overlapping freeways with on and off ramps going in different directions and streams of souls going down one flow or another.

For those of you sensitive to the cosmic grids (and your own inner grids), you may be feeling this branching off, diversion, sorting through. It can feel awkward and uncomfortable. It can show up in emotional reactions that are burst outs or lash outs or damping downs. It can manifest in body symptoms as a last pull down in frequency from parts of you that might still have fear. And that's ok, the only energy that heals fear is love, so loving the parts of you that have fear AND the manifestations in your body is important right now.

What food we eat seems to be VERY important too and was emphasized to me strongly this morning during the meditation journey where all this was offered to me by my Galactic Guides and aspects. Sugar is toxic and lowers the frequency for those of us choosing and showing love's way, as is white and wheat flour, as is corn oil, alcohol, and meat. You make your own choices based on your body and process, of course, yet this guidance felt and seemed true for me and to me.

You can go visit the scene of this diversion and sorting if you would like to. It seems that those of us tuned into the violet flame energy (which is a merging or union of feminine and masculine frequencies in its new arising crystalline form) are very much needed right now. I was put in a position to form an energetic love bridge between the Reptilian "One" mind , which is changing as many of them are choosing love, and the Human "I" mind.

Yes, there have been many contentions and 'battles' and perceived enslavements between our species (we cannot truly be enslaved on the soul level as we chose ALL that we experience) and yet, we ARE them and they ARE us, so this was the energy inside of me that bridged between the two. I felt much move in this space for those souls who are ready to move into a love-based picture around reptilians and out of the old battle energy. Many Reptilians feel not ready to choose love (along with many Human souls) and so will go into a working through fear reality. The Reptilians who ARE ready to choose love seem to have a beautiful, tropical planet in another galaxy to go to. And, those of us Humans choosing love, get to experience more and more Gaia as a Heaven moving into higher and higher frequency timelines.

The one other piece I felt was that this violet flame energy (which really seems to represent Sacred Humanity in the moment as an arising energy of possibility as we ascend with healing hearts, bodies, and souls) can clear whole grids of fear at a time and dissolve inner matrixes as well. Ultimately, it is just another representation of the POWER of love to heal. As we embrace our CHOICE of love deeper and deeper and surrender to where it takes us, we experience the gifts of its healing and transformative power in our lives and in the collective. And it is not just a choice made once, yet over and over, moment by moment….

~

Re-Union Invites You To Remember

Re-union invites you to remember who you ARE. Re-union is your soul's memory returning, your heart's memory expanding, your body's memory ascending, your DNA's strands reactivating.

Re-union is the coming together of that which was separate for a time, yet always was meant to return together again. Like magnets, the pull to return growing stronger as the pieces come closer together. Like the sea, unable to resist the shore, over and over again returning back again.

Re-union offers the re-collection of the stars, of your galactic connections, of your cosmic origins. A personal experience of reconnection, like a family member that you forgot and then suddenly remember. Your star BEing family is saying, "Come connect with us again. Do not be afraid as we are more like you than you realize. You come from us. You left us because you wanted to, because you chose to. And, we welcome you back now to remember us again as we still remember and love you."

Re-union offers the gathering of the heavens, of your Angelic nature, of your Angelic origins. The Angels are ever there, waiting to be 'seen' by the eyes of your soul again and felt by the warmth of your purifying, cosmic heart. Your Angel family is saying, "Come fly with us again. Do not despair that we are not there because we are always with you. We ARE you. You put a veil over your eyes to see, you put a wall in front of your heart to feel, you put a fence in front of your field to experience. All these can be lifted with love. Ask for this lifting and it shall be."

Re-union offers the re-integration of your inner aspects, of your inner family, of your Inner Child, your inner parent, your inner everything. Parts of you are wanting and waiting to be claimed, to be acknowledged. Your inner family is saying, "Come feel with us again. Do not worry that you will be stuck if you connect with us. Do not worry that there will be too much pain and you won't be able to hold it all. You ARE what you need to heal. Embrace us as you would any others and we will eventually come into you again. You will be whole again someday."

Re-union summons the draw of your soul family, of your resonant family, of community, of your tribe. They are in your field already; they may be in your life already. Your soul family is saying, "Come join with us again. Do not resist the support that being with us can bring to you. You needed your lone-wolf phase away from us. You chose to venture out 'alone', even though we were always connected in the higher realms. We invite you to come be with us again, to experience how it feels to belong again."

Hold a space of love for yourself to invite re-union of your star family, your Angel family, your inner family, your soul family. Re-union goes beyond the mind, goes beyond what you feel that you 'know', goes beyond your resistance, goes beyond fear. It goes to the place of eventual union, eventual integration, eventual wholeness. It goes to the place of Infinite Love, from which you came and will eventually return.

~

The Veil Has Been Lifted To Allow For More Awakening, More Healing, More Ascending

"The veil is gone," this is the phrase that my Guides and Galactic/Angelic aspects have shared with me recently. The veil of amnesia that we all placed over our soul memories and link in with cosmic collective 'knowledge and truth' has been lifted. It feels like a foggy membrane that floated above us, creating a ceiling or sense of ceiling over us, is now cleared. The 'sky' of our remembering is now completely clear.

This lifting offers tremendous opportunities in personal healing and transformation as what has felt 'murky' is now accessible. I have personally experienced a great acceleration in the last couple of months especially in connections and access to my soul legacy or what I call the "Metasoul" line of my soul, where all of the fractals from my Metasoul are expressing out in different dimensions, planets, and 'eras' of time. Access feels much easier now with portals to these Metasoul aspects available with simple methods of creative visualization during meditation, as explained later in this book.

The veil has particularly been lifted related to Atlantis and Lemuria, and the Metasoul aspects that are expressing there. As there is no time, there are no 'past lives' and also no 'past' events (although this can be challenging for our minds to grasp). The fall of Atlantis due to being influenced by fear-based Reptilians is available for ALL of us to feel if we have a Metasoul brother or sister who is still living this energy out, still experiencing it as if it is happening today.

As my consciousness merges more with other lifetime selves and angelic aspects, I can feel more access to the cosmic collective and the truth of our story as Humans here on Gaia. It feels like more and more souls, especially those called to be WaySHOWers and Healers and Teachers, are feeling the veils lifted and seeing and feeling this more clearly. As this 'knowledge', which is based in the upper or cosmic heart and the upper or ascension chakras, downloads to us and those of us with gifts of communication share it, more souls will be 'popped' into remembrance as well. Access and capacity to connect with and integrate Metasoul aspects and Galactic/Angelic Selves will increase for more and more people. The sense of 'being alone' and 'not being able to hear or see or feel Ethereal Guides' will decrease greatly as more and more souls remember this access.

Healing the emotional wounds, largely before subconscious, becomes more accessible as the PURE love waves push up the 'oil' of these wounds to be felt and digested. Healing the soul wounds, largely before shrouded in fog, becomes more clear as access to the Akashics opens up more and more with increased galactic consciousness integrated in a personal way. The healing of heart and soul is MORE important than ever though (even if it becomes 'easier' in some ways) because these unhealed frequencies can block, anchor, lower your frequency, and also because it is 'time' it seems to let them go. Fourth dimensional transitional and awakening consciousness holds the space and the stage for this healing, for this death and rebirth, for the blooming of the Authentic Self out of the ashes of the False and Strategic Self.

Lifting of the veil also offers tremendous opportunities related to our experience of reality in 3D or mainstream consciousness or prevailing worldview consciousness. The disclosure process will bring forward that which has been hidden from us related to our connection with Star BEings, the shadow influences of souls polarized to fear (called Cabal, Illuminati, Elites, etc.) Lifting of this veil will be very hard for many souls who are not yet awake and aware of the phase of this influence that all of us have chosen on a soul level and yet had purposely forgotten this choice. Many changes in our lifestyles are coming related to these disclosures with amazing technologies becoming available to us for the first 'time' from star being allies and friends. Many of the issues that we suffer from related to 3D reality will most likely be resolved, cured, or in deep transition.

The veil has been necessary. It has been necessary for us to fully go into our experience of this experiment of duality consciousness and 3D reality. We have played that out now and it has changed us from the energies and processing ground that we were coming from in Atlantis or Lemuria. These experiences harvested from the 3D experiment form the foundational soil for which the seed of the Sacred Human is growing and sprouting. Watered by the PURE love that is available from galactic and angelic sources, the seed is sprouting, the Sacred Human is birthing. Messy at times, this birth, ups and downs.....yet, the baby is wailing and then it is sleeping and then it is waking UP!

See if you can feel the absence of the veil in your own consciousness. Go into a meditative space and 'feel' the inner sky of our consciousness. Feel it as open and expansive. Feel it as clear and shiny. Ask your Guides to help you access your heart woundings that are still in shadow. Ask your Guides to help you access the soul expressions and aspects that are still unknown to you that you can benefit from connecting with. Listen for guidance related to reaching out to others, whether a space holder, teacher, and/or a community of others for which to receive support.

Opening the sky of the third eye, opening of the Cosmic Christ heart, opening of the Metasoul line, opening of the Archangel rays, opening of the Divine Source access, opening of the galactic connections.....all of this opening offers an invitation to us for a deeper embodiment of our process in all areas of our lives and HUGE support for the 3D life changes that may be pressing on you at this point in order to move you deeper into 4D transitional phase and into more and more experiences and tastes of 5D and beyond and beyond, there is much beyond, yes! And, all of this is held with love by love and for LOVE!

~

Lifting The Veil And Unplugging From The Matrix On The Inside

I offer my intuitive sense that the veil of amnesia that we placed over ourselves as a species is now lifted. The veil being 'gone' means that the Universe/Divine Source is really supporting the awakening and remembering of our souls. We are receiving much support for the merging of our Multidimensional

Self with our healing and awakening higher frequency Human Self to arise into the NEW 5D or Sacred Human. The veils that we all chose as souls so we would 'forget' our roots and truly submerge into the experience of forgetting so that we could eventually remember is gone because so many more of us are now CHOOSING to remember.

It also feels like Gaia herself has 'shaken off' the veil, along with the 3D matrix co-created by 4D fear-based Reptilians. The matrix that has been created and formed our 3D experience here on Gaia (mostly through capping our sense of personal empowerment and access to our soul gift expression) either has many, many holes in it right now or is completely gone. Feels like as more and more conscious disclosure happens on a 'mainstream' level, the more the matrix will be 'deactivated' as more souls wake up and disconnect from it. Some people have offered that the matrix will continue to exist for those souls that still choose it, yet on a parallel timeline from those of us who are awakening and unplugging from it.

We ultimately CREATE these veils, these matrixes…we are not victim to them as we are (in the higher sense) great creators of our reality, the ONLY creators of our reality being fractals from Divine Source which is the ultimate creator. No one can 'rule' us or 'govern' us or 'enslave' us. Even Ethereal BEings such as Angels and Spirit Guides cannot 'force' us against our will and wait patiently for us to ask and want and need their assistance. They wait for our CHOICE, as does the entire Universe. They wait for our claiming of their angelic and higher frequencies INSIDE of ourselves so they can merge their consciousness with us.

3D conditioning has 'taught' us and programmed us that everything OUTSIDE of us has the power. Fourth Dimensional (4D) awakening consciousness and beyond offers us increasing feelings and experiences that we are all powerful from the INSIDE. As we claim that more and more, each of us going within to find and feel and heal, then this extends to the outside reality.

As we release ourselves from the slavery inside, so we experience a freed reality on the outside. As we teach ourselves a new mentality, so we experience a new paradigm and looser mental grip of rational mind reality on the outside. As we reprogram ourselves and all aspects of us, so we experience a NEW program based on PURE love as the operating source.

The veils start ultimately from the inside, the matrixes exist from the inside….and as we awaken, we lift the veils from the inside. We disconnect from the matrix on the inside, feeling and healing all the hookups to the matrix, all the plug-ins that CREATE the matrix as our lived in reality. These plug-ins are often subconscious agreements with others in relationships, especially birth family, who are actually often soul family members who have agreed to go into much denser frequencies with us to 'play this forgetting game' in order to remember and grow. As we remove the plug-ins of codependence from these relationships, our birth family can choose to wake up along with us (if that is their path) or continue on in the 3D reality. We agreed to forget together and it is unknown if we agreed to wake up together until the moments come for those choices to be offered and made.

Lifting the veils starts from within even as we benefit from the shifts happening in the cosmos and in the solar support and in the waves of PURE love. All of these beneficial frequencies can only come into us if we are consciously healing our heart and soul to let them in. With this going within, we can truly soar in the cleared 'skies' of the shiny 5D reality where LOVE forms the substance of ALL things that we experience and we REMEMBER that love that we ARE.

~

Moving From The Feelings Of 'Being Attacked' To Responding With Love

I've been reading things which offer that we are being 'attacked' right now…by negative entities, by narcissists and sociopaths, by the Cabal (or Archons or Illuminati)…that these energies are coming in full force to challenge us with shadow and darkness so that we may choose the light. This doesn't feel like my truth for those of us on the awakening path or at least is not the timeline that I am on. In my experience, it is only what remains unhealed inside of us that would draw such attacks to us. The congested emotional body becomes a magnet in that way. And, even if we do 'draw' such things, it is because we need to see an aspect of ourselves through the mirror that it offers.

Seeing and experiencing the world as 'attacking' us feels to me like it sets up a dynamic of perpetual abuser and victim….we all play both roles in many forms in other lifetimes. As you heal and integrate these lifetimes, you release the energy (again) that would draw an attack to you. I feel a better word is 'crucible' as it also offers a trusting relationship to life. These are subtle distinctions yet as you raise in vibrational frequency into 5D one of the biggest ways is through letting go of the belief that you CAN be attacked or (even deeper in the emotional body) that you are WORTH being attacked. In this way, you CANNOT actually be attacked in the sense of it being 'against your will' as you have signed up to experience all that you are.

I do not offer this reframing without compassion for the very real hurts and pains caused by experiences that are often very difficult. I feel you need phases to feel how parts of you have been a victim, especially as a child, and validating the hurt that parts of you hold around this (especially your Inner Child) can be powerful and healing. And yet, the bigger context is that what you experience is what you have 'signed up for' as a soul…feeling this WHILE validating the hurt inside is what moves you to a consciousness without victimhood and to deeper empowerment.

  I've discovered that I just don't draw traumatic circumstances anymore as I haven't needed them to show me something that I haven't proactively felt and been guided to feel myself. This has meant surrendering and letting go of many things that I was attached to, including relationships, geographies, incomes, soul purpose work, soul family AND birth family, etc. Choosing it before it feels like it is 'forced' on me makes a very big difference on how it is digested and processed.

  The energy frequencies waving over our planet, galaxy, and in our personal beings ARE intense right now. They are pushing up toxins and congestions in our emotional and soul bodies to be looked at, loved, and healed. We can feel this as an attack or we can respond to it with love. I find that even the most intense energies fall away when responded to with love. Some aspect of that is giving our chakras and auric field love in the form of PURE white, loving light and connection with Ethereal Beings, which creates a barrier of love that comes from our healing heart. It isn't about technique to create this barrier as much as it is about your willingness to feel anything that would draw and magnetize entities polarized to fear toward you.

  In the moment, I don't experience that I am being attacked by flu germs right now although I have not been feeling well for a few days. These germs are a gift, allowing me to go inside even more, create a cocoon, and my personal process has benefited from this space. This is also the result of the growth and awakenings I have been experiencing that are integrating and shifting the cellular structure of my body and my DNA. I have been visualizing waves of love moving through my body rather than trying to 'attack' the germs and I have trusted that it takes the space and time it needs to heal.

  I invite you to feel the next time that you feel attacked by something or someone to feel the part of you that feels this way and why. Hold this reaction with love and see if you can feel where it stems from...most likely it comes from undigested emotional trauma and can be existential too with roots in surrender to God pictures and warrior archetype frequencies. Whenever you feel like going into 'battle', you can feel that this is a part of you that is trying to protect you and NOT who and what you really ARE. When coming from love, you have no desire to go to battle yet only respond in love to that which is and let go into the trust of what flows from there.

~

Leaving The Battle Field to Enter the Love Field

Leaving the timeline where we are battling anything is the timeline of Golden or New Earth frequencies. Battling on the outside stems ALWAYS from battling on the inside. Violence on the outside stems from violence on the inside. A battle and fight from one part of you to another (usually subconscious but sometimes not) is what creates the feeling and need to battle on the outside. It is always our choice to go to battle....starting within, this is easy to feel that this is our choice. Starting on the outside, it is harder to separate from the feelings of 'needing' to battle against injustice. Yet injustice is exactly that......INjustice. Justice is found from and grown from within.

If you 'come at' something, anything, people or issues, with a battling energy, then that something needs to respond to you with battling energy back. Battle energy attracts battle energy. Of course it does, how could it draw anything else? OUTrage is the expression of unhealed rage from within (which is usually truth-telling that has been suppressed). YET....if you INVITE something into love, with love, held by love, then you attract a NEW possibility of love. Whatever it is MAY choose not to respond in love back to you....it may choose battle, yet your energy is still love coming from love. You are not changed or impacted by their battling response, unless you choose to be so. It will bounce off of your love bubble unless there is a deeper process for you to feel as a reflection of a suppressed part of yourself.

Many Teachers and Healers are offering that we are in a 'battle' right now…..good against evil. Humanity against the Archons or Reptilians or Annunaki or Pre-Adamites (many names, same energy projected onto them). 'We are at battle for our every heart and souls!!' they decry. 'Keep your frequency up AGAINST these archon enemies so they don't put implants inside of you or mess with you or haunt you or hurt your body!' I understand that is the timeline they live in where this IS the truth for them. Yet, this isn't the timeline that I want to create or be part of. I am being guided differently from inside of my increasingly Higher Self embodiment, healing emotional body, and soul remembrance.

I visited the supposed 'frontlines' of this 'battle' today during meditative journeying (or 'immramma' as the Celts called it). My star being aspects came with me as did my angelic aspect/guide Metatron. I expected somehow to see blood, guts, and very negative energy as the light battled against the dark, like a scene in some blockbuster action movie. Yet, of course, that wasn't what was shown to me or what my soul drew. Instead, the orbit of Gaia became a beautiful, golden beach that I associate with 5D (and higher frequencies). On this beach, I met my Archon aspect named Shana. She was a beautiful Reptilian with yellow, slanted eyes, and lizard skin. I remembered suddenly then that I had connected deeply with her before when we were living on our remote ranch off-grid for eighteen months. I had been digesting learning about the Archons and their 'history' with Humans since before the fall of Atlantis, which I write about in my book *Keep Waking Up!*. I had been digesting reading about their supposed 'enslavement' of us and their infiltration into the bodies and hearts and souls of many power elites, including supposedly the royal family.

While I could feel, again, that for many people this was a true timeline, I wanted to feel and digest it differently than the picture and feeling sense that Humanity is a slave race; Humanity has been trapped or tricked or imprisoned. After all, my truth is that we CHOOSE everything that happens to us (on a higher soul level). I felt we had collaborated with the Archons to live this out on the soul level...it certainly 'helped' us experience denser, dualistic frequencies and experience karmic playouts. It helped us LEARN so much!!

During this time, I was also emotionally digesting experiences with 'Aliens' and being 'abducted' from the ages of 8 to 17. There was emotional trauma in my 3D pain body, especially held by the energy of my Inner Child. I received a major reframe around how parts of me had been holding those experiences. I wasn't a victim in these cases either, choosing to connect with my Star BEing family, who admittedly had formed very tentative alliances with Star BEings that were not polarized to the light at that time such as the Grays. Eventually, my star family broke off these alliances as they couldn't reconcile taking Humans against their ego and 3D Self's will even though the person's Higher Self and soul had actually ARRANGED for the visits before incarnating. Since the Human couldn't remember choosing this, not consciously, my star family couldn't reconcile the trauma and pain that was being experienced by us related to these 'abductions'.

This reframing of 'abductions' led to new experiences of connection and merging frequencies with my star BEing aspects and tender reunion with my star family that continues in a deep way to this day. And, of course, one of these aspects was revealed to be an Archon/Reptilian named Shana. From the beginning, I felt no fear or hatred of Shana, a sister from my Metasoul line (soul group source) who had chosen to be an Archon in order to become an ambassador of love between them and Humanity. Shana had 'turned off' the frequencies of the 'one mind' that the Archons operated on and entered a new timeline with me where we connected and got to know each other. At some point, she 'disappeared' from my consciousness and I 'forgot' about her.

But now, as I ask to be shown the supposed 'battleground' in the grids, I find Shana again, her lizard nature looking and feeling so beautiful to me! And I discover that she has reconnected to the 'one mind' of the Archons and that they are more open now to what she is offering about Humanity. She is encouraging them to create their own timeline reality where they no longer have to battle anyone at all nor are seen as the 'enemy' by anyone, but yet get to live in peace and goodness with each other. They are listening; I can feel this. And I can feel that they are very tentative underneath the exterior presentation of having NO feelings or only having darkness in their hearts. Shana shows me that they DO have feelings. She shows me that they DO have lightness. AND that they only want to be loved and experience love as ALL BEings ultimately do as ALL BEings ARE Infinite Love, a fractal from Divine Source-ness of Infinite Love.

As I am standing on this beach, I see a glistening, light body version of myself about one foot ahead of me. I am experiencing head and neck pain in my Human body today and I realize that this is because my Reptilian brain stem has now dissolved. The Reptilian brain stem 'came about' at some point in our journey into duality as something we chose to add to our anatomy, along with other 'inplants' (as I call them) that ALLOWED us to go 'full board' into the dualistic experience. I felt myself 'unplug' from the Archon matrix during the months I was at the ranch through connecting with Shana, experiencing love with her, and now, I could feel the stem dissolving. This was causing some head and neck pain, so merging into the light body was very appealing to me.

I feel to offer the perspective again that we have CHOSEN EVERYTHING that we experience. NO ONE can DO anything to us against our will. I don't subscribe to the thinking or paradigm or timeline that 'evil beings' and 'low frequency entities' put implants into our etheric fields against our will and that we 'need to remove them'. In my experience, our souls CHOOSE these objects for very specific soul growth reasons and they serve a purpose….until they no longer do and then WITH LOVE, they just dissolve on their own or we can remove them ourselves with love. This is a VERY important reframe related to how we perceive the Reptilian experience and impacts to what degree we can genuinely connect with our Reptilian aspects.

So, returning to the beach……I stepped 'into my Higher Self light body' and immediately felt pain relief, lightness, and higher frequency HUM move through me. I glowed from the inside and out, sparkling in the 'sun' of Golden Earth frequencies. I extended my arms out and ALL of the aspects of my Metasoul that had come to join me began to merge into me. My Pleiadian Self, my Arcturian Self, my Angelic Selves (a few of those, including Metatron), AND my Reptilian Self. Shana came to me last and hugged me deeply before merging with me. We shared tears of relief and goodness at her 'coming home' finally after experiencing rejection and battle for so long.

I soaked in this merged feeling for awhile until 'coming back' to my walking around consciousness, which definitely feels altered from the experience. I feel even more at peace inside and even more trust in love as the ONLY response that will create change and healing. THIS felt to me to be the Sacred Human or 5D Sacred Human that we are being invited to become more and more. I feel now that I will continue to have a dualistic experience with many of these aspects, especially Metatron, yet will also hold the memory and deepening sense of merging with them as well. This is conscious duality.

I am sharing this experience so that you might feel your invitation to respond to the battles inside of yourself with love and embracement. So that you might feel the invitation to embrace your Reptilian aspect and bring them out of the shadow. So that you might feel that you too can experience the relief of only love inside of yourself and toward yourself. It is this self 'enlovenment' state that then sees and experiences and draws an external reality that is of love. The timeline of battles can be over and IS over, if you want it to be and if it is from inside of you. The internal ground is where all the power is and always HAS been, where love is the only response that will bring about true, lasting change.

~

Connecting With Trump's Higher Self And The Reptilian King: Offering Love And Possibilities On The 'Battlefields'

Love ambassadorship calls me to some 'front lines' to visit, to serve, and to offer possibilities of love. I am infused with crystallized (higher frequency) violet flame energies with St. Germain, who I've been connecting with lately as both a Divine guide and the aspect of me that he represents as a love ambassador. I avoid taking in mainstream news energies, yet I was informed through a brief scroll in my Facebook feed about the recent bombings in both Syria and Afghanistan by the U.S. government. I can feel the energies of these bombings off gassing into the grids of Gaia and the fear frequencies that emanate from them. I am not too surprised when I am led by St. Germain, Archangel Metatron, and Mother Mary to a space 'above' the decimated land, bomb sight, in Afghanistan.

Moving into this space, I feel immediately that the higher self of Donald Trump is lingering there, drifting around, feeling very distressed. I can feel the distress immediately, the incongruence in the soul field that is created through acts of violence, even as it is part of the soul's journey to play it out and to serve in this role sometimes. I ask the Higher Self of Donald Trump why he felt the need to bomb others, to kill. "Because he believes THEY were killing. THEY needed to be stopped. This is how he and the others felt to stop them," exclaims the Donald Higher Self (who I will just call "DHS" from now on).

"The only way to stop fear or to move fear or to stop the fear expression of killing is through love, not through MORE killing," I say to DHS, who of course agrees and resonates with me right away.

"I feel this, yes. I KNOW this. But, he, 3D Donald Trump, doesn't know it or remember it. He is scared and, deep, deep, down, he feels small. He does these things….using these big weapons, because he feels so small and wants to feel bigger," DHS answers.

I nod, feeling an energy of forgiveness and compassion flow through me to DHS and ALL the others like him who energize the timeline in 3D and moving into transitional 4D where this is the wounded power playout from unfelt emotional pain bodies and unawakened souls. DHS takes in the energy of forgiveness and feels touched by it and begins to cry. "How can you offer forgiveness to anyone who has taken life, who is leading killing as a response to more killing?"

I feel Mother Mary come through me then, as a more embodied aspect of me through the many moments of receiving forgiveness waves from Her, going into the deepest places inside of me together of core unworthiness, soul karmic binds, and shame and feeling forgiveness as Her constant response.

I respond, "ALL BEings are worth forgiveness, as ALL are worthy of love. Forgiveness is a high frequency of love. Although forgiveness can be given and offered, it can only be received and let in by a healing heart and emotional body with self worth to let it in, balanced with an awakening soul that is able to feel genuine remorse for their killing and fear-based actions."

DHS takes this in and seems relieved by it, "I will try to communicate this to lower Donald during his dreams, sometimes he can receive guidance from me during that state." He fades away as then I am brought to the other 'frontlines' between the Reptilians and Humans that are still polarized to fear and 'battling' each other with supposed light-based frequencies. I have been here before. This time, I feel the power coming from the Reptilian representative, who is a high ranking 'official' it feels like in their hierarchy (as they are still hierarchal-based.)

"My name is Salvizar. I am president, yes, like a king of my kind. I wanted to meet you," he says to me when I come to stand near him. He is a beautiful Reptilian, very tall with iridescent scales that shimmer and glow. He has a kingly energy, much more used to leading mass groups then the DHS. And he is actually there with me as he is a fourth dimensional BEing. "I can feel that you offer new possibilities to my species and how some of them are turning toward and drawn to these possibilities."

I show Salvizar a picture of the tropical planet that is being offered as a refuge and sanctuary to those Reptilians who choose to leave Gaia. I have traveled to it with my Shana and it offers a natural setting of peace and tranquility for them to start over. He asks me, "Why would we be given this after all that we have done to Humanity for so long…..enslaving you, imprisoning you in our 3D matrix, feeding off of your lower energy emissions?"

I again feel the Mother Mary energy within respond to him, "You cannot do anything to another that is not in their agreement on a soul level. You have done the lower frequency, fear-based things you have done, yes. Yet, you have BEEN these frequencies through collaboration WITH the Human species. It has been a sacred aspect of both of your journeys for it to play out as it has between you. You mirror the shadow side of Humanity and they mirror yours. You are now being offered an opportunity to choose love and to move out of and beyond fear. You are given this choice because you have ALWAYS been given this choice and ARE always given this choice, moment by moment…..whether to choose love or whether to choose fear. There is nothing you can do or BE that will remove this choice from you as it is represents the Infinite Love that you ARE as a fractal from Divine Source. It cannot be withdrawn, it can only expand.

I feel Salvizar taking this in, receiving these truths, remembering something he has forgotten about his love essence and also DHS drifting back in the space to receive this message as well and pass it on to his 3D Donald. They both move away from me now as I continue to offer waves of love and forgiveness to them and they receive what they are able to let in.

My heart feels heavy from visiting the energies of these 'frontlines' yet because I have offered love in the midst of them and to two leaders of these 'battles', I can feel a sense of peace and accomplishment. I can feel how the waves of love are rippling through the collective unconsciousness web of ALL, touching and being let in by those who are ready to receive them. By those who are ready to choose love and remember who and what they really ARE as Infinite Love.

~

Offering Possibilities Beyond The 3D Matrix, Reincarnation, and Shadow Projection

Here is my response to questions asked to me in response to my writing about being on the 'frontlines' offering love and forgiveness to representations of shadow and fear projections in our culture (Donald Trump and the Reptilians/Archons) and the sense that we collaborate in situations on a soul level and agree to what happens, whether personally or as a collective. The questions were: "I've read about the Reptilians and the 3D matrix and was always confused on how they could do this to us when we have free will. And wondered if it was even true to be honest. Does ascension break your soul free of the trap? Is the trap reincarnation? Does this mean you won't reincarnate anymore once freed?"

As I feel into a response to these questions, I want to say that I am offering just ONE possible timeline of reality. The one that I resonate with and feels like is tuned to a higher frequency, Golden New Earth, love-based vibration, although it is not THE absolute truth or the ONLY truth as there are unlimited possibilities of timelines playing out in every moment. You'll choose the one that most resonates with you in the moment…might be the one I am offering, might be another one.

In my experience, the things perceived by people as evil and dark are ultimately disowned aspects of their OWN shadow (or aspects from other lifetimes) that they have not embraced, so they are afraid of them and there is an emotional 'charge' about them. Even though there certainly ARE BEings (Ethereal, Human, Star BEings) that are more polarized to fear rather than love. It is REALLY about your relationship WITH these fear-based beings as it represents your relationship with your own shadow aspects. Do you give them a lot of energy in your life of push away and resistance? Do you spend a lot of energy trying to 'wake up others' to their existence and feel rage and hurt if they don't 'get it'? Do you hold your relationship with them with a victim energy, feeling they have done things to you 'against your will'? Are you resistant to feeling how YOU have an aspect that they represent within you or as an emotional body/psyche or soul aspect?

Feeling into the answers to these questions can open up whole new areas of inner exploration for you if you feel drawn to go there. This outward projection of charged resistance to shadow aspects can be a sacred phase in someone's journey and a very necessary timeline for them to walk out until they no longer need or want to.

On one particular timeline, for the souls who need to experience it as part of their awakening process, the 3D matrix created by an 'evil' race of Reptilians they call Archons (and other names) is VERY REAL. I believe this 'outer' matrix is the representation of an inner matrix made up of undigested emotional and soul woundings creating the sense of limited or capped perception, self deception and manipulation of others, disempowerment, being a slave to something….all of these are 'chosen' by the soul as an aspect of the awakening journey although often this is not conscious to the person fused to the parts of them that don't remember this choice. For those who may not see or feel the inner origins of this matrix, they project out that it is coming from 'evil forces' of all sorts and kinds and being 'done to them'. Parts of them are afraid of these evil forces and this fear draws MORE of this experience to them. It is a continual loop for them until it is no longer needed for growth. This loop is again, VERY REAL, to the person experiencing it.

    I feel an aspect of this loop is also related to the timeline that 'believes' in reincarnation, however it is related to either as a necessary aspect of growth or as a trap. Because time in 3D reality FEELS REAL then so do past lives and, therefore, the idea of reincarnation. From a 5D and higher perspective, linear time does not exist and neither do 'past' lives in the sense offered by reincarnation. Beyond linear time, there is no 'coming back' lifetime after lifetime as the soul exists in the NOW spectrum.

    Offering a different timeline around this that I have experienced myself more and more is the sense I have that we have 'other' aspects of us, fractals off of a main soul source which I call a Metasoul (Metatron offered that word.) These Metasoul aspects of ours exist in different 'eras' and dimensions and their energy can be VERY influential in what we experience in the NOW. Connecting with them, healing with them, and eventually integrating them (the timeline they are on just seems to collapse and 'go away' eventually) allows for the you in the now to embody more of your soul gifts and soul accesses.

    Your consciousness sort of absorbs theirs over time and all their experiences. I have experienced this merged consciousness exchange many times on many levels....from parts from this life such as the Inner Child and the Inner Protector to aspects from other lifetimes such as a High Priestess from Avalon or a medicine woman to aspects from other planets such as an Arcturian, Pleiadian, and other aspects. This seems to be a very effective way to heal karma (which I hesitate to use that word for all the fear projection onto it).

The way to 'get free' of this loop of outward charged projection of shadow, reincarnation limited ideas, and the inner matrix is by going within to awaken your soul and heal your heart. Being open and willing to feel ALL that is within you in the shadow of your emotional body and your soul legacy and your energetic/chakral body.

Ascension into higher frequencies (while also focusing on healing the emotional body which can act like an anchor lowering your vibration otherwise) DOES shift you into another possible timeline where you have access to your soul in a very fluid and connected way where you no longer see or experience 'chapters' of your lives playing out in the way as offered by reincarnation. Soul contracts, reincarnation, and past lives all become 'ideas' that can feel binding, ultimately fear-based, and limiting compared to the dynamic, fluid, multidimensional frequencies of your SOUL ESSENCE as it expresses in the NOW. And, you also feel and hold more and more, that it ALL comes from love, is sacred, and is your soul's journey of remembering its essence AS Infinite Love.

~

Healing The Inner Punisher, Seeing And Feeling The Inner And Outer World From LOVE Rather Than Battle

FULL glorious EIGHT hour sleep last night, "gift from the Divine," says my body. Something calming and quiet inside for the last two days. Interesting that some people are offering that there was a big battle between dark and light yesterday, against Archonic/Reptilian energies, a stand-off or something. I guess I am just in a DIFFERENT timeline because, for me, something settled in softer, more surrender, more sense that LOVE will carry us through. I just can't vibrate with the battle, can't reSOULnate with it, don't want to put ANY energy into it….

Anything AGAINST anything else just doesn't feel like it actually heals or moves or transforms anything. The inner embrace of it ALL, not being against anything, moves the stuck grounds, the negative grounds, the dark grounds.... over and over, in my experience. It feels to me that this way of seeing the world as needing to be battled stems from an unhealed ground of Inner Punisher or Inner Critic part/subpersonality. The Inner Punisher is SUCH a strong energy in our collective and inside of us until it is connected with and healed.

I have had many versions of Inner Punisher over the years with sometimes intense energies of self hate, self criticism and then that frequency projected onto others in outrage, withheld (mostly) judgments without love, discernment with arrogance. I worked with a parts work facilitator for close to five years and this energy was a BIG one inside of me as my birth parents were very outwardly critical of me. This led to acute self consciousness about myself (esp. my appearance) that took years of self love and love with others to heal. I have worked with others holding space for these kind of frequencies for ten years as a space holder and I feel that we may ALL have this Inner Punisher and without connecting to this energy directly, it remains unhealed and therefore running as an underground stream in our 3D transitioning to 4D emotional body.

The desire to battle ANYTHING stems from this unhealed inner battle. The unhealed suffering loop between the part of you that punishes and then the part of you that feels shame can be VERY prevalent, yet unconscious. It can impact SO MUCH of how you experience daily life, relationships, and, yes, hugely how you view the world. It feels like those who hold strong energies of needing to do battle against something OUT in the world remain unhealed from the battle that is going on INSIDE and the resulting shame at the root of it. Also, there is often the idea that something can be done 'against your will' or 'to you without your permission' when, from a soul level, we CHOOSE all that we experience. Your 3D Self or unconscious ego may feel like it is against THEIR will, but your Higher Self and soul choose the experience actually in COLLABORATION with the Higher Self of the Reptilian because you have a Reptilian fractal from your soul group. It feels like an unhealed Punisher that would believe we could be trapped into something or held against our will as that is the exact energy it is vibrating at if it remains unhealed inside of us.

In this process of loving ALL that is within (including the Reptile and the Inner Punisher) we truly leave the battlefield behind and enter more and more the FIELD of LOVE, which is a different reality altogether. It really is a whole different timeline. Yet to enter it is not just a change in perspective about it, but a shift from the emotional ground, the unconscious ground from which so much of how we experience reality is formed and shaped. Related to ascension, these unhealed emotional frequencies in the 3D pain body can anchor your ascension process in lower vibrational energies.

From Shana (my Reptilian Self), she offered that there is a growing number of Reptilians (which they prefer to 'Archons', it is more like 'Humans', just describes what they are rather than Archons which has a negative twist to it) are wanting to stop battling, are wanting peace, are wanting something new. This group has moved to a new planet and left Gaia. Many people are saying that the 'evil has left', yet it is actually the forerunners or waySHOWers (like us only in Reptilian form) that are leading their species in a new direction. I LOVED the feeling of this, of the possibilities of this, and I offered to help her and her ROGUE group of healing Reptilians in any way that I can.

The way to free yourself from the matrix, free yourself from supposed 'slavery', free yourself from supposed evil is by BECOMING LOVE toward and with yourself firstly and then toward others. Sometimes a reframing around the whole reality is necessary, as I am offering here. It's not that I'm denying the existence of Reptilians calibrated to fear frequencies yet I'm offering that in their core is LOVE and I lead with the question, how can we come from love toward and with them?

If the Reptilian reality doesn't resonate with where you are at right now, that's fine. I do, however, encourage you to start getting in touch with your Inner Punisher/Critic. It can be an intense energy, yet if you connect with love in your heart, this energy WILL soften and, as always, in my experience, it has GOOD reason for being the way it is. A simple letter exchange back and forth with this energy and then a dialogue to get to know it can open up whole vistas of self love and healing. After enough connection ground with the Inner Punisher, then the inner shame frequencies can be felt as well and transmuted into innocence. Shame parts are often VERY shy and acutely self conscious and largely buried in shadow in most people so it takes negotiation with the Inner Punisher to get TRUE and authentic access to shame.

A space holder/facilitator/teacher who has done their own parts work in a deep way (which is rare, in my opinion) can be really important for this type of inner work as the Inner Punisher can be tricky and elusive. This is the space holding that we offer in SoulFullHeart and have journeyed this ground inside of ourselves extensively.

I offer a FIELD of LOVE in an outward way to you and through the transmissions in my words and in the space that I hold for others....it can water this field inside of you yet the true flow is created and comes from purifying your inner waters with self love, becoming conscious of the battle grounds going on inside to experience a LOVE FIELD reality more and more on the outside.

~

BEing Fast Tracked Related To Ascension

Wonderful afternoon unfolding, just arising from one thing to another, sitting in the sun, sharing tea and veggie sandwich at a cafe, no rush, just moving along to the next place and the next, taking our consciousness with us…..enlivening conversations with my two favorite Angelic Earth men on the planet my beloved mate Raphael and Gabriel Heartman. We talked about how it feels like we are all being 'fast-tracked' …those of us on this journey to ascend and heal and BE Healers offering to others.

  We feel this in SoulFullHeart as our personal processes are speeding up, quantum healing in moments, mega soul and heart healing happening fast, and continual creativity and ideas for offering and serving love. We are being fast-tracked because it feels like an intense phase is coming up with many of the old structures of the old timelines collapsing and falling away. Those of us, like you who are reading these words, with healing gifts will be very much needed. Those of us with a heart to serve and give will be in very much demand. Those of us called to serve love will be very busy it feels like.

  Part of the fast-trackness is claiming of your soul gifts and their expression, being bold to offer who and what you are, seeking to learn and train and grow so you can offer more, being willing to feel the self image attachments that may come up and heal them, being willing to feel the unworthiness feelings that come up in parts of you and heal them. Finding waySHOWers to offer a path and process perhaps that you can be part of and offer and serve love through. That is available through SoulFullHeart as a facilitator by the way, if you are drawn to that as it feels like we will be NEEDING more souls to serve as SoulFullHeart facilitators in the future.

  I have felt for many years the sense of collapse and recognized too that sometimes only through collapses and completions can the new be born. Out of the ashes arises the phoenix……this phoenix is the NEW Sacred Human. Some souls will arise into this, those of us who have been feeling this for maybe many years and on this awakening path for many years. Or maybe you have just 'popped' recently into awakening through intense awakening experiences that came about seemingly 'suddenly' (although orchestrated by your Higher Self all along). I am hearing of this 'sudden popping' from more and more people who seem to find themselves transported from 3D and into 4D and even into 5D and higher dimensional states in some ways very quickly.

  The eclipse coming up soon feels important as a 'marker' in time (even though time is not real); a placeholder to feel how we are entering a new phase of intensity in this intense year of 2017. What you have lived with that comes from a lower frequency will no longer be able to be justified or tolerated. Relationships that are being held onto out of safety will collapse. Jobs that don't serve love or your higher purpose will fade away with new opportunities coming to you. Geographies that don't speak to your soul will 'run out of ground', inviting you to explore and find new terrains, perhaps connected to a conscious soul family community. Soul mates/counter parts who 'signed up' to be in ascension will find each other more easily and things will probably progress FAST between you, no longer with years to 'get to know each other'…..you probably won't want to wait anyway!

  I feel for the Human body as it is stretched and reconfigured as it is fast-tracked too. As it is outfitted in a new 'suit' of crystallized energy to replace the carbon 'bodyprint.' This can bring body pains, body discomforts, body flus and body rashes, sudden congestions as the body shifts into a higher frequency. Recognizing when these symptoms are an aspect of the ascension process can help…sometimes the pains are 'old' objects and structures that your soul has held onto or are being energized in past lives suddenly dissolve and leave some residual pain behind. They are like scaffolding that is no longer needed or a vestigial organ that has ceased to serve a function any longer. This happened for me yesterday as my Reptilian brain stem dissolved. Head pain can be the pineal gland growing and shining and turning 'ON' too.

Self love is so important during the fast-track. Going within to find your grounding with Mother Gaia and going without into nature to connect with Her too in a conscious way. Going within to connect with Angelic Guides, Spirit Guides, Star BEing Selves…...even Archons-Reptilian Selves. Going within to breathe, to center, to clean and protect and activate your chakras. Going within to feel parts of yourself and their emotional reactions and digestions to ALL of the changes, especially your 3D Self that has been comfortable and secure in 3D life and maybe even comfortable too in the last 'vestiges' of that old life, content in shifting through the rubble of the old life.

Much love is available from so many sources to help those of us who are being fast-tracked. Love to you fellow fast-trackers! See you and feel you as we zoom through the timelines and multiple dimensions and collapsing and changing realities and experience of the self….. looking for love, resonating in love, BEing with love and offering/serving love.

~

Ways You May Be Experiencing The Intense Energy Shifts

It's only a couple of weeks into 2017 yet and, already, the tops have gone turvy and the timelines have gone from straight to curvy in response to the intense energy waves coming into our worlds, globally and personally. These boosts of energy can bring completions and beginnings; upheavals and creations; turning overs and tuning ins.

Here are some of the ways you may already be experiencing the accelerated momentum that will be the mark of this year as we shift into a higher gear related to ascension:

Altered Reality States – Reality as you have mostly known it is continuing to shift. More 'paranormal' experiences are leaking through your consciousness lifting the veils between 3D perception and reality beyond the five senses. You are experiencing an increasing sense of wonder and joy in moments, moved by the absolute magic and wonder of the moment.

You are not the same as you were, as if someone else is now looking through your eyes out at the world and living in your skin. Most of the time, this feels amazing and, sometimes, it can be overwhelming. Maybe you are losing words, maybe losing your mind (in a good way) for longer periods, maybe not experiencing time at all or definitely keeping less track of it. People around you may be noticing that you have changed and commenting on it with some of them coming along and others not able to resonate.

Deeper Access to Ethereal Beings – The new energies seem to support easier connection with Ethereal Beings such as Archangels, Spirit Guides, Ascended Teachers, and passed loved ones. All of the 'clairs' have been heightened: clairaudience, clairvoyance, clairsentience especially are dialed up. It's like you are a radio antennae and you've been turned up to a higher setting.

You may hear guidance much more clearly; see Ethereal Beings with much more clarity; feel intuitive reactions much more deeply. If you have lingering doubts about your capacity and ability to connect with spiritual beings, you are gathering the resources that you need to help you tune in and expand your capacities. The story of "I can't" seems to be being drowned out by the necessity of the Universe for you to connect with higher guidance.

Expanding Creative Visualization During Meditation – The older paradigm modes of meditating may not be working for you anymore, such as focusing only on your breath or repeating a mantra over and over. You may have already begun or already be engaged in creative visualization or shamanic journeying during meditation, where there are no limits on where you can go or what you experience. Following the leadings of your Ethereal Guides, you are taken on adventures into 4D and 5D (and beyond) consciousness states, parallel dimensions, other planets, and even galaxies. You are letting go of the 'practice' of meditation to let your soul and Higher Self take you to where you most need to go. You are drawing resources to help you remember these avenues that were once so natural, opening up to your intuition and creativity more and more.

Renewed Focus On Chakras – Taking care of your chakras is going from a spiritual concept to a beloved and critical aspect of your daily self love routine. You are able to feel them more deeply and clearly, see their vibrant colors, locate them with your hands and your inner eye. You again draw resources to expand your knowledge and connection with the seven main chakras (whatever system you choose to follow), feeling your relationship with them deepen and expand beyond mental understanding. You may be experiencing body symptoms of ascension such as flu, head and neck aches, shift in sleep patterns, change in appetite, etc. You are connecting these shifts with your chakras and noticing that cleaning and protecting them daily helps with these physical changes. You are empowering yourself around energy healing for yourself as you connect with your energetic essence and auric field.

Relationship Completions & Beginnings – Relationships are in a big transition and you are in various phases of experiencing these shiftings. You are finding an increasing need to set boundaries with people in your life, often saying 'no' to events and previous commitments and expected behaviors. As this creates rumbles of reactions in those around you, you find there is something more authentic at the heart of it all that serves you with the strength and confidence to keep going. As some relationships are completing, there is also an increase in relationships that are beginning or forming. You may find that you are suddenly in a romance with someone who feels like a soul mate and that it happened quite quickly. The previous holdbacks are dissolving and you feel compelled to explore it and see where it goes. Or if you are in a romantic relationship, you may be experiencing that ground of it is shifting with new dynamics of deeper soul bond frequencies coming up and lower dimensional conflicts reducing greatly. You may have the feeling of 'falling in love' all over again and your mate as someone that you are very excited to get to know even more deeply!

Trailing Edge Emotions Coming Up And Moving Out Fast – Trailing edge is that which is at your growth edge or what you struggle with or are 'working on' this life. It often relates to what is still in subconscious shadow within your psyche or emotional body. These energies of acceleration seem to be pushing up and out that which has been in shadow to be felt and healed. You may be experiencing that this process of feeling and healing is going much quicker. One moment you are feeling parts of you that are scared or resistant. And then, the next moment, you are feeling joyful and expansive. Deeper emotional movements are requiring your complete attention and self love and care, calling you to hold space for yourself during this intense transition. Resources come to you in different forms to serve your leading edge of being (your highest self) to feel, heal, and integrate.

During this time of transition and intense energies, strap your heartbelts on and go within through meditation as often as you need and want to! Going within will help you tap into the essence of Infinite Love that provides the motivation to ride the waves of all these shifts.

~

Anchoring To Fifth Dimensional Frequencies As You Remember That You Already ARE

"You've been anchored to the fifth dimension since the beginning of the year," the voice of my Guides/Higher Dimensional Aspects/Spirit 'team' offered to me this morning. They got my attention because they aren't usually so specific with me, although this is not a surprise either what they told me. There was a significant shift in the degree and depth of photonic light PURE love juice available at the beginning of the year.

These light waves have activated, in an even more intense way, those of us signed up to be WaySHOWers, trail blazers. This energy has created a sense of being 'fast tracked'. Slugging through mud for years in a quiet, disinterested room has been my experience in offering SoulFullHeart and now it is easier, smoother, with much more interest and reSOULance and the 'room' has expanded to feel like a vast sky of possibilities.

The start of a 'new year' isn't real, on one level, yet to our linear minds and 3D Selves it is VERY real and symbolic of change, transition, and growth possibilities. This is the energy of New Year's resolutions, of wishing and wanting for MORE in life, or for life to really BEGIN. The mantra I received from my Guides at the beginning of the year was "a year beyond fear"…for me, this meant acknowledging that there still IS fear (although not much anymore, I admit) and yet it is about moving BEYOND the fear in order to serve love. It was about 'putting my voice and teachings out there', to share my writings especially and then sort of 'stumbling on' the soul gift of voice transmissions, Light Language, guiding meditations, and video transmissions and sharing those more and more. None of this is strategic, I don't have a 'sales plan' for SoulFullHeart. I am not THINKING really about any of this. It is literally just wake up and see where the Divine creative flow takes me and where responding to interest from others takes me and where LOVE takes me.

Serving love is BEING anchored in the fifth dimension or New Earth or Golden Earth. Serving love IS serving self too….the two are actually NOT separate as more and more the service of love is just who you ARE. I am experiencing less and less 'me there' in terms of an active personality or persona and more an ENERGY of serving loveness in every moment, whether with myself, with others, with Raphael, with animals, with my house, WITH everything, WITH life. Even 'sessions' are becoming not any different than any other moment in the day, just maybe more a concentrated experience of serving love. In

PURE service of love, there is no self in the 3D way or even 4D way of parts and personas, there just IS an I AM that is offering, being received, and being in exchange. This 'I Amness' is without self consciousness, without personal tracking or filtering, and without self monitoring….this IS an incredibly freeing and wonderful way to BE in the self and with others.

Being anchored to the fifth dimension feels like a connection to a home frequency that cannot be broken or severed or gone back from. "There is no going back now" sounds a bit ominous but it IS actually reassuring because when you are in this place you don't WANT to go back to lower frequencies. You dip down in moments, you learn what dips you down or pulls you down and you set different boundaries……although these are needed less and less too as you just ARE your current highest expression and you INVITE others to join you and they can feel who and where you are and stay away if they don't want to raise UP to join you. Your energy sets the boundaries, love offers the boundaries and it dissolves ALL boundaries as well.

In those that I have served love with recently in what we've called 'sessions' I can feel how their anchoring to the fifth dimension, while still in process of deepening, is just THERE because it IS who they actually ARE as INfinite Love. AND, it's who you just ARE too. You are ALREADY THERE on a soul level, your Higher Self is certainly there already and much higher too. And there is 'no there there', so to speak, as it is not a place but rather a consciousness frequency to be remembered and embraced more and more deeply.

So, parts of you may feel like you are NOT there, that you are dipping down or pulled down many times a day and even for days or weeks at a time. And, maybe you are still connected more to 3D and 4D reality consciousness or really parts of you are still connected on the levels that are subconscious to you (until they become conscious.) You are maybe still very in 3D consciousness at your job or way you 'earn your livelihood'. Or you are 3D consciousness with your family, friends, and romantic partner. Or with how you relate with money. Or how you relate with body. Maybe you are MOSTLY a protective part energy a majority of the time, mostly guarding your heart, who is definitely connected in some ways to 3D reality.

Yet, STILL you are anchored to the fifth dimension and beyond as your HOME frequency, as your home bandwidth, as the tone you return to when out of the body. This is the frequency of your higher heart, your cosmic heart, the heart chakra that vibrates higher and higher and expands OUT to others and to the WORLD and to galaxies more and more. So, yes, there are some how's to anchoring to the fifth dimension in terms of how to EXPERIENCE that you already ARE anchored to it. The main HOW (at least in what I am here to offer) is to connect with and defuse from the energies and parts inside of you that are clinging to 3D consciousness still. AND to make life changes to transition to a higher consciousness in ALL areas of your life so that your I AMness can just BE and flow through all areas without dip downs and back ups again.

LOVE to YOU wherever you are currently connecting to in the moment at whatever consciousness level as ALL phases are sacred. AND, I hold out the invitation for the deeper experience and remembering of the anchoring in fifth New Golden Earth frequencies that you ALREADY ARE.

~

It Is Time To Burst Bubbles, Remove Compartments In Order To Serve Love

Bubbles are being burst and compartments are being flooded WITH LOVE. These bubbles and compartments served you for a phase as your soul has been awakening and the frequencies of expansion beyond your 3D conditioning have been SO needed. They served the learning and exploration as your mind deconditioned from so much academic training and programming about what reality is and isn't. They served you as the ground rumbled from within, quaking and shaking inside as you started to remember WHO and WHAT and WHY you are here.

These bubbles serve you until they no longer do. Increasingly potent waves of PURE love from Divine Source want to burst ALL the bubbles that remain in your life. Waves of PURE love want to swarm and reform the compartments that parts of you have created in your life to separate your soul alchemy from other areas that have not been ready to change and transform yet. A compartmentalized life is how the 3D Self can cope with the awakening of the 4D Self, it is how these frequencies are negotiated and even allowed to happen from within you. ONE area of life can change (maybe it is career or geography) but not ALL areas....this is how the 3D Self 'controls' the process of awakening until it can no longer BE controlled.

An example of compartments in your life is going to spiritual weekend workshops and retreats to get your soul watered and then coming home to or living with discordant and even toxic relationships that no longer serve your soul. Your unawakening mate may agree to this compartmentalization for a phase too in an attempt to preserve the relationship..it's OK for you to go to workshops, retreats, see your 'Healer' as long as the relationship stays the same and isn't impacted or changed. As long as you don't ask or invite your mate to JOIN YOU in the awakenings, then everything is 'fine.' The two 3D Selves 'agree' to this arrangement and the unawakened partner says they are being 'supportive' when really they are being suppressive and YOU are allowing them to be because somehow that serves part of you as well.

This compartmentalization can REALLY show up in birth family relationships as so much of the ground within them is based on 3D conditioning and role playing. Your birth family 'doesn't get' what your soul is awakening to and even judges it as 'crazy', yet your 3D Selves agree that the family bond gets to stay intact as long as they 'support' you in your path and you agree to remain in the family, do family events and holidays, not be 'too crazy or strange'. Again, this isn't actually resonant support but a compartmentalized and codependent agreement between 3D Selves. This can be the same dynamic in friendships too that are based on 'old' and previous life phases that you are outgrowing and moving beyond.

Another example of compartments in your life is continuing to do a job that is deadening, toxic, flat, not reflective of your soul purpose and reason for being here even as you SAY that you are here to serve love, be a Healer, be a Teacher. This is SO understandable for a phase as you transition to the expression of your soul purpose as your means of livelihood. But, watch and feel for the 3D Self keeping you stuck in a job that doesn't reflect your soul in order to shrink your bigness and keep you 'safe'. This part of you can use anxiety about money and existential trust issues to keep you stuck in a career and job that isn't serving love, which is the ULTIMATE reason for the soul awakening in the first place.

This is what bursts the bubbles and floods the compartments that parts of you have created and constructed….the DESIRE, the URGE, the COMPLETE DRIVE to serve love in ALL moments and in ALL ways. The service of love THROUGH you and TO yourself and WITH others is what provides the courage to complete the job, to complete the relationships, to complete the 'weekend warrior' seeker mode and truly CLAIM your soul expression in all moments. The service of love THROUGH you creates the NEW space to hold the reactions of parts of you as they transition and let go of the old structures and the energetic bubbles that form a 'second skin' over your auric field are dissolved.

The GRAND collective awakening that is happening in the NOW that we all agreed to participate in as souls has a force and energy to it that can be tapped into and downloaded in a personal way. Connection with Ethereal Guides in a way that is visceral and REAL for you, a way that allows you to

ACTUALLY make the changes you need to make in your life (the practical changes that you NEED to make) is available and they are SO ready to help you. Your Guides and Higher Self WANT to be life coaches for you, not just deliver higher frequency contextual messages all the time from 'on high' in some transcendent tones that doesn't really provide much relevant application to your life. Your Guides and Higher Self are VERY invested in you making the changes you need to make yet they can't go against the 'free will' (or stubbornness sometimes) of your 3D Self. ASK them to help you make the changes you need to make on the day-to-day living level, and then surrender into the transitions that are necessary to REALLY be expressing from your soul essence and stepping into and UP TO what you are here to BE and DO. Archangel Metatron in particular is a very effective life coach and project manager (he wanted me to add that!)

In all of my SoulFullHeart sessions with women recently, the main theme of our process together has been around what their compartments and bubbles are and what the next steps are to moving them forward. Feeling places and parts (we start with the Inner Protector) that have blocked their soul frequencies from coming in, rumbling the ground, creating and making changes, moving them on if needed from toxic relationships especially. This is 'practical ascension' and it is about REAL changes happening, not just reading spiritual articles online and sharing quote cards on social media or taking in spiritual phrases and ideals back and forth while you continue to suffer in your ACTUAL life. But TRULY changing what IS NOT working for you any more on a soul level. The Higher Self YOU already KNOWS what these changes ARE that you need to make….you have probably been thinking and feeling what they are even as you are reading these words.

Negotiation with your Inner Protector as you are supported by your most beloved Guides allows for the moving forward of these soul changes. Your Inner Protector is the aspect of your 3D Self that has been in charge of guarding and defending your most precious assets such as your Inner Child, your Inner Feminine (in both men and women), your Inner Teenager, your SOUL bigness and expression. This loyal aspect of you doesn't need to be battled or overcome to allow these changes but rather felt and connected to….to feel that he can NOW rest and have YOU take over.

Suffering in ANY areas of your life can come to a completion as you allow the frequencies that are available NOW of PURE love INTO all areas of your life. This means letting in and letting go, being willing to question and wonder about EVERYTHING in your life and WHY you have chosen it and feel into if it is serving love or if it is not. It is the willingness and openness to be REAL about what you have created in your life as you are NOT victim to any of it but rather THE grand creator that has drawn it all to you and for you. This means trusting in deepening ways that the changes that you ARE guided to make serve your soul essence as an expression of service of love in Human form.

~

ALL Are Being Invited To Wake Up!

"All are being invited to WAKE UP!"…..one of those messages I received that feels like a newspaper headline broadcast from the Divine Source News Station that we are all connected into as souls. ALL are being invited to awaken to the remembrance of this connection and to All That Is and to No-Thing-Ness too. ALL are being invited to awaken to their Sacred Humanity, the embodiment of their Higher Self (a higher dimensional fractal from Divine Source that we 'left behind' when we came into Human body here) along with the maturation of our emotional bodies and healing of our soul legacy experiences from other lifetimes.

The invitation for this waking up is coming primarily in the form of increasingly higher vibrational frequency love and light waves that we've all been feeling the effects of, in the last six months especially. The Schumann Resonance, which measure's the magnetic field vibration of Gaia, has been peaking at 120 lately....THIS IS HIGH! We are still adjusting as it rose from its consistent 7.83 HZ to 15-25 HZ in 2014 and now THIS level, which has never been experienced in our history of recording it. It seems to be a sign, some 'physical proof' of the higher vibrational frequencies that are caused by and are helping to cause the awakening of Humanity beyond our previous chosen caps, traps, and matrixes that limited our consciousness.

    Our DNA is waking up too, those sleepy strands that we put to bed after the fall of Atlantis (which is actually STILL happening beyond the linear time picture). Waking up DNA gives us access to so much more of our capacity as Infinite Creators, Infinite Awareness, and Infinite Possibilities in Human form. Waking up DNA helps us to remember, connect with, and integrate our multidimensional aspects that exist in the NOW, waiting to infuse us with expanded capacities in all areas.

    Our bodies continue to adjust to these increases, upgrading from carbon-based to crystalline frequencies, transforming into light bodies at the cellular level. Our adjusting bodies ask us for connection...for us to feel and hear and respond to what their shifting needs are. To be able to sleep when needed, especially, as that creates a 'reboot' and integration time. To connect with nature seems to help our bodies A LOT through this transition. For me, it has been daily trips to the beach, to bury my hands and feet in the sand, take in the sun codes, feel the salty water and ocean breeze. If I had access to forests, I would walk in the trees, put my palms on the trunks, connect in with their root systems. Even meditating, journeying to scenes with nature and the five elements can help right now.

    The increased level of light waves seems to create a sense of being juiced on caffeine, like there is all this EXTRA energy somehow if you tap into it from a soul place. It provides juice for creative projects, service of love projects, and clearer communication and access to the bigger picture and vision around these projects. For me, I have felt like I am constantly being downloaded creative ideas to respond to….I am getting better at navigating these downloads so I can also rest, meditate, feel the priorities, respond to service, be and feel balanced.

"ALL are being Fast Tracked!" is the other Divine Source news headline. Gaia is being Fast Tracked, so of course so are we as her Human guests. Fast tracked seems to mean an acceleration of the soul awakenings that you've been experiencing as your consciousness raises out of 3D reality processing and into 4D. Decompartmentalizations and bursting bubbles too that your 3D Self may have created around your awakenings. The previous compartments and bubbles that 'held back' the awakening from creating a rumble or changes in your life can be dissolved and collapsed FAST right now with linear time meaning nothing in terms of actual processing and digestion and decision making. Your soul is being supported to burst out of ANY container and express through you in any and all ways possible that serve love.

All this changing and transition brings our attention to our emotional body and the aspects of us that are still anchoring into 'past' traumas and pains, freeze frame stuck there with feelings of fear, resistance, being lost, disconnection, anxiety. These aspects of us NEED our growing awakening self (our soul infused self) to BE with them, to feel them, and to bring them into the current with us, into the now with us, into the new timeline with us.

ALL are being invited to wake up and to fast track this awakening. To enter this higher vibrational frequency timeline means letting go and most likely collapsing the one you are currently living. Shifting with love and inner negotiation into this NEW one with a NEW Earth experience with an increasingly mature emotional body, experience of a deeply nourishing inner and outer Sacred Union, a light-based Human body, and an inhabited frequency of our Sacred Humanity. A timeline which offers us increasing experience of our essence as Infinite Love walking, talking, and BEing here!

EMOTIONAL AREA

You can fly to the heavens and BE with angels. You can BEcome more of the transcendent BEing that you ARE. You have been more of this substance of light and AIR than you have been anything else. You have been more of the stars, then of Gaia and a Human body. You have been more soul than fleshy substance even if you feel that you have many lifetimes on Earth, what you might call 'past lives' although they are in the NOW...

Yet....As you go on your quest to the stars, how is your heart?

Your heart reflects your capacity to FEEL, to CARE, and to LOVE...the BEST of what makes you Human. Your heart also reflects your emotional body and your pain body, your 3D body....the place where the energies are stored of what you have experienced and felt as a Human in this 3D reality and what still needs to be digested. You can BEcome more and more transcendent, yet, your emotional body has pain and congestion and it will anchor you to lower frequencies. Its unhealed places will draw situations to repeat out suffering patterns for you to see and feel. Your soul frequencies, your transcendent nature, can be used by aspects of you that don't want to feel, that want to bypass heart healing, that want only light and no dark or shadow exploration.

As you awaken your soul, how is your heart?

As your emotional pain body heals, the anchorings lighten up, the aspects of you that guard, that hold the suffering frequencies, that are emotionally reactive in a charged way, that resist letting in love. These aspects transform into their higher frequencies, and eventually integrate into your Sacred Human/Higher Self embodiment. Your soul awakening can then ground into Gaia and into your healing and healthy Human heart. And, your heart vibrates at a higher frequency of health, it becomes more connected to the Christ Consciousness heart, the Mother Mary Consciousness heart, the cosmic heart.

As you become more of your cosmic BEing, how is your heart?

You are meant to take your heart WITH you on the journey of remembering yourself as a galactic BEing. It is your healing heart that brings in frequencies of vulnerability, compassion, reverence, humility, grace, surrender, relationality, connection, and healthy expression of femininity and masculinity. It is your healing heart that draws nourishing intimacies to you and relationships that water with love both your heart AND your soul. It is your healing heart that compels you to serve love as your highest purpose.

How is your heart? What does it REALLY want and need to experience and have felt in order to let in and BEcome MORE and MORE of the Infinite Love that you ARE?

~

Seven Areas Of Life: Introducing the Emotional Area Of Life And The Emotional Body

I discovered in serving others and holding space for my own process that it was helpful to think of the seven main areas of life and to use them as a lens to provide a locator on a journey that REALLY is often about getting and feeling very LOST as you find your authentic self and let go of what is not. With this so often feeling lostness, it is comforting to have SOMETHING to navigate with, to locate, to send up like a flare in the sky to see the landscape a bit more clearly for a moment.

The seven areas of life that we offer in our SoulFullHeart process and that we feel are the most important are Emotional, Spiritual, Mental, Social, Physical, Financial, and Environmental. Reality, of course, flows and weaves into all of these and cannot actually be categorized or compartmentalized. However, most 3D Selves seem to operate from a place of compartmentalization, so it can be a helpful bridge during the transition to the 4D Self and higher. For example, 'work life' can be very different from 'home life' with different aspects showing up to respond to these energies. Your financial life may feel quite 'separate' from your spiritual life. Your physical body health may be at a different consciousness than your spiritual and so on.

Another lens that can be helpful is identifying the expression of your 3D, 4D or 5D Selves related to each area of life. I've included questions for you to feel into in each of the sections that feature writings about the seven areas of life.

The 3D Self is the conditioned self, the version of you that received templating and conditioning from your birth family, culture, friends and in many other ways to reflect a more limited consciousness from the soul's expansive one. The 4D Self is in transition, awakening to your soul frequencies, sorting and letting go of what isn't authentic to the soul in all areas of life. The 5D Self is the embodiment more and more of your Sacred Human and the Higher Self (who is a fractal from your Metasoul that vibrates at a higher frequency and holds the memories and knowledge of all your other lifetimes).

I offer here the Emotional area of life and how the 3D, 4D, and 5D consciousness expresses and holds it. Feeling our emotional realities can be bypassed or transcended using spiritual awakening frequencies, positive affirmations, teachings that 'negative emotions are bad' and through Inner Protector aspects that 'lift' you up rather than allow you to be in the emotive ground. We have found that traditional therapies often don't 'touch' the actual ground of our emotional bodies as they are often processed or analyzing feelings through the mental body or mind rather than truly going deep into the emotional body. Psychiatry drugs our emotional bodies and mental bodies AND our physical bodies in an attempt to alter the chemistry of our emotions which usually only serves to numb us out and deaden our soul awakening possibilities.

Inhabitation and embodiment of our TRUE emotive ground and emotional bodies I feel rarely happens for most people as their 3D Selves work to avoid, numb, resist, and distract from feeling. This avoidance can keep you in an emotionally immature place as these places remain untouched and unprocessed and unfelt. Aspects of the awakening into 4D consciousness are so painful and push up so many reactions to be felt as you let go of so much of your 'old' life that feeling your feelings becomes almost unavoidable. It presses on you to feel yourself and to mature your emotional body beyond the places where it is stuck in 'past' toxic and traumatic experiences. Rather than being a smoothly flowing river, these stuck places of emotional congestion form like boulders, blocking the flow.

These boulders are energy, have distinct personalities and distinct likes and dislikes, they have particular 'modes of being' and strategies that they've developed over this life and pulling from other lifetimes and karma. We feel these 'boulders' as parts or subpersonalities or aspects (we use all these terms) and we directly work with, connect, and validate the reality of these parts in order to negotiate and navigate and awaken the emotional body. There is much more about working with parts in this section coming up.

The Emotional area of life includes your relationship to your emotions, your subconscious, your pain/emotional body, your emotional healing, your emotional reactions and triggers, your subpersonalities formed from this life and soul wounded experiences and your emotional expression or suppression of feelings.

3D: Your third dimensional (3D) Self is usually emotionally immature, in the sense of being largely unconscious about your emotional wounding and how it impacts your life. Your 3D Self can be emotionally reactive, easily triggered, and often play victim or use other strategies to divert taking responsibility for their lives, emotions, and life outcomes. You may fuse without consciousness to different parts of yourself while having brief moments of authenticity usually with very beloved people or in 'perfect' settings or situations. You may have done some emotional or psychotherapy work on your emotional body which creates some lightening up and preparation to move into 4D. It is the 3D Self that has been labeled with mental illness diagnoses whose actual root cause is in the congested emotional body. The 3D Self 'becomes' depression, anxiety, rage, mania, etc. without 'space' around the mood or emotional state. Emotions are generally seen as either 'negative' or 'positive' with active or passive suppression in play around expression of them.

A dominant motivation for the 3D Self is the use of many 'drugs' to numb emotions and wounding, such as codependent relationships, food, entertainment, content, distractions, alcohol, cigarette smoking, work or career, etc. Your main ground of relating to your emotions within third dimensional consciousness is typically 'suffering over your suffering' with repeated suffering loops. OR it is to suppress your emotions to a large degree or it can be somewhere between the two. How the 3D Self relates to your emotions is largely templated off of your same gender parent, whether to suppress or express is modeled to you and taken in or it is rejected and the 3D Self goes in the opposite direction. Much emotional congestion can be held in the chakras and as the soul consciousness is not connected to as consciously within the 3D Self, these congested places remain that way manifesting into suffering and physical disease and illness.

4D: The fourth dimensional (4D) Self is becoming aware of your emotional wounding and becoming more conscious of your own 'shadow' and trigger projections. Awakening of the 4D Self often comes about because of a life crisis that triggers dormant emotions that catalyze the opening and deep desire to move out of suffering. The life crisis could be a near death experience, health crisis, relationship crisis, sudden career change or retirement, or ayahuasca or peyote experience, Dark Night Of The Soul, or other spiritual awakening experiences. Or your awakening may be a gradual process over many years with many mini-awakenings.

In 4D, you seek out resources to help you with your emotional wounding, usually beyond just traditional therapy and some combination of psychology and spirituality. In the lower 4th dimension, your 4D Self may experience an often painful and dramatic roller coaster of emotions in order for your feelings to come up to be felt and move out of shadow and into consciousness. Your emotional body begins to wake up as it is not being numbed as much by the 3D self. This can be an 'alchemical purgatory' in terms of emotional reactions coming up, often ones that have been suppressed for this life or many lifetimes.

In the higher 4th dimension, your 4D Self is getting space from your emotions while still giving them room in your life. You embrace and respond to your feelings with love and curiosity rather than suppression. You 'hold space' for yourself and have others around you that encourage your authentic expression of emotions. You are more motivated by love than by suffering. You aren't interested in suppression as you are curious about every reaction that comes up and are consciously noticing and letting go of things that numb your feelings. Your 4D Self still has distinct subpersonalities and these parts of you extend beyond this life wounding to open out into soul themes, archetypal themes, karmic healing, trauma from other lifetimes, and tapping into wounds held in the collective unconscious. The parts of your 4D Self are integrating as they are felt and healing and the 5D Self is developing more and more to hold the process. There is less fusion to parts, less 'becoming' the emotions even as there are phases of intense emotional reactions and upheavals, especially in the lower 4D experience.

5D: Your Fifth Dimensional (5D) Self is balanced related to your emotions and has very few emotional reactions or fusions to reactions. The main emotions that you experience are joy, bliss, desire, curiosity, reverence, gratitude, innocence, vulnerability, creative inspiration, passion, compassion, trust, need to be authentic and tell your truth, and sadness (at times when mourning loss).You have metaspace around your emotional body and it is relatively or completely free of emotional congestions and woundings from your subconscious. You are 'current' with your emotions and share them authentically and vulnerably in the moment with yourself and others. You do not suppress or judge your emotions. As you are moving more into Oneness and Wholeness, you only have one or two parts (if any) that you are conscious of and it feels more like 'tendrils' of energies rather than very strong energies or very distinct personalities as it once did. You are motivated by love and serving love to self and others in almost every moment and have a deep inner reality of goodness and self love that draws more of the same from others. You do not experience suffering even as sometimes sadness or mourning is an aspect of your reality as you continue to discern, make choices, advocate, and sometimes set boundaries.

Questions For You:
How did you locate yourself related to emotions – as primarily a 3D, 4D or 5D consciousness and why?
What are your frustrations in the area of emotions?
What are your desires in the area of emotions?
~

Introducing Subpersonalities And Parts

This is writing from Raphael and me about the common subpersonalities and soul aspects that we have experienced in our own processes over the last decade and in holding space for others through SoulFullHeart:

"Unless we awaken to the consciousness process, the vast majority of us are run by the energy patterns (and subpersonalities) with which we are identified or by those which we have disowned," *Embracing Our Selves*, Hal and Sidra Stone

**

Let's turn the world as you have known it upside down for a moment. Let's offer that instead of one personality, what you know as 'you' or 'I', running the show of your life, that there are actually many personalities expressing in your life and many others that are off in the shadows. And, instead of seeing this condition as a pathological one, (i.e. the clinical diagnosis of multiple personality or cognitive dissociative disorders), we feel that this is normal life for all of us as we have adjusted to third dimensional (3D) consciousness reality. The clinical disorders/labels associated with having a fragmented existence in which personalities take over or possess consciousness without our awareness is actually an extremely wounded form of our universal subpersonal makeup. What is missing in these extreme forms, as we shall see, is a healthy 'Aware Ego,' or '5D Self/embodying Higher Self' mediating the subpersonal reality.

The sense of having more than one personality operating inside of us is one that most of us are actually more conscious of experiencing than you might realize at first. Using the words 'part of me' is quite common…as in 'part of me would like to quit this job and another part of me wouldn't think of doing that.' Most people can readily see that who they are at work or in social settings is a different version than who they are when they are alone or with family or mates. We also experience divergent and polarized energies inside of us, especially in times of stress, trauma, or during major life transitions. It can be a bit intense to feel how our moods can shift so dramatically or how we can suddenly just feel 'not like ourselves' when we are being highly reactive to a situation. It can feel like we are 'possessed' or that 'something is taking us over' during these times. It turns out that we are constantly being possessed (so to speak) by different aspects or parts of ourselves or subpersonalities. In the SoulFullHeart process, we have come to discover over time that each of these subpersonal aspects has a distinctive energy, tone, voice, likes and dislikes, environment that it lives in, appearance, life history, name that it goes by, and play out in our lives.

The foundations for the existence of subpersonalities and connecting with them goes back more than one hundred years, initially offered by Psychoanalyst Carl Jung and expanded by psychologists Hal and Sidra Stone over the last thirty years, which they offer as the Voice Dialogue method. Carl Jung used the word 'constellation' to describe the specific energetic and emotional formation of a subpersona or subpersonality and he further identified and differentiated the ego-consciousness, personas, the Aware Ego, the Self, and the Anima-Animus. We were initiated and trained in parts work facilitation through the paradigm of Emotional Body Enlightenment as offered by Theohumanity. The SoulFullHeart process has assimilated terms and approaches from these sources, as well as others, along with creating our own terms and processes that are unique to SoulFullHeart.

All of these aspects of ourselves or subpersonalities developed quite naturally in response to the environment we were born into and raised in within 3D reality. We received very distinct conditioning from our families and our school and social settings around which behaviors and energies were acceptable and which were not. Our 3D Selves learned quickly to adapt our behaviors to our caregivers responses, such as noticing and adjusting to when smiles garnered more smiles from our caregivers while crying or having 'tantrums' drew their disapproval or frustration. Based on this reward or disapproval structure, we started to express certain aspects of our personalities in our lives, while others became more suppressed.

Those subpersonalities and energy patterns that express regularly in our daily lives, such as at work or in social settings, can be called our Primary Selves (as offered by Hal and Sidra Stone), or our Personas (as offered by Jung). The word, 'persona' is Latin and means a mask or a character played by an actor. We hold that these Personas or Primary Selves (which we can also call the 3D Self) that make up our personalities are necessary and loving aspects of our being, but are all too often left out on their own and are like teenagers running a household trying to make up for an absent parent. Our 3D Self can put up a show of being unconditionally loving, able to meet everyone's needs, and being likable while suppressing feelings of overwhelm, frustration, and judgement. This suppression of inner feelings can lead to physical illness because our deeper needs are not getting met and our authentic self is not being expressed.

Some examples of aspects of the 3D self in expression are the Protector, the Controller, the Punisher/Critic, the Inner Matriarch or Patriarch, the Good Daughter and the Good Son, the Pusher, the Performer, the Perfectionist, etc. The 3D Self aspect that is usually first developed and formed is usually the Inner Protector as it is desperately needed to help us adjust to the brand new and often times energetically harsh 3D world we are born into. Our vulnerability held by our Inner Child is safeguarded by this part of us and, in most people, deeply and safely buried by the age of four or five years old.

Each expressed, 3D Self aspect usually has a correlating 'underbelly' relationship to a Shadow Self that may be opposite in expression and energetic tone. Usually the Shadow Selves inhabit qualities that are less acceptable in society, although we can also suppress or bury healthy expression of our power and our soul gifts. Some examples of the Suppressed Parts or Disowned Parts or Shadow Selves (all good terms) can be our Inner Child (who holds our vulnerability), our Magical Child, Anxiety, Rage, Shame, etc. For example, the Pusher would have a Shadow Self that is more laid back, relaxed, perhaps lazy even. The underbelly of our Primary Protector/Controller, as we previously mentioned, is very often our Inner Child, as this is the part that is most in need of protection.

Subpersonalities are created in response to our 3D environment and due to undigested traumas that we experience and go unfelt by our caregivers and in turn go unfelt and undigested in us. In this way, it wasn't a given trauma that constellates the formation of a subpersonality, but rather the inability to digest the trauma in real time with a heart open caregiver that is at root of the formation. Our parts digest and heal from the traumas they experienced as we become aware of them and, most importantly, as they are felt by a loving, nonjudgmental part of us that develops through the process. We could say that both the wounding and the healing pivot on this crucial issue of digestion. Another sense of digestion and profound sense of being felt that our parts can experience comes from the Divine – in both motherly and fatherly forms in Ethereal Guides.

Often, what creates the most healing and growth ground is the experience that a part of us has of being felt while they are feeling something by a facilitator or space holder who has also engaged in a subpersonality healing process. This goes beyond being listened to in an empathic way or merely being asked good, therapeutic-type questions. Only someone who has experienced these energetic tones in parts of themselves can resonate in a deeply feeling way that parts of us really need and didn't receive at the time the traumas occurred. A facilitator can't fake this kind of feeling tone with the subpersonalities, especially with the Inner Child, who simply will not come out of 'hiding' unless they feel matching tones of vulnerability in the space holder.

As we engage with the SoulFullHeart processes over time, we become more differentiated from our 3D Self subpersonalities and are able to inhabit more deeply our Authentic Self, Aware Ego, or 4D and 5D Selves. This is the loving, nonjudgmental aspect of us that can hold the energies within us in balance, remain more objective during decision making, and is more conscious about where our reactions are coming from. This part of us is who we were 'meant to be' as an expression of our Sacred Humanity and can also be felt as a subpersonality of the Divine for which we are an individual expression of and is the embodiment of our Higher Self more and more.

Our subpersonalities eventually vibrate at higher and higher frequencies and integrate into our 5D Self. For example, the Protector/Controller energies heal and vibrate at expressions of healthy management and self protection; the wounded Inner Child heals to expressions of vulnerability and joy and moves from 3D wounded to 4D magical to 5D crystalline; the Inner Critic or Punisher heals to expressions of healthy and humble discernment, etc. Some subpersonalities become a valued member of our 'team' or inner board of directors, yet allow the authentic self to run the show.

A unique aspect of the SoulFullHeart process is our work with the Soul Guardian aspect of the Protector energy, which also sometimes call a 'Daemon', which is Greek term meaning Inner Muse or Inner Guide. It is a transcendent energy that seems to protect and watch over our soul gifts, our soul purpose, manifestation of our soul power, and our connection to the Divine. The Soul Guardian seems to also connect us with Divine inspiration and our muse. Without conscious negotiation with our 5D or Sacred Human Self, the soul guardian can overly express in our lives or under express. Over expression or what we call 'fusion' with a Soul Guardian may be seen in someone who has prioritized the spiritual life over grounded, practical life and may have chronic health issues or difficulty in relationships. Or, someone who is 'enlightened' or 'awakened' and yet perpetuates patterns of abuse with their followers or in their intimate relationships. Under expression of the Soul Guardian can lead to a strong rational or scientific self who has cut off access to soul frequencies and experiences beyond the five sense perception. Also, under expression of a Soul Guardian brings up feelings of emptiness, despair, lack of meaning and disconnection from Divine Source.

The Soul Guardian is a loyal Protector and our most devoted guardian on mostly an existential/soul level. It differs from the energy of the Inner Protector, who is more concerned with your everyday, strategic, practical, and self-image-based life. Our Soul Guardian and our Inner Protector can 'work together' in many situations and ways in our lives, especially related to our relationships and life choices. The Soul Guardian is a disembodied, angelic or warrior looking, and usually a male feeling presence in your life. It has been 'assigned' to you by the Divine to serve as a guardian of your soul gifts, past life experiences, soul purpose this life, and to provide a pipeline of love to support your arising 5D Self.

It seems that somewhere along the way, as Human consciousness developed and yet we became more and more separated from the Divine, each other, our planet, and animals and into duality and 3D consciousness; our Soul Guardians were forced to become overly invested in our journey and our lives, lower their vibrational frequency and unity consciousness to match ours. As they became overly invested, they began to feel more and more separated from Divine Source and more involved in Human struggles, pain, and emotional wounding. They became 'fused' to their mission and lost the bigger picture of what their mission really was. The mission for our Soul Guardian becomes about protecting the Inner Feminine and access to the Divine Feminine-Mother in both men and woman. Like having an overly protective parent, we cannot access and express these frequencies in the ways that we most desire and need to with the Soul Guardian's energy blocking it.

The Soul Guardian itself started to carry a legacy of pain that expresses from almost every Metasoul fractal (explained in the Spiritual Area Of Life section) in the lower vibrational dimensions. The Soul Guardians have become fairly helpless to assist us in our Human emotional pain and wounding, in addition to being unable to heal their own pain, feelings of isolation and abandonment, and often violent and torturous experiences from past lives. They are torn between their own needs getting met (for the first time even realizing that they have needs!) and their "mission" from the mysterious Divine (which they feel disconnected from) to meet the needs of the Human they've been assigned to protect.

Soul Guardians need to feel us holding and healing our own Human emotional pain and young childhood aspects of ourselves that are hurting. They need to feel that there is an emotionally and spiritually mature, centered version of us there that can respond to them, be in practical daily life as a sacred practice, and connect with the Divine in a grounded and intimate way without turning it into a belief system, paradigm, or fundamentalist religion. They need to feel the invitation to rest and surrender that the Divine is offering to them and can only seem to accept this if they feel us getting what we need and if we are actively negotiating with them.

Through the SoulFullHeart process and sessions with your SoulFullHeart Facilitator, your Soul Guardian begins to trust the Divine again and starts to bring you visceral and authentic experiences of your Metasoul line and consciousness states obtained from other lives at a rate and pace that both your growing 4D and 5D Self and your soul guardian can digest in an embodied way. The Soul Guardian starts to collaborate with you in a negotiated way to awaken your soul frequencies, which includes multidimensional travels, deeper development of your soul gifts, and clarity about your soul purpose.

The deepening of this relationship with you and your parts can lead to profound changes in your life - in an internal way that opens up inside of you, yet also externally related to your professional and career choices, family and personal relationships, habits and coping mechanisms, and even your physical appearance. For women, much more femininity can begin to flood their being as they get more separation and healing from the Inner Protector and Soul Guardians' masculine frequencies. The depth and level of change is up to you, yet the amount of transformation seems to be limitless, and also paced at a rate that you can move through without suffering.

Parts work is self-directed, visceral, and proves its value in distinguishing the 3D Self from the 4D and 5D Selves, which leads to swift transformation that is beyond just self improvement. The energy patterns that emerge from the different parts are undeniable once you feel them in yourself and witness them in others. The part of us that denies the existence of subpersonalities is often the 3D Self, who wants to stay in control, resists being differentiated and felt, and doesn't want the Shadow Selves to come out of hiding. If you are feeling skeptical right now about the existence of subpersonalities, it is probably your 3D Self who holds this 'voice'. However, it is usually the 3D Self that is tired, run down, or just plain frustrated with running the show who then chooses to engage in a parts process for which they can finally get some relief.

Parts work allows for an embodiment and grounding of the spiritual experiences that come up through connection with our soul guardian and Metasoul aspects, the Divine and Spirit Guides. These kinds of experiences can be magical and yet also need to be negotiated with the 3D Self and sometimes the Inner Child as they can also be scary. Trauma can occur for people who have intense altered states of consciousness (such as what is accessed with ayahuasca and peyote) without inner negotiation and it can be difficult to integrate these experiences into everyday life.

It is when we are free to explore ALL aspects of our being – from our roots to our wings – that we most deeply experience our essence as Infinite Love and ourselves as a beloved subpersonality of the Divine. We embrace what is most Human about us, especially as embodied in our Inner Child and our Disowned Selves, while we explore what is most transcendent about us, as embodied in the frequencies of our soul guardian and other soul aspects. It is truly amazing the range that we can inhabit and experience without leaving any crucial aspect of ourselves in the shadows.

~

Integrating The Emotional Body As A Critical Aspect Of The Ascension Process

It is quite extraordinary the lengths to which our culture goes to suppress emotional expression. The 3D conditioning around relating to emotions starts at a young age as we are taught from our parents and social circles which emotional behavior is acceptable and which is not. We are rewarded for 'good' behavior' and punished for 'bad' behavior, which is usually connected to our ability to control our emotional reactions or not. We learn to hold back our tears, our hurts, and our pains. We learn that rage and anger are bad, along with other emotions such as shame, depression, anxiety, etc. We are told, "Don't be a crybaby" or "Get over it" or "Don't be so sensitive".

Aspects of us or subpersonalities form out of the wounded bed of this suppression. You experience traumatic situations that you cannot emotionally digest and clogs in your pain body are created. A part of you that is responsible for self protection and primary suppressor of emotions is formed early to navigate 3D life. The Inner Protector part of you uses control (and soul gifts) to manage life in order to minimize emotional triggering and to seek for safety and constancy. Other parts containing the energies and tones of unwanted emotions may be deep in shadow, buried away under layers of persona and self image-based personality.

The undigested emotional woundings of these parts act as an energetic anchor related to your ascension process. Their pain frequencies emit a broadcast that lowers your vibrational frequency. Your ascension into higher consciousness states is limited to the degree that these wounds remain unhealed. This goes beyond just advocating to feel your feelings; this is an invitation to travel into the depths of your shadow and pain body in order to feel, heal, and love these frequencies so that they can transform into their healthy vibrations.

In SoulFullHeart, we do this by supporting your inner exploration with aspects of yourself, both in your 3D pain body and integrating Metasoul fractals as well. Your higher self or 5D self integrates and embodies into you as you hold space for these lower vibrational frequencies of yourself.

Each aspect of you has 3D, 4D, and 5D frequencies or consciousness levels. For example, the Protector aspect of you in 3D is more defensive than open, vigilant about keeping you safe above all else, and afraid to risk the unknown for growth. As the Protector becomes more trusting through connection with your Higher Self and experience of Divine frequencies, it moves into 4D experiences of awakening, questioning, and exploration. It becomes more healthy self protection using strategies such as energy healing and support from Ethereal beings. In 4D expression, the Protector is helping you as the Higher Self rather than just 'taking over' your state of being. More feminine frequencies of responsiveness and stillness are integrating in with the previously dominating masculine ones in 3D. In 5D reality, there is little need for protection in the same way as you are discerning about the energies that you will be around and the relationships that you will be engaged with (the main ground that the Protector is trying to protect you in.) Also, you have fewer traumatic experiences as the magnet of your emotional wounding is not drawing them.

Each aspect goes through this kind of energetic transformation of consciousness, with eventual integration into the whole of the 5D or Higher Self. Another example of this transition is from 3D depression to 4D creative expression and risk-taking to 5D Divine alchemy and surrender to the death and rebirth cycles of life. Anxiety in 3D is about projecting hurt possibilities onto situations and lack of trust in life; 4D is transitioning to trusting SELF above all else and the soul; 5D is surrendered trust of outcomes to your soul and Divine Source and being more and more in the NOW without tensions related to the future. Control in 3D is about hyper and micro management and suppression of life; 4D is transitioning to healthy self management and letting go of control in all areas of life; 5D is embodied management of what CAN be responded to and letting go of outcomes for the rest.

The process of forming a conscious relationship with the 3D versions of these aspects seems to offer a catalytic and powerful ground for this transformation. As you get to know and connect with each frequency, aspect, and part in its expression and you are loving and curious, the energy can transmute, heal, and eventually integrate into your 5D Self.

The initial permission to feel your feelings again, to navigate beyond suppression and negotiate with your Protector to begin this process are all critical related to the depth of transformation that you can experience. As you go along in the process, you come to trust more and more that the ground of this exploration provides the real safety, which comes not from suppression but from integration. The safest place from which to interface with life is from the core of your authentic expression which INCLUDES your emotional reactions and emotional digestion as a critical aspect. It is the foundation ground of your embodiment as a Sacred Human and key to your reseeding of consciousness to a heart-based one that is being infused by your soul frequencies from higher dimensions.

~

Practical Ascension And Parts Work: How to make changes that reflect your soul

Practical ascension….this has been floating around in my head for awhile. What IS practical ascension? I was a small business/life coach for five years and we focused with clients on the 'what' AND the 'how'. The 'what' was the greater context and vision for their lives and business and the 'how' was how to get there. I've been asked a few times lately during SoulFullHeart sessions about the 'how' of making changes in life that reflect the soul's awakening desires and pictures about reality.

Going back to practical ascension for a moment…..it feels like where life intersects with concepts, where the spiritual

IDEAS that you've been learning, reading, and taking in actually implement IN your life and CHANGE your life. Another phase beyond the initial awakening of realizing the inner matrixes that block you and that you no longer resonate with the 3D conditioning you've received, and that MOST of what you've been taught about reality in school and in life is limited and based in fear.

The soul wakes up through this learning and taking in of ideas, this looking outward for inspiration and sources of guidance and advice. The mind is shifting in this phase, paradigms and entire schools of thought (taught through our schools mostly) are being dismantled. There is a whole bunch of rubble and ash during this phase, which I have connected with transitional fourth dimensional or 4D consciousness. This can mostly be happening INTERNALLY, however, as that is where it needs to start, where the seeds of change are watered.

And then, with this watering and baking and dismantling of ideas and shifting through emotional reactions does the soul energy begin to rumble to make ACTUAL changes in your life, to have the outside reflect MORE of your inner transformation. Some of these changes happen TO you as life moves you through the necessary death and rebirth (although nothing happens to you without your participation and choice on a SOUL level). More and more changes though can happen WITH you as you move into the phase of what we could call practical ascension and a more empowered sense of activation in your life fueled by your soul's momentum and out of the safety and comfort of your 3D Self.

This is when ALL areas of your life want to move into a higher vibrational frequency of expression as more and more YOU in your soul essence wants to express and grow. This is where the HOW comes in….as you then connect with aspects and parts of yourself to feel and negotiate with them around making practical changes to your life, especially within the areas which are causing you conscious suffering and capping your growth. It is the parts of us that hold the emotional body in confusion, remain blocked and stay in suffering. These parts are basically blocked or clogged frequencies. NEGOTIATION really is the key word here as it allows the movements forward at a rate and pace that the parts of you that are attached to the old way can digest WITH you ('You' being the growing authentic and Higher Self embodied version of you.)

Differentiating an energy of attachment or resistance or fear as coming from a part of you immediately creates objectivity inside of you (what we call 'defusion') as you can now address and feel these reactions. It creates instant metaspace to say, "Part of me feels afraid" and to then BE with and feel this part of you rather than BECOMING this part of you. We often start the process with your Protector part as it is negotiation with this aspect that allows for deeper access to the emotional body.

I have discovered no better HOW when it comes to moving life into a place of reflecting our deepest desires and soul expression then through the parts work process. There IS a way to actualize what you most deeply desire to BE in your life that I am inviting you into feeling if you resonate with or at least are open to exploring. Parts work is certainly not the ONLY way, yet I am pressed to find another that is as catalytic and effective as this one is. I have searched and researched for many years and yet always come back to parts work as my personal ground of healing and transformation along with what I feel called to offer others for close to 15 years now.

Navigating and embracing this parts work reality within myself and with the help of facilitators in the past is HOW I have been able to BE in a Sacred Union bond for nine years with Raphael and have it deepen, grow, and expand into magical terrains of goodness and MEGA love. Parts work is HOW I have been able to shift a highly self conscious and unworthiness-based relationship to EVERYTHING in my life to one of unselfconsciousness, comfort in self, and self worth. It is HOW I have healed lifetimes worth of karmic playouts and binds within a relatively short period of time. It is HOW I have been able to heal so much unconscious wounding in my emotional body and to experience life with little to NO emotional triggering or charged reactions now. It is HOW I have been able to inhabit and claim and express my soul gifts and serve love with others as my means of livelihood without compromising my values or soul resonance.

It is important to offer a HOW to you and not just a WHAT picture (although I love doing that too.) There are more and more Spiritual Teachers offering parts work as a key aspect of healing the emotional body wounding and more common language of Inner Child, Inner Punisher, etc. And of course Carl Jung blazed the trail here before us…the emotional body has been left out of spirituality for many years yet the continual 'proof' of its need for healing expresses out in abuse patterns, unworthiness-based and unaware ego (another word for the 3D Self) based frequencies, inability to make practical changes and navigate IN life and to integrate soul awakenings into everyday life, suffering loops inside and in relationships of all kinds. The emotional body is screaming to be included in the picture and parts work dives into the waters of the emotional body immediately with immediate access.

The love that you ARE wants to come in and move through your life…to change your EVERY moment experience of experience. Of course parts of you hold fear about these changes, especially when and if they relate to other people and relationships that are entangled yet still transact love. Being with and connecting with these parts and their fear leads to a more integrated self as they relax and integrate their energies over time and the stuck or wounded frequencies vibrate higher and higher. More and more then do you relate with life as a singular "I" that truly IS an I AM energy of embodied Higher Self frequencies pulsated with innate self worth AND visceral connection to ALL THAT IS.

~

Aspects Forming Of The 3D Self And Returning To Wholeness

There seem to be markers and milestones, moments along the journey that call for a celebration and marking of what has been moved beyond, what has been healed, and what has been awakened. You may need these celebrations as they are a recognition of the love that you are becoming and the love that you are letting in despite resistance and protection coming from parts of you.

Parts of you are waiting for these celebrations just as they are waiting for your love. Parts of you are energies or frequencies that give off a specific tone of emotional vibration. Some of these tones form into personalities and roles such as mother, father, daughter, sister, brother, son, lover, etc. Some of these tones are strong emotional frequencies as depression, mania, anxiety, control, rage. Some are energized very often and some are hidden away in the shadows. The ones in the shadow usually received little support from the world outside of you and were judged without love by others and then by you. These shadow frequencies are often of shame, rage, unworthiness, disconnect, and craziness. The conditioning you received and the conditioning you needed to grow as a soul was that it was not acceptable or OK to feel these things or to be these things.

The parts that become your personality (until you awaken to remember what you REALLY are and become more of your Higher Self) are those that are supported by others around you and by the culture you are in.

It was a need for love that formed parts initially inside of you. When your love needs didn't get met as you were experiencing traumas and pains, clogs were formed in your emotional body. These clogged and stuck places became 'fixed' in time during these moments of trauma and remain emotionally and energetically compressed there unable to raise to a higher vibrational frequency of love. Your love needs didn't get met for many reasons related to those outside of you and where they are in their own embracement of themselves as love. And, again, this is what you signed up for as a soul to experience.

If others have not remembered yet and embraced their essence as Infinite Love, they are not able to provide it for others. If their heart has blocks and congestions, stuck places and parts, then they are not able to flow out love to template for you how to hold that for yourself. This is especially true of the responsibility of parenthood. The 3D Self plays this as a role and has difficulty to allow a nonlinear arising of what they have become attached to as a daughter or son. This attachment becomes something you have to form and fit and thus parts of you are created to do this even as this isn't the natural state of your soul.

It was a need for love that formed parts of you into shields of protection from energies that didn't resonate with your soul BE-ing. These shields of protection were critical for you to survive life here on Gaia, in third dimensional (3D) processing, and in a dense Human body. Without these aspects of yourself, you would not have made it to the place you are today. The shields of protection are frequencies that came about inside of you in response to a world that needed them, just like plants and flowers that grew thorns and brambles and stickies to ward off predators. Your thorns and brambles are temporary, a part of the 3D processing system, and eventually there is no need for that kind of defense structure. The frequency at which you vibrate becomes ALL the protection that you need, which is energized for a time by Ethereal beings who template how to hold it.

The invitation is to return to wholeness, return to an integrated essence expression of your embodiment as your Higher Self. Returning to wholeness is to make real the parts of you that were created in the non-real. These parts are life and hold energy. Making them real gathers them into yourself and into your heart. It invites them to return to source with you, yet not in a forced way of 'doing this' but in the embracement of self love to them. You become the parent for yourself that is not attached yet deeply committed to your own journey, which includes the recognition of these aspects of yourself.

This invitation is the journey that we offer to remember the love that you ARE and as aspects of you heal and integrate, this remembering becomes more and more natural and organic.

~

Letting In Gifts From The Universe Through The Parts Work Process

SO MANY gems and gifts coming through right now, in insights and remembrances and putting things together. Gifts from Guides and Galactic Aspects, Angelic Aspects, Elemental Aspects, presented during everyday life and 'walking around' reality. Gifts coming in with the sunlight, every ray of the sun seeming to offer light codes to activate what has been dormant and wants now to wake up and be remembered.

With the sense of wonder in your heart, these gifts can come in to you. With a sense of goodness about yourself and your own worth, these gifts can be received by you. With a trust in love and Divine-Source, these gifts can be let in by you.

I have been receiving some comments lately on my writings and videos from some souls who are in a "I don't see it" and "I'm not experiencing this" and "I am not getting these gifts" phase on their journey. This is a sacred phase too, although not an easy one. Sometimes aspects of you need to refuse the gifts for soul growth reasons. Sometimes the gifts are blocked for emotional wounding reasons or karmic binds reasons. Sometimes the gifts are 'off your radar' because of core unworthiness or self judgment or self limiting thought forms that don't allow them into your BEing. Sometimes energies of entitlement from parts of you block them because the expectation of receiving them blocks their delivery.

The invitation then is to question yourself and WHY you are not receiving the gifts that are available to you in openings, awakenings, awarenesses, higher vibrational frequencies, and in

NEW experiences of love in every moment. Questioning yourself in a self loving way that is a quest to FEEL the whys of your emotional pain body…....Rather than 'fusing' to the self limiting and blocking reality of not receiving these gifts, you ask, "What part of me is blocking these gifts and why?"

Feeling these reactions as coming from 'part of you' and not all of you is important because this is the case. It is just part of you, an aspect of you, a stuck energy inside, NOT all of you feels this way. Saying and feeling 'part of me' can be VERY liberating. It creates space for it NOT to be the whole truth of your reality (whatever the difficult or resistant or defensive feeling tones are) but just PART of your reality. Just ONE aspect of it, not the whole truth.

If people could say, "Part of me does not see that anything is changing in the world," or "Part of me is blocking me from connecting with Guides," or "Part of me feels fearful about letting in gifts from the Universe", etc. they are making space for the possibility that it is NOT all of them. They are 'defusing' from the reaction and this allows the capacity then to have a relationship WITH it and not just BECOME it. This allows the possibility for it to move then and for a new reality and mindset and emotional reality to arise.

This differentiation of parts and aspects is so helpful for a phase of time, especially during 4D or transitional consciousness. In SoulFullHeart, these parts and aspects are beloved, felt, connected with, and through this process, more space is created of the Higher Self or leading edge of BEing. The authentic can separate from the strategic; the healthy from the wounded; the worthiness-based from the unworthiness-based.

This is SUCH an effective way to relate to the self that I haven't really seen nor been exposed to anything that works better at clearing and healing emotional and soul wounds to allow for the soul self to arise. Over 15 years of this parts work path, I now experience that the aspects I am most relating with are from other lifetimes (Metasoul Sisters mostly in other 'eras of time' and parallel dimensions) and also Galactic aspects, Star BEing aspects, etc. and that I don't seem to have many emotional pain body, this life, parts of me left nor much of any emotional reactivity from that place.

A lot of my process over the years, however, was about connection with my Inner Child (who transmuted from wounded and hurt to vulnerable, Magical Child to now Crystalline Child seated in my heart chakra) that has mostly integrated into my expression and comes out in bubbling moments of joy and wonder. I worked with many, many layers of my Strategic Self or 3D Self or lower vibrational frequencies of the ego and 3D self. This is the 'who we think we are' part of us, usually represented by our birth name. It is who we think that we are until the investigation and honest quest to discover our soul essence, and the letting go of what isn't who we are and doesn't represent us. This differentiation is what many awakening souls are going through only without directly connecting with the aspect that is going through the deaths and rebirths.

I can feel parts of people in so many ways that are very obvious, expressing and fusing and wanting to be felt. This is not a 'special attainment' or psychic ability but rather what develops over time as you work with and connect with your own parts more and more deeply. Even highly 'attained' Spiritual Teachers and Healers have parts of themselves, in their pain body mostly, that have not been connected with and this is easy to feel. Many of them may be 'fused to' their strategic, self-image-based self because they haven't directly connected and differentiated and deconstructed them yet. Many women feel masculine as they are still 'fused to masculine aspects of themselves' and so their authentic femininity is suppressed.

It feels possible that most of them have not done this direct connection work and so ARE their strategic or 3D aspects to large degree EVEN WITH the spiritual awakenings and soul accesses that they have (usually the soul guardian and control aspects). This Strategic Self can show up in 'how they live their daily lives out' and especially in their relationships and if they are toxic or codependent. This can show up in dis-integrity, inauthenticity, and hidden addictions or non-transparency, which has been a huge issue with Spiritual Teachers, Guru and devotees, lower vibrational cult-like groups, etc.

    I haven't led with this teaching of parts work in all my writings and yet it undergirds everything that I offer through SoulFullHeart. It is THE WAY that has led to the love and growth and joy and magic and wonder that I experience on a moment by moment basis. And the body health and vitality. And the intimacy ground of goodness with Raphael. And the self love and acceptance and self worth. Thank the Divine that there is this way available to those of you who are resonant with it. And those who are not will find their way as I don't feel there is just 'one answer' for all of us, yet many answers available. But, if this parts work way resonates with you, then you are blessed because it DOES work and it DOES heal and we have been walking it out for over a decade and so can offer it with you and to you.

    It is a challenging path to walk out, as the fusion of self to different parts and aspects is so prevalent and it takes practice and a willingness to be facilitated by a trusted spaceholder to truly defuse. We have to have an 'outside of ourselves' perspective in order to truly see and feel and defuse from the strategic and 3D Self because we just can't see it all ourselves. Yet, if there is trust and love in the spaceholding ground, SO MUCH healing and transformation is possible with this process and work. You will arise into the version of yourself that you long to be and desire to be while experiencing profound levels and layers of self connection and self love.

    The parts work path feels like a Divine gift to me. And, of course, it can be refused or, again, just not felt to be the resonant one. If you remain open and curious and it resonates for you, HUGE vistas of change and transformation are possible when you are open to letting in the 'part of me' reality with the ultimate experience of MORE integration and wholeness. When you are open to experiencing more and more LOVE.

~

It's OK Not To Be OK

I am sitting in the back seat of my parent's car. I am looking out the window, my head turned away from the chaos in the front seat. I am looking out the window but I am not seeing any of the landscape. The tears that slide down my cheeks are silent. I have learned to cry without sound from many years of practice. I cannot completely numb my reactions to the tension, the negativity, and the hate that fills this car, that staggers from him and crawls from her. It has sharp teeth, harsh words, energy that cuts to the bone.

Part of me tries to protect me. Put up a shield. Put up a barrier. Create a bubble of light space around the growing girl. Tries to turn off the tap on the tears that flow from the pain of feeling like I do not belong. The craziness of feeling like this is not my family, cannot be my real family, not my soul family, not my family of heart. So eventually the tears go deep in, get buried, and my other feelings as well. And the part of me that protects my heart breathes a sigh of relief as a possible crisis of self revelation is avoided.

It starts so early, our conditioning to suppress our feelings, our emotional reality, and what our actual reactions to situations are in the moment. Through this conditioning and the pain of not being able to be real, we have to develop aspects of us that can fit in with the non-feeling environment around us. It is a necessary self defense mechanism. It just seems to happen so naturally and organically.

The message of, 'It's NOT OK to NOT be OK" is so strong in our culture. The conditioning around not expressing our feelings starts so young when children are first told not to have tantrums or to cry. Tantrums feel to me like releasing the unfelt emotional energy of the parents and the surroundings. We tantrum and then we reach a stage where, to get and keep love in the form of approval, we develop parts of us who become very good at suppressing what we are feeling. And parts of us who become very good too at form fitting our environment to not draw attention to ourselves and our vulnerability.

I described a scene above that encapsulates so much about why my defenses developed the way that they did. In my process through SoulFullHeart and previous subpersonality work that I have done, I have 'gone back' to these moments of extreme hurt and pain through the aspects of me who became stuck there. The emotional body has no sense of 'time', so these pains are present and current, energizing in the now until they are moved.

I sat in the car with the part of me that holds hurt from this repeated experience of my parents fighting that I experienced during childhood and I felt her tears with her. I became the loving adult, heart filled with support and permission to feel, that she didn't have at the time. And this version of me, no longer needing to be quiet or suppress her tears, could lean into this adult version of me. She could be felt and the pain from this moment and other moments like this could heal. And, I could become more current to myself.

To be able to go into places like this painful scene with parts of me has needed to be negotiated with the loyal Inner Protector part of me. This has happened through a growing sense of trust that I will be able to 'handle it and hold it' and that it is safe to release it and feel it. Over time and development of our authentic self or 5D Self, protective parts of us begin to feel that they can relax their strong protection of us, which can come in many different forms and energies. Through conscious negotiation with them, we can open our heart up more and let others in more deeply, also sharing ourselves more vulnerably and authentically. This leads to more experience of love transaction inside of ourselves and with others.

Through the SoulFullHeart work, you reach a place where you no longer really want to be around people (or in many environments) in which you can't BE authentically with your feelings or express them in the moment. Or, you choose to stay home or go to a secluded spot in the woods…..somewhere you can feel yourself. It becomes the ultimate priority over 'fitting in'. We have created a place and space inside us for this that then is expressed in our community where it is truly OK to NOT be OK.

    Sessions with us are just a practice ground for this dedication to yourself, to feeling, to being not OK if that is what is real, to be with the parts of you that resist feeling and why, and to be supported by someone else for it. And, eventually, this regular practice moves into and influences your choices in everyday life in a natural and organic way where you are desiring to be authentic with those you are in relationship with and in whatever soul purpose-based vocation you are serving love through.

~

The Essence Of You

    Beyond personality, beyond ego, beyond conditioning, beyond what you have learned and been taught is the YOU that just IS. Your essence is this arising you that you have within. This YOU is your soul essence in expression through your Human body, your Sacred Human Self, we can call it. Your Higher Self consciousness in embodied form. This YOU is without filters or barriers or limitations. Beyond reactivity of emotional woundings, this YOU is free-form energy blending and merging and responding and serving. Beyond the mind's ideas and boxes and concepts, this YOU is beyond the mind yet in dance with the mental gifts you have and can offer to others. Using the mind rather than the mind using you.

    Beyond the roles, beyond the duties, beyond the obligations, beyond the routines, beyond the usual, beyond the ordinary, beyond the boredom...there lives a YOU that is unknown to boredom and lives instead in the magical possibilities of every moment.

SO MUCH can quell or dampen or squash or limit this magical expression, this magical experience, this magical relationship to life. What is quelling this YOU? What have you created on your outside from your inside that is creating a shrink in this YOU? To move beyond the shrinking and quelling is to feel and identify what is causing it and what needs to be felt inside to create a new reality outside. Going inside out rather than outside in.

Beyond what you are experiencing as 'outside' of you is what is actually inside of you and starts THERE. Everything starts from THERE, inside first. Beyond the conditioning that outside is what matters (this is 3D conditioning) is the actual experience that ONLY inside matters because only from the inside can anything actually change on the outside. Inside is where your essence IS and the rest is formed on the outside of you.

Beyond the outside version of you is the inside, the essence, the core of who you ARE which is NOT a you at all but energy in different frequencies responding to other frequencies. Beyond the you version of fitting in is the YOU that cannot fit in because you only just fit inside of you and you ARE limitless without boxes or barriers....

This YOU is eager to be born, is 'spring-loaded' to express as it is expression and yet beyond expression to you. This YOU just IS and as it is embodied more and more, it is so much more natural than the conditioned you. It is so much more natural to be this rather than what you have form fitted to be. This YOU arises rather than conforms. This YOU responds rather than reacts. This YOU connects rather than is triggered.

Welcome this YOU into your world, let this YOU create a new world for you made for love by love and with love.

~

Embracing And Healing Our Fears To Experience More 5D Consciousness

"How do we dissolve and transcend fear contracts that we have created while in 3D reality so we can be clean for 4D and 5D experience?" This question was asked of me by someone to respond to from my perspective. This is probably a good time to offer that while I often have a strong sense of inner clarity, intuition, and guidance that comes from many years of inner work and soul integration, I also hold an open question about what I offer and do not claim to possess the Absolute Truth about reality. Only you can feel if what I am offering resonates in your heart and soul as a truth that you also are remembering and, therefore, we will find our resonance there.

The first place I feel to go in response to this question is the ideas that parts of us can have about fear. Our Divine or Higher Self doesn't have fear as it is a resistance to love and our Divine Self is remembering that we ARE Infinite Love. Yet, in the process of remembering this and because we are so influenced by the cultural and societal conditioning and programming around us, then parts of us are formed and created that hold fear or a very visceral resistance to love.

The way to heal anything is with love; it is the only frequency that can and does heal and transform energies. Resistance to love is healed with more love. Rather than resisting our fears, we connect with, get to know, and love the parts of us that hold the fears. These are parts of us that have been conditioned to a 3D reality where fear is expressed in politics, in religion, in society, in education, in many ways and forms love is resisted and not embraced. Our fear is actually trying to show us where our resistance is. When I feel fear I celebrate it (at this point, for me, after many years of this awakening process through parts work I don't feel much conscious fear anymore) because it is showing me another place inside of me that needs more love.

When I feel fear, I become very curious about where it is coming from, how it lives inside of me, and I go in deeply to be with it.

When I feel into the idea of 'fear contracts', it doesn't have an alive frequency for me. It feels like a binding idea, an idea of old paradigm binds with legalistic roots. It's not a word that I have used over the years even as I have felt deeply the fear that exists inside of bonds with others, which is what I call the 'binds' that exist. There can be many layers to these binds between souls, many cords of codependence, many chapters living out even in other dimensions and other lifetimes. Those that are most intimate with us are usually the ones for which we have the most grounds of transaction of both binds and bonds. These souls are also the most powerful mirror for us to see ourselves and both our trailing and leading edges.

If both people are engaged in a consciousness awakening and heart and soul healing path, they can be WITH the fear that comes up to intimacy (again, a fear of love), feel the aspects of themselves that are in fear of love, and come back to the mutual ground to process it. Going in as an individual, going in 'vertically' (you to you) rather than focusing on the 'horizontal' (you to other) ground is so important here as it is the only place that we actually have the power to heal or transform fear to love.

I also don't use the word 'transcend' as it can imply not feeling or not being in the body, not embodying our emotions and fears. Again, it is the embracement of the fears and shadow that heals them. Embracing without going into suffering loops is a delicate balance and one that I have needed space holders at times to guide me in, to be a mirror outside of myself so I can see myself. I believe that this support from a heart-open other person is critical to this process of healing fears and awakening to our Divine self. Also, to be in a community of others who are on the same path is hugely nourishing and transformative as well. I do not feel that we were meant to do this alone. It is from within community that both our wounding and healing occurs. It can be the fear of love and the fusion to the 3D sense of separation that keeps us in a solitary place around our healing, suffering, and not asking for support.

It can be very tempting to parts of us to just escape our 'pain body' (where our subconscious woundings live in heart and soul frequencies) rather than 'go in' to them. Parts of us are literally afraid that we will die or go crazy if we go there. These parts of us will use spiritual frequencies pulled from the 4D and 5D consciousness levels to bypass feeling these things. However, I feel that we cannot really avoid our own healing. It comes back around in a parallel lifetime to be faced and held. It is why we are here after all.

With this 'inner embracement' of fears it is not that they dissolve so much as the parts of us that hold them eventually integrate into our 5D Self until we experience more and more Wholeness of Being and more sense that we ARE Infinite Love. We experience more and more the frequencies of fifth dimensional consciousness (and beyond) as we let go into what we really ARE beyond the fear.

~

To The Part Of Me That Protects My Heart/Guided Meditation

To the part that protects our hearts....This is written to the part of us that I believe we all have who is our Guardian and Protector. They do their jobs so well and we would not make it through life without them....AND this is an invitation for them to begin to rest and so that we can let in MORE love:

To the part of me that protects my heart,

Will you let me thank you? Will you let in my gratitude? Will you lower your shield a moment so that you can let in my appreciation?

I want to thank you for existing. I want to thank you for coming in during the moments when life was the hardest, when there was the most pain, and when there was the most struggle.

I want to thank you for creating a bubble to ward off energies that would have harmed even more and for transmuting the harsh things so they landed softer. I want to even thank you for the numbness that descended at times so that life could be navigated.

I want to thank you for stepping in when there were no others to protect me. No one else could have cared as much as you have nor been so dedicated to your duty.

I want to thank you for every moment that you have spent in vigilance, watching over, not letting down your guard, not falling asleep on the job. I want to thank you for soaring the skies and the multiple dimensions and for being at the side of my childhood bed.

I want to thank you for all of this, and……..I want to invite you too into something new.

This something new is a relationship where you get to rest more. Where you get to trust more. Where you get to experience love for yourself. Where you get to help open the heart and not just guard it.

This something new is a relationship where I show up to hold my life as an Authentic Self and you get to help me. You are on my team, yet I am the leader now. I wasn't there before and I am sorry, but now, I am arising and I have desires.

I want to open my heart to let in others. I want to flow with love and surrender to that flow and wherever it takes me. I want to dance with the currents of change and allow them to sweep me somewhere new.

I want to dance to the music of love without self consciousness or worry about what will happen next or your worry about if I will get hurt

I am asking you to start resting even as I acknowledge how much you have done for me and that I need you on my team. Always. To help me set healthy boundaries, to help me defend myself if needed for my own safety or self love, to negotiate the rate and pace as I delve into heart and soul terrains.

I need you for these things and you need me to love you. This is new for you, but I feel your needs for love and rest. I am extending my open arms and heart out to you and I am inviting you to collapse into them when you are ready. For the first time, I am here and I can hold you now.

To the part of us that has protected our hearts….thank you and….it's time to start letting go.

~

This is usually the first aspect that we work with and connect with in SoulFullHeart sessions with people as it is negotiation with this Protector energy (also manifesting as a controlling energy) that allows for deeper access to the Inner Child and more suppressed aspects and energies. Through connection in sessions, journaling, dialogue, energy healing, the protective part differentiates from YOU as the arising authentic and embodying Higher Self.

This differentiation can lead to SIGNIFICANT changes in how you experience life, relationships, and love with much more openness, trust, and capacity to let in. The Protector often presents itself as masculine and as a knight or warrior. They can have karmic ties and binds to other lifetimes and energize or appear as Etheric Guides or Guardian Angels. They have different 'weapons' too, sometimes swords, sometimes energy shields (or both). Identifying how your Protector uses weapons and in what situations (and WHY) can be really helpful to understanding when, where, and why your heart feels 'opened' or 'more closed'. It is amazing how universal this energy IS as we have so needed it to navigate 3D life here.

A way to connect with yours is to write a letter to it/him expressing something similar to what I did above and anything else you feel about how protective energy shows up in your life. It's important to be loving, open, and curious in your emotional tone to your Protector, even as you are inviting them to rest. Then, wait for a response and write it down from your Protector. You can then begin a dialogue back and forth on paper (and eventually out loud) to get to know each other. In SoulFullHeart, we provide dialogue questions for you and also help to differentiate and identify this energy, which can be challenging to separate or defuse from. It is also the feeling ground of space holding with an open-hearted facilitator (who has differentiated from their Protector and other 3D aspects) which helps to heal and transmute this energy.

You can also connect with your Inner Protector through creative visualization during meditation. There are guided meditations that I offer during group call sessions. You can hear the recording of this meditation and others on our SoulFullHeart Experience YouTube Channel. The text of a meditation to meet your Inner Protector is below:

Meditation To Meet Your Inner Protector:

Close your eyes, go within, concentrate on your natural breathing in and out.

Imagine yourself in a space of pure white light. The light is surrounding you, holding you, and guiding you. The light is inviting you to vibrate higher, to move your frequency UP to a higher one.

Feel this pure white light moving through you and through each of your chakras and through every cell of your body. Allow this light to move through and activate and clean each of your chakras, from your highest one to your root. Feel the grounding from your feet down into Gaia and the connection that is there.

See yourself in a forest surrounded by the pure white light. The forest is beautiful and vast. It offers the sense of exploration and journey, a sense of adventure to unknown places. There is a stream nearby, running through and weaving through the trees. You can hear it babbling at you. Take in the five elements of fire through the warmth of the sun; water through the running stream; air through the soft breezes; Earth through the grasses and trees that surround you; and spirit through the sense of your own soul and your connection to Divine Source and other

Ethereal Guides you may be working with in the moment. I can feel Archangel Metatron here with us and also Mother Mary as they are going to help us with this meditation.

You go to stand by the stream that is nearby, next to the trees. Feel the purifying energy of the water. Cup this water in your hands and then pour it into the top of your head, into your crown chakra, allowing it to flow down your field. This water is clearing your energy more and also offering you an invitation to go into your inner depths, your emotional depths, even as you are at a higher frequency and especially because you are at a higher frequency to hold these feelings. If you notice feelings now, send love toward them with your cosmic heart, do this by picturing your heart and heart chakra filling up with light and love. Hold the feelings in this water love and any oil that may come up.

Allow the water to move through all of your chakras or energy centers and down into the cord at your feet that connects you with the center of Gaia. Feel the water washing out any energies that you've collected.

In this moment, we will call on Archangel Metatron, asking him to connect with us. Prepare to receive his energy. Picture him as a wise older man with a very high frequency of golden orange light coming from him. Metatron offers running a golden orange column of light through you, a honey light into and through you. Feel his golden light flowing through every chakra.

We will also call on Mother Mary, who has frequencies of both light pink and blue in her energies. She is comforting and nurturing, offering you a reflection of your innocence. Mary comes forward into the woods.

Mary takes your left hand and Metatron takes your right hand. They lead you down the path in the woods that you see before you. You may feel excitement as they lead you on this path into the unknown, you may feel some fear, embrace all that you feel as it comes up.

The path winds through the woods and ends at a clearing. In the middle of the clearing is a large castle. Picture this castle however you would like to, see it in front of you. Notice too how it FEELS to you as you approach the castle. Begin to open up to the sense inside of this castle is your essence…..is your most authentic self, is the embodiment of your Higher Self. Inside of this castle is your most precious treasure of Sacred Humanity, and your deepest vulnerabilities, your Inner Child. Let this into your heart and begin to connect to this energy.

As you approach the castle, a Protector of the castle steps forward. They have an energy of protecting the castle and they come toward you. Notice what this Protector looks like. It is male or female? Is it wearing armor or not? Do they have a weapon or shield? And what do they FEEL like to you? Notice if they say anything to you and make space to hear what they have to say.

Mother Mary and Metatron both smile and send love to this Protector, who is YOUR Protector inside, the part of you that protects your essence and your most precious gifts and your Inner Child especially. The three of you approach your Protector. Feel your heart open to your Protector, inviting them with your energy to connect.

Invite them to relax and allow you to connect with your essence more, to embody it, to claim it. Feel the reactions of your Protector to this invitation for conscious connection and negotiation with you. Ask your Protector to show you (without moving into the castle unless invited) where your Inner Child is. It may be locked in a room, or under a bell jar in a room, or in the dungeon, or high up in a turret. Ask the Protector if you can visit your Inner Child in the future to be with it. Listen to the Protector's response and take it into your heart. Feel the possibilities of future connection with your Inner Child as your Protector's trust and love with you grows.

Say goodbye to your Protector now and offer that you will connect with them again in the future. You walk back through the woods with Mary and Metatron. Eventually they too fade away yet their template of masculine and feminine stays with you. Infusing and offering you a sense of balance throughout your day.

~

You Are Not Broken: Ending The Punisher-Shame Suffering Loop

It is important to offer that you are not broken. You do not need fixing. You will remember this or maybe you already do. As your essence is Infinite Love, there cannot be anything really 'wrong' with you either. This sense of being broken, needing fixing, needing help, that something is wrong with you….none of this is what you really ARE and is just the conditioning you've received in 3D reality ABOUT reality.

Having unworthiness and feeling wrong doesn't mean there is anything actually wrong with you. It just points to a place in you, aspects of you, that need more love in order to let in more sense of the Innate and Infinite Goodness that you actually ARE. This place in you needs MORE water of feeling love from your Higher Self, from your relationships, from the Divine, in order to remember that there is nothing wrong with you.

The conditioning you have taken in has many messages that reinforce an overall sense of wrongness and unworthiness. This conditioning can be overt, such as that in religions, some spiritual practices, and the educational system. Or it can be subtle and subconscious, such as what can transact in 3D birth families and relationships.

Unworthiness is the root ground of most relationships and it is there not because it is true, but because it just hasn't been loved enough to heal into goodness. Both people in the relationship have this untouched unworthiness inside of them and it reaches out for connection, often settling for binds of karmic knots rather than bonds of deep nourishment and love. There is nothing wrong with this either, as it is perfect for each person as it plays out…..until you remember that you are much MORE than this and can experience much MORE within relationship. As you remember this about your own goodness, then your desires in relationship change and you want different things, often with different people.

There has been 3D conditioning you've received that has offered this limited picture of you TO you, over and over again, for many different reasons. This is an aspect of the veil that you have placed over your soul to not remember. The feeling of being broken is a very effective screen used by your 3D Self to block out the sense of what you really are as Infinite Love. You eventually come to remember why you put this veil up and the growth reasons why it was better for you NOT to know….until you do and then you are seeing and feeling the veil. And then you are seeing, remembering, and feeling beyond the veil. Your eyes are opening wide, your heart is opening too, and your soul is waking up beyond suffering.

Suffering feels more real than love because of the conditioning that you have received that teaches you this. Almost everything in third dimensional (3D) reality is founded on either the continuation of suffering patterns or the numbing down of it. Some of the most prevailing suffering messages have to do with attainment, whether of material possessions, physical perfection, career ambitions, money accumulation, romantic mate idealizations, Guru-based enlightenment pictures, and educational achievement.

The attainment picture as offered by suffering is that you are not enough as you ARE, that you need to be or do or have something else in order to be happy and nourished and that Love is not real unless you have reached this attained state. Some souls spend their entire existence in this loop of suffering around attainment.

Awakening and ascension that comes from embodiment of the Higher Self is not about attainment in this sense. It is not about getting something and then you will be happy, fulfilled, worthy, and worthwhile.

If you are not broken and do not need fixing, then why go on a journey of awakening, healing, and ascending? You go on this journey not because anything is actually wrong with you, but because you start to shift from relating to life from a place of suffering to a place of love and so then you want more and more love. And you want more and more to experience yourself AS love and you start to awaken to what isn't love inside of you and what is love. You awaken out of suffering in reaction to life and into relating to life with love.

From a place of suffering, most of what happens to you and your 3D Self offers more evidence of that suffering. Experiences add to the suffering or prove the suffering or make the suffering real. Almost everything you do or engage with or have in your life (when you are coming from your 3D Self) is there in order to numb the suffering or make life bearable related to the suffering. Or it is there to continue the suffering in some way or both. The parts of you that believe suffering to be MORE real than love draw circumstances and situations that keep the suffering cycles happening.

Suffering cycles happen outside of you, in external circumstances, or they seem to anyway since the true source of suffering is from WITHIN you.

A suffering loop between a punishing aspect of you and a corresponding aspect that feels shame and unworthiness in response to the punishing aspect is a common suffering loop. This punisher-shame suffering loop is one of THE most effective ways to keep the veil in place. This is inside of you, in self talk mostly, the critical 'voice' that you hear in your head and also the corresponding shame and unworthiness that washes over you in response to that voice. This can happen very subtly and near constantly until you become aware of it. This punisher-shame talk creates an energy inside of you that projects outside too, pushing away love as it it energizes you are not worthy to receive it.

You are not the part of you that punishes and criticizes you. You are not the parts of you that respond in shame and unworthiness to this criticism. Responding to these aspects of yourself with love as your 5D/Higher Self, once you become aware of them, brings in the possibilities of discernment without disdain and the transformation of shame into innocence and of unworthiness frequencies into innate goodness frequencies. Responding to this punisher-shame suffering loop with love and curiosity to understand where it comes from and the conditioning you received that seeded it within you allows for the loops to happen less and less. Eventually, you have rooted so much self love into your BE-ing that there is no ground for self punishment and shame to take root inside of you.

You are NOT your suffering, as real as it can feel to you in moments. You are not the truths that your suffering offers you either, although it can feel very true in moments. Suffering offers the filter of more suffering to come, that is just lurking everywhere, ready to pounce and come again. Suffering offers the sense that all of life is not to be trusted and acute anxiety can come up in response to this. Yet, again, you are not this filter ready to see more suffering in everything. And, you are not the anxiety that doesn't trust the goodness of life, yourself, or anything.

Suffering can be useful when it acts as a motivator for awakening and for ascension. At some point, the degree of suffering is enough in terms of the lessons that your soul wanted you to learn from it. You wake up to wanting something more, to wanting more love, to wanting to remember that you ARE love and that you ARE goodness. You wake up wanting to feel that the world and life are inherently good and offer love, not more suffering.

This waking up happens because of a crisis in life caused by health or relationships or near death experiences or spiritual awakenings. This happens because of repeated patterns of suffering that become so apparent that you can no longer *not* see them. This happens because you are ready as a soul to be woken up to your Higher Self and your essence. This happens because you meet someone, a teacher or guide or romantic partner or community, who offers you a taste of love that is so good and pure that you remember what you really ARE.

As you waken to love, you begin to let go of suffering. Letting go of coming from suffering does not mean that you no longer feel any pain or anything that you might label as 'negative.' Letting go of suffering means that you are moving out of 'suffering over suffering', out of filtering reality from the lens of more suffering (either anxiety that more suffering is coming to you or a sense that more will inevitably come to you), out of feeling that more suffering is what you deserve.

As you connect with your Inner Punisher, this punishing and critical (of both self and others) transmutes into humble discernment WITH love for self and others. The discernment is able to see and know with love while being open to new possibilities and with an understanding that you ARE innocent and good in your essence and you are able to move out of suffering over your suffering and into BEing in life, feeling your way through.

~

Openness To Feeling Our Feelings As An Aspect Of The Awakening Process

This afternoon, I experienced a sense of feeling unhappy, which is admittedly rare for me most of the time. It was a vague feeling of unhappiness without a strong charge, but really felt more like a restlessness. I couldn't feel specific content which created this feeling, but I sensed it has something to do with changes that are coming, both personally and for our community. Changes that will provide a crucible for growth and self understanding, as change always does. It felt like part of me was tense about these changes and how they will impact us and what they will push up to be felt.

There was a rare breeze moving through this afternoon and it seemed to reflect my impatience back to me. As has been my spiritual and emotional healing practice for many years, I asked myself: "Which part of me is agitated?' and 'What is going on in my life right now or what has been previously subconscious to me that is now coming up?' Finally: 'What do I need to be open to feeling?'

This openness to feeling the source of my reactions has led me to the place I am now most of the time….can it be called, 'awakened'? Or, even, 'enlightened'? I suppose it could be, seen through a certain filter. Or, at least, that I have had tastes of being awakened based on the experiences I have had and continue to have. Why, then, if this is true, am I feeling restless and, even, agitated? Isn't all that supposed to be 'behind me'?

I feel that these questions are at the heart of the distortion about being awakened or enlightened. As if, suddenly, like receiving a bolt from the sky, we are free of our feelings and reactions. As if, we are released from our Humanity and no longer 'plagued' by shifting moods and emotional tides. Maybe for some souls this is true….maybe it was true for Buddha as he was described by others. And for Yeshua and for Krishnamurti perhaps. But, it seems to me that these saints and sages must have had passing moods and feelings too. They were Human after all, even if they had ascended to a place of consciousness that is well beyond what most of us experience every day. While I admire deeply the great saints and sages, I don't look to them for a model of being without feelings but rather as templates of how to hold higher states of consciousness and our Humanity in one individual expression of Infinite Awareness and Infinite Love.

For those of us interested in personal and spiritual growth, I feel that what we are after is understanding and awareness about our reactions and moods. We want to understand and, therefore, ultimately heal our pain and suffering to experience more joy and wonder about our lives. And through this understanding, be able to make choices that feel more in alignment with who we authentically are and our soul purpose reason for being here. Perhaps some of us want to experience our nondual nature in magical moments freed from the tight constraints and filtering of our minds. Or, we want to feel the arms of the Divine around us, guiding and holding us, even as in moments It sets us free to fly our own routes, sovereignly following our passions and our desires.

The SoulFullHeart definition of awakening is not about being liberated from feeling anything negative. It is about having the consciousness and heart capacity to hold the reactions, move through them, and gain invaluable healing and understanding in the process. Being with my feelings in this way is what has opened my heart and soul to let in the altered states of consciousness that I have experienced and the overall joyful and magical way that I relate to my life. Yes, 'bad' moods still occur for me, but they are held with sacredness and honor. And, they move quite quickly rather than sticking to a deeper, unconscious depression and suffering place inside of me as they did before I began my growth process.

Within the SoulFullHeart community, we invite everyone to share reactions and feelings that come up – as I will do at dinner tonight with my mate Raphael and others after checking in with myself and my Guides to feel into the source of my feelings. Being able to share our vulnerable feelings with others who can feel us and love us is another key to awakening to our essence as Infinite Love. Without a support for our inner world to come out, our 3D Self (comprised mainly of our Protector part) suppresses it and part of us pretends everything is fine. This suppression comes from a sense of feeling separate from each other, which then makes it necessary to hide what we really feel. When we are invited to be authentic with ourselves, with others, and with the Divine from a place of connection and Oneness about what we are feeling, we experience the reactions move and heal. We experience that everything about us can be held with love and sacredness, even what we would have previously judged as 'negative' or 'unenlightened.'

Now that I am finished writing this, I feel better and lighter. My heart is filled with the truth of what I am offering and my desire to share this with others who are tired of suppressing their feelings and pretending to be what they are not. The agitated mood is moving along like the breeze, not gone for good but ebbing and flowing until I need it again.

~

Shifting Your External Circumstances By Shifting Your Internal Experience

Being YOU no matter the context, situation, or environment is a profound invitation for growth and awakening. Being the version of you that is spacious and sees the bigger picture, feels the deeper connection to life and Divine Source. And then, slipping and dipping, going down, being triggered, being 'fused', feeling emotions. And then, back up again to yourself when you can find yourself again and the situation is 'right' and the day is set up for it and the circumstances support it.

The circumstances offered by relationships, jobs and careers, geography, money, etc. impact you in these ways of lowered frequency, of not feeling like your Higher Self, when you need that reflection still, when you need something to rub up against, when you need the grist that it provides. These circumstances are sacred (as pain is sacred), yet, too, there is an invitation to consciously feel what the circumstances are reflecting to you and IF this is still YOU or not. The invitation is to feel if you want to BE what the circumstances are reflecting about you or not.

This is where the Universe invites you to go within, to FEEL and LOVE and KNOW yourself. Your 'outer circumstances' ONLY change when your inner reality does. There is NO other way. In 3D reality, it has been presented and we've been conditioned the opposite to this: WHEN my circumstances change, I will be happy. WHEN the externals of my life get better, I will feel joy. WHEN the situation outside of me improves, I will feel whole. However, the deeper truth that our soul knows is that only WHEN your internal experience changes and shifts does the external reality shift to reflect it.

This is where your POWER is. This is where your responsibility lives. INside. In self intimacy. In-to-me-I-see that is intimacy. And in this seeing of self, you can see what and who you REALLY are versus what you have been conditioned to feel that you are. You can lift the veil of amnesia you chose as a soul and start to remember and see who you REALLY are and your multidimensionality and how much power you have. If your external circumstances are making you consciously unhappy and you are suffering over them, then this is who you ARE in this phase of your journey. Is this being of YOU as you are seeing ok with you or do you want to BE something different? If you are consciously unhappy and looking for answers to not be unhappy anymore, then you are most likely wanting to see and feel something different.

As you awaken and heal your heart, your soul, your body, your mind then you raise your vibrational frequency. The wounded frequencies create a magnet inside of you, drawing more wounded experiences and circumstances which perpetuates the cycle of suffering. You need this cycle until you don't need it anymore. Until you have experienced enough love inside to let it go and your frequencies are healing and higher so that you are drawing more higher love frequencies from the outside to reflect your inside.

This is a transition, this being and claiming of true self expression and then having your external reality reflect this. I feel it is ALWAYS a transition in some form or another as we are ALWAYS growing in some form or another. Yet, too, there is a tipping point in this ascension journey where you no longer draw nor desire an outer reality of suffering, unhappiness, or frustration. You still make room and hold space for pain that comes up from inside of you, yet you are no longer 'flooding the decks' of your ship with unhappy waters triggered by current circumstances. This IS possible as you go within, seek support, DO and BE something different in how you relate to self. This IS possible as you experience more love, reach a saturation point, and feel more and more that you ARE love and deserve love.

What You Resist Persists; What You Embrace, Arises

When you react with resistance to something that comes up inside of you or outside of you, then it will persist. When you resist to feel and go inside to feel and resist holding space to feel, then it will persist. The oppositional energy, the resistant energy itself creates a polarizing effect on whatever it is that you are resisting. The edges rub against each other creating more tension and more friction.

When you respond with embracement to something that comes up inside of you or outside of you that is difficult or hard, then it is able to arise. When you embrace feeling and going inside to be and feel and understand, the loving energy creates a loving effect on whatever it is that is needing your attention. The edges of separation dissolve, opening up the possibilities. The difficult or painful or hard energy can then arise into something ELSE, something that comes up in response to love.

This applies to your inner world and then, what you experience of your outer world too. If you resist a person or the mirror they are offering you of YOU, then that negative energy persists between you and usually creates a loop of entanglement and suffering in the relationship. If you embrace the person and the mirror they are offering you, then the energy between you can arise into something else, something new, something made and coming from love. Even if you feel to take space from that person, YOU are different and what you experience of the situation is different because you ARE love even if they have not changed.

Feel the energy you are responding with....is it resistant? Is it embracing? Is it pushing away? Is it bringing closer? Is it open? Is it closed? Is it edgy? Is it soft? ALL reactions are sacred and embraced even as they are invited to move and to heal.

And with ascension, if you resist the transformational and alchemical energies that are flooding Gaia, they will still persist yet you will be in opposition to them or even in denial of them rather than in flow and surrender WITH them. Embracing these energies that want you to grow and that will support you to transform allows YOU to arise WITH them into infinite possibilities in every moment.

~

Holding Space For Your Pain So It Can Move And Heal

I am making space for my pain today. Does this sound strange? I guess, from a certain perspective, it IS strange. From a third dimensional perspective, pain is to be avoided, numbed out, covered over. Pain 'gets in the way' of what 'needs to be done', so it is usually not allowed any space at all. Whether that pain is sourced from the body, the emotional pain body, the mental body, the spiritual body....in the 3D perspective it is all just wrong and needs to be cured, drugged, or gotten rid of somehow.

Yet, in my experience of awakening and ascension into higher consciousness frequencies, pain is something to be honored, something to be held, something to be digested, something that is a sacred aspect of the process until it isn't anymore. In this honoring and space holding, the pain can provide to you messages about what and where it is coming from. It can identify its root origins to your core woundings.

There is SO MUCH information in pain. Information about our heart struggles, our body shifts, our soul challenges. Most of our pain comes from suppression of the pain we experienced in the moment it happened to us, it comes from lack of digestion, lack of 'being felt' in the moment. So, it collects and pockets and is stored at a cellular level in our DNA and as energetic and emotional blocks in our emotional, physical, and chakral bodies. Life situations and circumstances and relationships trigger this pain and we are 'alerted' to it. If we respond to this alert with love and curiosity, then we have the opportunity to actually heal the pain at its root and this creates the end of suffering.

Holding space for pain is not the same as suffering over it. 'Suffering over your suffering' is when the pain is amplified and dragged out and mulled over and stuck to…'fusion' we call this in SoulFullHeart. The part or aspect of us that holds the pain is 'fused' to it and we BECOME the pain rather than hold space for the pain to be felt and moved. Our Higher Self and Ethereal Guides can beautifully hold space for our pain and they want to. They know that with love and care that going into the pain will lead to going THROUGH it. And this has been my experience the last 15 years and in serving others. I have not experienced nor experienced with others that anyone has gotten STUCK in their pain when they have been willing to feel it, but rather moved through it and only able to feel what they could handle to feel anyway.

The pain I am holding space for is related to my body and experiencing painful menstrual cramps for twenty years now. I have tried many herbal and energetic treatments. I have come at it from many angles. I feel now that this pain lives in the cellular memory of my body, in the DNA, and is wanting to shed and let go as I move into inhabitation of more of my light body. So, I will be with it, listen to it, and feel it. See where it wants to take me and where we can go together. With so much joy and love coming into my field lately, I can feel more easily where this pain is part of the 'old' and is ready to let go now.

What we resist, persists…..including our pain. What is yours trying to tell you? Are you making space to listen to it or are you avoiding it? Often it is trying to tell you of changes or of soul stories or of heart woundings that need your attention and love. Often it is trying to tell you of unfulfilled desires or dreams or purposes. It is offering the end of suffering and when loved and healed, another place for which love can enter in.

~

Digesting Post Traumatic Reactions Stored In The Emotional Body

Yesterday, while Raphael and I were out sitting at a cafe, I thought I saw a woman from my past. In the immediate sense that this MIGHT be her, I felt a knot of anxiety and tension in my third chakra or solar plexus area flare up. After confirming with Raphael that it wasn't this woman, who I will call 'Jane', I felt the tension move out of my field replaced by a sense of calm and love.

In digesting my response to seeing who I thought was Jane, I gave my solar plexus some loving energy as I felt into what the reaction had been. Jane was once a very close friend of mine, true soul family and sister. Almost ten years ago, we were both part of a spiritual and emotional healing group for close to five years together. The same group for which Raphael and I met and eventually left together. I left the group in a highly intense way, after receiving a choice from Daniel – the leader of the group and a man who was like my surrogate father – to either break up with Raphael for a year or leave the group as we were deemed too codependent to be together in a healthy way. This choice was given to me after only three weeks of dating and years of me being in the group within the inner circle and serving as a facilitator of the work for a few years too.

It was a very difficult decision on one hand yet, also, my soul was guiding me that it was time to leave this setting which had brought so much love and healing to my life but for which much of it I had outgrown. I heard a strong "No more" in my head which I feel now was my Higher Self and my Guides. I said 'no' to the frequencies of control, power OVER those in the group, the gossiping and competition amongst those in the facilitator circle. I said 'yes' to my own sovereignty and my choice to explore relationship with Raphael, a man who felt like the deepest mate of heart, soul, and body that I had been desiring for many years. When I left the group, none of the people who I felt to be soul family would or could talk with me any longer.

    Jane and I were living together at the time of this dissolution with the group and it was very awkward. We tried to have a friendship 'outside' of the group, but she was still very much involved and wouldn't listen to my growing clarities about the shadow frequencies within it. The separation with her and her disapproval of me was so challenging for me to digest when we had experienced so much love together. Eventually, we went our separate ways, with love, and with her choice to continue in the group. We haven't spoken in over nine years even as the group fell apart two years ago with Daniel finally being called out for his behaviors by all those in the group.

    I am sharing this story, I believe, because it was interesting to feel how even though consciously I have reconciled this experience, my emotional and energy body still held trauma from it. I connected with this energy in my solar plexus last night (and the nasal congestion that came up too) and also cut any karmic bind cords with Jane and yet sent her love too in case it was the Universe telling me that she was thinking of me. In my experience with serving others, this is how our emotional and energy bodies work…they store undigested pain in this way, as pockets that release when they are triggered to release (what Carl Jung called 'being constellated'). We can trigger them to release through consciously connecting with the part of us that holds this energy as we offer and hold space for in SoulFullHeart.

    Ultimately, I feel gratitude for my experience in this group and my experience with Jane especially as I trust that our souls signed up for it and it brought me so many gifts of realization around heart-based leadership that invites others in and respects their sovereignty, which is the place I come from related to SoulFullHeart. This group also introduced me to the emotional body, parts work, and the importance of healing at this deep emotional level. Because of the dark night I experienced in leaving the group and 'being rejected by' all of my soul family connections that I had at the time, I appreciate the connections that I have with others now in a much deeper way. And, my bond with Raphael was instantly solidified and strengthened by our moving through the trauma of leaving together and we really had no 'choice' but to be completely vulnerable with each other. This experience also helped me work through and heal karmic patterns around rejection, being dominated, dominating others (I connected with my inner Daniel part at some point), shadow side of spirituality, authority, etc.

If you find yourself in or are digesting having been in a relationship with some of these frequencies (and this can happen in romantic and family relationships too, usually what is called the empath and narcissist relationship), it takes time to heal and recover from them for sure and much inner strength and soul resolve to complete them. In fact, 'time' doesn't really exist to these places of trauma as it is stored in the emotional body, which doesn't relate to time. The feeling and connecting with these places through negotiation with the Protector part that is protecting them can lead to MUCH movement, growth, and healing with lots of self love and care. Held in a container of love, the lessons are integrated and the tensions are moved with much transformation and deeper embodiment of the Higher Self as a result of our willingness to feel it and hold space for it to move.

~

Going Within, BEing with Self

A day spent yesterday of being with me, relaxing, feeling mellow, being more inward than outward, moving some lower frequency/subtle toxicities through…not my usual JOY and high energy frequencies yet these are good days too actually! A 'recharge' of the love batteries from going inside which leads to offering more in overflow to others, especially for our group call today and right NOW in this moment of shared creativity.

There are times where self space holding is not specific or something big to process, yet just a sense and commitment and desire of BEing with self. A true desire to BE with self, not an 'obligation' or 'should', but because there is NO ONE you would rather be with than yourself. Making space for self and not 'giving out' too much. Feels like an incubator space created for one that we can return to over and over again!

I was an only child growing up and also a 'latch key kid' and my birth parents didn't get home often until late. So, I had glorious hours to myself after school and these were my moments to BE with self, to play pretend, to dance, to sing, etc. Sometimes I played with friends or hung out with others, but mostly I cherished this time to myself as it was for and with ME and it helped me digest the intensities of the day and from the sometimes toxic and complicated dynamics with my birth family. In this way, I believe I chose to be an only child in order to build up this container of sense of gloriousness about self time. I rarely have experienced being lonely this life because of the sense of a rich inner world that has bubbled over into my life.

In 3D, everything is outside. There isn't an internal incubator because everything vibrates from outside of the self. There is no 'there there' inside and the inside is like an empty chamber, yet with ping-pong emotional reactions clashing around (largely unconscious) and soul karmic frequencies simmering and bubbling (again, largely unconscious). There isn't a strong self love and awareness fireplace to hold the fires that come up and so ALL of what comes up in self gets burned in the process. There are smoldering fires and ash everywhere inside of the 3D Self.

The outward focus then is seeking for things to entertain constantly, to divert constantly, to control constantly, to numb constantly in the 3D Self as conditioned by a 3D world. It is a constant search by the 3D Self for the NEXT activity, thing, person...that will maybe even provide ALL of these aspects of entertainment, control, diversion, and numbness. So much of 3D cultural expression is based on this underground NEED and, really, obsession with outside distraction.

A big aspect of 4D awakening is the awakening to SELF and the glorious pleasure of creating and experiencing a growing self fireplace and incubator. And less and less NEED for outside distraction, numbing, and diversion. You are more just content with what is inside and going inside through meditation becomes the entertainment ground with vast rich terrains opening up inside of you. Not used for distraction though but actually in order to feel, in order to heal, in order to grow, in order to INtegrate the soul.

The 4D Self has ups and downs, deaths and rebirths, discoveries and integrations, yet it is held in a CONSCIOUS and AWARE context of growth and awakening. THIS is a big difference from the 3D unconscious letting life just happen and being reactive consciousness that draws drama after drama to be victim to. The 4D Self more and more feels how everything that you experience OUTSIDE of you is a reflection from INSIDE of you.

In this growing lived-in truth is empowerment. There is the completion of feeling like a victim and as if life is happening TO YOU. This is the growing sense of trust and surrender to your connection with All That Is and Divine Source. This is the transition into the frequencies of unity-yet-individual consciousness that is 5D and beyond (conscious duality) where the self is revealed through the peeling and burning away with self love ALL the layers of persona, self image, and 3D conditioning to REVEAL and REMEMBER the soul that is a fractal from Divine Source in Human expression as Infinite Love.

~

Holding Space For Your Tensions To Move Into Trust

The tensions inside offer a communication to you about what is going on in your heart. The tensions are a broadcast signal pinging and ringing inside to get your attention. The tensions are energy that is stuck and fixated at a certain place and in a certain part. The tensions are a sacred thing as it is sometimes in the contrasts that you get the most data about what is going on within you.....until you no longer need the tensions to 'alert' you to anything.

The tensions so often are about desires, about frustrations, about things and ways that cannot BE in the moment. The tensions are about fears of change or going into the unknown that parts of you may hold and feel. The tensions are about unexpressed or suppressed feelings that didn't come out in the moment when they needed to. The tensions are perhaps about the gap between the current YOU and the current circumstances and the current relationships with what your dream self, dream life, and dream relationships are wanting to arise into.

When you feel the tensions, when you look to them for information, when you respond to them with LOVE, then you can get to the heart of where they are coming from. You can give them a voice, give them a tone, give them a tuning in, give them somewhere to land. You can give them a hug, a helping hand, a soft container for which to express.

Part of you can try to cover them over with things and activities and BUSYness, yet still, underneath, the tensions simmer and bubble. The substance of them, the root of them, does not heal, does not 'go away' until you feel and face, until you cry or scream or sleep or just go within or share with those you need to. The things that numb them for the moment eventually don't work anymore as you become more conscious and self aware and tracking with your heart in every moment what you are feeling and BEing.

Your Guides, Angels, Star BEing selves, all want to help you move these tensions as they can block their higher dimensional frequencies from coming into your field. Angels especially offer trusting frequencies, Infinite Love tones and energies that make all the tensions OK, permission to go to the heart of them, even as they dissolve in the loving energies. Divine Feminine energies from Mother Mary wrap the tensions in a loving pink container of support and compassion that allows you and invites you to release.

As you do this and as you ARE this space holder for the tensions, then more and more does the root cause of them (the heart wounding causes, the soul wounding causes) heal and integrate into your loving and spacious Higher Self who has NO tensions about existence in response to the moment. More and more the contrast of tension versus trusting is not needed and you live in the trust. You ARE and BECOME more and more the trust in the moment and that whatever happens is perfect just as it is.

In the meantime, embrace the tensions rather than resist them. As you do, the possibility arises then for something NEW to transmute from them, something moves, and then your heart is open again, you are trusting again, you are spacious again. You are love again as you have responded to ANYTHING inside of yourself with love and so it becomes. And so it is.

~

Why Must You Be Safe, Hidden, And Afraid?: Soul Cry Of Awakening

Oh, why must you be safe? Your heart is crying for MORE.

Oh, why must you be hidden? Your soul is aching to SHINE.

Oh, why must you be afraid? Your courage is wanting to LEAD.

Oh, why must you be settling or shrunken or LESS? Your BIGness is right there waiting.

Oh, why must you be lonely? Your soul family and your Sacred Union mate is inviting you to join them, to deepen with them.

Oh, why must you live in these 'musts'?…these places that FEEL real and yet are not? The places of 'shoulds' and 'have to's' that just feed the conditioned self, the masks, and the personas.

Letting GO, Letting IN, Letting God, Letting LOVE…..washes away the musts and the shoulds and the fear and the hiding and the loneliness and the conforming and the shrinking too. This is NOT an easy thing….all this 'Letting' that replaces the 'Musting' and the 'Shoulding'.

This is SO painful at times to be almost unbearable, this process, and it can't be floated over or bypassed or transcended or just made 'light'. Letting Shadow, Letting Dark be illuminated by the LIGHT of your courage to love ALL that is inside you. To crawl into the deepest recesses, your heart beaming with love, and bring love THERE….even there, to the places and aspects that have been disregarded and disowned. To re-parent them, to re-claim, to re-member them back into love and reunion.

There are times in the awakening and remembering that you feel like you are cracking, the skin you have known is peeling away to reveal the REAL you, the essence that wants to BURST through. And loving even THIS cracking and THIS false skin and not feeling them as bad, just necessary for while they were to be in 3D frequencies.

Feeling how there are NO places inside of real evil or darkness, nothing to REALLY be afraid of or that can't be transmuted by love. No pain inside that can't be held and moved by love. And this changes too how you feel about the outside world, about others…how you feel and see everything outside of yourself as ultimately being worth love and forgiveness and made OF love.

Letting Go, Letting IN, Letting God, Letting REALness, Letting Feelings, Letting Love……THIS is the ground of awakening and remembering. This is the ground where the pain can be held and has a sacred purpose. The sacred purpose of being YOU into realness, into your bigness, into your emotional body being current, into your deepest ground of Sacred Union of self and with your mate, into the embodiment of YOU as Infinite Love.

~

Walking Through Your Valley Of Shadows Of Death During Awakening

You are walking through a valley……crawling on your knees at times. Completely lost and feeling like a ghost at times. Totally submerged in pain and mourning at times. Ash in the Air, filling the Air at times. THIS is the valley of the shadow of death place that awakening brings you to, invites you to…..yet it is not a place on the outside. It is not a place to GO to, yet rather, a place that you BECOME inside for a phase in order to move beyond it.

You are BEing with the shadows that are inside during this phase. The shadows are echoes of fear, of wounding, of trauma. The shadows are energies from other lifetimes wanting to become visible again so you can connect and heal and integrate them into your soul expression AS a Human again. The shadows are what is inside of you that has been repressed and disowned, cast away, and rejected.

You are BEing the death that is happening inside. The death is of the false YOU, the version of you that you agreed to be until you no longer needed or wanted to be anymore. Until you started to remember that you are not THAT, but really SO MUCH more. The death is of the old world that used to be nourishing and no longer is. The death is the letting go of relationships that require you to shrink and to settle and to conform.

You are crossing from the old way, the conditioned way, the veiled way…and into the NEW, shedding the layers of what is NOT you along the way. This crossing is dangerous to the old way and pushes up fear and resistance. The crossing asks more from you at times than you imagine that you can possibly give or have. Yet, somehow, there is always something there to keep you moving forward.

Even though you walk through the valley of the shadow of death, you fear no evil, because you realize that there is NOTHING evil inside of you. There is nothing truly evil as it ALL can be returned to love WITH love. You fear no evil because you are with YOU. YOU are there to BE with the shadows, to BE with the aspect of you that is dying, to BE a guide during the crossing and the dying and the letting go.

You are supported during this inner valley walk by a growing Sacred Human YOU. This YOU is infused with and held by Divine love, by love from your Guides/aspects that become you more and more. This YOU can hold and respond and LOVE all that comes up inside of you AS sacred, meaningful, and important. This YOU sees all phases (especially the death and rebirth one) as sacred, meaningful, and important.

You are walking through your valley of your shadow during the death of your false self…..responding to change with trust…..responding to death with possibilities…..responding to growth with desire……responding to fear WITH LOVE.

On the other side of this valley is the land of self-love milk and self-worth honey. The riches of self love and self worth that flow like rivers from your expanding mind, your embodying soul, your opening WIDE heart. This land of riches is of SELF beyond self image, unaware ego, personality and persona. This land is rich with the sunshine of your higher consciousness coming in and BEcoming you. It is rich with intimacies with others that are nourishing, catalytic, and based in mutual love and respect.

It is rich with a sense of being WITH Divine Source and also FROM Divine Source and also BEing Divine Source. This is the place you feel and remember as you cross the valley, that keeps you going, that reminds you of who you are MEANT TO BE as a Sacred Human.

~

A New Timeline Is Calling You To Heal And Feel On The Inside

Beginning again and again....YOU will emerge from the ashes of your purposefully burned down previously beloved life. The moments of your phoenix self emerging out and UP, those moments of being FREED UP from what was tying and binding and confining YOU.

So many hooks and binds fitted in and slotted in and configured in your 3D Self that call you to unplug, over and over, feeling the places that are connected in. Aspects of you sitting around the living room of your conditioned life, watching the television of programmed reality, believing the timeline offered of suppression and smallness and suffering. Aspects of you 'stuck' in frozen moments of trauma and pain, living there still, freeze framed beyond time, still feeling the PAIN of this then. Aspects of you co-created with your birth family, them constantly energizing "this is you" and so the hologram-like you arising from this projection and matching what they want and need you to be.

ALL these aspects of you needing YOU…..your love, your soul juice, your heart tones to help them leave the living room of programmed and conditioned reality……to help them turn off the old TV (literally and figuratively)…..to unplug from the matrix INSIDE…..to heal the grids INSIDE……..to unfreeze them in the stuck moments, to meet them there, feel them there, and then MOVE them on into the NOW moment…..to turn OFF the hologram-you projection created by your birth family through boundaries and taking space so the TRUE you can arise.

These aspects of you and the stuck energy of them that manifests in rage, depression, anxiety, tension, despair, control, suffering, body pains, insomnia, toxic relationships…..can MOVE into the higher frequencies of joy, magic, bliss, trust, creativity, truth telling, Sacred Unions, and SERVICE OF LOVE frequencies for which YOU REALLY ARE.

This process of unplugging, deconditioning….it ALL is held with SO MUCH love and support by the Divine, by Mother Gaia, by your BEloved Guides, by your soul family (who is witnessing on the higher soul level), by your Sacred Union mate (who is WITH you or is waiting), by your Higher Self (who is embodying into you more and more), by your star family and star BEing aspects…..they are ROOTING for you and want to support you in this process that can be SO challenging, yet inevitable too, if it is what you have signed UP for to experience here.

This support and this love from others, from outside can come INSIDE more and more as you feel and heal your inner landscapes…it is the ONLY way to experience a new reality on the outside. A NEW life, a new timeline is calling you into these higher frequencies of emotional, spiritual, mental, physical, and social health, nourishment, and abundance….can you feel it?

~

You are NOT a victim

You are NOT a victim. You ARE a powerful creator.

This can be hard to remember and difficult to embody. It can FEEL like to parts of you that you very much ARE a victim to circumstances and relationships and life situations and the 3D matrix and illnesses and your boss and your mate….and just about everything that you have experienced and are experiencing.

Yet, the soul REMEMBERS how you CHOOSE all of the circumstances, situations, and relationships that you experience in this life in order to grow and transform. Your soul remembers that you chose to line it all up for yourself to play out in this 3D

Gaia experiment.....this very short life span, to 'power pack it' with growth opportunities because it offered so MUCH chance to learn. Your soul remembers that none of the people in your life are 'against you' but have actually AGREED to be with you in this life, playing certain roles for you and you for them, in order to heal and move patterns in your Metasoul and soul group.

Also, if you chose a particularly painful and hard life, it is because you are a BIG soul who needed to go through a lot......in order to offer healing and service of love to others AS you overcome and remember and awaken. I feel there are those of us too that came here to heal our emotional bodies specifically and to lead this ground of exploration into bridging a healing emotional body WITH soul frequencies in order to arise Sacred Humanity. THIS is a BIG picture indeed and context around the painful things we have experienced in life!

If you can hold this soul perspective WITH the parts of you that feel like a victim and offer it to them when they are feeling hopeless and powerless, it can lead to MUCH healing and sense of empowerment. These parts of you, especially the young parts such as the Inner Child, can be responded to with compassion around their feelings of being a victim.

When you tell the story of your life, do you hold it with reverence and the sense that you CHOSE it ALL? Or do parts of you tell it with despair, depression, powerlessness and rage? Do you blame and shame others or yourself in your 'story' as you tell it? If those emotional tones come up, that's a clear sign that there are parts of you stuck in your emotional pain body with undigested wounding and traumas. You can unstick them with self love and compassion....and by offering this higher soul perspective too. This is not just 'thinking differently' about what you have experienced...it is BEing different, coming from a trust place and these soul frequencies are able to transmute the victim places into empowered places. It really does work this way, in my experience over the years.

ALL that is IN your life and that you experience of it is there because you have allowed it to be, because you have chosen for it to be. Feeling this then leads to the question: "Do I want what is currently in my experience of life to continue and why or why not?" And also, "WHY have I chosen this? What is it telling me or teaching me?" THESE are powerful questions because you can feel the WHY at the deeper level (at the parts level is what I would recommend) and then make choices of action based on the answers that you discover.

Staying victim can be used by parts of you to keep you safe, to keep life safe, to keep you from risking or growing beyond where they feel you can go. It can keep you entangled in toxic relationships that no longer serve your soul and are more 'scared' unions than sacred ones. It can block ACTUAL self love and compassion from flowing to the parts of you that really need it (and ALL of them need it actually!) It can block connection with Divine Source where you can feel and let in and TRUST that the Divine (and your Guides) are WITH you in this life experiment and support you with love in all moments.

You are not a victim. You are a POWERFUL creator God or Goddess fractal from Divine Source in increasingly Sacred Human form! As you remember this, so do the places inside that FEEL less than this, transform with SO MUCH love!

SPIRITUAL AREA

You are arising from the ashes of your purposefully burnt up life, choosing the match, the heat, the way in which your now feeling false world will burn

You are BEing reborn from that which has been cast off, birthing out from that which is true as the only REAL thing that can remain

You are resurrecting your form out of a dying and collapsing reality, claiming a new way of BEing as your Sacred Humanity

You are serving love as your greatest purpose, feeling in every moment how you can BE THIS MORE

You are moving beyond fears of an unenLIGHTened soul, accessing your awakening soul's courage and desire for UNION

You are co-creating a NEW Golden Earth possibility, feeling in every moment how you can BE THIS NOW

You are opening and healing your higher heart through PURE love, connecting with the energy of your Star BEing and Angelic origins

You are awakening from the deep sleep of the forgetful soul, remembering the LOVE from which you came and already ARE ~

Jelelle Awen with Christ Consciousness/Yeshua/Christiel/Jesus
Written on Easter morning, 2017

~

Becoming Childlike AND Angelic

Becoming childlike, you remember the innocence and purity of your Humanity. Embracing your Inner Child within, your Inner Teenager, your 3D Adult too......the joys and the hurts, the magic and the pain, both held in your heart with tender love and curiosity. The vulnerability emerges through this holding....the magical access emerges through this loving....the reverence emerges through your reverence for self.....the authenticity emerges through this genuine holding.

Becoming Angelic, you remember the expansiveness and sacredness of your Divinity. Embracing your inner Angel within, your Galactic and Higher Self, connecting from the 'outside' with Guides in order to remember and become the Angel that you ARE more and more. The soul bigness arises through this holding.....the soul purpose expression arises through this communion....the soul gifts sharing arises through this exchange of self-to-self soul gift love.

Becoming a Sacred Human, you remember the BEST of what makes you Human and the BEST of your sacred, soul nature. You remember and, also, BECOME something NEW in this embracement of roots to wings, integrating the Human consciousness experiment into NEW frequencies of Divine expression. All is held with love, all the capacity, the FULL range of your BEing in its Creator God and Goddess expression.

~

The Spiritual area of life includes your relationship to your spirituality, soul gift expression, soul purpose, ethereal Guides, the Divine, and chakral/energy body. It is the metaphysical, multidimensional, and transcendent expressions of reality coming more and more into your lived-in daily reality. This aspect of our experience of reality has largely been 'deconditioned' out of us by 3D mainstream conditioning that caps our multidimensionality as an aspect of the veil that we chose as souls to put over ourselves to experience life here. Soul awakenings bring spirituality back into our consciousness more and more as our trust deepens in what cannot usually be experienced with the five sense reality, but offers very meaningful experiences.

3D: Your 3D Self is hugely conditioned by birth family and social relationships related to spirituality. Due to your 3D

Self's inclination to adapt and survive, you 'take on' whatever spirituality paradigm offered to you by family. You will accept religious conditioning, for example, without much question or protest and even often with deep embracement. Or, you will accept a no-God or no-spirituality paradigm in the same way. The soul's frequencies are rare to come out in 3D consciousness (although they peek through, of course) and when they do, this is the awakening of your 4D Self.

You may have some authentic connection to the Divine or a spiritual practice or spiritual guru yet it is related to as an 'outside authority' and can be more superficial than deeply meaningful or is more about getting social needs met. The veil is thick related to connection with your higher self and soul. You usually do not have access to memories of other lives, a sense of your soul purpose, or much expression of your soul gifts, although there are usually hints of these things in your lives if looked at from this lens.

4D: Your 4D Self is in a transition from what your conditioning has been, moving into embracing and discovering what truly and deeply resonates with you as a soul. Soul awakening is happening, including memories and recall of other lifetimes and a deepening sense of soul purpose. In the lower 4D, there is often some sort of Dark Night Of The Soul experience or deep spiritual awakening experience(s). There can be a fixation and break off with a group and Spiritual Teacher/Guru as an aspect of this that brings about big awakenings and realizations. In the lower 4D, outer authority is looked to for guidance and validation, replacing the authority of your birth family and your culture, with sometimes mixed results and experiences. Polarities of good and evil still exist here and are experienced in different ways to heal soul themes and legacies. Archetypes such as Hero, Priest/Priestess, Warrior, Shaman are starting to infuse your BEing and heal into more positive expressions from the shadow expressions.

In the upper 4D, you have increasing clarity about soul purpose and are drawn to serve others in some way with your soul gifts. There are usually claiming and educational choices that come along with this even as the shift of earning money and livelihood from soul gifts maybe hasn't come into manifestation. There is usually a deep and rich experience and relationship with Ethereal Guides such as Angels, Ascended Masters, the Divine - in both feminine and masculine forms - Star BEings. The connections are becoming more and more personal and less generated by an outer authority.

5D: Your 5D Self operates from a sense of deep personal authority related to spirituality yet also a large degree of surrender of outcomes to Divine will. Your 5D Self can operate in paradoxes such as this. Your 5D Self has a rich inner world and realizes that everything that you experience as 'guides' is actually YOU as you embrace the Metasoul perspective. You are connecting with Guides and aspects from other lifetimes in a bigger context, quantum way, with integration to wholeness happening more and more. Your 5D Self has a visceral experience of being a fragment of the Divine AND the Divine both. Your 5D Self remembers that its essence is as Infinite Awareness and Infinite Love having a Human experience. Your 5D Self is embodying the Higher Self more and more as your vibrational frequencies increase more and more. Serving love and your soul purpose are manifesting with income and gift exchange connected directly to expression and offering of your soul gifts.

Questions For You:

How did you locate yourself related to spirituality – as primarily a 3D, 4D or 5D consciousness and why?

What are your frustrations in the area of spirituality?

What are your desires in the area of spirituality?

~

Lifting The Veil Of Connection With Ethereal BEings

Divine Source is offering this invitation to you to remember the love that you ARE. Divine Source becomes the voices and forms and energies of Angels, Ascended Masters, Spirit Guides, elementals, Unicorns, all such magical and love-based arising creations. For a phase of time, you are invited to relate to these beings as outside of you. You are invited to feel their higher vibrational energy as a template for you to move out of 3D frequencies and into the transitional fourth dimensional ones and increasingly into the fifth dimensional ones. These beings vibrate at such a higher rate than the 3D Self that we need for a time their energy to infuse ours and lift ours UP.

These Ethereal BEings are the first to remind you that you ARE them and they ARE you. They remind you that they are not better than you even as they vibrate higher than you and are free from the density of the 3D Human body. They are freed from the veil of not remembering that you have chosen as a soul to place over yourself so that you can engage in a process of remembering.

These BEings represent your Higher Self in energy and tone, amplified and taken in to the degree that you can and are meant to in any moment. Claiming a connection with them is an important aspect of the ascension process because it allows your 3D Self to feel something bigger than them. Your 3D Self developed aspects of them that felt bigger than everything and everyone, which was just a compensation for feeling deeply unworthy related to everything and everyone. The 3D Self then projects this 'bigger than but actually unworthy' energy onto God, mostly through religious pictures and lower vibrational frequency spiritual practices.

The Awakening Self can hold the truth that these Ethereal BEings ARE higher in some ways and have much to teach and ALSO that they are no bigger or higher than you and that they all

COME from you and inside of you. Holding this kind of truth is not something the 3D mind can do but can only come from experience of this ground over and over as you ask for connection and seek it out, experience it and realize eventually that it all comes from within.

My 3D Self put a veil over my natural love for the Divine and my abilities to hear, see, and feel Ethereal BEings until I was awakened to these frequencies in my early 30's. My Higher Self agreed to this veil and it was necessary for the time that it was for me to be here in 3D life. I always had a very active 'imagination' though and never 'outgrew' playing pretend games and scenarios. I would have long conversations with people who were not physically there and I would often have them go and flow the way I wanted them to versus how I experienced the person in real life. I realized later that I was actually communicating with the higher self version of the person and transacting at a higher vibrational frequency of possibility timeline with them! And, some of it was fantasy too as I created a better reality than I was experiencing in daily life.

Imagination, make believe, and fantasy all are rejected by the 3D Self or maybe bubbled off and kept private like mine was for many years. The 3D Self values the rational and the proven over the imagined or the created. This dominance of the left brain and overdevelopment of it has been undone in order to move into the world of connection with Ethereal BEings. To make real, with your heart open, that which doesn't seem real because it cannot be 'seen'.

People who have remembered their gifts of imagination and creativity and present themselves then as channelers of this energy, of ultimately these aspects of themselves, can offer useful teachings to others. And, sometimes, it is a fourth dimensional process for them to not attach to a self image around this capacity. A back and forth process with the 3D Self who attaches to self image, to the way others perceive them, serves as a compensation for an unhealed unworthiness in their emotional body. Those who have parts of them who are always in knowing and present their teachings as 'absolute truth' are usually hiding core unworthiness that lives in their emotional body. Becoming a channel or medium can feed this cycle of compensation over unworthiness.

Your 3D Self may look to others as the channel and message for other BEings and, for a phase of time, this may be necessary. Your Higher Self knows that you are a channel too. It knows that everyone is a channel for these energies, as we are all sourced from the same Divine energy and will someday return to it. Ethereal BEings will remind you that everyone is a channel and as you experience more and more connection with them then you will remember it too because you will BE it from inside rather than projecting it onto others as being a special attainment that only they have.

I will share conversations that I have with Ethereal BEings and especially the BEing and energy known as Archangel Metatron as his energy is one that I am in the process of embodying more deeply FOR and AS myself. I share these conversations not from a place from having a deeper attainment or higher status than you, but rather as a template for the inner exploration that I have given myself permission to remember and embody. And, I am sharing meditations and journeys that you can go on to find this out for yourself and empower yourself to claim back your ability to channel energies that cannot be seen until they ARE intuitively seen and felt by the upper chakras opening up.

Metatron has a strong knowing energy yet, I also feel his continual curiosity and wonder at the Infinite possibilities of every moment. Every Ethereal BEing that I have connected with has this same combination of deep inner knowing and clarity in combination with an open sense of possibility. This is how I feel Divine Source at its deepest essence is as well. Our existence is the result of this curiosity to discover something beyond what the Divine could know as It split itself off into fractals with free will, individual soul spark consciousnesses, so it could experience life and Itself in a new way. This is one of the pictures that has been offered by Metatron and other Ethereal BEings as the origins story of life. It's one that I like as it has this sense of play and wonder about it.

Lifting the veil to remember your connection with Ethereal BEings brings many gifts with it. You have the visceral sense that you are not alone and never have been. You feel their energy around you, especially angels, and it infuses you with a sense of being loved and feeling comforted. It helps your 3D Self feel safe enough to go into the jagged spaces and shadow places that are uncomfortable, fear-based, and hard to feel at times. Angels especially hold an energy of anything is possible and nothing is to be feared and that nothing is wrong with you. This unconditional acceptance of you floods your BEing and helps to heal the places that have felt unacceptable and rejected.

Teachers that ascended out of the physical body after incarnating here and are now available as Ethereal Teachers can provide a bridge for you to feel their experience of life on Gaia that has now transmuted out of the body into higher realms. Being the student is easy with these BEings as they invite you to lean into their wisdoms while empowering you to embrace your own. They provide a template of being a teacher, how it feels to teach from a place of egolessness and without self image. How it feels to teach purely from love. Some of the ascended teachers that I have connected with have offered me beautiful wisdoms, opened my heart up hugely, touched me deeply, and all have helped me remember my essence as Infinite Love. Some of these teachers have been Kuan Yin, Mother Mary, Magdalene, Kali, Dark Mother (Divine Feminine frequencies)…..and Yeshua, Buddha, and others.

Ethereal BEings are there to guide and support, yet the real 'work' of the process of remembering and healing is yours. They cannot take away your pain if you are meant to feel it and heal it yourself. They cannot make better what is yours to sovereignly go through, even if you ask them too. What you have signed up for as a soul to experience is what you need for growth. The 3D and even 4D Self can cling to angels and other BEings to make life better for them and to take away their pain that they don't want to feel or take responsibility for. The 3D Self wants transcendence because the emotional pain can run so deep and has so long been suppressed. This is just another form of not taking responsibility for what you create in your life and what lives and breathes inside of your heart to be healed and in your soul to be healed too.

    This is a delicate ground to walk. The more you embody your Higher Self, the more you can feel when you are not taking responsibility or not holding something deeply enough inside of yourself and looking too much outside of yourself for answers. An example of this is to feel when you are seeking for others to take away your fear or your pain rather than to hold it yourself, to seek yourself, and sometimes to experience others as a support for this holding. This is a big one, a big crucible for the 3D Self transitioning to 4D and beyond. Even now, as you take in my words and energy, you may have aspects of you who are looking to me for answers as an outside source. Yet, truly, only what lives inside of you as YOUR truth and then is represented by me as a reminder of YOUR truth will really resonate inside of you in that heart and soul way that keeps you eagerly reading on.

    The Higher Self holds connection with Ethereal BEings as a blessed experience, a necessary one for a phase, and also that it (or you as you become more of your Higher Self) are also an Ethereal BEing in your essence. The Higher Self holds outside sources as templates for inner resonance and remembering. Outside sources are there to trigger what you need to remember as your own truth but they do not hold MORE or BETTER truth than you. They are there to help you remember your soul's truth. With unhealed unworthiness, it can be difficult for the 3D Self to hold and feel this. This is a transition that takes love and patience to be with and practice in your own connection ground with Ethereal BEings is key to deepening this ground.

~

Introducing Archangel Metatron: Frequency Of Ascension

Archangel Metatron is offering this invitation to you, to undertake this journey of remembering your essence as Infinite Love. He is available for you, especially if your desire and intentions are to raise your vibrational frequency to embody your Higher Self as a fractal of Divine Source. Metatron is the Lord of Light frequency, the voice of what we have felt to be God. He speaks for God as God and even physically (when he shows a physical form) is that of an older man with a white beard and long, flowing hair – the usual picture of God. He shows this form because it is comforting to many people. His actual form is of such a high vibrational frequency of light that we cannot see it with our Human eyes nor let in the full force of his radiance.

His energy is golden orange, feels like the warmth of the sun amplified by a thousand. You let in what you can of his energy and form. You see what you are ready to see. You hear what you are ready to hear. You feel what you are ready to feel. When beginning your connection with him, you may feel very strong emotions of reunion, gratitude, and remembrance. Or you may feel a slight warmth in your heart with a sense of being glad to feel him again. You may hear his voice very clearly or not at all for awhile.

Trust that whatever happens is what is meant to happen. It is what you can let in at this current moment based on where you are in your journey. As 'author' of this book, I am surrendered to where Metatron would like to take it in moments if it is his energy that wants to lead. This has meant that it is not a linear journey laid out for the mind, as he doesn't 'do' linear, but rather a spiralling and nonlinear sharing meant to engage your higher self consciousness and open your heart and trigger your emotional body. Reading these words is to take in a transmission of ENERGY, as much as is ready to come through to you in this form.

Metatron wants you to begin your own connection with him as you read this book, as I provide a template for what it feels like to be in communication with him and as his energy is shared through the writing. He is already part of you and you are part of him. This is true for all souls on the planet Earth or Gaia at this moment. Not all will choose to claim this connection. Not all are meant to claim it. If you are reading this book, it feels as if your Higher Self is offering that you are ready to claim it. Your Higher Self drew you to this energy, to the bridge that it provides, to the message that it offers and to the energy that it shares.

I will share some communications with Metatron and meditations for you to begin your journey with him, which hopefully will coincide with and be supported by reading this book.

~

DNA Activation Made Simple: Conversations With Archangel Metatron

Archangel Metatron came to me when I called. I didn't call him personally but, rather, held in my heart a desire to understand more about DNA activation and asked for an Ethereal BEing to help me. The concept of 'hidden' DNA strands that when activated raise our consciousness level was intriguing to me. The articles I had read online about this topic were often written in a way that were difficult to understand, almost as if I had walked in on a conversation already underway for many years!

I was engaging in a white energy staircase meditation and holding the question of DNA activation in my heart, asking for guidance and help from any angels that would like to help me.

In this very simple meditation, you visualize a staircase surrounded by pure white light. You count out each step as you walk up it, only on the inhale so that you are really feeling and experiencing each step up. You will feel it when you can go up no further and are as high in vibrational frequency that feels comfortable for you. It will feel as if you are crawling up the stairs and then you will sense it is time to stop. Sometimes it will take 30 steps before you feel this way or 200 or more. Some of this will depend on how low or high your vibrational frequency was when you started. This is a great beginning meditation to start your daily meditation and connection space with Angels and other high frequency BEings.

On this day when I first connected with Archangel Metatron, I was around the 111th step. I felt the presence of my Healing Angel, who is named Coral. She has a comforting and loving energy, yet she immediately seemed to be in a more intense and focused mode than usual. I knew intuitively that she wasn't going to answer my questions, as her gifts are more in the domain of chakra activation, protection, and clearing. She is a Healing Angel, after all, and she has shared with me that we all have one, although most people never consciously connect with theirs. The Healing Angels usually have names that correspond with Earth elements such as stones, crystals, or other natural formations.

Coral and I stepped into the 'elevator' that sits off the platform on floor 111 and shot up to floor 222. I felt a surge of energy move through my body as the elevator journeyed upward. We reached this level and she pushed the next button, landing us on floor 333. In the past, I had been quite vigilant about progressing up each individual stair at a time, but Coral told me that I was ready for a more accelerated ascension. This was after a week of being physically ill with many symptoms similar to the stomach flu. It had been a challenging time and I felt deeply 'cleaned out' and cleansed from the experience. This was also a detox reaction to being in a new environment. I felt lighter and that I had purged some necessary toxicities in the process. My emotional body felt less attached to fear related to the ascension process.

We stepped out of the elevator and were surrounded by golden white clouds swirling around our feet and all around us. It felt lighter and more airy, similar to traveling to a higher altitude where the air is thinner and it becomes a bit harder to breathe.

I asked my question again about DNA activation and I heard his voice respond to me immediately.

"I am here to help you and answer your questions," he said to me (in my head in that way that all Ascended BEings and Angels seem to do.)

"Who are you?" I asked, trying to feel out if he was polarized to the light or polarized to the dark. I can tell by my heart's response if an Ethereal BEing is coming from love or from fear. I couldn't feel much of anything coming from him other than the clear vibration and timbre of his voice, which I liked very much right away.

"I am Metatron," he said.

"Megatron?" I replied. "That sounds like a robot or something!"

He laughed, heartily, in my head. "I am going to give you some advice which helps you understand my name. Always keep the big picture in mind. Do not get lost in content and remember the context."

"Ok, yes," I said. "I get it. You offer a 'meta' perspective on life. I'll just google you when we are done connecting to read more about you. I think I have read your name somewhere. You are an Archangel, yes?"

"Yes. I like to make complex concepts more simple and easy to understand for as many people as possible to grasp."

"So, this concept of DNA activation is one that needs some simplifying, I believe. And it needs to be more accessible. There are Healers out there charging $5,000 to activate people's DNA codes and 'teach' them how to do it for others. Surely, it is simpler than this and something that anyone can do?"

"This is why I am here to help you, Jelelle. Your soul is a bridge and I want to assist you in doing that. I love that you will not pretend to know something that you don't know and actually enjoy being both the student and the teacher."

As he was offering what he loved about me, I could finally feel a wave of it in my heart chakra. It was a sweet feeling that I let flood over me for a moment. He seemed to pulse with love and light for many moments before continuing to speak again.

"It will take some time for you to feel me or to see me more clearly as I am at a much higher vibrational frequency than other BEings that you have connected with in the past. You have a strong clairaudience ability which is why you are able to hear me now easily," he paused to let me digest this. "Now, back to DNA activation. The Human species currently has two active physical strands of DNA, which carries the genetic code, and is shaped like a twisted ladder called a double helix."

He sends me a picture of the double helix, which is familiar to me from biology class in college. "Your species actually has twelve strands of DNA, two that you can 'see' in your third dimension and ten that you cannot that exist in higher dimensions. In your Human history, you have used more strands than you are now. I won't go into the reasons for their shut down right now. But, returning to operation from all twelve strands is a key aspect of the process of ascension and to raising the vibrational frequencies of mainstream consciousness out of fear and into love."

"So when all twelve strands are operating, we can more easily experience our essence as Infinite Love and union with our Divine creator?"

"Yes, exactly, Jelelle, and also the reactivation of the latent, unused areas of the brain along with the reunion of the right and left sides of your brain. As this starts to happen, you begin to feel the powers you have of manifestation, overflowing creativity, psychic and paranormal abilities, clear past life recall, and access to the Akashic Records, among many other things."

That all sounded wonderful to me and exactly what I have been wanting to accelerate in my own life.

"So, how do we activate our DNA codes?"

I felt a wave of energy move through me and the picture of the double helix appeared in front of me again. I also felt my chakras light up one by one from the root to the crown. "We energize and reignite them using golden orange energy together. And, even more importantly, you continue to shift your emotional, spiritual, and mental filters of life by healing any blocks, woundings, congestions, and self limiting patterns in order to lighten your energetic field."

"Oh, ok," I responded, almost feeling disappointed that it wasn't a more dramatic process.

"You are already activating them through your awakening process, Jelelle. As is anyone who is engaging in heart and soul consciousness work…the process is already in motion. Rather than some dramatic 'moment' where all the DNA codes are suddenly activated, it works best if you let time and your process organically allow it to happen. It is the most kind and self loving method for the body and the mind."

I know intuitively from my own experience that he is right. Yet, it seems so tempting to just 'get it over with' somehow.

"We will continue to talk about this over time as there is more I want to share with you about DNA and its connection to the chakras and to dimensional communication as well."

"Thank you, Metatron, for what you have offered me today. I am starting to feel the love that you are and the love that you have for Humanity and it is deeply touching to me." Tears begin to roll down my face as I speak these words. I feel that he is touched and another wave of love rolls over me. I feel our mutual respect for each other and I can feel the student inside of me that is eager for another Ethereal teacher, as I experienced lovely openings through previous conversations with the Divine Feminine Ascended Master Kuan Yin, who I have been connecting with for many years.

I then finished my meditation and after sharing with my beloved mate and co-creator of SoulFullHeart Raphael what I had experienced, I turned on my computer and was soon looking at paintings and images of the beautiful BEing that I had just had the honor of connecting with…I was excited for the new questing adventure that had begun and the places that he and I would go to together!

~

Importance of Heart-Based Awakening: Conversation With Metatron

"Only From The Heart Can You Touch The Sky," Rumi ~

The light is so bright I feel like I need to squint my eyes, even though they are already closed. The light is coming from him, it IS him, and it seems to invite me to remember that it is always what I am made from and of too. It's been four months since I briefly connected with Metatron. At the time, I hadn't even fully remembered his name or what his purpose and gifts are to others. I hadn't remembered yet what a gift he has been to my soul and how deep our connection goes.

This time I am crying. I feel the love that he is, and I can see his facial features too where last time I could only hear his voice. He looks like a thinner Santa Clause. He looks like the traditional God picture with a white beard and long, flowing white hair. There is nothing stern or formidable about him, even as he is very powerful and vibrating at an extremely high frequency.

We are meeting in the Akashic Records, a place in a higher dimensional frequency that has the look and feel of a very bright, spacious, and beautiful library. The Akashic Records are so familiar to me, I feel comfortable there. There are arched windows on my left, twenty feet high at least and there doesn't seem to be a ceiling in the traditional sense. There are 'files' or books for every soul stored in there, along with all the wisdoms and knowledge of both the collective conscious and unconscious.

Metatron wanted to meet me here as it is a halfway point in vibrational frequency between where he normally dwells (too high for me in the moment) and where my frequency is at most times (hovering between 4D and 5D). I can feel the intense recalibration, detox, and upgrade process that I have been in the last months and how my frequency is much higher now to be able to connect with him. Yet, still, the tears come without body reaction at all, no runny nose, just waves of reunion, soul recognition, letting in love that is pressing against places in my heart that are still learning to let it in.

Metatron tells me that he appreciates my tears. He says that he loves my heart. I step through a portal or doorway that he opens for me of one of my other lifetimes in Atlantis where I was very focused on studying the mysteries, working with intense energies of the Earth and the cosmos. I was not much in my heart it feels like even as I was working with very strong energies. I already know from my own soul legacy exploration that my soul theme has been around healing my heart, embodying my emotional reality and relationality as a priority this life along with my spiritual development. This was my primary focus for many years even as spiritual awakenings, connection with Guides and the Divine, energy healings still happened. I am here this life to heal my heart and to open up and integrate the soul consciousness from this heart enlovened place.

This has not always been an easy journey, especially after leaving the spiritual group I was in. Many times in my life I have been turned away from intense development of my soul gifts in order to go back into my heart, into my 3D pain body, into my emotional wounding. This time, I am taking my heart with me as I ascend into higher dimensions, really open to soul awakenings, and I am inviting others to do the same.

I feel a lot of support from Ethereal BEings and our Higher Selves to bring this message to you. The message is to not leave your heart behind in your awakening journey. You cannot really anyway. The hurts and pains remain and they show up primarily in relationships with others. I feel this is why so many Healers and Spiritual Teachers struggle in their personal lives to embody and transact what they can access in the spiritual domains. Often this leads to a dis-integrity around what they are projecting from their leading edge of being and what their actual daily life is like from their trailing edge (where the wounding is.) This transaction is blocked by aspects of them that are still protecting them, protecting their heart, caught up in moments of trauma from childhood and from other lifetimes.

You can clear the channels to remember and integrate your soul gifts and even soul purpose, yet if you do not have access to your heart consciousness (which only becomes available as you go into and heal your shadow, your subconscious, and aspects of yourself) then you are not able to infuse it with the deepest gifts of your Humanity, your compassion, your sensitivity, and most importantly, your vulnerability.

SoulFullHeart is a reflection of my focus on my heart first and the gifts it has given me of experiencing life from a place of really feeling it, really being relational with others, and in such a meaningful and nourishing relationship with Raphael. SoulFullHeart leads to many soul awakenings and is quite catalytic and effective at it because of the way it starts with the heart first, works with the protection that is there, and offers self empowerment for you to lead the way.

In denying the heart, you may soar higher in the skies of the soul, yet you will experience more light than heat and somewhere, deep inside, the pain goes on screaming for your attention. To remember our essence as Infinite Love is to embrace that which has been formed from fear, all aspects of ourselves, and our heart most deeply of all.

Letting In The Pure Love You Are Receiving: Message From Archangel Metatron

I am here. I have always been here and I always will be. I have been with you through your soul's journey, all the lifetimes that your soul expressions are energizing in all the places and eras of time that they are expressing. I am with every soul in this way…..Always and in ALL WAYS.

I am close to Divine Source, so close that We are One in one way yet Divine Source is formless energy of Love so I take Its form and so do other Archangels and teachers in the Ethereal realms. My purpose is to be the voice and scribe of Divine Source as we are ONE and I am VERY close to feeling this and so I can energize it for you to be close again too.

It is your sense of separation which has made you feel hurts and pains. Your sense of separation from Divine Source is an illusion. A necessary illusion that you CHOSE as a soul when you put a cloak of forgetting over yourself in order to take on the form of Human with Gaia. The illusion of being separate from Divine Source makes you feel lonely, deep down in a core way, that NO relationships with other Humans can really help or cure. The ONLY cure is to connect with Divine Source again and to heal ALL of the blocks that divert the energies of Divine love waves that are CONSTANTLY coming at you.

If I look at most Humans' auric fields, there are waves and waves of love coming AT them. PURE love from the Divine, PURE love from Archangels, PURE love from Guides and Teachers in the etherics, PURE love from their Star BEing family and Galactic Selves. This PURE love is raining down, like a waterfall, on their fields. ALL Humans, by the way, not just a select few who are special or who are angel souls or who have decided to 'activate their upper chakras' or who have 'activated their hidden DNA' or who are 'enlightened' or 'awakened' or are 'gurus.' ALL souls receive this GIFT from the UNIVERSE of

PURE LOVE. Please do take this into your heart as it helps to heal the separation illusion.

As ALL Human forms (and animals) are fractals, children, from Divine Source, so ALL are worthy of receiving PURE love from It. This waterfall of Divine Love is splashing down on ALL, yet MOST Humans are blocking it. They have created layers and layers of protective blocks to experiencing this love again. These blocks are made of unhealed karma. These blocks are made of unshed tears from hurts and pains. These blocks are made of fear. These blocks are also sacred and necessary until the soul wakes up and decides that it is time to REMOVE them.

SOME souls, like Jelelle and her soul group expressions, are very focused on healing and removing these blocks in order to be a Human channel for this PURE love from Divine Source in whatever forms it wants and needs to come through for whichever soul is receiving it. There is no specialness in this, in one way, as ALL have the capacity to be this kind of channel. AND, Jelelle is special too (I'm feeling her struggling with typing and sharing that sentence but I want her to feel that it is true.) If you are reading these words RIGHT NOW, then I invite you to feel that you are a soul who is also dedicated to this purpose and that your Higher Self would like you to REMEMBER this.

It is an exciting phase as your Gaia Herself wants to ascend to higher vibrational frequencies. She has chosen this and you are Her guests, so you get to come along. If you are a version of you that blocks Divine Source love it will be harder for you to come along. You will experience being dragged or forced or you will just not be able to come and so leave the Human body you are in in some form or another. Gaia wants to experience frequencies of unity in her inhabitants. She has held beautiful space for the Human dualistic experiment because She too offers PURE love if you connect directly with Her energy. She has also had many personal pains and hurts done to Her from Humans and is now shifting to higher frequencies in order to end this cycle of suffering.

I will offer more to YOU directly if you'd like through Jelelle and her beloveds through the channel they call 'SoulFullHeart' and I would like to. I am also available to you RIGHT NOW....all you have to do is ask, open your heart, open your third eye, go within, clear the decks of your life of ALL that is false and not YOU, clear it of all that blocks PURE love from coming through. If you are ready and want it, you will experience me again as I am already there WITH YOU always and in ALL WAYS. It is NOW. And so it IS.

~

Light Wave Influxes Offer Support, Not Suffering: Message From Archangel Metatron

We do not want you to suffer. Many messages from teachers and light workers coming forward about how 'hard' and 'intense' it is right now as the influx of photonic light (PURE love) waves from the Universe come in, wash in, and rinse out and push up. Sometimes, unknowingly and innocently in a way, these teachers are supporting a suffering and self punishing response in the hearts and souls who take in their messages. Many heart cries go out in response to this interpretation of what is happening in the cosmos and then how it may impact you on an emotional, spiritual, and physical level.

These waves of PURE love are NOT meant to make things difficult for you but rather to offer a support, a boost, and a means for you to continue on in your remembering journey. These waves are meant to encourage you that life as you have known it on your Gaia is changing to the miraculous, the magical, the joyful. These waves of PURE love are to encourage you that it IS moving into frequencies of love, it IS moving into Sacred Humanity, and unknown expressions of divinity in higher frequency Human-from-Gaia form called Sacred Human or 5D human.

The PURE love available to you in ALL moments is only challenging if you make it challenging. It is only painful if you make it painful. It CAN push up oil to be felt, to be with, to make space for, and then move out. Yet, what if, it doesn't have to be painful and challenging? These waves of PURE love are not there to test you. They are not there to see if you can endure the intensity and all that is pushed up. They are a GIFT from Divine Source to offer you support to ascend with your mother home Gaia.

There can be parts of you that suffer over suffering, this is an easy loop to get into as it has been the default energy of 3D for thousands of years and is in the collective unconsciousness. Suffering over your suffering,…your soul, your Higher Self can feel when this is happening inside. Your soul can feel when 'holding space for your emotions and what is pushed up' has moved into the area of suffering over your suffering. Your Guides can feel this too if you ask for their help. And if you cannot access Guides then this, too, is suffering over suffering because we are a VERY available and accessible resource to ALL Humans right NOW.

We want to offer the END of suffering altogether and so the end of suffering over your suffering. We have had to give much invitation to FEEL though as so much has been suppressed in your emotional bodies as it was hard to feel it in the denser 3D reality space with any kind of separation. This invitation to FEEL is not an invitation to suffer over your suffering, but rather to make space, hold space, to ALLOW the feelings so that they may then move. And the invitation is that this space would be held by love for love and with love at a rate and pace that you can bear.

The consciousness that awakens in 4D is receiving infusions of Higher Self guidance, wisdoms, soul retrieved lessons and gifts, connection to the Metasoul source of your soul, Divine Source. With these infusions, more 'metaspace' is created inside in order to allow for the process of de-fusion, de-conditioning, de-attaching from the 3D persona, personality, and aspects of ego that are connected to development of the 'strategic self'.

Metaspace is heart space, soul space, objective space, Infinite Love space that 'holds the space' for relationship TO and WITH the feelings and reactions and woundings and pains and sufferings. This metaspace-infused self grows more and more as the inner world shifts, more soul embodiment comes in, and external choices are made in alignment with your soul.

We offer you this gift of light infusions that provide Metaspace if you let them into your 'higher heart', your Christ Heart, your Cosmic Heart. Connecting with your ascension chakras can help with this. Taking in the sun's rays can help hugely with this too. Connecting with Mother Gaia can help with this too as it roots you as you connect with your Cosmic Selves, creating a bridge or column of light that I call the 'Sacred Human or 5D blueprint'.

The Universe, Divine Source, does not want you to suffer or especially to suffer over your suffering. If you are experiencing very intense emotional and physical reactions in response to the light waves and activations, please feel if part of you is in resistance to feeling them as a loving invitation. Feel if part of you is in a suffering over suffering pattern. Feel if you need a space holder to help you navigate the difference, such as the beloved souls in SoulFullHeart. Feel what you need to support you to ride with these waves rather than get tumbled by them, or 'whooshed' as Jelelle calls it.

The Universe is MADE of LOVE as are YOU. These gifts given to you in these accelerated light codes are gifts….they ask for some adjusting but, again, all of the capacity you have to accept and thrive in response to them is inside of you as, also, they ARE you. I love YOU. I am here to HELP you remember the aspect of you that is me. And so in this remembrance, become One yet not the same….. again united and connected in love. And, so it is!

~

Keep Being The Light: Message With Metatron

Touching message from Metatron this morning during my meditation, we feel it is for ALL of us called to serve love in any of the forms and ways that we do and ARE….

Keep being the light. Keep offering the light and your light will shine the way for others.

Keep being in your heart. Keep offering your heart and others will respond with theirs. Your Cosmic Heart, higher dimensional heart, will beacon to others and light up theirs and you will be lit up by theirs in return…spilling over into love and more love.

Keep being in your soul. Keep coming from your soul and your soul will call to others. Your soul will call to your soul family to rejoin, it will call to your soul mate, your Counterpart and Complement Soul, to rejoin. It will call to your Soul Guides to rejoin with you.

Keep seeing the light. Keep feeling the light even in the death and rebirth, the darkness that comes, the difficulties and pains that many will feel. Your light will serve their way out of the shadows and for them to find their own again.

Keep becoming your Star Self. Keep merging with your Star BEing selves and their consciousness can come through to others too, inviting them into this experience too of reunion with their star roots and galactic consciousness.

Keep fulfilling your purpose. Keep feeling your SOUL reason for being here with Gaia at this time of great transition and change, of great awakening and rebirth. Stay connected to this reason and it will infuse all that you do and be and are with great meaning.

Keep making changes. Keep feeling the changes that you need to make, are now ready to make, in your life and feeling the letting go process of ALL that does not serve your Higher Self, higher purpose, ALL that does not serve love in your life.

Relationships, careers, geographies......feel what serves love and what does NOT and let go of what does NOT.

Keep letting me into your heart, into your soul, into your inner spaces as an Angelic Guide and to BECOME as well. Keep inviting Angels into your heart and so they will come, the ones for which you resonate and match, the ones for which you are part of and ARE.

Keep being PURE love in your Human form, still growing, always learning, perfect as you are RIGHT NOW too. Keep offering this PURE love to others and they will receive and pass it on. And so it IS!

~

Teachings and Conversations While Connecting With Christ Consciousness

The following are teachings and wisdoms that I've received while connecting with Christ Consciousness, which I have experienced as a fifth dimensional energy and higher that is available to ALL. This energy transcends religions, belief systems, and even shadow projections onto Jesus Christ. This energy is the energy of New Earth, and what we are moving collectively into as we ascend into higher dimensions of consciousness where we experience more sense of Oneness, peace, self love, and reverence for all life. This is the energy that I feel alive in the most nourishing aspects of Christ-mas celebrations, inviting us beyond material gift giving and into the frequencies giving and receiving love with ourselves and others. This is the energy that we are birthing into BE-ing as we embrace our Sacred Humanity and both the best of what makes us Human AND what makes us transcendent, multi-dimensional souls.

*

An empty vessel cannot give love. Heal your heart and its pain by feeling them. Heal your soul and its painful legacy by feeling them. Purify through your tears and your openness to feel it ALL. Then, as you are this, will you be able to transact real love, Human frequencies with others who are in the same process….you will be able to let in Universal Love frequencies that light up your Infinite Love essence…and you will be able to give with a healthy heart and soul.

*

Be in the world, not of the world…..yet care for the world.

You are in the world, bring your heart with you, feel your surroundings and those who call you into connection. You are in a Human body, bring your health to it, feel your embodiment as sacred and the desires that flow from it. You are in a culture, bring your celebration of it, feel how it impacts you and forms you.

You are not of the world, it is not a reflection of that which you are really made and ARE. Participate in the world even while remembering that you are not it…not your name, your occupation, your body, your income, your home, your history, your culture. Remain with some separation from it so that you can retain the essence of what you ARE as Infinite Love.

You are care for the world, bring your compassion with you, feel the tears of the world and those cries that call you to respond. Serve love as the greatest gift for yourself, others, and with the Divine God in all Its glorious forms, including YOU. Remember to respond to fear with love, not more fear, and you offer a new possibility to each moment.

*

I am still digesting my connection time with Yeshua this morning during meditation. I experience him as an Ascended Teacher energy, a loving and provocative presence available to anyone. For me, connection with him transcends religions and belief systems into a space where just love matters.

We were floating on a golden white fluffy cloud together, sitting Indian style. It felt like we were in a higher vibration frequency, a higher dimension. I was taking in his energy, feeling the warmth and love of it moving up and down my chakras like a cascading flow.

We sat in silence for a bit and then he asked me, "What do you see?"

I looked around and the first answer that came to me was, "Nothing." This felt strange to me because, after all, I was surrounded by beautiful clouds and sitting next to HIM.

He seemed to take that answer inside of his heart though and then asked me, "What do you feel?"

"Everything," was my first response.

Again he seemed to take this answer in deeply.

"How can that be though?" I asked him, confused. "How can I see nothing and feel everything?"

He smiled at me in the way that sends golden waves of love straight into my heart and replied, "That's actually the purest way for which to feel."

As I sit here now, digesting this message, I feel that what He is offering is that we can 'see' so much with our minds, filtering everything, 'busy mind' in addition to so many people with 'busy life'. In this state, it is so difficult to really feel anything, we are numb from over stimulus.

When we open up ourselves to seeing 'nothing', to just being, then we can start to feel everything in a more pure way. Our hearts can open up and feel the All That Is for which we are made. And tastes of Infinite Love too.

This is my explanation anyway....Yeshua would probably just smile and offer for me not to think about it so much, just feel it.

*

Embrace that which you are in this moment.
Feel that which you desire to be.
Understand that the gap between these two is an invitation.

An invitation from the Divine God, from the Divine Mother Aspect, from the Universe…..to experience your essence as Infinite Love through the form of your Sacred Humanity.

This invitation is open, it waits, it doesn't push, but it does call…and it is always your sovereign choice if you will answer and how you will answer.

And if you choose not to respond to this invitation, Divine Source will go on loving you just the same and just as much.

*

To look in the mirror, to really look, is to be open to seeing that which is hard to accept, difficult to love, and most in need of attention. That which lurks in the shadows of your soul, the tight corners of your heart, and the darkest regions of your mind.

Going into this darkness with full consciousness is what illuminates the soul spark that you are and reveals the Infinite Love that you are. Going into this darkness with willingness to feel it ALL reveals the Divine light that you are.

Sometimes life will bring you to this darkness and sometimes you will choose it…..whatever way you find yourself there, feel how it is the beginning of the true lifting of the veil that falseness has placed over you.

If you have not had this experience of the crucible of darkness, seek that which will guide you in it and through it rather than letting your false self cling to a light that is but an echo of the real thing. When what is false has been repeatedly burned away in a conscious process which includes the dark, you can trust the light that emerges from it as being real and a reflection of the Divine spark that you ARE.

*

Everything is made of love energy. Everything. Yet, also, there is the fear of love that can have equal or greater power at times when it becomes more real than love. This fear of love manifests in many ways and expressions.

The only way that fear of love heals is with more love. It cannot be ignored, suppressed, or made to 'go away' because you do not want to look at it. Fear grows if it is related to with more fear. Only love has the bravery to look at the dark, to feel the fear, to be with what is real about it.

Calling it 'love' and not acknowledging the existence of the fear of love that is often underneath it is NOT real love.

~

Worlds Within Worlds Are Within You To Discover

All is magic arising in every moment to be seen, felt, and let in. Worlds within worlds inside of you to explore, to discover, to uncover. Let in the magic that you ARE and SEE it all around you as your filter changes. How you see the world is how you see yourself. How you feel about the world is how you feel about yourself. How you experience the world is how you experience yourself.

In a place of self loving discovery, you are curious about all the dimensions and expressions of yourself. You are collecting and investigating your soul aspects, the fractals that come from the same source, the versions of you in so many different forms and expressions.

As you are curious about the Star BEing YOU, the Galactic you, the version you have been much more than you have been Human and for so very much longer…..this aspect of you can begin to give you messages and show you signs of your galactic nature. You may hear and experience and feel this as 'outside' of you and you may become a channel for this energy and the messenger of the stars. Yet then when you embrace these Star BEings as versions of you does the intimacy go so much deeper. They can take you on a journey of remembrance and embodiment, they can bring you UP into higher frequencies. You become them more and more and their frequencies integrate into you, become you, and you are that much more galactic because of it.

As you are curious about other lifetimes in other 'periods of time', versions of you living different experiences in different settings connect with you. Stepping through the portal that opens with your heart eagerness and your soul's desire, you are transported to the scenes that these Parallel Selves live in: the courtyards, the stables, the castles, the fields, the spaceships of light, the mountains, the churches. Backdrops that hold the setting for these scenes of soul expression. You can dial in a year: 1930, 1100, 1880 and then see what you can see. You can go there to these places and be with and feel the aspects of your soul in these settings and what they are experiencing. You can help them heal and move on. And you too can become them eventually as they integrate into you and the energy of their existence is released and ascended.

Worlds within worlds are inside of you to discover. Sign up for the trip, earn the trip by your self love and willingness to go within and with your willingness to feel. Follow the guideposts to the next place and the next.

Life IS magical and so are you. Believe it, feel it, live it, experience it. And so it IS.

~

Portals Opening In Your Living Room

Multidimensional realities are opening up in more and more 'merged' moments where you may not be sure where you are but not all HERE and not all THERE. Not inside and not outside. Outside is becoming inside. Inside is projecting outward. Life seems sometimes like you are watching a TV screen or a computer screen. Watching and yet ARE it too. ALL of it somehow.

Words are forgotten in mid-sentence and names slip too. Naming things is a strange 3D practice anyway when really every THING is a WOW thing arising in the moment. Once it is a 'spoon' or a 'clock' or a 'sunset' or a 'person' then the wowness of the magical nature gets put in a box, tagged somehow, limited somehow. Losing names allows wonder to arise.

Time goes from segments, one tick at a time, seconds counting down into minutes....to more fluid sweeps of experience that are sped up and then slowed down. Condensed tighter and then spread out like a deck of cards, seeming to last forever. The past is fuzzy, more blurry, like it happened to someone else and yet is STILL happening. The future is unknown and yet already happened and happening NOW.

The light waves coming in, washing in, rinsing and ringing you out are inviting you UP to slurs and blurs of time and realities. Inviting you to allow more merging of Multidimensional Selves. To see the spaceship interior where your Star BEing self walks around as clearly as you see your living room. What is imagined and what is real? This question will become more and more difficult to answer even as you care less and less to define what you are experiencing in these terms at all.

Surrendering to these shifts, discovering your role in it all, riding the waves, checking in and tuning in become the priorities.

Surrendering to these shifts looks like a trust in where it is all headed in goodness and that it is being held with love.

Discovering your role in it all looks like claiming your soul gifts and serving love, serving the movements in whatever ways you feel called to do so, ways that your heart sings to you and life draws the means and hows.

Riding the waves looks like being open to being in the unknown pretty much ALL of the time and in every moment as life is 'usual' and yet it is very much not.

Checking in and tuning in looks like holding the space for the inner journeys that bring guidance, awakening, inner support, Ethereal help, visions, and clarities.

The portals want to open up in your living room. Invite them in by blurring your inner multidimensional experiences with your lived in reality. And when they open in whatever forms they do, dive in and trust it will be held with love!

~

Teleporting To The Place Of Infinite Possibilities

Where do you want to go? Your consciousness can take you there, wherever, whenever…this is teleportation. Teleporting to other dimensions, other galaxies, other realities begins in the super conscious mind, in the 'imagination'. Someday we will take our bodies too. It helps to be in the Now moment, close your eyes, use Solfeggios or other music, dedicate the time without outside distractions…..go within.

For me, today, during what I call 'meditation', I was teleported to a room made of stars…not really a room as there were no walls. A place made of stars where Higher Selves were hanging out. I had conversations with some of them, people that I needed to connect with and understand where they were coming from beyond what their conscious personality would tell me. I have been doing this since I was a very small child and then called it 'make believe'. My 'make believe' world has always been very rich….it continued into my adulthood and only stopped when it transferred from 'fantasy' to multidimensional travel. Some people would say (those fused to 3D reality) that I still make it all up or it is all fantasy. I am ok with feeling that I 'make it all up' as what a wonderful thing THAT IS! I certainly hope that we all make up our reality as that is where our POWER Is.

In the star room (and other super conscious landscapes) I feel like I can breathe. This is my home frequency. The rest of the time I am bridging 3D with this more natural reality. I've been having womb memories lately as the rest of the 'past' releases away. In the womb, I was unwanted and feared. Maybe that's why I left the womb six weeks earlier than expected, to escape this energy. Womb processing is really the end of the road it feels like for the 3D pain body and I am certainly ready after a decade of feeling and healing it. So, I was also teleported back to the womb today and it was helpful because the letting go process of my 'this lifetime' past continues to move.

Where do you want to go? Back to the womb? To other lifetimes? To the akasic records? To what we call 'Golden Earth'? It is a relief from 3D reality, the density, the earthboundness, the five senses, to go away on adventures in the etherics, to have conversations beyond what the conscious personality or 3D Self can track and understand. You can remain grounded to the Earth and go on these adventures. Gaia likes to hold space for them it seems.

Dare to be deluded. Dare to make it all up. Dare to be in fantasy for awhile. The rewards are a return to the frequency where you feel like home, where you feel love, where you feel Infinite Possibilities.

~

Meditation As An Inner Journey Of Remembering

For many years, I did not know that I was actually meditating. I thought, or my 3D Self, thought that meditation had to follow a specific path and process, a mantra needed to be repeated, or to track the space in between breaths. When I tried to meditate in this way, I was not able to focus or concentrate much at all and my creative mind was restless. I eventually came to understand that my whole life had moments where I was experiencing BEing in living meditation. Whenever I would have conversations with people who were not there or place myself in scenarios of being a movie star or musician or create entire scenes to play out and then did play them out, I was in a meditative space beyond the physical. I was accessing the deepest recesses of my imaginative mind, activating my pineal gland, opening my third eye, using creative visualization to experience (to really FEEL) worlds beyond the physical.

I also experienced that in nature, during a hike or walk, I would slip into a space beyond thoughts, a higher consciousness reality. Nature would release me from the past or future and move me into the moment by setting a template for BEingness. When I was in a deep emotional process with an aspect of myself, I would often go to nature to hold the process with me and give me energy to transmute what was going on. When I would connect with parts of myself through 'dropping in' to the energy of the voice and tones of the aspect, it was a form of meditation or trance or self hypnosis state that held the space for this exploration.

Eventually, I discovered shamanic journeying, creative visualization, or what was called "Immramma" by the Celts (for which I have a deep Metasoul legacy.) I drew the teachings that I needed so I could see that what I had been doing with my 'make believe' scenarios and in nature was actually a form of meditation and deeply going within. I could walk around, conscious, and access this state. Then, I began devoting energy, space and time to closing my eyes, being in a contained space, lighting incense, holding whatever crystal and rock friends were helping me in the moment. I write about the Immramma journeys that I went on during an intense phase of Higher Self awakening in my book, *Keep Waking Up! Awakening Journeys To Avalon And Beyond.* I leaned into the wonderful imagery, self permission, and perspective shared by Jhenah Telyndru in her book, *Avalon Within*.

During this awakening phase, I went on the journeys into Avalon over and over, discovering this wonder world of imagery, felt senses, and spiritual awakenings. Avalon really was within me and I could 'go there' whenever I wanted to and it felt like a fourth dimensional place as well. I was living on our remote ranch in Mexico at the time with no internet, no electricity (off grid, with a solar panel), very few people, no industrial noise and few cars. This natural and beautiful setting held the space for this inner exploration combined with the deep grounding offered by spending most of my day in our organic gardens. I was in a phase of letting go of serving others through our offering of SoulFullHeart, even as I deeply wanted more people to join our community.

In discovering meditation in this way, I discovered a bridge to the rich imaginative world that I had always experienced as a projection outside of myself. In holding space for others over the years, I had created this bubble of safety with them to go into other lifetimes, emotional terrains, bring up often very intense energies, access Ethereal BEing and Divine source energies. I could create this bubble because I had created it for myself over and over again as a comfort and process ground. I believe that my Higher Self created this cocoon space for me, outside of me, as I needed it and then, I was able to claim it inside as well.

Creating a cocoon space within during meditation every day brings in a rush of self love and self awareness. The setting of Avalon or the woods or Golden Earth or the beach, or whatever setting most resonates with you, allows for the emotional body and the soul to release woundings and densities. This space is created by the sixth chakra or third eye with help from the pineal gland, both of which can be covered over and blocked by soul woundings and karmic congestions.

The 3D Self does not 'take the time' for self exploration in this way of inner reflection and journeying. The 3D Self is so focused outside of self, on others, on material things, alternating between fixation on the past or feeling lack about the present or worrying about the future. It does not 'take the time' or 'make the time' because it has not been conditioned to do this and core unworthiness messages that it is not worth the 'time'. Everything else and everyone else is worth 'time' but not inner exploration and container space to get to know and remember self.

The Higher Self understands that only through inner exploration will anything change in the outer experience of life. As everything originates from within, the journey within to explore, to connect, to be, to cry, to chant, to whatever arises in the moment, is what activates the alchemy and draw to experience something new in the outer experience. The Higher Self and soul understands that there isn't really an 'out there' anyway; that all things and people and experiences originate from an inner projection and nothing is actually separate from us.

I am not big on structured meditation, I feel that it just doesn't offer enough freedom to explore and be creative for the way that my soul most resonates with. I can follow an outlined journey (such as is offered in *Avalon Within* and also beautifully in *The World Of Archangels* by Sufian Chaudry and also in books by Diana Cooper.) These outlined journeys provide a template and guide, a way and means to go that have worked for the authors and are often downloaded from higher dimensions by Ethereal BEings. Exploration of these and also the ones available on you tube (including ones that I offer on our SoulFullHeart Experience YouTube Channel) allows you to find what resonates with you during the phases that you need it. The guided meditations offered in this book provide that as well.

The repeated mantras or the meditations based on religious doctrine or practice feel too confining for me. Maybe they will work for you, yet, I encourage you to open up your creative imagination and the places where your inner muse and Divine inspiration ('awen') can take you away. All of us can picture a place in our minds and follow along with a story with our third eye, this is what we are doing especially when we read fiction books or listen to someone tell us a story. It is this capacity to visualize and picture that allows for the openings into soul frequencies that can be remembered. It is this capacity that gives us access to the Akashic Library and our files and portals we can go through to visit other lifetimes that are not past at all (since linear time is not real in 5D) but are still happening in the Now moment.

This access to the metaphysical, beyond 3D reality ground, beyond what we experience with our five senses opens out more and more as we go within during meditative space. Negotiation with aspects of ourselves that resist taking the time for meditation may be necessary to allow for it to happen in your life. Part of you may relate to it as a 'should' and that's ok for a phase because eventually it will become a necessity for you to navigate your life from the grounding of this inner space that has opened out.

~

White Staircase Meditation And Connection With Archangel Metatron

I am walking up the stairs, visualizing pure, white light all around me. I feel a lightening up in my body as I ascend up the stairs with every inhale and rest on the exhale. I count out each step as a means to keep my mind active while I start to feel a sense of pulling from my crown or seventh chakra. I climb as high as my body will go until I feel resistance. I see a door to my right and I walk through it to enter a large, open space with an extended platform.

In my physical body, I feel as if my torso is elongated and stretching out with my two hands (which are resting on my crossed legs) seeming to be quite far away from my head. It is a unique feeling and I am enjoying it, already feeling how it could be a simple thing to travel out of my body following this method.

I begin to feel love and desire flood through me as I repeat over and over a call for Kuan Yin to come be with me if it is the will of the Divine. I exclaim, "I AM God," feeling a shiver of recognition move through my body of my expression as a fragment of the Divine source. I see the outline of Kuan Yin start to appear before me, framed in a brilliant white light. She is so radiant that I squint my eyes, even though my 'physical eyes' are closed.

We don't exchange words at first, but just bask in our communion with each other. I am in awe, I am in love, I am grateful just to be near Her. I feel all this in Her presence as I have felt since first connecting with Her many years ago.

The only thing She says to me is what She has offered me in a previous meditations, "I am you and you are me." I take this in as the love, gratitude and awe that I am projecting onto Her also lives inside of me.

This simple meditation in which you climb a staircase to access higher dimensional realities while asking for connection with ethereal BEings is offered in a very expansive and transformational book called *World Of Archangels* by Sufian Chaudhary.

Explains Sufian in his book, "The Human body has a very low vibration in order to maintain its physicality. The higher in vibration you manage to achieve, the more you will perceive yourself as a powerful energetic source rather than something limited to the physical world….the most effective communication with ethereal BEings takes place when both parties alter their vibratory level in order to meet each other on middle ground."

I have been connecting with ethereal BEings such as Spirit Guides, Angels, and Ascended Masters for several years, yet I can feel a difference now in the purity and intensity of the connection that can be experienced after engaging in the staircase meditation and 'meeting' these BEings in a middle point. Such a simple meditation and, yet, one offering seemingly limitless possibilities of experience!

~

Go Within And Remember The Love That You ARE

Everything impacts your vibrational frequency; sounds, smells, foods, and especially the energy of others. Your 3D Self (unaware ego/mind fusion) has layered you over with densities, literal protection shields, so that you cannot feel how impacted you are by all these things. In this layered over place, you cannot feel how your vibrational frequency is going down. Or if it is going up.

The only way to feel this is to go within, to reconnect to your inner energy system, to your emotional body, to your 3D Self (and other aspects). The 'you' that goes within is the version that is splitting off, differentiating from the 3D Self and being infused with energies from your Higher 5D self or Divine Self. Your Higher Self is always with you, waiting to arise, like a seed in your consciousness that is waiting for the water of good energy and good love to bloom.

Your Higher Self may be mostly outside of you. It may feel like when you connect with it as if you are reaching for something outside of you, similar to how it can feel to connect with Guides, Ascended Teachers, and the Divine. And, that's OK because the important piece is that these energies, while feeling outside of you, can still infuse you with frequencies that you need to raise your base tone. They offer you light codes to activate your light body to arise and start glowing, to begin the transition from carbon-based body to crystalline-Christ Consciousness body.

Eventually, then, you realize that your Higher Self is within you and IS you more and more. As are the Guides that you have 'channeled' or looked to others to provide the messages of their channeled Guides. Validation from outside of us, people who are embracing their higher self wisdoms and personal experiences, can be very helpful. It can light up things that need to be lit up. Support from others who have journeyed in places we want to go deeper can be very helpful too, along with a community to resonate with.

And, then, you return to you, back inside where the power is, where the Universe is, and where the only source of Love that you can ALWAYS count on is. Going within, exploring within, learning about what is within…..the message is the same in so many different forms and yet, when you are too much your 3D Self, you may find many ways to not do this and not to begin this.

Looking outward may be easier for your 3D Self than looking within.

Try this, right now. Pause from reading for a moment. Close your eyes. Become present to the moment. Become present to yourself. Feel what you are feeling. Check in. Feel where your energy is at. Feel any other people that have entered your 'field' while you have been online, as it is a virtual 'room' containing many energies that you absorb like a sponge.

Feel your heart, is it open or more closed? Why?

Breathe in, Breathe out. Feel the world that is YOU that is waiting for your exploration of it. Stay in this inner focused space for as long as you need to and as long as you like.

~

Energy Healing As A Key Aspect Of The Ascension Process

We are energy…..everything is energy. What we are experiencing of experience is energetic. Energy moves, transforms….vibrates from lower density to higher density. Vibrates faster or slower. Vibrates at a denser frequency or a more porous, higher one.

3D conditioning doesn't allow for energy. It doesn't make space for it, teach it, or see it as 'real'. This limiting perception is like a box over your capacity to experience yourself AS energy and everything you experience AS energy. This limiting idea that energy is not real because it cannot be seen, is one of ways that the veil has remained over our remembrance of our soul essence, our soul gifts expressing, our soul self being inhabited and embodied.

What you suffer from related to physical, emotional, and mental distress is sourced in energy. Emotional wounds are energy and made up of energy. Karmic wounds are energy and made up of energy. Suffering is energy and made up of energy. Mental 'illness' (which is not how I would label it or feel it) is made up of energy. Relationship discords are energy and made up of energy.

As you move into 4D reality, as you awaken…..a major aspect that awakens is your tracking of energy and how your own personal energy is impacted by others, by environments, by geographies…by both inner and outer experiences. You may seek out Energy Healers to remind you of your own energy healing capacities, both towards self and others. EVERYONE has the capacities to heal with energy since everyone IS energy. Even if someone is not conscious of being an 'Energy Healer' they are one every time they transact love with themselves or with others.

The highest vibrational frequency of ALL is PURE love. PURE love is the frequency which can move and heal the emotional stuck energy, the karmic stuck energy, the mental stuck energy, the physical stuck energy, the relationship stuck energy. PURE love is a wave of VERY high frequency energy that we let into our BEing more and more, as it arises inside of us as we heal, as it arises inside as we integrate Soul/Star/Angelic aspects, as we draw others in relationships based more and more in PURE love frequencies.

PURE love energy = PURE love experience = end of suffering over suffering…….this is a simple thing to understand yet harder to embody because the stuck energy can be SO thick and congested, like concrete in some people. The stuck energy takes the form of protective aspects, fearful aspects that use your energy to form barriers and guards and shields and weapons. This stuck energy needs to be negotiated with in order to let in the PURE love experience.

In our SoulFullHeart process, we do this very consciously with these aspects…we connect energetically with the energy of the protection and guide you to lead this exploration. As these energies are felt with PURE love, they begin to shift into higher vibration, they become unstuck, they move into Higher Self expression. Protective energy becomes healthy self protection and eventually integrates into the 5D Self as it isn't needed in the same ways.

BEING with energy at this level of differentiation can open up major, major soul awakenings and emotional pain body healing too. I always come back to offering SoulFullHeart because it provides a bridge from awareness to transformation, from knowing to living, from being inspired to being transformed. I come back to it because I feel it offers a PURE love source (coming through still Human, growing and learning hearts and souls).

You ARE energy and that energy can be a beautiful flow of swirls and vortexes. A beautiful flow of LOVE as you recognize it as such, as you let it in as such, and as you experience YOURSELF as a loving energy more and more....

~

Cleaning, Activating, And Protecting Your Seven Main Chakras

Chakras are energy centers, points of flow, in our etheric bodies. They are alive, have a consciousness, and can even be dialogued with. I have most extensively worked with seven chakra centers in my energy healing work with myself and serving others over the years. There is a lot of information available online about chakras, what they represent, and where they are located, so I will focus on sharing the daily meditation that I engage with to activate, clean, and protect them.

As with all meditation, find a comfortable place to sit and practice deep breathing for as long as it takes for you to feel centered with your mind (somewhat) quiet (usually 5 to 10 minutes).

Ask for the help of whatever Ethereal BEing you are connecting with in the moment or would like to connect with. Right now, I am working primarily with my 'healing angel' named Coral. A healing angel provides healing frequencies for both self healing and in serving others. They are at a slightly lower frequency and dimension than our guardian angels and, therefore, easier to access and connect with. According to Coral, every one of us has a healing angel and we subconsciously connect with them during moments of injury or in serving others. Our connection with them only becomes conscious if we ask for it to be so.

Calling on Ethereal BEings is as simple as feeling your desire for it and then asking to connect with them. Meeting them halfway by raising your body vibrational frequency (through meditations such as the white staircase mentioned below) increases the degree that you will experience them. You can feel in your heart's response if the Ethereal BEing you are speaking with is connected to the light and has a love-based connection to offer to you.

Engage with the white energy staircase meditation to raise your body's vibrational frequency before engaging with your chakras. It seems to help with the process of visualization and with energy flow. As you connect with the Ethereal BEing that is going to help you, climb the stairs slowly on the inhale and rest on the exhale. The usual place that I get off is the platform at stair 111, as it holds a strong vibrational energy. Visualize white energy around you as you sit down and begin to imagine your chakras. I have been offered by Kuan Yin to visualize each chakra as a lotus flower, imagining when I first see them that they are closed up and then I see each petal opening and unfolding wide.

You can imagine any kind of flower that you resonate with or just a whirling circle of energy. This activates the chakras and if you haven't done chakra work before, you may feel a sudden surge of energy in your body as the flower/chakra opens up more. Move up your body starting with the first or root chakra, imagining the color that they are (as represented in the above picture), and then through to your seventh or crown chakra visualizing all of the flowers opening up.

Then, visualize a flow of white energy entering the top of your head and moving down your spine, showering each of your chakra lotus flowers with white light. Chakras can have many layers of congestion over them and you may need to focus just on this meditation for a while to get them open and clean with good energy flowing through them. The congestion will look gray or even black with sometimes pockets or balloons of this dark energy surrounding the chakra or trailing off of it. Allow the white energy to sweep up and cleanse the dark energy in a swirl. Then move it out of your root chakra or visualize a grounding cord connected to the Earth for which the energy is swept out of. You want to make sure to move the congested energy that has been loosened out of your etheric body, either into the ground or up into space.

You may also encounter objects in your etheric body or surrounding your chakras. I have seen and felt many objects in myself and others, such as corsets, suits of armor, arrows, Christian crosses, crowns of thorns, etc. These objects take on a symbolic form for us to interpret and feel and are often related to other life traumas that our soul is holding on to. If you find an object, see if you can get a sense about why it is there and what it represents. You can then negotiate with your Healing Angel around if and when you should remove it using more white energy and for guidance around why it is there. Holding a quartz crystal in your hand while meditating can help with this process.

After devoting your meditation to activating and cleaning your chakras, you can then create a protection around them to help prevent negative energies from coming in. This is especially important during the first weeks of your dedicated practice when you are 'opening up' to new vibrational frequencies and will become much more energetically sensitive. To protect your etheric body, visualize a wrapping made of white energy forming to fit your entire body. You can picture a suit of armor or any other kind of 'outfit' that works for you. Bring in strong white energy through your crown chakra (or top of your head) and infuse the outfit with it. Ask your healing angel to help make it 'the strongest material in the Universe.'

Regular chakra activation, cleaning, and protection is very important to physical, emotional, and spiritual health. Engaging in a daily meditation to undergo this process will raise your frequency to a higher, more love-based one and clear out dark energies that will eventually led to physical illness and emotional suffering patterns. This kind of regular chakra love along with a heart work healing process brings vitality and health to all areas of our lives.

~

Why It Is Important To Energetically Clean A Home, Website, and Any Space

Do you notice how you are drawn to certain spaces and repelled by others? They could be nearly identical in décor and location, but the energy within them either repeals you or draws you in.

Why are some restaurants full of people and another one with equal quality of food and location sits empty? The energy inside the restaurant that is projected by the people who work there and the customers either draws people in or it pushes them away. Why do some places just give off 'bad' energy and others seem like a beacon of good energy?

We are all sensitive to energy, whether we are conscious of it or not, because we are all made up of energy and are not actual solid matter even though our very narrow visible light spectrum reflects us as being solid. If we could widen our spectrum of visible light, we would see that we are made up of tendrils or tentacles of mostly white energy that look similar to fiber optic cables.

Since we are made up of energy this means that the energy contained in spaces, and that includes virtual places such as websites, deeply impacts us. Usually this is an unconscious or subconscious reaction, although for those of us who have 'woken up' to our energy sensitivity, we are very aware of this and track it carefully. We avoid places that don't feel energetically good to us and move toward those that do. We also transform spaces by clearing and cleaning out old energy and keep them cleaned out on a regular basis.

I became aware of my energetic sensitivity to spaces many years ago and since then, I have consciously interacted with the spaces that I live in and visit on an energetic level. We recently moved into a new apartment and the previous tenant was someone who seemed desperate for money and would lie and manipulate to get what he wanted. When we went to 'see' the apartment, it was difficult to feel that it was desirable even though it had features that we wanted, because this person's energy filled the whole space. Most people would have walked away from it because of the energy that occupied it. I could feel that it was going to require a few days of concentrated effort to clear the space but that the 'bones' of it were exactly what we wanted. Beyond the decorative changes that we plan to make (new paint, beautiful things on the wall, plants), I knew that it was the energetic cleaning of the space that would make the most difference in its livability and desirability.

Energetically cleaning your house, space you are visiting, or even websites that you visit or manage is not difficult at all. The first step is becoming conscious of how energy affects you in these spaces. What does 'good energy' feel like to you and what places represent that? What does 'negative energy' feel like to you and what places represent that? Certainly if you are a non-violent vegan then visiting a butcher's shop or a website about meat would not hold good energy for you. You would probably consciously avoid things like this but, sometimes, we are subconsciously being drawn or repelled by energy and aren't aware of it. Bringing it into our awareness is the first step.

Then, engaging in a simple visualization during meditation can move the negative energy out and clear the space. If it is your home, visualize a white glowing orb of energy in each corner of your house. Activate the orb with energy that you pull from the white energy that is all around you at all times. Move it through your seventh or crown chakra and pulse it into the orbs. Visualize the orbs collecting all the gray or black energy in the space and then shooting it up and out into outer space. Or you can imagine the orbs with grounding cords connecting to the core of the Earth and the negative energy is moving out of them.

Engage in this visualization process every morning for the space that you live in and especially in the space that you work in every day. A big aspect of the antsy feeling that we get at the end of a work week (especially if we work in a building with florescent lighting in cubicles) is because of the accumulated energy that has built up and is being off-gassed by people all the time. Most people are completely unaware of the energy that they give off in person and especially through email, Facebook, or other virtual communication. People who are conscious of their energy then 'take care' of their energy every day through cleansing it in their chakras.

Using sage or other cleansing herb can be very helpful in moving energy out of a space. Here in Mexico, there is a wonderful product called Copal, that is resin from a tree, and burning it or sage regularly can make a big difference. You can take the stick of incense or sage stick and wave it around the room, visualizing as you do the smoke moving the energy out of the room with it. You can combine the white orb visualization and the cleansing smoke one if you want.

When you go into a public place or visit someone's house and you want to clean the energy, just visualize (even with your eyes open) a white tornado swirling around the room, swooping up all the dark energies, and then moving away with them. You can do this in seconds without anyone even noticing and it can make a big difference to how much you enjoy yourself. I especially do this if I am entering a busy public store (such as a grocery store), public transportation, or a restaurant and especially if I can feel that the space has never been energetically cleaned by anyone (which most have not).

The same approach applies with any website or Facebook page that you are visiting online. Most pages have never been energetically cleaned because most people don't think of them as places even though they are as real as physical places. I think of websites and Facebook timelines as being the same as visiting the room of someone's house. I am very particular about which website pages I visit for this reason as the energy can linger for awhile even if I clean it first. To clean a website, visualize a white energy swirl moving through every page of the website and every post on the Facebook page. This can be a fast and efficient swirl that collects the accumulated energy and deposits it away.

I clean my Facebook page and the SoulFullHeart website and blog nearly every day. We get positive comments from people about the good energy of our websites and Facebook pages and I think this is one of the reasons why. Remember that every person who has taken in your posts or websites has had an emotional reaction (usually subconscious) of some kind to them which off-gases as an energetic response. Even if they are mostly positive, this still builds up over time and can make it 'very crowded' in a virtual space. The worst feeling websites to me are those that draw a lot of comments from the general public about topics that are highly charged such as politics, religion, etc. Parts of people can be cruel, aggressive, and very 'kicking' in these forums and usually no one has cleaned out this energy and so it draws more of the same.

I want to finish this with some signs for you to start tracking in yourself so that you can become more conscious of how energy in spaces is impacting you. We often manifest energetic reactions in our physical bodies since it is our etheric or subtle body (including our chakras) which is actually most interfacing with our external environment. Body reactions such as headaches, light headedness, allergies, cold or flu symptoms, and nausea can indicate that we have been impacted by negative energies. Headaches in particular can mean this as it is the third eye or sixth chakra and the pineal gland that is so sensitive to energies.

Tracking our reactions to energies and being conscious about cleaning the energy of spaces that you live and visit allows us to be much more consciously discerning about the energies that we want to be around, because we don't want to have to do a bunch of clearing! Doing this regularly can clear up our capacity to let in the joy, goodness, and love all around us.

~

Connecting To The Consciousness Of Your Chakras And What They Are Trying To Tell You

Chakras are full of information, data, and clues that your soul is offering (as is EVERYTHING). A phase of the awakening experience seems to be the growing awareness of chakras with the learning about them and where they are, what color they are, which glands and organs they connect to and meridians in the body, hand positions (such as the ones used in Reiki) and the 'cleaning' of them. Being able to 'see' and visualize them with more clear clairvoyance. The mind opens up to the idea of them and their metaphysical existence.

You may be quite experienced in working with your chakras and even offering energy healing to others as well. The invitation is to deepen this connection to a place beyond the known and into the realm of bridging with your emotional body. The question is….how connected are you to what your chakras are wanting to tell you about YOU and your emotional body?

Try to connect to the CONSCIOUSNESS of your chakras….to really FEEL and BE with them and to HEAR them too. To tune into what they are trying to TELL you and share with you about your heart, about your soul, about other lifetimes and the pain that still is energizing there, about your physical body and the stuck places of potential and perhaps manifesting disease and illness, about your social body and where it is receiving nourishment in your relationships and where it is not.

The emotional body is deeply connected with the chakral body, as both are 'beyond the mind' and into the terrain of visceral experience, unfiltered experience, beyond what the 3D Self can control and manage or even 'get to' or access most of the time. Parts of us also connect to, attach to, and associate with our chakras as well. Sometimes parts of us 'live in the world' of our chakras. They also 'live' or energize in parts of our body as well. It is ALL connected ultimately and going upstream to the root cause of the wounding in the emotional and chakral bodies that is then manifesting downstream in our lives can bring A LOT of healing.

Each chakra is ALIVE, has a consciousness, and can TELL you things that are useful. The seven main chakras offer a good foundation and also there are the 'ascension chakras', which I resonate with the ones based on a model offered by Spiritual Teacher and author Diana Cooper (although there are others too.) The stellar gateway, soul chakra, causal chakra, and earth chakra offer multidimensional access, galactic and cosmic connection, more lifting of the veil around our soul experiences in other lifetimes, rooting and grounding with Mother Gaia and more. Connecting with these chakras brings the next level of growth, awakening, healing, and awareness into your life.

I feel chakras more and more lately in myself as energy fields, swirling vortexes of energy that aren't really delineated in the way that we have related to them. They are merging together more and more….a less literal sense than, 'the root chakra is at the base of the spine, the sacral chakra is the lower belly,' etc…..they feel more like fields of particular tones and consciousness to me. AND their vibration is changing as I move more into light body, 5D frequencies, their color is changing. They are feeling more crystal, to put it simply.

Because I have focused so much on the clearing and healing of my emotional body, my chakral body is pretty 'current' in terms of emotional congestion. As access to my multidimensional existence as a fractal from a Metasoul source becomes more developed and fluid and I connect and integrate more with 'sisters from my Metasoul line' who exist in other dimensions and 'periods of time' (what was previously felt as 'past lives'), there is less congestion too from other lifetimes and karmic bind playouts. All of this healing at this level is possible because of the negotiation ground I have created between myself and parts of me, especially my Inner Protector(s), Inner Punisher (when I had that frequency inside me), my 3D Selves, Inner Child, Inner Teenager, Inner Matriarch/birth mother…..this negotiation has opened the way to access the deeper consciousness of the emotional body, the chakras, the Metasoul.

Becoming conscious, open, negotiating, learning, exploring with self love and curiosity, expands your experience of yourself into these fascinating terrains inside of you, especially your chakras! ALL of it serves your remembrance as the Infinite Love that you ARE.

~

Sacred Human Column And Activation and Cleaning Of Ascension Chakras Meditation

Close your eyes in a quiet space. Breathe in and out many times as you relax your body. Feel yourself surrounded by pure white light and all lower vibrational energies moving out of your field and aura. Engage in the pure white staircase meditation (previously shared in this chapter) to raise your vibrational frequency.

When you feel you are vibrating at a higher place, feel yourself surrounded still by pure white light. You are next to a very large tree, any kind that you like with branches going up into the sky and roots going down into the Earth. Connect with this tree, sit by it and feel its template entering you, soaking into you.

Feel the voice and energy of Mother Gaia coming through this tree. She is inviting you into reverence, into beauty, and into joy. She is inviting you to connect with her. She is inviting you to ground into Her like the roots of the tree.

Feel the breeze on your skin as you sit by the tree. Call in the energies of air to aerate you, bringing in wisdoms and inner knowing and guidance from Ethereal BEings and Guides. Feel the warmth of the sun on your skin as you sit by the tree. Call in the energies of fire and warmth to act as a catalyst in your life, burning away all that doesn't work for you, bringing in passion and energy and change into your life and your relationships.

There is a gentle stream running alongside the tree, it is babbling, and talking at you. It is offering rejuvenation and refreshing energies. Call in the energies of water to purify yourself and your energy and to provide the safety to go into deeper emotional spaces, into shadow, into the hurt and stuck places.

Call in the energies of spirit and soul to illuminate, to help you remember who you ARE and the love that you ARE. Call in the energies of angels and Star BEings and Guides to support you in the service of love. Call in your Higher Self to connect with you and begin the process of embodying your Higher Self.

Call in Archangel Metatron now. Ask Him to connect with you and to prepare to receive His energy. Metatron may appear to you as an older man with white beard and white hair. He may just be a shimmering form of very bright light. You should feel safe and very loved being around His energy.

Metatron begins to run a golden orange column of light through you, a honey light into and through you. Feel His golden light flowing through every chakra. You may start seeing geometric shapes floating around you in the air, pulsing with energy. Every cell of your body becoming pure honey-golden light and Metatron places His hands upon you. His energy floods into you and everything around you, including the tree, become brighter as He amplifies the light level of the energy. Ask Him to dissolve anything within your body, aura, or fields that has been an issue during the day. Ask Him to hold the perfect level of light within your body and field at all times, day and night.

Metatron now connects you with your chakras, including your ascension chakras. He runs his honey light through them all and they spin and respond at a higher vibrational frequency then before, including in new colors than you may have seen or felt before.

Picture and feel these ascension chakras as Metatron moves light and love through them:

Stellar gateway- about 15 inches above your head, looks and feels like a golden sun. It connects you with galactic frequencies and All That Is and the Great Cosmic Sun of the Universe.

Soul star chakra- 7 inches below the stellar gateway and is bright pink. The soul star chakra offers access to your other lifetimes, your Metasoul or soul group frequencies, and your soul gifts.

Causal chakra- behind your head and is pure white. The causal chakra connects to Star BEing frequencies and galactic languages, communication frequencies, and consciousness beyond the matrix of 3D conditioning.

Crown chakra- It is a thousand petal lotus that is a golden white light of wisdom.

Third Eye chakra- It is indigo and located on your forehead.

Throat chakra- It is light blue and opens up access to Light Language and gifts of communication.

Cosmic Heart chakra- It is white with touches of pink and is THE center for which your ascension process is seated.

Solar plexus chakra- It is over the rib cage area and lungs and contains golden colored wisdom and knowledge.

Naval Chakra- It is over your belly button and is radiant orange providing connection to all through the collective umbilicus.

Sacral- It is a couple inches below your belly button and is pink.

Base- It is at the root of your spine and sparkling platinum.

Earth chakra- It is black and white and about a foot below your feet, offering you a deep grounding and connection with Mother Gaia.

Feel the golden energy from Metatron flowing through each of your ascension chakras, swirling through them in a ascension light flowing. Feel yourself expanding into your fifth-dimensional blueprint and light body. Feel every in-breath as pure Source energy and every out-breath as pure light. Metatron is now surrounding you with light of protection and to help you ground into your body.

Feel your earth chakra connecting deep inside of the Earth. Feel and connect with Mother Gaia, who welcomes you into Her arms. Feel the connection with Metatron that He has opened up and what Gaia provides in grounding, feel the column of your Sacred Humanity

~

Etheric Implants, Energy Healing: All Held There And Put There By Love

I was reading about etheric implants last night and am still digesting what I had read with what my experience has been as an energy facilitator. I am not one to study things deeply as I am more intuitive than intellectual. I pick up concepts very quickly on a contextual level and am not so great at remembering or tracking fine detail or 'facts' at all. So, most of what I offer in terms of teaching and serving comes from an intuitive remembrance in the form of inner guidance or knowing and Ethereal Guides. I experience or remember or download something and then I might go do a little research into it or be guided to read a book (usually very quickly, skimming for concepts). Then the digestion begins, the resonance is found, the bridge identified to teach it, and quite shortly the offering of it to others....always with a 'near as I can tell' energy and not absolute truth as I don't feel anyone can have the absolute truth about reality and consciousness.

SO, back to implants. I have been feeling my way through energy facilitation over the years, letting my Higher Self and soul come through, and always been very collaborative with whoever I was holding space for and with. I talk out loud and transparently about what I am doing/feeling/seeing, teaching as I go, and involving the person's Higher Self with me and also negotiating with their protective part of them if necessary (if fear is coming up for them or resistance. I'll stop energy work altogether to be in the feelings if that is what is needed as I am primarily an emotional body facilitator). This is also how I facilitate emotional movements as well. It is SO powerful when someone's soul is leading in response and in collaboration. So, often there is no structure to energy facilitation with me, beyond the main chakras being cleared and activated, and beyond that, it is always a magical journey into the unknown.

And, implants...I am struggling to be linear today as it is becoming less and less my orientation to life! Ok, yes, I have experienced 'implants' as not so much something 'put into the etheric field by negative entities polarized to fear and lower dimensional frequencies' (as is the usual read on it.) I have experienced more and held it more that each SOUL chooses what is in their field and for reasons that further the growth and transformation of that soul. It may even sometimes be IN COLLABORATION with these lower density BEings (called Archons, Dracos, etc.) for reasons that actually WORK for the soul. This is not done out of lack of self love either, it is done for GROWTH, which is the reason that we even chose to come here to Gaia.

When I have discovered objects in the etheric field with people, there is ALWAYS an emotional and spiritual component to them. There are deep tears and processing and we quite quickly can connect the reason for them to their bigger process as a soul this life. Often, the person themselves does this as I create a bridge to their Higher Self so they can 'hear and feel' them. We remove the objects together and that too is an emotional and very touching journey and we only remove them if it feels like the right time. All of this is negotiated with the person, their higher self, and whatever aspects or parts they are working with in that moment. All of this is held with much tenderness and feeling tones.

  The energy that some Energy Healers and practitioners have around 'removing implants' feels cold to me and, in some ways, fear-based. It is as if they aren't trusting the REASON that the objects are there and how NOTHING is done to us without our Higher Selves' permission and in union with Divine Source. There can be a victim-based energy to their relationship to it and, also, a sense of vigilance and defensiveness. It feels like these Healers are going to 'battle' with these implants and the symptoms of recovery they describe afterwards such as being very ill, etc. feel to me in part because it has all been held with battle-like energy rather than love. All of these frequencies of battle, vigilance, defensiveness…..lower OUR vibrational frequency because we then believe that we are victims to these entities, that they have done something to us 'against our higher will', etc.

  I feel it is more about being an Ambassador of love to ANYTHING that is going on in our bodies, minds, hearts, souls, and etheric fields. Responding to it with love and trust that it is there for a REASON, that we've needed it until we didn't need it anymore, and the Universe is a place offering an exploration ground of love ultimately as we were birthed from love out of a Divine source of LOVE. Removing these objects that can block energy flow and even 'cap' your growth and awakening can shift some amazing things in your experience of reality. However, this can only happen – in my experience – when it is time for it to happen and when it is led primarily by you and by your Higher Self.

Over time, as your heart pains heal and your energy field clears out, you can easily track when and if entities are hanging on to you or if there is another object to be lovingly removed. You become your own energy facilitator with the help of your Higher Self (which becomes more and more YOU) and with Ethereal Guides too if you need them. THIS to me is the endgame of all of this……the empowerment and remembrance of EVERY soul back into wholeness, a return to love, a return to self care and love at such a high level where things like implants or etheric objects are no longer needed at all.

~

The Universe Sings Of Your Radiance: Unicorns On The Beach

You are on a beach, fingers digging into the sand, toes wiggling around. The sun is warm, soaking into your skin, forming crystals, activating DNA. Light codes in the rays recalibrate your aura. It shines and shimmers; it sparkles with life.

The waves attach and reattach to the shore, claiming the sand and moving back out again. The cycle is relentless, you float away on the rhythm, feeling the beat of the waves in your heart. You seem to hear the smash and crash inside of your soul.

Mother Gaia is smiling through the gulls, the pelicans, the tiny fish that create the food chain. She is inviting you to feel your magnificence that is grand and great as the smallest particle to the largest objects in the deepest of space. You are vast and noble as the stars and as humble as the Earth. She invites you to ground, connecting with the chakra below your feet. She is the umbilicus, inviting you to feed from Her deepest Earth dwellings, providing a steady nourishment of grounding.

The Angels are here in groups. They are drawn to the beach because of the negative ions, the mists, the portals near the shore. You can slip in easy wherever you'd like to go and they show you how, over and over, flying on currents of energies to unseen destinations.

You are as radiant as the sun. A million light rays broadcasting from a higher dimensional frequency of Divine Source expressing as You in Human form. As you tune into this frequency more and more, your crystalline broadband echoes out to the ethers and more Ethereal BEings are drawn. As you heal your pain body, your heart pitch rises emitting both heavenly tones and radiant light.

Your unicorn is there, a guide waiting patiently for you to call it. It is waiting to be 'of service', to serve love to and with you. Its enlightened state creates a wand of pure light emitting from its third eye….not a horn or bone, but pure energy. You call your unicorn to you, reunite with each other, he or she has been waiting for you in the higher dimensions. The loyalty of his service touches you deeply.

Your tears are of joy, of reunion, of remembering. They are the substance of hope, desire, and love. Your tears are the language of the healing Human heart; they are your capacity to feel all of the joys of the beach in a multidimensional way. You open always to the possibility of feeling more, whatever needs to be felt, not good or bad, but just what Is and what needs to BE, coming up to be released.

The Unicorns, the Angels, the fish, the waves, the sand, the sun, Mother Gaia…..all seem to celebrate your existence and your mission, your deeper purpose to serve love. They sing it to you, remind you of why you are here. They sing to help you claim your place and your space, support you in healing anything that limits or holds you back.

The Universe sings of your radiance and you…….smile back.

~

Connect With Your Unicorn Meditation

Breathing, relaxing, floating, connecting within. In a quiet space with journeying music playing (or not), you create a cocoon for yourself. A safe space where you can soar the inner skies of your magical inner world.

You bring in the fire of alchemy by lighting a candle or some incense or some sage. You bring in the Earth by grounding to Gaia through your root chakra at the base of your spine and through the earth chakra that is about a foot below your own physical feet. You bring in water by seeing yourself dipping into a pool or standing under a waterfall, allowing the waters to purify the lower denser energies that may be in your field. You bring in air by breathing deeply, in and out, inhaling loving light and exhaling whatever needs to move out.

You stand in an open meadow with trees on all sides. There is an increasing calm and peaceful feeling inside of you.

You call your unicorn to you, asking them to join you once again. The one that fits the image of your imagination comes forward to you. The one that has just been waiting to accompany you and be by your side once again comes to you.

Their glimmering horn that is made of pure energy sweeps over you, offering love and nourishment to your heart and soul. You take in this energy with gratitude and appreciation, so grateful to connect again with this magical creature of the higher dimensions. You feel tears at the reunion with this mystical BEing who offers you such deep frequencies of loyalty and joy.

You are riding on the back of your unicorn. You are going up, rising up, moving up. The clouds call you, the higher realms and the places where Angels and Unicorns fly in the sky. The 'sky' is full with them and they call to you with images, hand gestures, and Light Language. Light Language is just waiting to be expanded out in you and some bursts of it come out without self consciousness and without worry if it is 'right' or not.

The higher frequencies invite you to open your heart, expand your soul, and lighten your 'load'. You are surrounded by golden white light. This light gets warmer as you go higher, it is as warm as the sun. The orange gold energy is flooding into your Being, into your aura, into each spinning and whirling flow of each chakra.

Your chakras accept this golden warm flow like hungry sponges, increasing their swirling vortex energy. You connect with each one, feeling intuitively where they are located and what they are offering for you. For now, it matters less all the specifics of where and what they are, you just let the golden warm energy move through your field and out your feet again.

You soar through the skies as long as you feel to, opening up to connection with the angels that flow around you and other Unicorns too. You open up to connection and conversation with your Unicorn, sharing and exchanging your soul names in Light Language. You open up to the next places you will go as you continue your ascension process and dedicate yourself to the journeys within that bring such expansive frequencies to your life.

When you are ready, you land with your Unicorn back in the meadow where you began. You embrace your Unicorn and thank him or her for reuniting with you and for taking you on such a wonderful journey. You remember now that you can call on them whenever you need and want to. You remember that they are there to help you, assist you, and serve love with you even as it serves them too.

You bring this energy with you into your day, into your world, into your bridging of this higher dimensional frequency energy within every moment and within all of your relationships. And, you feel glad and so, so loved.

~

Everyone Is A Channel: Conversation With Archangel Metatron

We are sitting in the courtyard in front of the Akashic Library. The courtyard is surrounded by trees, grass, and flowers. Everything is encased in a golden light, the perfect lighting that I recognize from higher dimensional frequencies as the visible light spectrum expands beyond what we experience in third dimensional or 3D reality. Metatron is sitting next to me yet I still can't look directly at him for too long as his frequency is so high and intense.

He is pure white light. He is presenting himself to me in his grandfather form, long white hair and long white beard. He knows that it is comforting to me and easier for me to take in his teachings when he is in this form. What his actual form is (way up in the 12th dimension) feels like would be impossible for me to even imagine or resonate with.

He wants me to be as current and transparent as possible in sharing with you what he is teaching me. The floods of information and teachings coming from him are quite full in the moment. He wants me to claim it AS him and to be more comfortable with offering myself as a channel of his and where my teachings are originated from as an aspect of my Higher Self embodiment process.

"Everyone is a channel," he says to me as we 'sit' on a bench in front of a particularly stunning tree that looks like an Oak tree but doesn't feel like one as it is emanating a very strong rainbow colored aura. "Every soul has the capacity to channel and bring forward energies of higher dimensional BEings such as Archangels, Spirit Guides, Ascended Teacher frequencies. You are ALL sourced from It, so of course you can channel It."

"I have about five questions that I want to ask you about that, Metatron, but I'll start with this one. What do you mean when you say that we are sourced from It?"

He shows me an image of the Flower Of Life, sacred geometry, for which I am becoming more familiar recently. He communicates to me in the form of shapes sometimes and especially during energy healing where He uses Triangles, Tetrahedrons, or 'Metatron's Cube' to move through my auric field to clear it out.

"The Flower Of Life is found in all major religions in the world in some form, the story of creation. Google it if you need to know more about its history," he says, with humor in his voice. One of Metatron's favorite expressions seems to be, "Google it!" He seems to find the Internet an amusing and amazing source of information and so it IS!

"Anyway, the Flower of Life shows how everything originates from the center point. This center point has been called the Void, the Nondual, Big Bang, many others things. I like to call it Divine Source. Divine Source is All That Is, Ever Has Been, and Ever Will Be. And it is also No-Thing At All. It is Infinite Love, Infinite Awareness, and Infinite Possibilities."

"I can feel the resonance here as this is what I have been feeling for awhile that each of us ARE Infinite Love in our essence and that awakening is about remembering this," I say.

"Yes," he nods at me in happy agreement. "You've had an intuition about this provided to you by your Higher Self and connecting with Higher Dimensional Guides like me. You've had tastes of this Infinite Love essence in moments as you raise your vibrational frequency and mostly because of your work to heal your emotional body. The emotional pain body, which is created out of traumas experienced in third dimensional or 3D reality, is the biggest drag on your and everyone's consciousness ascension. The emotional body in a healthy form is not, it is a gift from the Divine to the Human species."

I'm starting to feel dizzy with all the questions I have and also because what he is offering validates my own focus and the work I offer to others through SoulFullHeart. Before I can respond or ask a question, he continues on:

"Let's go back to the Flower of Life and my origin story, shall we? So, Divine Source is the source of all existence, which you can see demonstrated graphically in the Flower Of Life. Its energy pulses and surges in a very high dimensional space, you could call it the 13th dimension if you wish. I like the number 13 for many reasons, so we'll use that. You can feel Divine Source, yet you cannot have a relationship with it as it has no duality or relationality."

"Divine Source decided at some point that it wanted to experience different fractals of itself and, also, that it was bored," he says. "Maybe not bored, but definitely I get the feeling that It wanted something to witness and live through. It wanted to get to know itself through a different expression than Its vast Infinite Love-ness. So, it created some first degree fractals of itself. These are the Archangels, like me. Archangels are 'tasked' with holding back the intense energy frequencies of Divine Source. We act as pillars to contain the energy, hold it back for it would 'wipe out' all of creation if it came through unfiltered. It is both Great Destroyer and Great Creator."

"Ok, I see how that is represented on the Tree of Life as the first circle there," I offer, pointing to the Tree of Life image that has appeared before us in the air.

"Yes," he says, continuing on. "Divine Source then split off all BEings from the Archangels, just like the Flower Of Life shows. It is not a linear splitting off but rather a circling outwards, like shown here. In addition to the Archangels' existence in the 12th dimension, we also respond to the heart cries and needs of all the fractals that split off after us. We can be in all places at all times as time and space are not real for us. We Archangels are also fractals off of what you been calling the Metasouls. Of course, I love that name, Metasoul, as it contains part of MY name and also because it perfectly captures the energy."

What he is offering rumbles through me. Already, being a Healer and Teacher, I can feel how this perspective could serve people in their ascension process.

"Yes!" he exclaims. "You are already feeling the ramifications of what I am offering. Since all Human BEings originate from Metasouls, you are fractals or projections from us Archangels too. Therefore, you can learn a lot by identifying which Archangel you most resonate with, connecting with us directly, and claiming your Metasoul origins connected to one of us. EVERY sentient being comes from one of the 13 Archangel Metasouls as every being comes from Divine Source. There may be others that could be considered Archangels but let's stick with 13 because, again, I like that number. Angels, Ascended Masters, Spirit Guides, are all higher dimensional fractals off of the 13 Archangel Metasouls."

"How does the Higher Self fit into this picture?" I ask.

"Your Higher Self is another fractal, a higher dimensional one. It vibrates at a higher frequency from the 3D one that you live in and experience life from every day. Your Higher Self is a soul fractal deposit that you left in a higher dimension to guide you in your way. One key aspect of the ascension process is about raising your vibrational frequency to eventually embody your Higher Self consciously within your Human body. To merge with your Higher Self eventually"

"Ok, yes, I have been aware of that one for awhile now. I'm sure there is a connection here, but since you tend to be nonlinear, I want to bring it back to the point for which we started, which was about channeling."

"Yes, of course! Thank you for keeping me 'on task', Jelelle! Many souls have the capacity to channel higher BEing consciousness and 'hear' the messages. As I said, this is nothing special since ALL BEings come from the Archangels and Divine Source ultimately. Yet, often, the person channeling these energies has to go unconscious to bring the energies through. Or their channeled messages sound and feel strange, affected, not

Human like, and fewer of the relational tones of warmth and compassion. This is because their Higher Self is not embodied inside of them. Their Human-based bridge to the higher dimensions, which is through a healthy heart, is blocked and clogged from pains and traumas."

"You said earlier, Metatron, that healing the 3D emotional pain body is key to embodiment of the Higher Self because that raises the vibrational frequency enough for the Higher Self to come in. This is also what allows the channeling of higher dimensional BEings and hearing their voice (clairaudience) and seeing them (clairvoyance), yes?"

"Yes, but also the integration of your Metasoul fractals (those fractals that split off from the same source) that exist across spans and eras of 'time' helps with raising vibrational frequency and embodiment of the Higher Self. As you have felt for awhile, Jelelle, it is both the healing of the heart AND the soul which leads to ascension, enlightenment, transformation, healing….whatever you want to call it."

"This is the work we are doing in SoulFullHeart, yes, and you have been expanding that out lately with access to Metasoul portals in the Akashic Library that we can access to connect with our soul legacy and other lifetimes. But that feels like a topic for another writing."

"Yes," he says, smiling his bright, bright LOVE grin at me. "There is much more to offer about the story of creation, the connection to Archangels, and Metasoul healing, but we'll let what I've offered today go in for now. We don't want to blow any fuses, do we?"

I am starting to feel a familiar pressure at the top of my head and third eye/forehead area which usually means that I am at the full point in terms of letting in new consciousness frequencies and ideas…..it does feel a bit like 'blowing a fuse' but in a good way.

We smile at each other as he begins to fade from my vision and I start to drift into the deeper sleep that allows for integration of these ideas into my BEing to be formed later into words to share with others.

~

Introducing The Metasoul

I'm feeling, experiencing, and becoming open more and more to the sense that Guides (Angels, Ascended Masters, Spirit Guides, etc.) are versions or fragments of what I call Metasouls (similar to the concept of Oversouls) which exist in a higher dimensional reality and project onto different 'eras' of time and dimensions many versions coming from their original source essence and energy. I feel as if when we are experiencing Guides, we are experiencing in some ways an aspect of ourselves, a fragment of the same Metasoul. Or we are experiencing a fragment from a Universal Consciousness Metasoul (which would be fragments such as Yeshua, Kuan Yin, Buddha, Magdalene, Archangels, etc.) These Universal Consciousness Fragments or Aspects seem to be available for anyone to connect with.

If fear, resistance, or just inability to access Guides comes up it feels to me like it just isn't the right time for integration of that particular frequency. There is other 'work' to do first, usually within the emotional body (often connected to unworthiness) or with an 'other lifetime' aspect that may be feeling the fear or resistance due to unhealed issues of persecution when inhabiting soul gifts, abuse of others related to soul gift expression or being a recipient of abuse, etc.

Getting to know, connect with, heal, and integrate the aspects that are usually known as 'past lives' allows for navigation of your Metasoul's legacy and themes. These legacy and themes are often connected to archetypal frequencies and the collective unconscious.

I experience my other lives as existing in the NOW until their 'time is up' and their energy can ascend and integrate back into the Metasoul that we originated from. This way of relating to other lifetimes is dynamic, visceral and emotional yet also brings huge gifts of higher vibrational frequency access as some of the 'fragments' are in higher dimensions (such as Avalon, Atlantis, Lemuria, other planets, parallel dimensions, etc.) Because time is an illusion, 'past lives' are not really past and the energy they generate and take up (esp. related to emotional and soul traumas) can be huge and I think goes largely untouched in many people. There can be a lot of energy caught up in these other lifetimes that influences and impacts our current lifetime. This especially seems to be the case when the other lifetime(s) is one in which being famous or still currently well known is involved.

Raphael and I (along with Gabriel and Kalayna) have been connecting to the Akashic Records recently yet before then discovered it to be quite simple to access these other lifetimes (and we feel it is simple for others too when the time is right in their process), meet our Metasoul brothers and sisters (as we are calling them), and form a relationship through creative visualization during meditation, verbal dialogue exchange, and journaling. A simple creative visualization process can open up this gateway as well, especially if your upper three chakras are open, healthy, and activated. It is within this mutual relationship between you and your other lifetimes that healing occurs on BOTH sides.

~

Healing Karma And Integrating Selves From Other Lifetimes

"You are not wrong. Nothing you can do is wrong. Nothing you can be is wrong." So says my heart to yours. So says my sense of Divine Source to your sense of Divine Source. So says my Higher Self to the parts of you that feel like you are wrong or have done something wrong.

Karmic wounds and binds, soul entanglements, and the playout of soul themes and patterns over and over can make you feel 'wrong' or that you have done 'wrong' actions. Yet, still, even in these things or scenes that feel intense and where you have been accused of wrong...you are NOT. You may have done things that are not polarized to love, especially in other lifetimes when the consciousness was much lower and during a Dark Night Of Your Soul phase. You may have explored grounds of influencing others or being influenced yourself to do things and be things that vibrate at a lower frequency of fear and even hate. You may have caused harm to others or allowed harm to be done to you.

As souls, our Higher Selves remember that we CHOOSE these explorations to grow, to transform, to understand more about the polarities of life, and to ultimately return to the love essence that we ARE. To heal these karmic wounds and to understand the soul patterns is to LOVE ALL that you have been and done and all fractals of you from your soul group (which I call Metasoul and has also been called Oversoul and Monad), all expressions of you, parallel selves of you spread across many eras and periods. To heal these karmic patterns is to integrate these soul fractals with LOVE, to embrace them into your heart where forgiveness lives and breathes.

In SoulFullHeart, we explore this karmic ground through an aspect differentiation process during sessions. We serve love with you to open up portals of exploration into these other lifetimes through meditative creative visualization journeys. This is primarily accessed through the Akashic Records yet can also be a simple doorway meditation process too or whatever 'way' comes to you as your way. We can help you to raise your vibrational frequency, activate your seven main and ascension chakras, and connect with Guides (especially Archangel Metatron) who can assist with this process of accessing your 'Metasoul line.'

You step through the portal or doorway into the 'scenes' of other lifetimes which we help you access and remember through your own deepening connection with your Higher Self. Your intuition guides you to where you need to focus. Usually there are impulses and interests to certain time periods or eras. There are draws to watch certain movies from specific time periods or about Aliens or space exploration. Dreams can reveal the next places that the soul needs to go through images and memories. Your Star BEing Selves (Arcturian, Pleiadian, and so many more) begin to get your attention through offering channeled messages from others to you or through activation of Light Language or Star Language.

This goes along beautifully with your emotional pain body healing process too. They weave together wonderfully as every Parallel Self has pain to heal and move and often this pain connects to your current life patterns and play outs. You then form a relationship with this other aspect of yourself, this Parallel Self, this Metasoul Brother or Sister from the same soul group, and in that relationship gifts are exchanged, wounds are healed, and energy is released. Then, integration happens and you organically move on to the next and next. It is limitless healing and transformation with limitless possibilities released.

This way of feeling and healing karma is so effective and efficient that you can move lifetimes worth of patterns and issues quite deeply yet rapidly (all in its own 'time' of course). The intention and holding love is what moves it. The forming of a relationship with it is what moves it. The curiosity about the soul patterns is what moves it. The supportive space holding with an open-hearted facilitator is what moves it. This is quantum healing of karma that allows for truly leaving it behind to arise into the new.... freed from the anchor of the karma and unhealed unworthiness, guilt, shame, disconnect.

"You are not wrong. You are perfect as a love expression from Divine Source. All you have done is perceived and held with love." And so IT IS.

~

Moving From Fear Of Aliens To Embracing Your Star BEing Self And Family: Our Heart Is A Beacon

All of my life I have felt a fascination and curiosity about Alien BEings, outer space, and travel to other galaxies. Yet also, beneath that curiosity, there was a lingering sense of fear and trepidation. Like most people who experienced Alien abduction or 'visits' with Extraterrestrials during their childhood, I didn't consciously remember it until many years later.

I started to remember my Alien experiences during an energy healing class. I was lying on the table and the group stood around me to identify my chakras or energy centers as instructed by the teacher. I suddenly remembered and saw myself as a young child lying on an examination table on an Alien ship surrounded by strange looking BEings with grey skin, very big eyes, no noses, and small mouths wearing doctor coats. Feelings of terror and discomfort came back to me in that moment, which the teacher was able to help me process.

I was surprised to discover that I had experienced at least one Alien encounter when I was visiting my grandmother in rural Kansas at the age of eight. The one clear aspect that I could remember of this experience was flying in the air over the rows of corn on her property. It didn't feel like flying as much as it did being tugged or pulled through the air. It was both frightening and exhilarating.

I didn't explore into my abduction memories any deeper until many years later, when I began to read anything I could about alien encounter experiences from an expanded viewpoint beyond a fear-based and victim picture of aggressively hostile Aliens bent on destroying Humankind. I began to let in the idea that I was a star seed, or soul who had spent many incarnations on other planets and in other galaxies. Reading the book *Abductions* by John E. Mack was very helpful to facilitate my remembrance and put it in a more positive frame through his expansive therapeutic work with many people who experienced alien encounters.

Eventually, through a self-led hypnosis process during meditation practice and due to the emotional healing work that I had focused on for many years, I was able to remember some of the visits that I had with Alien BEings. These visits started at a young age and seemed to continue into my late teens, where they then stopped. Going into a meditative state, I would engage in creative visualization to imagine the examination room with the Aliens shuffling around the room around me and also doing things to my physical body with various instruments.

At first, the feelings of terror were so strong that I had to picture myself as a young child lying on the table in the alien ship rather than re-experiencing it *as* me. It was as if I was watching a movie that I resonated with on a deep emotional level, rather than actually experiencing it myself. I stood in the room as my adult self and sent lots of love to the young version of me that was crying on the table. I discovered that this was an effective method of healing the extreme sense of powerlessness and helplessness that many people feel who have had alien encounters.

At some point, after witnessing the examination, I watched as the young version of me stopped crying and screaming and started to negotiate with the Aliens, especially the short grey-colored ones in the doctor coats. She told them that she didn't like the tests they were doing or the probes they were putting into parts of her body. She said that she didn't like that they didn't ask her first for her permission before doing these things. She told that she wanted to be their Ambassador and connect with them, yet they needed to be respectful toward her.

At this moment of advocacy, I felt a huge surge of relief flood through me as I consciously shifted the way that my subconscious was relating to the experience. I took my power back in that moment. The Alien BEings were a bit confused but seemed to understand what my young self was saying as they were quite exhausted and weary from so many Humans being resistive and afraid. This is also when I met and started connecting with a much lighter and higher frequency Alien BEing that I came to relate to as my Guide. She was taller than the others and had a bluish tint to her skin. She felt like a different species to me than the others. I could actually feel the love and remorse that she felt for what they had done to me as a child, whereas the others felt unemotional and more robotic.

    This Alien, who asked me to call her Binkh, took the hand of my younger self and helped her off the table. I trailed along as the two of them left the examination room and began to float around the light-filled ship together. I could feel then how deep my bond had been with this being during these encounters and how I had even felt her to be my 'true' mother in some ways. She showed my young self to an amazing room that seemed to be like a biodome. This room didn't seem to have a ceiling or walls and held many species of animals and plants from Earth. Binkh explained that this was like an ark and that her kind, called Arcturians, were saving these species as they were starting to go extinct on Earth. They were storing them here until the Earth's and the Human Species' vibrational frequency was high enough for them to come back.

    She showed my younger self (and me) a picture of cohabitation with her species (and other benevolent ones) on Earth at some point in the future. This was very touching to the younger version of me. I began to remember that after the frightening examinations, I would always get to play with the animals and in the trees. This was a joy for me and something that I deeply, subconsciously missed when I was returned to my life on Earth. I also connected my lifelong capacity to make up pretend and imaginative worlds to my Alien experiences. As a child, I would miss the higher dimensional reality that I experienced in the ship and try to recreate it through elaborate scenarios and eventually astral travel.

After discovering that there was a much deeper meaning and interpretation of my Alien encounters, other aspects of my awakening process took priority for a while. About a year later, I was more ready to connect with Binkh again in an intimate way as a beloved Guide and Soul Sister. I learned from her that I had chosen as a soul to come to Earth during this time of great transition and ascension. I digested with her how I had experienced the visits as intrusive and fear-based because they felt like they were against my conscious will and the will of my 3D self. Then, I learned that these visits had also included awe-filled explorations of other planets and galaxies and that I had a role as a Love Ambassador between Humans and Alien species.

The following is an experience that I had with an Arcturian healing circle that offered a beautiful sense of the gifts we have to offer Aliens (which I now call 'Star BEings') in terms of our emotional capacity and the gifts they have to offer us. If we are in loving exchange with them, benevolent Star BEings offer us higher dimensional frequencies of peace, unity, and telepathic communication. When we move beyond our fears of the unknown related to Star BEing connection, so many wonderful things become possible!

**

I am in a circle with the Arcturians, these tall BEings from the stars with bluish-white tinted skin that reminds me of Dolphins. I am in that floating space of in-between physical body, astral body, and crystalline/light body. The hurt and fear from remembering the visits I had with Aliens as a child is gone. Also, I have already learned that these visits were led by another species of Star BEings called Grays, who are polarized to denser frequencies of fear and without much compassion.

The Arcturians went along with the 'abductions' in the early 80's and 90's to learn and help Humanity and yet, eventually, they stopped participating because of the fear and trauma that it caused us. Plus, taking Humans against our conscious will (even if our souls had 'signed up' to experience it) didn't go along with their peaceful and respectful nature.

These are a circle of Arcturians, a benevolent and loving species, who feel like they are my star family and seem to verify that I am indeed a Star Seed soul. I am sinking into how it feels to be with them and the absolute peace that comes from no sense of separation between one BEing to the next, even as they are still individual sparks of Divine consciousness. Having led and participated in many Human healing circles, I understand the flow of energy that moves when given a circular structure. Yet, with them, these BEings from the stars, it is amplified by thousands. The energy is not from outside of them, yet just *is* their essence. They have physical form and long flowing gowns, yet, do not have any form at the same time. Their vibrational frequency is so high that every cell of their 'bodies' seems to dance in light, be in light, and *is* light.

Tears are leaking from my eyes as their love comes to me in light waves, rippling through me. They are love and I am love. These are tears without running noses, just leaking out. These are tears without pain. These are tears of joy, of reunion, of the soul, of remembering what I am and what we all are. These are tears of remembering that there is no 'they', only 'we'. We are merging; me in my enlightening Human form and them in their Arcturian ones.

Binkh stands to my right and, yet, also, seemingly in the same moment, I feel her merge into me. We become more than Soul Sisters then; we are the same. As we become one, I feel the muscles in my mouth try to form smiles as she plays with my mouth from the inside. It is awkward because she is not used to smiling and being expressive like I am. I feel her tenderly touch my face, feeling wonder at the tears running down my face and the flood of emotions in my heart.

As much as I ache to be like them again, to be in such peace as they are, to be in such Oneness feelings as they are; I also feel their delight and reverence in me, in my Humanness, and in my tears. I feel how they desire to smile, to laugh with joy, to cry tears of wonder, to be overcome with emotion, and to be swept away.

    I began to understand at an even deeper level, because of this and other experiences with the Arcturians, why so much of my focus the last ten years has been to heal my emotional body and allow the spiritual growth to flow from that. I usually realized at a deeper level why I have taught, held space, and created a healing process that allows for transformational emotional healing along with spiritual awakening. Spiritual growth is inevitable as the soul signs up for it, yet emotional body growth, emotional ego maturation, and emotional healing is our new ground of transformation as a species.

    Psychology has opened out this healing of the heart ground with offerings that are a blend of psychology and spirituality becoming more and more popular as more souls wake up to the need for both. This is a crucial ground that, if not tended to, can leave our hearts out of the picture as we awaken and ascend our consciousness. The wounded aspects of us hold our heart frequencies hostage and we have to free them up by deep feeling led by self care and love. And, in my sense of it, we need others to hold a loving space at times and in phases for us to go into the heart healing inside of us.

    My healing and open heart was what the Arcturians were drawn to, as I was drawn to the expansiveness of their consciousness. As we were merging and becoming One, a new energy was being created. Perhaps it was a new consciousness or a new species, a new expression of Divine Source.

    They were showing me that it is our heart and our emotionality, that is arising and desired by species in many other worlds and galaxies. Our heart is a beacon. It is not about us becoming like the Star BEings or about leaving behind all that makes us Human in order to become Star BEings, as some people offer. It is not about becoming aggressive with them and trying to blast them from the sky. It feels like it is about truly claiming the sacredness of our Humanity, our capacity to feel, and to bring that so preciously 'along with us' as we ascend and experience higher and higher dimensions of consciousness.

Our hearts can get us in 'trouble', yes, especially when they are troubled and weighed down with hurts and wounds from the past. As we are cleared and healed of these frequencies that block our love flow, our expansive heart-based consciousness can lead the way. Our hearts are our ambassador to other realms and dimensions – both inside and outside. Healing our hearts is what allows us to move beyond our fears and traumatic reactions to alien experiences and let them in for the transformational ground they offer us. The heart is the gateway to other Universes – both within and with-out. It is this that the Star BEings/Aliens honored in me and that which they honor in all of us. Coming from our hearts with them and not being afraid, we can dance in heart frequencies and soar into love's limitless skies together in this galaxy and beyond.

~

Message From Arcturians And Pleiadians

Arcturian and Pleiadian Messages with me, Jelelle:

We are in no time, no space, no place. We reach out to you from this here and NOT here. We communicate with you from this place and not place.

Our language is Light Language, language of the multidimensions, language of the stars, you could also call it Star Language if you wanted to. Yet we will offer English now and one word after the other even though it is not our natural way.

We would like you to remember Light Language so that we can communicate with you in freed up tones and places. Less mind. You have busy mind from being in your dimension of density. Shut down to the flow of multidimensional language that is layered and spiraled, where many meanings can happen at once. As you remember this language, it will help you to write it down and to speak it out loud, to sing it too. It will help you to heal and clear your throat chakra, raising its vibration to fifth dimensional frequencies.

All chakras need to be raised to fifth dimensional frequencies. This is harder for the lower ones, the 'survival' one at your base or root especially. It may be that some are vibrating higher than others and that is all right. Your cosmic chakras of stellar, soul, and causal will open as your frequency is higher and you are ready for what you will access through them. Opening these will lead to big growth and movements, transmissions and transfusions of light and raising of frequencies.

We are not so much channeling through you, Jelelle, as you are remembering the 'we' for which you have spent most of your existence. You have been a 'we' much more than you have been an 'me' or a 'you' or a 'I'. Channeling in many Humans is done from disconnection, a taking over of star frequencies or Etheric or Angelic frequencies to bypass the Human consciousness. The person becomes and fuses to these energies and then sees them as separate somehow. They are not separate and we are NOT separate from you.

You have created communications and dialogues with so many aspects of yourself, mostly in your pain body but also your soul aspects, and you are practiced at feeling energies that feel outside and bringing them inside while also remaining YOU too. This practice allows you to remain as 'Jelelle' while you are connecting with our message. You are 'with us' and not separate from us. You intuitively have felt this and now you are remembering how this is so.

Everything you can imagine and want is ALREADY in your life. Remembering this and feeling this helps with feeling lack and to move you on to the next place in your journey. We do not experience lack or scarcity as we do not relate to life like this. Life is abundant as it IS in the moment, since there is no time then there is nothing to relate it to like Humans do. We do not compare the present moment to the past or to the future in what might 'happen' or has yet to 'be'. We can feel and see and experience it all happening NOW and so it is now and it is good.

Through our Human Selves, we have learned much about Human consciousness. We have felt there are good things about it and we have learned from it as well. We are especially interested in the experience of emotions that are different than what we experience. Some of them are very hard, very low, and we do not want to be there long. Yet others are layered, like our Light Language, and always they are beyond the mind. Emotions come from a place that intrigues us and, yes, it is a beacon to us and other Star BEings.

Through our Human Self, we have experienced the lows of the emotional range and the highs of it too. We shed tears with you as you do and are amazed at how the tears can contain so much and so many layers of feeling. Like our Light Language symbols which have many layers of meaning in one symbol.

We would like to talk with you much, much more and also to merge with you into your consciousness and experience things with you as you do as we are very curious. Thank you for receiving this message from us. We love you! We ARE you!

~

Light Language

Light Language invites us to go beyond the mind, beyond what we have been conditioned to feel as language, what we have learned as language in school. Light Language or Star Language (as I've been offered by my Star BEing Selves to also call it) is multidimensional, nonlinear, based on wave-form energy transmissions. It forms in the higher dimensional throat chakra and is downloaded and transmitted from openings in our 12th chakra or stellar gateway. We pick up these downloads as we tune into them from within, as we connect with our Galactic Self more and more, as we feel how we our roots are from the stars.

Star Language is heard, yet it also comes through in hand and body gestures and movements, and sometimes in written symbols. The written symbols are nonlinear, often presented in circular form as mandalas, and sometimes just 'appear' to float in the air. The sounds may be present without the gestures or the symbols without the sounds or vice versa. It seems to come through in the ways that will best land in the heart and soul.

    Rather than trying to interpret Light Language in a literal way, it invites you to FEEL it and in the feeling of it to REMEMBER who you are and where you come from. It helps to lift the veil of amnesia that we placed on ourselves to come into the denser frequencies of Earth at this time. During this time of transition to higher consciousness or ascension, Light Language is one of the things that we are remembering and needing to remember to facilitate our processes individually and collectively.

    As you listen to recordings of Light Language and especially one of mine which is listed on the SoulFullHeart Experience YouTube Channel, I invite you to allow Light Language to come to you in response to it. It may happen spontaneously in response to the tones here that are coming through me. It may feel strange at first or you may feel as if you are 'just babbling.' Yet, you will feel it in your heart if you are accessing it and moving it through. You may have deep tears of reunion and a deep sense of 'returning home' as the waveforms offered by me or yourself trigger the frequencies of your star origins.

    Whatever happens is what is meant to. It is also helpful to raise your vibrational frequency as often as possible so that you can tune into the higher frequencies of Light Language that are 'floating around' in the air. Your Unicorn can help you to activate your chakras at a higher frequency and especially your throat chakra. Also, Unicorns communicate mostly in Light Language so you can 'practice' with them as you ride around the skies of your third eye and into higher realms. Angels and Spirit Guides also love using Light Language with you as it is closer in frequency to the way that they communicate with each other -

which is usually beyond language all together and is more about One Mind-One Consciousness in which all shares each other's thoughts and feelings.

Light Language opens the heart and expands the soul. Held with love and curiosity and play, it is expression of the Divine coming through you and serves your remembrance of the Infinite Love that you ARE.

~

We Are Here To Connect And Merge With You: Message From Your Angelic Aspects, Star BEing Aspects, And Higher Self

We know it is has been hard and IS hard in so many moments. Moments where you want to give up. Moments where you want to 'go home'. Moments where you are consumed by pain. Moments where your heart feels like it is breaking. Moments where your tears fall and sobs shake your body. Moments where the sky feels so dark and cloudy and overcast with unexpressed pains.

We feel you in this and we see you in this. We are with ALL of our hearts WITH you in this. It has been SO hard for you at times, this journey of forgetting, this traveling road of separation. This road has many curves and dips and turns. We see all these with you, we witness how you crawl at times. How you lay at times. How you feel like giving up at times.

Yet, your heart beats on. Your desire lives on. Your need for love echoes strong inside of you. You do not give up. Your soul carries you forward.

We watch you crawl through glass at times and yet you keep going until the way is clearer. You fight your way 'back' to your heart over and over and then, the fight rests and you are just moving forward because it is what you are called to do on your way to remembering.

We know that you often feel like you are alone. How you feel sometimes that no one else understands and no one else GETS what is happening to you and how you are changing from who you used to be. We feel for you and this struggle that you sometimes go through alone. We feel your loneliness and we ache for you in it.

Yet, this we offer, that you are NEVER alone. Your eyes may see no one else. Your heart may feel sad and alone. Your birth family might reject your changes and who you are becoming. Your friends may not come along. Your mate may not come along or get what you are awakening into. But, you are NEVER alone. As we are always with you and we will NEVER leave.

We feel how you sometimes think you are wrong or unworthy. How you feel that the struggle and suffering are what you deserve. And we want to offer to this part of you that this is NOT the truth. You cannot do anything wrong. You cannot BE wrong. We want to offer to this part of you that you ARE worthy of love, you ARE worthy of awakening, you ARE worthy of connection.

We feel how you forget that you ARE love. You forget how you ARE infinite possibilities. You forget that you ARE infinite awareness. This forgetting was part of the process, the experiment, that we all agreed to. We are here watching over you in the forgetfulness and we feel how you ache to remember again. And, it is TIME for you to remember again (if it is time for you remember).

If you are reSOULnating with these words, then we INVITE you to connect with us. Reach inside for us. Find us INSIDE. You don't have to look outside of yourself. You don't have to look to others, unless you feel that you want and need to. You don't have to be at a special place of attainment or have special gifts. You ARE special just as you ARE and we are RIGHT HERE inside of you, ready and so eager to connect with you.

We are the aspects of you that you feel are TOO MUCH or you have forgotten or you have disconnected from. We are the aspects of you that are from and of your SOUL. We are the multidimensional aspects of your BEing. We are your Angel Selves. We are your Star BEing Selves. We are your Spirit Guide Selves. We are your Divine Selves. We are your other lifetime-Metasoul Selves. We are your Councils Of Light Selves. We are your Star Gates inside and your portals inside and your Star Dust Selves inside. We are your Crystalline Body Selves and your Crystalline chakras merged into one. We are your Merkabah and your inner gridwork connected to Mother Gaia's new gridwork.

Connect with us and we BECOME you. We merge into you more and more and in that merging the feelings of loneliness, the feelings of pain, the feelings of separation, the feelings of unworthiness, the feelings of despair and suffering, the feelings of wanting to die….ALL of it can and will move with this embracement. Embrace us AS you in a process of connection, deeper and deeper, and so you BECOME this. Have a relationship with us as you need to and for as long as you need to as we benefit from this too. And someday, we will become ONE, more and more, and your sense of you will keep changing and changing until you don't really have a sense of you anymore as you just ARE. You just ARE the Infinite Love and Possibilities and awareness that you were MEANT TO BE in Human form.

We love YOU and we wait right here for you, inside you. Come and get us with an open heart and we will become one again. And so, it IS……

~

Conscious Duality And Merging With Our Star BEing Aspects And Metasoul: Journeying With My Pleiadian Self Leeza

She travelled with me today during meditation to one of the 'sister' planets in the Pleiades constellation; sharing the name in Star or Light Language, so it is difficult to translate into English. She is telling me now to just call it, "Moora May" as that is close enough. Moora May is a lush world with bountiful waterfalls, deep jungle landscapes, exotic animals and birds....so many animals! Animals are never eaten here, treated as equal in consciousness (in fact felt to be higher dimensional Guides often from other planets), communicated with telepathically and in Light Language. I am 'visiting' this amazing place to reconnect with one of my many 'home' frequencies, connecting with one of my galactic roots in order to integrate it into my experience here with Gaia.

Leeza offers that our paradigm around Star Seeds is a bit limiting. "You as a soul exist in many dimensions all at ONCE," she explains as we sit on shore of a pool formed from the spill over from a particularly stunning waterfall. "You are not seeded or originated from just ONE planet or galaxy or dimension as your 'star seed paradigm' has offered. You are split off from Divine Source, then your Metasoul represented by what you call as 'Archangels'. From this Metasoul expression, you then prism off into many fractals of you-ness expression. All of these versions of you exist in many timelines, dimensions...."

I feel my soul remembering this, it is soaking it in like the water pooled at my feet. Yet, my mind is struggling, so much 3D conditioning in linear time and in 'past lives' and even in the 'only one star seed origin' paradigm are shifting around and letting go.

"I am just one aspect of you that you are experiencing as 'separate' from you although I am not," she says, her smile so genuine, her teeth so white, her hair bright as sunlight. Her 'beauty' is physical, yes, yet goes so much deeper as it is the peace and integration of her soul frequencies which most radiates out and is perceived then as beauty.

"In my experience with you, we are merging consciousnesses more and more," I respond, smiling back. "You are coming into mine, such as when I am cooking or at the beach or, really profoundly, when I am making love with Raphael! You are coming into all my bodies – emotional, spiritual, mental, physical – and are bringing your consciousness in with you."

"Yes! It is such a joy too. I so enjoy to experience your duality, even though some Humans have made it so bad and wrong. Yes, unconscious duality has led to many wars, violence, greed, hate, separation. We experienced this too as Pleiadians. BUT, conscious duality offers such possibilities! It is the merging of our Oneness experience of life with the beautiful edges of your Human experience. Your capacity to feel emotional states, your experience of feminine and masculine….for example."

I feel my heart and soul and mind light up with the possibilities of conscious duality as her enthusiasm infuses mine. "This message is so important, isn't it, Leeza? We can frame our Star BEing aspects or Star BEings that we 'channel' such as the Galactic Councils as being so much higher than us, as being better, as feeling that we are so 'fallen' and 'dualistic' and 'young' and 'dense vibrationally' that the end goal MUST be to become more like or just like you higher dimensional Star BEings and Angels. I've heard this framed as 'leaving the Human behind.'"

"Aspects of the Human, yes. You are invited to ascend beyond the lower consciousness aspects of Human expression. Evolve into the Sacred Human…..beyond the third dimensional aspects and eventually even the fourth dimensional, in order to experience fifth and much, much higher. YET, the grand Divine experiment is to take the BEST of the Human WITH you, Jelelle. Your capacity to feel, for example, when healed as you have done of so many woundings, is SO wonderful. As I have experienced with you…..your tears of joy, your tears of reunion, your tears of love, your smiles of joy, your smiles of gratitude….oh, I could go on and on! As I have experienced with you this range of higher emotion, it has gifted me with an expanded consciousness and appreciation!"

I take this in, even though she has offered this to me before and is what we have been experiencing together. My Arcturian aspect and guide, Binkh, has also offered this message and energy to me....one time 'coming in' to my body and lovingly touching and appreciating with awe the tears that were flowing down my cheeks and the emotions in my heart. I feel how her and I (and Leeza and I) have much more to explore and learn and teach about this together in the future to help bridge this merging for others as well.

We smile at each other, holding hands, feeling the energies of peace and goodness in this 'place' on the outside and feeling the possibilities of increasing this feeling on the inside.

I am brought out of my meditative space by Raphael, who wants me to take in the two beautiful whales who are splashing together in the bay. I come out onto our balcony to watch them with him....it feels like a male and a female. And in their play and splash, I can feel Leeza's energy and also Leviathan, who is Raphael's Pleiadian Aspect, Guide, and Male 'Counterpart' to Leeza. They are entering our dimensional reality to greet us, to play in our waters, and to invite us to explore the goodness possibilities of our merging our consciousness together. They are offering love in a physical form and I am deeply touched by their efforts to bridge their consciousness with ours on Gaia. And I feel how there are so many awe-some experiences TOGETHER to come!

Bridging Your Emotional Body With Your Star Consciousness

Galaxy in your heart, the stars in your soul....creating a bridge through traversing the waters of the emotional body that hold the pains of undigested experiences from this life, from other lifetimes, from the sense of 'abductions'. The bridge has been purposely blocked by your Higher Self as an aspect of the growth journey. Clearing the blocks is about negotiation with the blocks themselves, offering them love, over and over, until the energy shifts and moves and integrates.

Connecting to ALL THAT IS, following your higher heart consciousness, going beyond your mind, to navigate the multidimensional life, to open beyond what you've been conditioned to believe is real. 3D conditioning, our 'education', what we've learned from our birth families, is SO pervasive, often we can't even consciously know how deep it goes.

All this 3D conditioning creates a filter, an inner matrix, over us and IN us that filters out magic, filters out Infinite Possibilities, filters out shifting timelines, filters out abundance. We choose this filter as we needed it to really GO ALL IN to the experiment of this density. Our 3D Self is created to handle this density and it does this filtering to form a protection layer UNTIL we are ready to see and feel and BE without the filter. Until we are ready to remember and arise into our 4D and beyond self more and more. Awakening removes the filter more and more and LOVING negotiation with the 3D Self to let go and drop away and eventually integrate.

Accessing the Inner Child, connecting and feeling…healing them INside to move from wounded and sad to magical 4D to the Inner Star Child who holds such curiosity and capacity to BE the bridge to the stars. The Crystalline Child energy is in our higher heart. It sits in the seat of our higher heart. It is the 'key' to unlock the Star BEing frequencies, connection with our star family, merging with our Star BEing aspects, hearing the messages, speaking the language. This can trickle in, yet the flood of it comes as the Inner Child feels YOU as a loving energy holding the space more and more so it can let go of the wounded frequencies and vibrate higher.

The Universal grids going crystalline to match the inner grids that are awakening and ascending….tending to the inner grids is what accesses the outer connection. Light waves from the Universe wash in, come in as the heart and soul blocks are healed and 'let down' and 'let go'. Without this negotiation with the blocks this can be painful and hard on the body, symptoms showing up in ringing sounds, heavy bones, hurting heads and necks, sleepy and drifty. All the bodies are connected (emotional, physical, mental, social, chakral, astral) and all impact each other.

Galaxy in your heart, the stars in your soul…..the TRUTH of this becomes revealed as you go within to bridge your emotional body WITH your soul awakenings, your inner space program to connect the inner galaxies with each other, mission to Infinite Love and beyond…YOU are the rocket, YOU are the fuel, YOU are the destination, You are the emotonaut/astronaut. Feeling, healing, INvestigating who YOU are and being willing to not kNOw the answers opens up the vistas of ALL possibilities and experiences BEYOND the self of Infinite Love.

~

Negotiating Your Soul's Desires For Change

Your soul stirs, drawn forward by deep impulses. Like a magnet, your soul is drawn to the light, drawn to love, drawn to growth, drawn to inner transformation that arises then in external manifestation. Your soul wants to move out of suffering and into LOVE, even as the 'suffering' is held as a necessary ground of growth until it is time to let it go.

This soul draw is PURE and connected to your Higher Self, the fractal of you from Divine Source, your Divine expression, your Sacred Human. This draw is resonance, that vibration of "yes!" that vibrates in true tones. This draw is compelling, it invites you to return to it over and over again.

The push and pull, the openings and closings…these are reactions in your 3D Self, within parts of you that have learned to modulate desire and draw. These aspects hover over the aperture of your heart and soul; opening and closing, adjusting based on their perception of safety or comfort or fear of getting hurt again. This adjusting of the aperture can be largely unconscious to you and happens in seconds in reaction to many triggers.

Your soul negotiates, feeling compassion for the push and pull aspects of you. Your soul understands and feels with compassion the fear of change, the fear of being hurt again, the fear of rejection, the fear of re-union because there might be more loss that comes, the fear of the unknown. Self love and compassion in response to the fear is what heals the fear, this your soul knows and remembers.

With loving negotiation, the parts of you that are in fear can move into love and trust. This I have witnessed in myself and others over and over.......when fear is held with connection to it, with desire to understand, with TRUE and PURE compassion for self and others then it can let go INTO love and so becomes love.

Yesterday, during a space holding session with a beautiful soul, we could feel together how all of the life changes she had made very quickly had moved her toward her soul and were inspired by her soul's awakening. Yet, there was a part of her that was still 'sifting through the rubble' of her old life. Ah, it was so tender to see and feel this part of her who was now 'homeless' and in shock in response to so much abrupt change. This part was definitely oriented toward 3D life, and yet, had so many soul gifts to offer her too! I invited her to connect with and feel compassion toward this part of her, to 'collect' it from the rubble site and give this part love so that it could lean into trust with her (the Higher Self frequency that comes through when we 'separate' from the fusion). We also felt that any future changes and shifts in her life could be negotiated with this part of her so that less shock would occur and more acceptance.

Life, the Divine, the Universe, Gaia, your soul family, your soul mates, your own soul desires and awakenings will invite you into making changes and going into the unknown. At first, it may be primarily motivated by getting relief from suffering and yet, also it will be motivated more and more by experiencing more LOVE. To bring the push-pull aspects of yourself WITH you is to consciously connect with these energies inside of yourself. Not to make wrong resistance and fear, yet to feel it and love it is what moves it and heals it.

In SoulFullHeart, we offer space holding sessions that create beautiful room and space for this exploration. From roots to wings, integrating the 'this life' emotional reactions and feelings and woundings with the soul frequencies, karmic playouts, soul gifts of other lifetimes, Galactic Selves, Higher Self expression, etc. is the space that we template and create with you and that you experience on your own more and more. It's a beautiful thing!

The soul will stir, desire, be drawn….it is 'peeking through' in some form of expression in ALL of us. The degree it can vibrate and express AS you is related to how you navigate its desires and longings and draws and the resistances that come up.

~

Responding To ReSOULnance

You feel that soul 'yes!', that reSOULnance, that 'this is ME!' feeling….. what triggers this response, what pushes it up, what elicits it, what calls it forward….THIS is the direction to go in. This feeling of 'YES-ness' is a guide, a marker, a big ARROW of….. 'go THIS way'!

Your soul vibrates with this reSOULnance. Your soul allows the space and room for this vibration that ripples into your world. Your soul allows the tears and smiles of reunion, of remembrance, of longing and desire, of wishes and dreams. Your soul wants MORE of this reSOULnance and seeks for more. Your soul is activated in the process of the remembering and the feeling of reSOULnance facilitates this journey into reclaiming and re-minding.

And, the response from other aspects of you comes often without awareness or consciousness. These aspects, vibrating in lower frequency 3D conditioned places and sometimes in 4D transitional spaces, immediately and so often without consciousness, go into 'quell it' mode. These logical and rational and SCARED aspects say, "That can't work" or "I don't have the money" or "This is too hard" or "This relationship is stopping me" or "It's not the right time" or….many, many such things and ALL with an energy of hopelessness and limited possibilities. All with the energy of fear.

Coming from fear, these 3D Selves of you don't want to get hurt again, they don't want to feel pain again, they don't want to risk for fear of pain coming again, they want to keep life safe and comfortable for as long as possible. They don't want to risk for LOVE because love feels uncertain and, often, unknown. These aspects often have 'good reasons' for feeling this way and the roots of these feelings, when felt by you, CAN heal and let go into more trust and love.

The self limiting thoughts and beliefs conditioned into these 3D aspects comes from our hugely suppressed culture, from birth families that ingrain these energies into our BEings, from relationships in which you shrink and suffer yet keep remaining, from separation and isolation, from capping and blocking the merging of higher frequencies into your consciousness.

What have you felt reSOULnance with lately? What has pinged your soul, chiming and ringing? What has LIT you up and made your sky open up? Maybe it is these WORDS right now!

And, then what? What happens after these words or other things which cause reSOULnance, are digested? How long does the feeling last? What feelings or thoughts come in to suppress it or shift it or close it? What aspects of 3D conditioning raise up to 'argue against' the rising tide of awareness and consciousness?

Feel this and track this inside of yourself and you might be amazed at how prevalent the quelling of your reSOULnance is. And how much energy these fearful thought forms have and how much they impact your capacity to manifest and BE the YOU that you most want to BE, living the life of your soul and heart expression.

ReSOULnance is a gift. A gift that wants to reflect your bigness back to YOU and is NEVER about the source ultimately but about YOU. ReSOULnance speaks of LOVE. It invites LOVE. It IS LOVE…..so, this is the arrow of 'go THIS way' which is ultimately the WAY OF LOVE. The 'right' way is the way of PURE love.

~

MENTAL AREA

The Mental area of life includes your relationship to your intelligence, knowledge, nonduality, and mental-based intuition. We are so much conditioned in 3D life to lead with, develop, and come from our minds….this is the ENTIRE focus of our educational system. We are taught how to kNOw, not how to kNOW. The bits of data and information are stored in our minds, keeping them busy and full and stressed with content and details. Mental content blocks the flow of our intuition and creativity, which comes from a different stream of Higher Self consciousness. The mind dominates our 'space' until it can begin to relax and rest through infusions of soul consciousness frequencies that invite it to let go.

Parts of you 'gather information' during your awakening process to support the shifts that are spring loaded to happen from the source of your soul. Your mind is participating in this learning, as it has been trained to do. At some point, you begin to go beyond your mind and what it can track and learn and into the experiences of soul frequencies coming in and the emotional body, which is nonlinear, beyond time, and beyond the mind. It is not about being 'against the mind' but rather going beyond it into the realms of the imagination and hyper mental activity that cannot be explained or learned, just experienced.

3D: Your 3D Self is conditioned in a big way by the educational system that you engage with from a young age. The public educational system is focused on academic achievement and mental development, which overly develops left brain thinking over right brain, which is more about intuitive thinking. Thinking over feeling is usually the focus, especially in males and masculine-feeling energies in women. Thinking can be used to suppress emotions, intuition, and spirituality.

There can be a strong self image and identity related to mental intelligence which covers over core unworthiness. Lack of relationality usually comes in with high intelligence as core disconnect goes unhealed. The mind dominates your 3D Self as you are fused to it and think it is what you ARE. You can be slave to your thoughts and they tend to be polarized to either positive or negative most of the time, with most leaning towards negativity (depending on what your parental templating was.) You may have 'busy mind' with cluttered thinking, inability to multitask or instead hyper tasking, short attention spans or inability to focus, etc. Rationality can block intuitive thinking and creativity with a high need to have things 'proven as real', especially by science or data or facts.

4D: Your 4D Self is shifting from mostly left brain thinking to right brain thinking. More opening of right brain leads to more intuition and creativity, more capacity to grasp the bigger picture and deeper context. More 'open mindedness' and less rigid thinking. More trust that something is true if it feels true rather than needing everything to be proven through facts. More trust in personal experience over data. As your soul consciousness awakens, your mental capacities shift from just the mind to something much deeper and starts integrating with the awakening heart-based consciousness.

Thinking mixed with feeling is developing and balancing more naturally. Thinking is more clear and, with meditation and other processes, there are less cluttered thoughts, scattered thinking, and busy mind. You may be able to focus for longer periods of time on activities, especially ones that are directly connected to your soul purpose and soul gift expression. You are consciously tracking your thoughts and reframing negativity by being with and feeling the parts of you that hold on to these filters. The upper 4D Self is having tastes of nondual awakenings and loosenings of the mental filters of life.

5D: Your 5D Self is in deep partnership with your mental capacities, which are following behind your heart-based intuition. Your mind is looser, with fewer mental grids to filter reality through. Experiences of the nondual nature of reality are happening more and more as your mind relaxes and lets go of its tight reign on your consciousness. Integration of soul aspects from other lifetimes with sagely access to these frequencies infuse your 5D Self to remember the nondual aspect of reality. Your 5D Self is curious and wants to learn, is always a student, yet the learning is not attached to or used to build up a self image. Learning comes primarily through experiences and remembering and integrating your soul's knowledge and wisdom in balance with your open heart.

Questions For You:

How did you locate yourself related to the mental area of life – as primarily a 3D, 4D or 5D consciousness and why?

What are your frustrations in the mental area?

What are your desires in the mental area?

~

Moving From kNOwing To kNOWing...

In the awakening journey, in this process of ascension.....it becomes more and more about what you kNOW rather than what you kNOw. This is more than just playing around with capital letters. I kept getting offered this over and over and now it has become a sort of mantra to invite us to go beyond the mind. kNOWing comes from higher guidance, soul wisdom frequencies, reSOULnance, weaving in with the higher/Christ Consciousness heart openings. kNOWing is the 4D Transitional Self and the emerging 5D Sacred Human merged and embodying with Higher Self frequencies relating with life through exploration, through curiosity, through risking into the unkNOWn in every moment.

kNOwing is the 3D Self, leading with what the mind has learned, analyzed, digested, filtered and packaged. Non-vulnerable and rigid, kNOwing caps the frequencies of joyful magic that could and can arise in ANY moment. With kNOwing, nothing can arise or surprise as it is 'figured out', its essence drained of possibilities through the figuring and defining.

kNOwing creates a resistive frequency relationship to life and love.

kNOWing creates an open frequency relationship to life and love.

You've been conditioned to kNOwing by a culture that cultivates this frequency as a safety bandwidth. Changing your frequency to kNOWing happens through negotiation with the 3D Self, through letting go of what is safe and known (what has become just TOO comfortable and isn't offering growth anymore.) Letting go of what numbs and dulls and flattens everything into the kNOwing space. Letting go of the mind more and more and moving beyond it, in relationship WITH it yet the soul and heart are leading.

Moving into the kNOW is letting go of the comfortable connections sometimes too and risking to leap, to fly, to lunge off of a cliff and into Infinite Possibilities. A deepening connection, a personal sense of the Divine Source waters the frequencies of inner kNOWing, not book kNOwledge. This HAS to happen inside FIRST, over and over, in a loving self held space (and with a space holder too in phases) creating safety INSIDE that also allows room for trust to arise in the unkNOWn on the outside.

This safety and trust inside makes the jumping-off-the-cliff feeling movements on the outside bearable, enjoyable or INJOYable. It is an internal YES that then can move downstream to the external YES to the kNOWing possibilities in every moment…..

~

It All Comes From Within

Many intense days of body adjustments, realignments, DNA activating, frequency upgrades. I have been in a personal cocoon space to hold it all. I feel like this is ALL so important, this ascension process, and yet I already knew it somehow. I am remembering it. I have been 'receiving' messages, higher dimensional messages for many 'years' yet I never have called myself a 'channeler'. Why? Everything has been so within. That is what has felt natural. Making a relationship with energies inside and calling them 'parts of me' has felt natural and yet, not, at the same time. It has felt temporary. A temporary way to connect. Because, ultimately, I am WHOLE as you are a WHOLE.

The voices and energies that I have 'heard' and experienced of the Divine Mother, Magdalene, Kuan Yin, Yeshua, Metatron, Divine Father, Star BEings, Morgaine and others from Avalon, Guardian Angels, Soul guardians and Spirit Guides…these energies have somehow come from within. I am starting to remember this now. The 'travels' to other dimensions, Avalon, Golden Earth (fifth dimension), and beyond have felt like they are from within my own landscape, which is as big as the Universe.

My mind is trying to digest what my soul already knew. My mind hurt all day trying to understand. My soul felt and feels at peace. The portals are within, the Star Gates, the High Star Councils, the Star BEings. All exist INSIDE. This is simple. And it is from this place that I have guided others to come from….inward, within….only from themselves can awakening, remembering, ascending arise and not from anyone else. It cannot originate from anyone else.

My mind is often looser, and it wants to loosen more. To let go of linear and perfect words, to let energy flow through me, even if it doesn't make mental and linear 'sense.' To be free to let the energy flow that is from within me, the energy flow of (more and more) PURE love.

I have long felt I was a Love Ambassador. Yet, my mind thought that it was from me to others….me to Star BEings, me to Humans…now I can feel that it is me to me that the ambassadorship Is. Me to me, and because we are not separate, me to me is me to you. You to you is me to me.

My mind wants to know if this is 'right', the 'right' approach and feeling. Yet, it just IS, so it is what is remembered and, therefore, right. I don't want to judge right and wrong anymore, or dense versus porous or awakened or not awakened. It is not what we really ARE, only what the mind has filtered us to be.

Letting go of judging, I had to be with the Inner Judger inside, be an Ambassador Of Love to my mind and ego's judgments. 'Ego' and 'Mind' can be judgments too, maybe new words will come to describe these energies, which are just energies of not remembering.

I feel grateful for what is flowing through. I want to jump in joy, my heart does. There is still much to remember but going within, inside, is natural for me. So, there, I am discovering what I am again. What I have always been. What I will more and more reawaken into….and YOU will and ARE too….

~

A DripLine Of NonDual

A couple of months ago during an intense initiatory phase, I asked my Guides for a strong infusion of energy while I was in a meditative state. My Primary Guide/Metasoul Sister Morgaine, who is a High Priestess who lives in the fourth dimension reality of Avalon, provided me with surges and pulses of energy, which ran up and down my chakras and slithered along my spine. It was familiar and yet, also, powerful. I didn't realize how altered I was until later in the day when I was planting seeds in my garden.

I felt relaxed and yet, also, I was struggling to track anything mentally. At one point, I 'lost' my sun hat, which I had placed in the garden somewhere. I had to go up and around the paths many times to find it. This struck me as funny since I designed this garden; I know every path like the back of my hand, and it is not big at all!

Then, I misplaced other things as well and it became difficult to even concentrate on the act of putting seeds in the ground. I got distracted by the wonder of a seed: how it holds all of the DNA for the plant to create itself in all of its form. A seed is in hibernation, just waiting for soil, water, and sun to burst free of its dormant shape and arise into its potential. Much like Human BEings, actually.

I finally decided that I couldn't 'do' gardening anymore and needed to head back home. It felt like it was going to be a long walk, with my altered state of consciousness, yet I also felt a bit giddy with how different things felt. On my way out of the garden, I kept getting distracted by the leaves on the trees. Every leaf seemed to flash its molecular structure at me, a glittery burst of its real essence. There seemed to be a shimmer to everything. I was reminded of how tiny a spectrum of what is actually going on can we see through the narrow bandwidth of visible light.

Although it is normally only about a ten minute walk, it felt like it took much longer to get home. I didn't have many words to share with my Raphael about what I was experiencing, but he could feel I was altered. I didn't want to try to explain it too much as it felt like it would dampen the experience if my mind tried to understand it. And I couldn't seem to do that anyway! When I helped him to get lunch ready, I struggled to get my body to do what my mind wanted it to do. And I couldn't do anything at my usually brisk pace, even in the kitchen. I kept getting distracted by the 'truer' essence of things that seemed to have no relationship to anything else as I would walk by them or go to use them. For many moments, I held an arising wonder of black plastic in my hands before being able to remember that it was a 'spatula'. This 'state' continued on until the late afternoon when finally I could write again and think somewhat normally.

I feel that this condition was, to some extent, what I call a 'drip line of the nondual.' The nondual being a state of consciousness (even though it is not a state) where there are no contrasts, no opposites, and only essence or Arising Isness. The seeds, the leaves, even a common kitchen utensil all took on magical qualities when experienced through the lens of no-thing-ness. Before we were trained to use our minds to dualistically label everything with names and filter reality through comparisons, it feels like this is how we could have naturally experienced life.

In SoulFullHeart, we feel that it isn't about the supremacy of the nondual over the dual or that the ultimate attainment of the nondual is the goal. Rather, it is bringing them into balance again so that our experience of reality flows between the two in a beautiful stream of ebb and flow. Raphael feels that we are 100% of both and have just overly focused on the dualistic side. To bring our consciousness back into balance and awaken to our essence of Infinite Love, we feel that opening the drip line (which could turn into a gushing flow over time) to the nondual is a critical aspect.

For me, the best way I have found to open up my nondualistic nature is during meditative journeys during meditation and energy transfusions which transcend the mind, engage with our true nature AS energy, and bypass our defenses and 3D Self to some extent. I have also had drip line tastes of nonduality through a dualistic relationship with Kuan Yin, an ascended teacher and bodhisattva. Through my connection with Kuan Yin, I am able to receive transmissions of nonduality even as it is coming through a dualistic channel. I don't feel that one cancels out the other and both can be used to experience the other. In this embracement of both, we aren't making one 'bad', which is actually a dualistic way to see it.

It seems that when we resist one side of our nature in order to embrace the other that we become in fundamental struggle with ourselves. This struggle locks down our access to Arising Isness because the 3D Self feels that we need to be 'enlightened' or 'attained' or spend hours and hours in meditation in order to transcend our dualistic nature. Maybe some souls do need hours of meditation every day, yet, my sense is that parts of us have made all of this much harder and more 'exclusive' than it actually is. In my drip line state of arising wonder that day, it felt as natural and easy as breathing. Because my mind was loosened and relaxed, it couldn't evaluate or compare what was going on. It just 'was.'

I look forward to more drip line experiences (with maybe some gushers in the future) and bringing my nature back into balance between the dual and nondual. And I look forward to experiencing and facilitating others in this exploration for which I am hoping that we will discover even more naturally arising ways to experience our essence as Infinite Love in both dualistic and nondualistic forms.

~

A Preschool Beyond The Mind With Kuan Yin

I originally wrote this writing about a visualization visit that I had with Kuan Yin in 2010. I began to experience visualization visits with different faces and energies of the Divine Feminine after I received Reiki energy healing attunement from a Shamanistic Healer. The transmission of Reiki energy seemed to spark soul access in me related to clear communication and experience of the Divine Feminine. Not channeling, per se, as I remained conscious the whole time. I interacted with four specific faces of the Mother and one of them was Kuan Yin.

Before I began to connect with Kuan Yin in the visceral way that I describe below, I had never read anything about Her even as I had received some sagehood teachings from my former Spiritual Teacher, who had practiced Zen Buddhism along with many other things. It was later, after I read more about Kuan Yin, that I was touched to feel how I had seemed to authentically experience Her energy and guidance even without mentally knowing much about Her. My experience went beyond what my mind could know to the place where only my heart and soul could access.

I am sharing this piece of writing again because I have very recently begun a renewed surrogacy time with Kuan Yin. I am engaging in daily meditation with her, inviting Her in for visits with me, and receiving Her guidance. My ultimate desire is to feel our union with each other; to feel how I am Her and She is Me. To feel how none of us are separate; no BEing is higher or lower than the other. I still feel a strong tendency in my soul group legacy to feel I am the student related to such Divine BEings, so this will take some practice. The meditation that I am engaging in is one offered by Martin Birrittella in his book, *The Field: How To Experience The Field Of Love* and it is based on a practice of Hindu saint Chidananda Avadhuta.

    In this meditation, you find a quiet place to sit in comfort. Feel your breaths going in and out. On the inhale breath, repeat the mantra, "Ma" and on the exhale breath, the mantra, "Om". Concentrate on the form of Kuan Yin in front of you or on another face of the Divine Mother. Have your mind become as still as possible. Feel love and honor in your heart for Kuan Yin. See Her all around you, above, below, and beside you. Visualize that your body is merged with Her body while you continue to repeat the mantra of "Ma Om."

    Touch all parts of your body as you continue to repeat the mantra, feeling yourself connect with Her. Continue to touch your body as you repeat the mantra, over and over with love and trust. Feel how you are Her and She is you. As you walk around the rest of the day, feel your hearts merged and connected to each other.

    For me, I also experience a dialogue with Kuan Yin during this process, where She guides me and offers reflections to me before the sense of unionizing begins. She talks more than I do, which suits me just fine.

    Below is the experience I previously had with Kuan Yin in 2010:

    Here is it and I am here. This "it-ness" has been called a "Monday" and each moment has been given a category of a "second" and then a label of a "minute" and "hour" and "date." These are false to the true reality of the moment as there is no time actually, yet only the arising magic of the Divine exhale and inhale that is the uprising breath of the moment. This naming and categorizing every moment in a linear way is false food to comfort the mind, yet I have eaten this diet of dualistic thought forms my whole life.

 I am in preschool again; a preschool that is the real school of life where there are no rules to follow, dualistic concepts to learn, or linear realities to accept. This preschool is where the beginner's mind is not educated and conditioned to become an expert in dualistic reality. It is where the beginner's mind is celebrated and encouraged to become even more childlike and simple and unlearned.

 I am guided by Kuan Yin. She tells me to move beyond past associations and we track lovingly my mind's wanderings together. We track together my mind's seemingly obsessive need to connect and associate everything with something else from my past.

 "Be in this moment," she tells me. "Be stillness in this moment."

 This is helpful. I can BE stillness again after finding myself wandering off into content and into thoughts that only clutter rather than liberate. She offers me the picture of a very still lake and we are sitting, lotus style, at the shore. Peaceful, quiet, stillness, depth.

 Yet the most helpful to me is Her repeatedly saying, "Arise and dissipate." I see trails and streams of life and energy in these words, which repeated often enough cease to have any meaning at all.

 I feel a purifying inside. I feel stillness. I feel liberation from the past, and I feel sleepy. I doze all day, in and out of consciousness and not in pure sleep yet somewhere else, somewhere "not here" and yet "not there" either. Repeatedly Kuan Yin asks me if I am ready to learn more and go deeper. She is a kind yet dedicated teacher, making it safer to explore this unknown ground, the one I have always yearned for. Repeatedly,

I answer Her with a "yes", surrendering my day to spend in this place of not place.

When I take a walk in the park near my home later that night, the flowers arise. The irises in the garden unfold and wink at me. The birds fly very close, nearly crashing into me, and I feel how somehow I have become more of their substance and more of where and what they are. They do not feel separate from me. They feel more kin than the people busily walking by, people not being but doing, and that is OK. I forget words for things and the things become more alive and miraculous in the forgetting.

Arising and dissipating.

I am in awe of the bigger container and canvas of the Creatrix for which all of life is painted upon. I am in awe of the whiteness backdrop of Her genesis.

This is a gift; this no-place yet all-place place that I am in. I wish for it to last forever even as I am offered that, "Forever is as it already is as I AM and All That Is Is."

This makes my mind hurt and get confused in a good way.

The next "day" offers different spaces, different challenges, emotional turmoil, yet the feelings and memories and template of the stillness and arising place remain. They hold it all and She holds me, bearing gentle witness to all that arises and dissipates in my journey deeper into myself with Her.

~

Becoming The Birdsong With Kuan Yin

Sunrise here in Mexico brings an orchestra of bird calls. It starts with the crooning of the rooster at the first hint of the new day and sometimes as early as four o'clock in the morning. The rooster says, "Get up! Get up! A new day! A new day!" This is the first time in my life that I have been woken up not by an alarm clock, but by an animal bred for this function. It is mostly wonderful.

The birdsong then escalates as dawn approaches, so many different kinds of chatters and trills that it seems impossible to identify them all. It is a flurry of noise and, while 'silent' from industrial sounds such as motors and engines, it is by no means quiet here in the early morning at the off-grid ranch where we are currently staying.

This is the time that I feel most open to meditation and connection to altered states of consciousness. I have learned to mostly 'block out' nature's sounds and it becomes background music while my process takes center stage. More about the birdsong in a moment...

This morning, I am floating in "Ma Om" mantra, seeing if my mind can let go and rest in longer stretches without actually thinking about something every few seconds. But, then it is my mind that is tracking if it can go without thinking! Sigh.

As I open to Ma Om, my two quartz crystals I am holding in my hands become burning hot with energy moving through me. Kuan Yin is more of a blur today, less solid, and more an energetic presence. I can feel Her energy but I am struggling to feel my love and adoration for Her this morning. Usually it flows through quite freely and sometimes I can even let in Her reciprocating love for me. Something is blocking my letting in capacity and I suspect it has to do with letting in love on my birthday a few days ago.

Then, I am suddenly engaged in an etheric conversation with Padma – who feels like a Metasoul aspect of mine who lives(d) in India in the year 1930. Padma has been recognized as 'born with strong Atman (internal Godhead) with a strong connection to Brahman-God.' She tells me that she left her family at six years old to go with her Master, Nomanji, to live in his ashram and become a great yogi and saint. This is considered a great honor, but I feel her loneliness.

She is now 18 years old and can't remember what it is like to be a 'normal' person. "All I do is meditate and sleep," she tells me. I ask her if this makes her unhappy.

"If I think of what I am missing...if I think of myself as a self, then I can get sad. But, there is no 'I' there," she responds.

I tell her that I want to help her feel her sadness. Immediately she admits to me that she would like to leave her Master, who is not cruel to her, but she does feel that she has outgrown him. She would like to start her own ashram and she says that there are those who want to be her devotees. I agree to support her emotional process (which she has suppressed and transcended) if she helps me with opening out my consciousness to transcendent frequencies and to liberate my mind more fully.

After we make an agreement, I feel her energy leave my presence and I am alone again with "Ma Om." I feel more open in my heart chakra now that Padma's sadness has moved out. This is when I become aware of the birdsong around me, which seems to have just increased suddenly in volume.

There is one particular bird that is singing at a length and volume that seems to penetrate my field.

Kuan Yin offers for me to, "Follow the birdsong," so I do, turning my attention to it.

At first, I am just listening to the chatter back and forth of this bird and one of its kind in another tree. Then, I feel rumbles of energy move through me with each refrain from the birds. It feels like their song is inside of me. It is a jerky thing because I'm not sure if I like it at first.

Eventually I surrender to it and then I am in flight with every tweet, in motion with every twitter. It is a liberating sensation.

I try not to interpret if there is a message from the birdsong, even though I can feel how they are communicating one to me. I can feel how Kuan Yin is communicating to me through birds, which seem to be one of her favorite creatures to use as a communication medium. This is fortuitous since I happen to live on what is essentially a bird sanctuary, with some very rare and endangered species of birds here.

I just *am* the birdsong and I feel Kuan Yin's encouragement. I am reminded of Her showing me a lotus offering that it knew more about who and what it was because it didn't know and was just Arising ISness. Becoming the birdsong offers the same kind of not knowing and BEing in ISness.

The song tapers off at some point and my attention moves back to me and the start of my day. For a few hours afterwards, I feel a lightness in my mind and a sense of suspended moments without mental tracking…..what I call, 'loose brain.'

And, I am more aware of the birdsong around me and its offering of communion, lightness, and freedom.

~

Going Beyond The Mind, Not Against It - With Kuan Yin

I start these processes without knowing where they will go or lead me; not knowing how they will unfold to offer consciousness expansion for myself; not knowing how they might serve spiritual and emotional consciousness awakening and expansion in others. I follow a desire and from there the form unfolds.

I was led recently by a desire to deepen experiences I have had (even though they aren't 'experiences' in another way) of altered states of consciousness over the years but particularly in the last 18 months. I call these experiences a 'drip line' because while they are strong in the moment of happening, they move on eventually. They feel like a drip rather than a gush, so far. I trust this drip is what I and parts of me can let in right now.

I have a relationship with Kuan Yin that goes back several years to when I was awakened to Divine Feminine consciousness after becoming attuned in Reiki energy healing. The Shamanistic Healer and Reiki Master who attuned me also offered that I turn to Kuan Yin as my personal Spirit Guide and Teacher. My immediate response to her suggestion was to burst into tears. Just the mention of Kuan Yin (who I wasn't really familiar with at the time) brought up a huge surge of heart and soul longing.

Kuan Yin is both (at times) stern sounding but affectionate mother and penetrating Spiritual Teacher. I feel both comfort and discomfort around Her energy. She is both familiar and foreign; nurturing and, at the same time, without a form to wrap around. All these contradictions seem to work for Her though and my heart trusts and loves Her deeply even if my mind can't quite grasp Her. But, that's the point actually.

This morning, during our meditation time together, She inspired me to share regularly about my experiences with Her during this time of surrogacy together and offer whatever message She would like to express through me. I have long ago embraced my soul purpose as Divine messenger and scribe; it is at times a very blessed thing to be and at times can draw misunderstanding and strong resistive projections from others (just as the Divine Mother Herself can.) I feel that we all have the capacity to connect with various forms and energies of the Divine Mother and receive Her messages. Millions of people already do in the form of what the world's religions offer, such as worshipping Mother Mary, even if their religion can tend to filter the purity of Her heart and message.

As I repeated my "Ma Om" mantra while touching my body and feeling my love for Kuan Yin this morning, I noticed the crazy activity of my mind. How the thoughts and mental digestions seemed to 'interrupt' the process every few seconds! My mind wanted to process and package the whole experience before I'd even really had it. I would move my attention back to the mantra and, again, after a few seconds, would discover I had drifted again.

Kuan Yin was with me in this, seemed to feel my growing concern, and we began to dialogue about it.

"Busy mind, yes," She said to me in her penetrating way.

"It is SO busy! I try to still it with these mantras and it gets bored. It seems to rebel and want to gallop away like a wild horse," I responded.

I do believe She chuckled then...laughing with me, not at me.

"Yes, like wild horse. But, why you go against it? What does it want?"

I felt and thought about this for a moment. "My mind says that mantras are too boring. It likes dialogue and conversation. Or to go on creative visualization and etheric journeys like we used to. When it is occupied in 'helping' with these things, then it can let in energies such as Kundalini or the Nondual."

"So, why you not let it?"

"I didn't think that was Ok?" I admit, feeling very much like a beginner in that moment.

"Who say it not OK? Who know what is right for you other than you? You've got a very imaginative mind, Jilly Bird. It is beautiful. Let it help you move beyond it."

I contemplated this for a moment (and so did my mind) and we both felt this sense of goodness about that. Rather than trying to 'tame' my mind, I could flow with it. All of my most altered states had come through letting my mind help take me on an imaginative journey, as Kuan Yin said.

"And," She continued, "Just what do you suppose is helping you talk with me right now?"

I could feel my mind get a bit puffed up, but that felt better than putting it down. "For the last ten years, my process has been about forming relationship WITH and creating negotiation...whether it was with parts of me or with the Divine or with my body. Forming relationship is a dualistic approach though..."

She cut me off with, "Calling something 'a dualistic approach.' These are just words. Other people's words. You follow your own heart, as you have always done. As you teach others to do."

"I offer a path that has worked for me and then, yes, support others to find their own heart and soul way along it."

"So, same for you, J-Bird. Same for you."

I was left with a primary message today that it isn't about going against the mind but rather beyond it. Taking it with you as a helper, but journeying beyond it….where life can then fully take flight, allowing the mind to help you in the journey beyond it rather than fight against it to 'get somewhere'.

~

The Wonder Of Magic Available In Your Inner Child

The wonder of magic is available in the NOW moment....around and through and AS you. The light codes from the sun shining down and inviting the experience of wonderFULL joy and connection to the magics all around. Mother Gaia offering Her PLAYground of natural magics and exploration. The PURE love waves that are all around in every moment are inviting you to experience it.

The wonder of magic can move you beyond the doing. It can move you beyond coming from the mind, the mind tracking EVERYTHING and so experience can't come in. With the busy thoughts of the mind....usually thinking of yesterday or tomorrow and rarely in the NOW......these busy thoughts block the wonder of the moment. These busy thoughts and busy mind coming from a busy aspect of you labeling arising wonder and making it a name. These labels dampen wonder.

Knowing can dampen the wonder of magic too, it can kill it before it can even come into BEing. Knowing that comes from the busy mind and the 3D pain body is about numbing and making reality flat....making it kNOwn so that it can be safe. This is different than heart wisdom or soul wisdoms that are remembered and yet allow for exploration into the unkNOWn in every moment. This knowing is lower frequency and it has layers of unworthiness underneath it and lack of trust in life, love, and the Divine.

The wonder of magic is within your Inner Child and is spring loaded to burst like a comet across the sky. Children feel and come from wonder yet are conditioned to suppress it and to conform and dampen it. Children are conditioned in 3D reality to DO and to KNOW first and foremost...often leaving BEing in the moment far behind as they get older. Yet, it is still inside of you, this Inner Child, and these frequencies of BEing in wonder that you had as a child.

Healing, feeling, connecting with your Inner Child moves you into more and more wonder and magic that eventually expresses as your Crystalline Child essence in 5D. We feel this as an important aspect of ourselves to connect with in SoulFullHeart, many frequencies of hurt and shame and unworthiness contained in the unhealed Inner Child expressing in our lives that through space, time, and love begin to heal and transmute.

The wonder of magic is yours to let in and experience again....it lives inside your Inner Child and can be revealed again as you go within, reclaim and love and embrace this energy inside until it can arise as LOVING WONDER again.

~

SOCIAL AREA

As I reach for me, I reach for you and find that both are right there….every time.

I change and shift and in these twists and turns, you come along by my side…in your own way.

Leaning into me while held in your arms makes the journey that much deeper, better….filled with love.

For this now moment, we belong to ourselves while we respond to this love….moving between us.

You become both more known to me and less known……a comforting mystery.

As I discover myself, I discover you in the same way….the glory of Love arising anew. ~

~

The Social area of life includes your relationship to birth and soul family, friendships, romantic mateships, and Star BEings/star family. As your consciousness shifts to higher vibrational frequencies of love, the type of relationships that you are drawn to and that you draw changes. Your 3D Self sought comfort, while your Awakening Self (4D) seeks challenge and growth in relationships. Your 5D Self or Higher Self, as it becomes more embodied within you, seeks for union while remaining an individual soul spark of consciousness.

Romantic relationships shift greatly too. Perhaps your heart is still hurting from past wounds and hurt experiences within relationships where your 3D Self was most in 'charge'. Your relationships were more about healing karmic binds from other lifetimes (that are still happening) than about transaction of love frequencies in the moment. You are still feeling the energetic binds and cords that run between you and your former partner(s). Feeling leads to healing, mourning what was and what couldn't be and what isn't enough, letting go of the possibilities in order to let in what your awakening self really wants and needs.

~

3D: Your 3D Self receives your main conditioning related to the social area of life from your birth family culture and educational social experiences. Your family conditioning runs particularly deep in this area as it is the practice ground for all of your relationality and impacts you hugely to the degree its influence is unconscious to you. The 'role' that you play in your family forms into a key subpersonality in your 3D Self, especially related to the order you were born compared to your siblings (oldest child, middle child, youngest child, or only child). Your relationships with your siblings, both same gender and opposite gender, impacts the way that you relate with others and parts of you form based on these relationships depending on their impact and influence on you. The relationship grounds tend to be codependent with subconscious agreements to 'love each other no matter what' and without healthy boundary setting. Your 3D Self romantic relationships are more about healing karmic binds from other lifetimes (that are still happening) then about transaction of love frequencies in the moment.

4D: When you are being led by your 4D Self, you are consciously asking questions about yourself, your soul purpose, what you really want in and from relationships. You are looking around with an opening heart and curious soul, wondering if the people currently in your life can come along. You start testing the grounds of these relationships to see if they sustain or if they run out of room to move. You may find that others, even beloveds, are not awakening in the same way that you are. You begin to realize that their journey is different from yours. Your needs are changing as you are changing and awakening. You go through a push-pull with others, perhaps even tugging on them to come with you. Perhaps they tug on you to remain the same. Yet, at some point, you probably realize that you cannot change them, only invite them to come along. And if they don't, you reach a place where you have to let go and trust the deeper love that exists at the core of all relationships.

As you transition into fourth dimensional consciousness and awakening, it begins to become a priority to heal yourself, to love yourself, to mate with yourself first and foremost. You woo yourself, date yourself, give yourself what your previous partners couldn't. You connect with the aspects of you that need parental love, your Inner Child, your Inner Teenager. You find and draw resources outside of yourself to help with this healing of self. You find and draw a soul family community to help with this healing and loving of self. You discover union within, the masculine and feminine inside, and heal the drifts and splits that exist there.

As you become more of your 4D Self, you may draw a new mateship based on heart, soul, and body connection, a true Sacred Union with your Counterpart Soul. This union feels both familiar and also is stunning in the new avenues and vistas that it opens up in you. You are creating inner safety first and foremost, so it feels safer to be vulnerable in this new bond. You are able to express your sexuality more fully as you are opening up sexuality inside of yourself and feeling more and more your own desirability.

You also become more open in 4D consciousness awakening to your star seed roots and origins and to reconnection and reunion with your star family. If you have trauma in your emotional body from 'Alien abduction' experiences, you seek healing from these woundings to be able to become open to reconnection with your Star BEing Aspects, Guides, and family. You may go through a phase of research and learning about Star BEings, transitioning from feeling them as 'Aliens' as you have been conditioned in 3D reality to increasingly familiar and beloved to you.

5D: As you move into 5D consciousness, your relationships deepen and you feel at a fundamental level how everyone is YOU and YOU are them. Previous triggers and reactions, competitive feelings or comparisons are dropped. You are in the moment in your relationships and you are current with whatever reactions or feelings may still come up. You feel moved by the beauty that is every Sacred Human, wherever their 'level' of consciousness is. If you have signed up to experience a deep soul mate union to assist with your expression of your soul gifts and serving love, your 5D Self energies will draw this mateship to you.

You are discerning about who you want to be in relationship with and probably have fewer intimates than many acquaintances with strong soul resonance forming the main ground of connection. Your 5D Self is discerning about the energies that you take in and are involved with, inviting others to be in your higher vibrational frequency with you rather than lowering yours to make them comfortable. And your heart and soul are a beacon drawing others to you as you step into your soul bigness and your gift expression and the reason that you came here this life.

In 5D consciousness states, You embrace and integrate your multidimensionality along with your Star BEing family, aspects, and origins. Their unity consciousness infuses you with frequencies of Oneness and you offer them your ground of ever increasingly healthy and awakening conscious duality. Their consciousness merges in with yours more and more in moments of 'shared consciousness' experience together, shifting between their galactic world experience and your Human one.

Questions For You:

How did you locate yourself related to the social area of life – as primarily a 3D, 4D or 5D consciousness and why?

What are your frustrations in the social area?

What are your desires in the social area?

~

Moving From Sticky Binds To Soul Bonds In Relationships

Entering into relationship is to walk through a doorway offering so many possibilities and opportunities for growth. Relationship with self, relationship with a mate, relationship with soul family, relationship with Guides and Angels and star family. Relationship has been my most important teacher and I its constant student, always learning and growing in response to the invitation of the into-me-I-see that it offers. Exploration of relationship is the exploration of conscious duality for which we hold a consciousness of being separate and distinctive WHILE we feel that we are also One.

In fourth dimensional consciousness, relationship becomes the ALL important ground for exploration….not just ANY relationships or those that you inherited when you were born or through going to school or through duty and obligation or that you drew through personality or persona expressions. But you begin to draw and be drawn to relationships that your SOUL is choosing more and more because of the reflection they offer of YOU, what you can see of yourself and feel of yourself as offered by that person. Your soul chooses consciously; your 3D Self can think it has NO choice. Your soul chooses growth; your 3D Self wants comfort. Your soul chooses to experience joy; your 3D Self will settle for suffering.

The transition from 3D to 4D within the ground of relationships offers so much growth! It can be sticky as the clings and binds are felt, tested, let go of. It can be VERY painful as the soul bravely sees that it is NEVER a victim to any relationship that it is in. The soul accepts ALL relationships as being formed from the choice to experience them or not, in every moment this choice is made, whether consciously or not. The soul spurs on the desire for change, for transformation, for NEW beginnings and holds the fear of the unknown with grace and trust. The soul holds heart space for the aspects of you that need to be felt in their fear, anxiety, depression….ALL are responded to within relationship with you and not resisted or judged as wrong.

Shrinking to fit' in relationships with others is one of the biggest ways that we cap our soul bigness and keep our hearts more closed related to transacting intimate love with ourselves, others, and the Divine. These shrinking dynamics happen when parts of us conform to others' expectations, ideas, and role playing about who we are rather than being who we really are.

Instead of shrinking to fit to maintain the 'old' and comfortable ground of transaction, we begin to stretch and challenge that ground as we awaken and heal into more expression of our authentic self. Real and authentic connection between people cannot be lost, it only deepens and is revealed with healthy shifts and changes in each person. If it doesn't deepen yet instead completes, then the connection was based in more grounds of compensation, codependence, and emotional binds than it was in resonance, interdependence and healthy bonds.

This can be a VERY painful process of completion with much opportunity to feel the deeper aspects of ourselves that were being mirrored and projected in the relationship onto the other person or people. Held with love and an open heart, the process can be very transformational with a possibility of new openings in the future in the relationship.

The intense energies of PURE love that are washing down on us and the shifts in the consciousness frequency that is available to us as a species to help us ascend ARE impacting our relationships of all kinds. The soul cannot live in inauthenticity for long especially with the help of these love waves. The soul WANTS more love, not to settle for crumbs, it wants the full MEAL deal in all areas of relationships in our lives.

These PURE love waves are reminding us of our relationship with Divine Source AND our origins as a fractal from Divine Source. It is a reminder that we ARE love ultimately and all of our relationships can reflect this love that we ARE. If your relationships are not reflecting this but are rather reflecting unworthiness, disconnect, conflict, tension....this can be a sacred and necessary phase for your growth. Yet, also, you can move OUT of this phase if it feels like it is time to do so. It feels like more and more souls will be choosing to complete and move on from relationships that do not deeply nourish their souls and reflect their growing self worth and embodiment of their soul-Higher Self expression and healing heart.

The most important relationship, of course, is with yourself and the energies for which you hold and respond to yourself and all aspects of yourself. This can be challenging with unfelt textures and feelings in the 3D emotional pain body, subconsciously buried, that are wanting and needing to be felt, healed, and integrated. The self to self LOVE relationship invites these aspects into reality and does NOT deny them even if there is strong soul access to higher frequencies of love and light. What you resist persists anyway and the emotional pain will be there, waiting, until it is responded to with love. You cannot really avoid or bypass it. And, in the meantime, your outer relationships will probably reflect this unfelt pain in same way or form.

Relationships are KEY in ascension. Being unconscious about them (again with self AND with others) does impact your capacity and ability to experience higher vibrational frequencies. It does impact your experiences of reality. And, beyond that, SO MUCH nourishment and love is there, just waiting, within the possibility dynamics of any relationship based in the soul and healing heart!

~

Is It Time To Complete Your Lone Wolf Phase?

You are not alone. You were not meant to do this journey alone. You come from a Divine Source that invites you to embrace and remember this. In this embracement, you no longer feel alone. Divine Source is the home frequency for which you can return over and over to remind yourself of where you came and where you will eventually return.

The sky of your third eye or sixth chakra (energy center) world is filled with Light BEings that want to support you, care for you, and infuse you with their higher vibrational frequencies. You come from them. You ARE them and connection with them creates the foundations for the remembering of this. In the most vibrant and radiant Archangel is the reflection of your sparkle, your glow, your warmth.

In your Lone Wolf Self is the habit to be overly self sufficient. It has been a necessary phase that your soul chose to navigate the denser frequencies of third dimensional reality. This lone wolf energy, this self protection, has been necessary to move through life with an overloaded emotional pain body and undigested karmic infused soul field. It is overloaded and feels tired from carrying this 'burden' alone. This lone wolf needs to feel that there is a higher self embodying YOU that is ready and able to ask for help to carry the load of what you are here to heal and feel as a soul.

Golden community, higher vibrational community based on soul resonance, offers the lone wolf in you a place to land, a pack to join. This can be challenging as so much wounding is experienced in birth families that vibrate in 3D frequencies of separation, comparison, fear, and unworthiness. Karmic binds and ties that remain unfelt and unforgiven and undigested create a pack of codependence rather than interdependence where each individual soul is honored yet still a cherished aspect of the collective.

Healing these karmic binds is a ground found through going into intimacies, especially with those for which you feel soul family resonance ground. Within these intimacies, you start to feel safe to heal, to explore, to express, to journey. These intimacies can be a soul mate bond, soul friendships, and, as will form more and more, soul family communities based on awakening, authenticity, and connection. This type of higher frequency community is what we are exploring in SoulFullHeart. Within it, I've found the deepest ground of healing, awakening, and ascension in relationship with others on the same path.

You are not alone. You are not meant to do this journey alone even as part of you may feel that way and resists asking for guidance and help from another. A loving space holder and guide can provide a space to land, to feel what has been too painful to feel, to access what has been unable to be reached on your own. You cannot see and hold all aspects of this journey and sometimes need someone else to walk along with you who is travelling the same ground.

The Universe supports the asking of help, the reunion of needing each other in ways that actually empower and light up your sovereignty. The Angels and even the Archangels are available instantly once you ask for their love and guidance. They are eager to help. The Divine wants to support your surrendered leaning into of the best of what It can provide at whatever level you can let it in.

Reach out. Ask for what you need. Get ready to receive and let in. Hold the parts of you that are afraid with lots of care and love. It is time. You can no longer do this alone nor were you meant to. Claim what is your birthright and all that you need will become available from there.

~

Opening The Cosmic Christ-Universal Love Heart Chakra To Feel Forgiveness And Compassion

Opening your Cosmic Christ love heart chakra is to open your heart to feel the cries of the world. The cries of the world are easy to pick up as the pitch is so high and so pressing right now, yet they can be difficult to digest. Feeling the cries of the world can lead you through necessary phases of activism and advocacy. In this phase, you are compelled to fight for justice and to shift the exterior realities of the world.

And, you may move through this phase into a place of acceptance and seeing that every soul chooses their own journey. EVERY one. You may feel how the injustice actually begins from within and that the real protest originates from within. Every person and situation that you have advocated against lives inside of you (most likely in shadow) somewhere. As you shine the light of self love on the shadow within that comes from your undigested pain body, unhealed karmic binds, and within the collective unconsciousness, the frequency of protest shifts to forgiveness. The frequency of outrage shifts to compassion. The frequency of separation shifts to connection.

As you shift your sense of authority over your life to within AND to a surrendered sense of the Divine and your higher self, you no longer feel that any outside authority is doing anything TO YOU that can cause you suffering. You cause your own suffering by drawing these frequencies to yourself.....until you no longer need them. Until the frequency of love has replaced the suffering.

All of these phases are sacred and necessary and every soul is different. We are receiving so much support from Archangels, Angels, Spirit Guides, and Star BEings to move into a higher vibrational frequency of heart, to open the cosmic heart chakra of Gaia (which seems to be located in the new crystalline grids around Glastonbury, England), and this energy cosmic heart frequency is available to all sentient BEings on Gaia to choose or to reject.

Your compassion, gratitude, and forgiveness are higher frequency vibrations templated by the Cosmic Christ heart. Feeling them firstly and most deeply for yourself opens out their access for you to feel them toward others. This allows you to feel the cries of the world, to serve love, yet not become the cries of the world, tied into suffering over suffering.

The cries of the world are easy to feel. These cries vibrate in so many ways, especially the lower frequency ones of pain and suffering. So many souls incarnating on Gaia during this time of great transition have chosen to experience the ground of suffering as their growth path. The lessons learned and the gifts gained from moving out of a suffering relationship to life and into one based on love is a profound one. Each soul is walking this path of remembrance of moving out of suffering in their own sovereign way at their own sovereign pace.

When I first could feel the 'cries of the world', it was overwhelming to my emotional pain body, which still had many layers of resonant woundings and relationship to suffering over my suffering. I was awakened to this frequency of feeling the world after becoming Reiki attuned in 2010 and experiencing powerful surrogacies with the Divine Feminine Ethereal Teachers and Angels, Kuan Yin, Mary Magdalene, Mother Mary, and Kali or Dark Mother. This is also an aspect of the moving through 4D awakening consciousness, to 'wake up' to the suffering on a collective scale. In response to this activation of what is often called the 'cosmic heart' or the 'Christ Consciousness heart', parts of me became outraged at the 'conditions' of the world. Part of me was looking for someone to blame, someone to hold accountability for all of the suffering in the world – the hunger, the violence, the greed, the devastation of Gaia, the cruelty toward animals. I watched documentaries that were hard to watch, as emotionally sensitive as I was, and I cried and cried and raged too for the people, animals, nature that was in suffering.

It was an important phase for me as it also opened my compassionate heart eventually toward those who part of me felt had done me harm or hurt me. If I could feel compassion for the ENTIRE world and its suffering, then certainly I could feel it for myself and those who had supposedly 'wronged' me? Compassion is the root of forgiveness as is gratitude. It was a process of holding space for myself with the loving support of Raphael and my Guides and eventually holding space for others too that healed the root wounds inside of me that blocked compassion, gratitude, and forgiveness.

Eventually, the need to advocate and be an activist in a 'going to battle' energy faded for me. The sense of truth about the state of suffering and pain didn't leave my consciousness, yet I shifted to feeling how I could inspire and teach and serve love through sharing MORE love and offering safe space for the exploration of suffering within. It feels like in the awakening out of third dimensional consciousness of separation, many souls need to become advocates and activists to push away the conditioning that they have received and claim something that resonates more deeply with frequencies of justice, truth, and love.

Some souls get 'stuck' in this place, looking outside of themselves for the changes that can actually only happen from within. They are looking to authorities to lead them and to guide them, to have power over them….until they are ready to claim their own authority, lead themselves, guide themselves, and feel how true power originates from within. When we look to an outer authority (such as the government) to determine our fate, we are in a space of helplessness and powerlessness. This is the same way that we felt as children related to our parents and other authority figures.

On some level, protesting against anything outside of us is a reflection of an inner protest that is going on related to part of us. This stems from either an undigested and unfelt part of us that has been placed in shadow (such as our narcissistic side, our judgmental part, our suppressor of others, etc.) It is so challenging to even admit that we have these aspects inside of us yet we ALL do as we are ALL connected to each other and to the collective unconscious.

When you are willing to embrace these aspects of yourself, you stop protesting them inside and this changes how you feel and react to the representation of them outside of yourself. A personal example is how I related to my former

Spiritual Teacher Daniel and how my feelings toward him shifted as I connected with an aspect of myself that was just like him. Daniel served my heart and soul awakening to so many amazing frequencies for which he bridged the access that was already inside of me. Shadow aspects of him that needed control over my process and all the others that were part of his group played out because each of us allowed them to. After close to five years in his spiritual group and three years as a facilitator of his Emotional Body Enlightenment process, I reached a ceiling in remaining in the group anymore.

I was waking up to my own authority and autonomy, which was just amplified and mirrored by the deep love and soul connection that I felt when Raphael and I began dating. We were only dating for three weeks when we received an ultimatum from Daniel that our relationship was deeply codependent and we could not see each other for a year if we wanted to stay in the group and if I wanted to continue being a facilitator. Raphael had been having sessions and involved in the group for three years so this was a very big deal for both of us.

The decision to leave the group, while very difficult, was made easier by the commitment that Raphael and I felt to explore and be with our relationship AND a voice of guidance that I felt resonate inside of me saying, "NO more suffering." I left the group and the very close and intimate soul family members of it that felt that they could no longer talk with me (and they really couldn't because Daniel would have 'kicked them out' too.) Oh, such a wave of emotions for the next year (and on) as I digested this dramatic shift in my life.

I felt like I was in the Dark Night Of My Soul with no desire to heal or teach or learn. Parts of me felt so devastated and rejected and angry. I went through a necessary phase of researching about and advocating against Spiritual Teachers like Daniel, whose unhealed shadows play out in abusive and controlling patterns with their followers. I wrote and read many articles about cult leaders and the dynamics in cult-like groups, wanting to digest my feelings through understanding others' experiences in similar dynamics. I published a book about my experience in the group and received positive feedback from others who felt it helped them digest their experiences too.

Eventually, and now nine years later, I came to accept that my soul had signed up for this very specific experience with everyone involved agreeing to 'play their part' ahead of time for the benefit of all. Daniel was playing out karmic binds with me in an often confusing playout of father, teacher, romantic interest, and God projection. I came to a place inside of feeling genuine forgiveness for him as I more deeply forgave myself for drawing and needing the experience. I came to a place of even feeling compassion for him when the group that had been so loyal to him for ten years and more crumbled around him and rejected him. I knew what it felt like to be lonely and to lose almost everyone that you felt that you loved deeply….even as he had created the situation himself.

Forgiveness and compassion, even for those we feel have harmed us, is a big aspect of the opening of the higher or Christ Consciousness heart. When we can genuinely feel forgiveness, even if we choose NOT to be in relationship with the person, then we are 'freed up' from any energy entanglements with them. We can truly 'move on' in the grounds of our emotional bodies and there is new space made to let in the nourishing relationships that we most want and deserve.

~

Moving Into Unity Consciousness: No Longer Needing To Contend, Prove, And Judge Ourselves Or Others

Some things came up in the interview that Raphael and I did for the YouTube channel Nature Of Reality that I felt to expand on more. We were asked a few times to make distinctions and clarifications, to get specific in a detailed way related to ascension, sometimes with an energy being invited to prove what we were saying or a 'how do you know?' related to what we were offering about reality.

While some specific distinctions and delineations can be useful, there can also be a lot of intense energy caught up in defining and proving....there can also be a lot of contention too between different viewpoints within spirituality, wanting to argue against this or that perspective with much labeling going on. It feels to me like the mind wanting this definition, the 3D self and the unaware (or fused) ego, rather than to be in the unknown and also parts of people that are in a battling place inside and so projecting that on the outside.

To argue against anything, to contend, is lower vibrational energy. This doesn't mean that we agree with everything and have no personal opinions. We ARE and BE in our inner truth that comes from our hearts and souls and offer it to others to resonate with or not. We INVITE, not contend. We allow our reality to BE and invite others into it. Others either resonate or they don't yet we don't feel a charged reaction or a need to defend or contend or prove if they don't resonate.

Being able to feel this sense of self worth and self containment, this sense of OKness without contention, has arisen inside us primarily through the parts work process we have engaged with where we respond with love to any energies and aspects that want to contend and be against, that want to fight from within us. We feel and hear them, connect with them INSIDE and negotiate with them and with love the fighting energies move and settle out of frustration or need to fight and into love. This is an inner process though that changes how you feel and relate to others on the outside, which is the only way that anything changes of your outside experience

I also offered a few times in the interview that EVERY phase is sacred within every soul's journey. I don't resonate with using the word 'sheeple', for example, to describe those souls engaging in the 3D consciousness journey because it immediately cuts off love in how it is held. It contends for something

AGAINST others, rather than feeling that those souls are where they need to be and that it is a sacred place they are in. A place that I have been many times as a soul and spent some of life in during THIS life. I don't judge my inner 'sheeple' as I LOVED this part of me and worked and connected with her for many years in order to have my soul consciousness come in to offer her a new possibility of awakening beyond what she had been conditioned to. Because this inner love of my 'sheeple', I can invite others into experiencing something MORE from a place of true self love.

    There is much comparison in spirituality too....amongst who is more awakened or enlightened and who is not and why. I don't feel to engage in this energy either as it creates separation and fear, it feels like it comes from unhealed Inner Punisher again, an energy that judges without love. Discernment WITH love invites others into resonance and then lets go if they don't and yet STILL loves them even if not able to be in relationship with them. Also, when we are coming from true self worth then we don't feel the need to compare to others around where they are 'at' in their spiritual journey in order to prove to ourselves that we are further 'ahead'. We can feel the sense of BEingness about our reality and, again, invite others to share in it and serve love WITH them if they feel that we can as they become more empowered in self love WITH us.

    I do not hold absolute truth about anything that I offer or teach or share, yet rather an arising sense of possibility inside of myself, an arising timeline really, that I offer with a clarity that just resonates inside of me in the moment. It is not THE truth as I feel there are Infinite Truths, Infinite Possibilities playing out in every moment. I offer A truth.......usually a different way to see or feel something, hopefully love-based, coming from someone who has spent many years deconstructing and deconditioning from so much of what we have been taught as reality, offering a new reality and alternative to what has been based in fear.

Even as I am offering this, I feel love for the souls that need the contending, the defining, the proving...as, again, it is a sacred aspect of their journey. I had my phase of this too, especially related to awakening to the conditions of suffering in 3D reality of so many people and animals. There is a phase of being outraged and advocating for change and, on a certain timeline, it seems to be necessary. I am in a different place now where the outrage has been replaced by a sense of trust that it is all playing out as it should, no one is a victim in a higher soul sense, and it is all held by and offered by love finding its way back to love.

~

Let Them Arise Anew For You In Relationships: Conversations With Archangel Metatron

I am sitting on a step that is part of a circular round of steps, in a place high up in frequency surrounded by golden white light. It feels like high altitude and my consciousness goes in and out, drifting here and there, returning to the denser dimension and content of where my body lies on my bed and back up again.

"Where are we?" I ask Archangel Metatron, who is 'sitting' on my right side. He sort of hover sits, crouches really, sometimes appearing to float above me and then sit next to me again, often in the same moment. This sense of his multi-dimensionality and physicality being in different places at seemingly the same moment helps me to feel how time and space are not real and certainly they are NOT linear.

"We are in what you have called in your religions, 'Heaven'. What you've conceived of Heaven from your 3D perspective is actually the fifth dimensional consciousness realm – or what you call 'Golden Earth' that Gaia is now moving into as a planetary consciousness. Where we are now is higher than that. It is what is called the Seventh Heaven or seventh dimension."

"I feel joy at that, Metatron, and being in this place. It doesn't feel as important to figure out what its name is or to locate it in some kind of cosmological picture. It just feels good to be here and…..heart opening," I say, with a smile on my face. This smile is just there when I connect with his energy, even when something emotional is moving through. Often I have tears too, leaking down my cheeks without runny nose, just pure joy and reunion, higher frequency tears. I know this is when I have taken my heart with me to these higher frequencies. This is when my Cosmic or Christ Consciousness heart is open and letting in at the emotional body level and not just the astral, etheric, or sixth and seventh chakra level.

"Yes, your tears are a sign of your heart lotus opening and coming with you," he says, 'reading my thoughts' as we are communicating not out loud but on multiple levels at once. Sometimes I just see geometric shapes hovering around me or feel huge surges of orange gold energy that feels like the sun move through or we exchange many words spoken in Light Language or multidimensional language, which I have asked him to help me remember.

"It feels so important to bring our heart consciousness with us as we explore these higher frequencies. I mean this is a repeated message I have received over the years from Ethereal BEings. I explored this on my own through the emotional body healing path I was part of and got a big lesson in karmic binds, and deep healing, too through being part of that group and then leaving it when the lesson had been learned. Then, I connected deeply and remembered my soul legacy of Divine Feminine frequency awakenings and the energies of Kuan Yin, Mother Mary, Magdalene, Kali….they all came through to support this message of necessity for heart healing, for emotional body healing."

I feel the energy then, a light pink and light blue energy of Divine Mother frequency which begins to surround us like a warm bubble. I breathe it in deeply, into all of my chakras…all seven main ones and the five cosmic ones that I am reactivating with Metatron's help. The Divine Feminine energy invites me always deeper into my heart, into my forgiveness of self, into my acceptance of myself, into my love of others, into service of love.

"Thank you so much for coming here," I say to Her, the Divine Feminine, the Divine Mother, the heart of my soul, the heart of the Universe, the heart of the Divine.

I feel Her energy move into my heart chakra, which is feeling more and more like a lotus with many petals, each petal symbolizing a karmic journey and a heart chord bond and heart binds too. Each petal opens as it receives more love and healing through more connection from within and from Ethereal BEings and the Divine Feminine energies especially. Metatron adds his masculine, golden orange energy to Hers and I am lit up, heart expanding, tears flowing.

It feels as if the whole Universe is inside of my heart and I am inside of theirs. A deeper sense of the connection between us all accompanies this feeling and surges of Divine Masculine and Divine Feminine energies dance together, play together. It is this union of masculine and feminine that invites us to journey into our hearts, which initially and in phases feel like a dense pain body to us. But I can feel with the lightening of the emotional body, the healing of pain in so many layers, how the heart is NOT pain at all and that there is NO pain body, it dissolves as it is felt with love, heals, and transcends into something else.

I feel the tendrils and chords of love and bond that I have with the most beloved souls in my life and the sparkling new energy of those who are entering my soul field in response and resonance to what we are offering with SoulFullHeart.

"Let them arise anew for you," offers Metatron, with a fresh wave of his energy seeming to rush through my body. I feel a new lighting up of my Merkabah (or fifth dimensional light body and energetic flow vehicle for multidimensional travel) with this and a deeper connection with All. In his offer of arising anew, all those souls that I know and have known and will yet come to know seem to, indeed, come alive and new for me.

I feel a sense of mystery, awe, and invitation about everyone in my life arise in me, even about Raphael. He is still in the same physical form, yet, we have experienced in many moments as we deepen in our awakening and ascension journey together and we continue to go within in profound ways that we become both more known to each other on a soul level as we remember our connection and, also, we become more unknown in the ways we have previously experienced here in 3D filtered life.

I take the message of "Let Them Arise Anew For You" and the powerful invitation of feminine and masculine dance that I received deep into my heart and into my day. And I invite you to feel into this message related to your own life as well. What does it mean to allow someone to arise anew for you in your life? Can the relationship arise anew? Is it based on enough soul resonance and transformative edges to allow for this experience? Is it more karmic binds or soul and heart bonds? As you shift and grow and change, does what you experience as other, outside of you, grow and change with you?

It is a powerful message, offering much invitation for new experiences and perhaps necessary completions and shifts. Whatever transacts it is held with love by love and for love....this you can trust.

~

How You Allow Others To Treat You

How you allow others to treat you is always a reflection of YOU....others represent aspects of yourself that are in shadow or in light, need love from you, need connection with you. Others can't do anything to you that you don't ALLOW to be done. Often it is subconscious (and soul buried) woundings rooted in unworthiness that draw these behaviors, actions, and reflections from others.

When you are loving yourself, ALL Aspects, and healing your own worthiness, you no longer NEED these reflections from outside of yourself. You no longer draw them. Your vibrational frequency of self love and worth is too high to draw them to you anymore.

You are not a victim; you are all powerful and all that you experience in your environment or outside of you that you have created from inside and agreed to be there.

To feel this and let this in reconnects you with your inner power, inner worth, and inner soul bigness. There is so much love available from within and when you tap into this source, it then overflows to your outside experience with others who reflect the love that you ARE back to you.

~

Why It Can Be Challenging To Set Boundaries In Relationships

I feel setting a healthy boundary with someone in a relationship as being about the sense that we can no longer be in relationship with them or we need space from the relationship because it isn't healthy or self loving for us to do so or because we just don't have the reSOULnance value ground to BE in relationship any longer (even as love remains). A 'porous' boundary would be one that is open to being changed if the person changes or if the ground of the relationship becomes healthier through inner healing work, soul awakenings, or shifts and choices that happen.

This process of boundary setting and perhaps taking space in relationship or breaks is an important one related to our ascension process and arisement of our 5D Self as every relationship we are in is an energy exchange. It is a key aspect of growing and arising into our soul self as every energy we engage with is a reflection of us. This process of sorting through relationships and setting and BEing boundaries is an aspect of the transition and awakening into your 4D Self.

Every boundary has a door, just as every fence has a gate. Healthy boundary setting can be done with an open heart, with love and compassion for both the person and ourselves, and before the relationship reaches high levels of toxicity or codependency that is harmful to both sides. This is challenging in our culture, however, and most people struggle a lot with this and how to BE with it.

Why is it so challenging to set boundaries with people in relationships, even when the level of abuse and toxicity is obvious to us? There are many possible answers to this question that could be applied in a universal way even as every individual situation is different.

1) One of the reasons it is so challenging to set and BE in healthy boundaries is because most of us received no modeling on how to do or be this with our caregivers AND we weren't 'allowed' to set any boundaries with our families prior to adulthood.

We are such sponges, absorbing all the energies and emotional tones of our families as we grow up. By the time we are teenagers, we are so filled up with these tones and energies that part of us begins to rebel against what we had no choice in absorbing, which is a form of boundary setting. Some of us continue this rebellion until adulthood and eventually our boundary setting with family may end up being a complete push away or break from them for a phase of time or for life. Most of us as children are not invited to set boundaries with our family members and we wouldn't anyway because of our food and shelter needs that they provide.

3D conditioning is that we are required to deal with whatever we are given or however we are treated without advocating or defending ourselves and without the opportunity to say, 'No'. So, we learn how to live with what we inherited and the cost to the expression of our authentic self and the development of the ability to set boundaries out of self love is hugely impacted. Basically, we literally have 'no idea' how to set healthy boundaries because we didn't 'see' and 'learn' how to do it from our families.

2) This leads into the second reason, which is that we don't have enough self love or core self worth to lead this navigation of boundary setting. In SoulFullHeart work, core self worth is something that emerges after much processing with the parts of us who don't find us worthy and yet are tasked with protecting and defending us, such as our Inner Punisher-Critic, our Protector, our Inner Matriarch-Patriarch, etc. These parts of us have developed as internal voices and energies inside of us because of the energies and tones we took in from our caregivers.

It is actually an aspect of our self-defense structure to develop these parts of us that keep the messages running that we 'are not worthy of love' or 'are unlovable' or 'are crazy' or whatever the message is. These parts are actually trying to keep us safe by knocking us down first before someone else does (which is what happened in childhood) or before we get too 'big' and do unsafe things. I know this sounds strange, but over eleven years of working with people in subpersonality work, I have seen this over and over again. And, of course, I have felt this in myself. Without an innate sense of core self worth and self love, it is very difficult to say 'no' to unhealthy frequencies. Saying 'no' means that we are saying 'yes' to what nourishes us and that we feel that we are worth it.

3) Boundary setting can be challenging because we don't know which ones to set and which part of us is doing it. Sometimes it can feel like we are setting healthy boundaries because part of us has said 'no' to something or a relationship and is shutting it out, but it actually IS necessary for us to go into it or it could lead to our next growth place to go into it. Parts of us (the Protector again primarily) actually like saying 'no!' but it

can be misdirected and misplaced. This part of us can say 'no' to people who are trying to help us by no longer enabling us or by bringing us a tough truth that we don't want to see. Or this part of us can say, 'no' to changes that we need to make or tough conversations that we need to have that could bring conflict and more changes. So, this can be a confusing ground to navigate and asking, "Which part of me wants this boundary and why?" is very important.

4) Boundary setting can make us look 'bad' or 'not nice.' For the parts of us that care about our self-image or how others perceive us, it can be very uncomfortable if we are judged by the person (or others) that we are setting the boundary with as mean or not nice. We are so conditioned in our culture around 'being nice' and that it is a 'good thing'…..even as most relationships, if you go deeper, have a layer of toxicity and falseness in them that has nothing to do with being 'nice'. Many people would rather preserve the self image of being nice even with someone who is NOT nice with them and actually treats them badly. This behavior pattern has usually been strongly modeled by one of our parents or both of them.

5) It's challenging and nearly impossible to set boundaries with others if we haven't set them with parts of ourselves. This is a crucial aspect of parts process work: learning when to set a boundary with a part of us when we identify and feel that we don't want their behavior to continue because it is isn't self loving. We literally have to set a boundary with them as the 5D arising Higher Self sometimes in order to be 'bigger' than the part of us. For example, we feel love for the Inner Punisher even as we set a boundary with this part of us to stop beating us down with self judgments. Or we have to say 'no' to certain things which parts of us use to keep us numb to our deeper feelings. Our growing 4D and 5D Self learns to do this in a loving way that is both strong and open. When parts of us feel this energy of healthy boundary setting arise in us, they lean into it. They have been waiting for it our whole lives and parts of us become

relieved because finally an 'adult' is home to say what is nourishing and healthy and what is not.

Boundary setting transforms relationships, either by closing them down for a period of time or by opening them up to something new. In my experience, both sides benefit from healthy and porous boundary setting, even if one side is leading it (which is usually the case.) Boundary setting doesn't have to be a 'one time' thing in relationships with a dramatic declaration and big fallout, although that is often what happens if it hasn't been done consistently.

In healthy and authentic relationships, boundary setting is something that is being talked about and negotiated, something that just happens organically and, in an intimate relationship, sometimes several times a day. And, it is porous…meaning it shifts and changes based on the current conditions. It can be porous if both people are working on healing their hearts through subpersonality work and if they are dedicated and committed to serving the LOVE in the relationship. And it feels like in relationships that are mostly based in 5D consciousness frequencies, boundary setting is not even necessary as the Oneness connection and soul ground flows within the relationships in most moments.

~

Making Heart Room For Your Mate To Enter Your Life

I felt him before we were together. I could lie in my bed and feel his arms around me, sense his heart beat flowing along to mine. I had conversations with him that were so provoking, the deepest of context, the most enlivening of content. My laughs responded to his smile, his wit, his humour with absolutely no meanness. All of his passionate energy focused on me, I unfolded in his arms and in his heart gaze, over and over returning to the essence of me through what he could see.

This is how it felt for me even before Raphael and I began dating each other eight and half years ago. Many nights before we went on our first date, I could feel his energy in my field as my 'next and probably most important mate'. I didn't know that it was him specifically but feeling into it now, it is so clear that it WAS him. And similar to how a pregnant mother begins building a nest for her new baby, I started to build a nest in my heart and in my life getting ready for him.

This all feels so romantic, this story of falling in love and being in love and arising in love, even many 'years' later still we are falling in love together. And, it is, yes, romantic. Yet, also, love like this with what is truly your heart, soul, and body mate is a challenging crucible. Often when this kind of love enters your life, much has to be let go of in order to let it in. All the furniture of your old life gets rearranged in rapid fire. Relationships get sorted out fast. How are you going to let this intense new energy into your life? How are you going to make room? What fits with these soaring, new, enlivening, heart opening, and soul expanding frequencies and what doesn't?

For example, within weeks of starting to date each other, Raphael and I experienced the collapse of the spiritual practice, paradigm, and group that we had been deeply involved with for many years and within which we met each other. I was a facilitator of this work for years, deeply committed to my process as was Raphael. And then, we were challenged to choose our new emerging love over that which we had previously placed our devotion, which was the group.

The choice was easy in one way as my heart and soul just knew there was no going back out of this kind of love. A love I had been wanting for so very long. So, I said 'yes' even without knowing if it would continue to open out between Raphael and I. All of the people in the group, my deepest and closest soul family at the time, no longer would be in relationship with me, so I had to let go overnight of so many previously very meaningful connections. And of the paradigm and process which had felt like my soul purpose path. The heartbreak of this spiraled me into a Dark Night Of The Soul where I literally felt like I was splintering into many pieces, going crazy, and the only heart rails I could feel were the incredibly touching love with Raphael and a supportive frequency of love with the Divine.

Many other shifts and changes have come and been chosen over the years, catalyzed by the love that moves between Raphael and I. Geography, relationships, money earning, belief systems…we have let it ALL go many times over the years. Yet, we have always let go of it together. And, in some moments, we have uncomfortably held the possibility that our union too is complete and that we need to let go of it. Always our own individual growth is primary and comes first. Fortunately, so far, our togetherness has served our growth and so we keep on finding our way together.

My heart is opening in this moment in large part because of what I experience with Raphael on a daily basis. We are two individuals, yes, and we are also within a union of feminine and masculine. This, I believe, is truly possible for anyone who is awakening and healing their heart and soul woundings to open their capacity to give and receive love. This process sends your beacon out into the world, which your mate hears and feels.

I do believe mates are 'already within each other' as the poet Rumi offers. So it is inevitable that yours will find you and you will find them. And, most likely, your life will change in very significant ways once you do. In the meantime, you can prepare your heart and soul through truly getting to know yourself. Building your nest out of self love and beaconing your heart out to the world. Letting go already of that which does not serve the Infinite Love in Sacred Human expression that you ARE in preparation for the stunning reflection of your bigness that is to come.

~

Eclipse Of The Heart: Shiftings, Re-Unions, And Completions:

The moon passes in front of the sun, the warmth of the rays are blocked for these moments, and the energies shift across our world as the recent eclipse offers us. Most of us will not be able to actually see and view the eclipse yet our souls will feel it, our Galactic Selves will feel it, and our Higher Selves are already calibrating to its influence and energy.

Most of my focus as a Teacher, Healer, and Facilitator has been on the inner cosmos, especially on healing and awakening the emotional body as it integrates and weaves with the soul expressions and embodiment of the Higher Self. So, my focus has not been so much on reading the grids or cosmic connections or astrology, etc. Recently, though, I have been integrating more and more aspects of my Star Selves, connecting with my Star Family (especially the Arcturians and Pleiadians). This organic process has infused me with more cosmic awareness, more sense of connection OUT there, which is really rooted inside, like everything else.

I have become more sensitive to how playouts and movements and events in the stars impact our emotional states, spiritual awakenings, ascension process, and our relationships. I feel that as an Emoto-Spiritual Teacher, it is important for me to bridge what is happening in the sky with how it might manifest and relate to what could be happening for you inside of you, in your personal worlds, in your inner cosmos.

When I feel into the eclipse, I get this sense of covering over and then revelation again of the sun, mostly in the heart domains. Just as the sun gets to 'arise' again after it has been obscured by the moon, what has been 'veiled' over wants to be seen anew. Experiencing darkness in the middle of the 'day' is a waking up to what you may be taking for granted. What has been in the dark, wants to come into the light. While the soul awakening frequencies have been amping up and up for so many on this ascension path, these eclipse energies feel PERSONAL to the heart, getting to the REAL heart of the matter for many people.

The comments and questions that I have received lately have mostly been about relationships and specifically romantic unions that have been energized for many years, even decades. Within these relationships, there can be a sense of 'living with' what has been while consciously dreaming and desiring MORE....more love, more connection, more resonance, especially in the soul areas. There can be a 'living with' what has been not as nourishing and even a settling for shrinking of body, heart, and soul desires that are blooming from within, yet cannot express in the current ground of the relationship.

What you experience on the outside is a reflection OF YOU and, often, in your romantic patterns with your partner (and other close relationships with friends and family), you are experiencing a version of you that wants YOUR attention that is represented by them. If someone feels stuck to you or not awake or not in synch or depressed or too linear or much more literal….you can look inside and FIND that you have a part of you that is JUST LIKE THEM, but has been suppressed.

The part of you that is judging them (even if there is true discernment there, you can feel it is judgement when love is being withheld, primarily toward yourself!) is actually deeply judging the part of you that is JUST LIKE THEM. I am emphasizing this being just like them piece because it can be such a suffering loop and trap to feel what your partner/friend/family member is somehow NOT just a reflection of some part of you. You become in argument and fight against them on some level then, just like is happening inside of you from one aspect of you to another.

As you can bring the reflection that your partner (or friend or family) is offering and find the place inside that is like them, connect, and heal and feel this aspect…THEN the ground of TRUE discernment is available to you. THEN you can feel if you want to continue in the relationship ground or not, even as there is still love there. It is possible that the relationship ground will collapse and complete once you feel the part of you that was needing to be felt and being expressed by your partner. Although it is also possible that a whole new ground will arise between you and the partner as it clears of the projection energies.

If you feel as if you are 'settling' in relationships, this you have allowed until you no longer need to allow it because you are connecting to and healing the previously suppressed part of you that you NEEDED to have reflected by your partner or friend or family until you didn't any longer. This need to have this reflection is what people can mistake for resonance in relationships, when actually, it is what a facilitant of mine recently called 'sticky' or codependent at its roots. Sticky relationships are based primarily in subconscious unfelt need RATHER than health and soul bonds.

The SOUL, the 5D Higher Self, WANTS to seek for revelation inside AND outside. The SOUL is OPEN to eclipses of the heart. For things to be revealed and in that revelation to arise new or to fall away and complete. The soul doesn't want to spend moments settling; it wants to move on and experience the possibilities of growth that come from letting go of what needs to be completed while love remains in the heart.

ALL phases are sacred, of course, and necessary for your growth and are there because you have allowed them to be there, on a higher level. YET, there is so much support for this revelation into honesty, to take an honest look at your relationships and feel them from this ground of heart AND soul nourishment. And then to take action, make changes, based on what you see and feel. This transition, if it leads to completion of the relationships, can be held with SO MUCH self love and love for other. It is a difficult and painful transition to be sure, as the unbinding happens of the hookups and connections AND the goodness that is there too.

I do not offer this is in a casual way as relationships and relationality are, to me, the PRIMARY ground for which our soul growth and awakening moves and I hold very high reverence for them. The relationship within which then expresses outward being the main ground for transformation....

The eclipse offers us a symbolic picture of what can happen inside of us; the obscuring of the light, the re-emerging of the light into our experience...the digestion of the 'event' which then brings about shiftings that lead to re-union or to completion. And ALL of it held by love in service of love.

~

Heart And Soul Recovery After Relationship Completions

Your heart will recover. It cannot really break, only gets bent, only gets cleansed, only gets reminded. The reminders can be painful, sometimes the most effective ones are the MOST painful. The reminder is of your worth, your goodness, your true essence. The reminder is that you are so much more than you have settled for...if you have settled.

If you have settled and are on a consciousness path, you can trust that whatever happens is a mirror and is for your own growth. It is a way for you to see that which you have settled for and invite you into so much MORE.

The so much MORE is found within you. The so much more becomes available as you let go of what is less. The so much more becomes available as you discover and love aspects of you that broadcast pain, unworthiness, doubt, and fear. The so much more becomes available as you collect fragments of your soul that are spread over eras and dimensions living out realties from many different levels of consciousness.

Your soul will recover too. It cannot really be defeated, only gets woken up, only gets recharged, only gets realigned. The realignment can be difficult, sometimes the deepest realignment brings the most awakening. If you are in a place of shrinking your soul in some way in your relationships, in your career, in your geography, in your physical health, in your emotional healing, in your spiritual growth....the realignment comes as a gift from your Higher Self, the Divine within and with-out.

You will wake up and feel that something just isn't enough anymore, maybe you do already. You move from suffering into love. You move from being motivated by suffering to being motivated by love. Your desire for more love and less shrinking moves you into new inner terrains, inner unknown places, inner vistas and avenues.

You realize that everything you experience in your outer world is a reflection of your inner world. Your soul remembers this is true even as your heart always knew. Setting boundaries, letting go, moving on...you seem to say more 'no' than 'yes' in this phase as you move out of 3D consciousness and into 4D and 5D.

You start vibrating higher, faster, brighter. Your radiance is beaconing out to others as you discover the radiance from within that is released as you get to know and love the previously unlovable inside of you. Your sense of self love and goodness is becoming unconditional. You feel this form within and so your relationships reflect and transact this more and more.

In this growing sense of center and of self, you somehow feel more sense of connection with everyone and less separation. Your individuation has brought you the gift of Oneness. Your maturation has given you the sense of union. As you feel inside, so you feel about the outside. Your inner union has delivered you to union with others.

You will more than recover; you are recovered already. You are whole already, even when part of you feels broken. You are whole as you ARE even as you discover more and more because the possibilities are as infinite as you ARE.

~

Celebrating Eight Years In Sacred Union

Eight years ago, I joined my intention to Raphael's....in the moment and for all moments that followed that would be in mutual desire and resonance. On some level, it all felt like a whirlwind....we started dating in July and married by March (after knowing each other for a couple of years) having already moved through two major geography changes finally JUST settling in Canada when we married. And, the collapse of our whole social and spiritual world by leaving the spiritual group we had both been part of.

Our courtship was the highest highs of desire moving through, my body calibrating to what it feels like to REALLY be wanted by a man and my heart letting in what it feels like to REALLY be cherished by a man. AS I was also going through a Dark Night of letting go of ALL the souls I had been close to for more than five years in the group. Ups and downs, bittersweet, and yet, always was he there for me, over and over, in complete devotion and utter eagerness to be together.

Those ups and downs have settled over the years as we found our way together through many changes and transitions yet, always, arising our way through it in union. We took our wedding rings off last year, feeling like it had been other parts of us (going by our birth names Wayne and Jillian) who had exchanged those rings even as the core of us was there. We felt so different after years of parts work, being in the crucible of Sacred Union together that had burnt away so many layers, letting go of incomes and geographies and just about everything there was to let go of other than each other.

We even felt that the significance of this day was a memory from the past and we were arising in the NOW together. Yet, I do feel in my heart a tenderness for this day, this anniversary, and where we were at that time and who we have been through the years and who we are arising into now as Raphael and Jelelle.

Our USness keeps expanding as we do and keeps vibrating at a higher frequency at all levels and in all areas – sexually, emotionally, spiritually. We are more and more connecting other lifetimes together (energizing NOW) such as in Atlantis (a couple of those) and also our Star BEing aspects. Very little conflict between us, fewer words needed, more soul connection...

I feel we are Counterpart Souls to each other, which I prefer to the twin flame paradigm. I can feel how our relationship could feel like a fantasy or idealized, yet it is not, it IS very real, and we have had to go through the dark together to illuminate the light and the love that was always there. We have had to commit to awakening and to our own personal process OVER everything else, including the relationship. The goodness overflow in a relationship can only deepen and grow if the partners are committed to their OWN growth first. Being my counterpart, Raphael is like me yet NOT me and it is the beautiful blend of masculine and feminine that offers SUCH growth and mirror for our own inner union.

So I celebrate a love today that I am SO BLESSED to experience and have been so blessed to experience for these 8.5 years....

~

To Be With A King Man

What is it like to be WITH a King man, a vulnerable man, a man that pursues with ALL of his heart, a man who holds space for himself and ALL the feelings that come up inside of him? This is what I felt moved to share today......what it is like to be with a King man from a Queen woman's perspective experiencing our USness ground with Raphael in Sacred Union. I felt moved to share what it is like to be with a man opening out into the capacity and potential that I feel ALL men have inside of them....like a seed just waiting for the water of SELF love, SELF worth, and PURE love with and from the Divine to grow and to bloom!

To be with a King man is to feel him cross the space toward you with clarity and with desire. To feel him CLAIM the exploration between you into deeper grounds of intimacy than either of you have EVER known. Raphael crossed the space toward me shortly after we met many years ago. We were sitting in a local Starbucks in Ashland, Oregon, and he rolled out his attraction to me after being around each other during two recent seminars connected to the spiritual and emotional healing group we were both part of. I felt the goodness of him IMMEDIATELY, his big heart and his immense capacity and purity. Parts of me weren't ready for all this then and the ground between us (as lush as it was) wasn't transactable between us yet as also he was just out of a 23 year marriage and leaving Christianity and his whole social world behind. He then brought his attraction again to me several months later and I again 'turned him down' as it didn't feel like the timing was right for either of us.

A few years later, the timing was right for both of us and Raphael AGAIN risked to cross the space to pursue me and to claim an exploration between us. NOW I was open and ready for him. On our very first date, he literally cleared the restaurant dishes out of the way when we were done eating, reached out across the table and grasped my hands in his for the first time. The rush of love and desire that moved through me feeling his skin against mine, the tender yet passionate way he held me and US....offered all I needed to 'KNOW' about our love and the possibilities of where it would take me. A few moments later, he reached over again towards me and we were kissing passionately on the sidewalk, not caring who saw us or witnessed!

To be with a King man is to feel cherished for ALL aspects of you and their expression grounds. Raphael has wanted me passionately as a physical woman from the beginning. Other men in the past wanted my soul frequencies or my spiritual gifts or priestess frequencies….Raphael could feel all those capacities but also he CRAVED my BODY deeply too! That craving continues to this day…..he notices and comments on every bit of clothing that I put on my body and feels a visceral physical response to what I wrap my body in and the way I physically move through space. He FEELS my physicality and responds to it in an alive way. This is SO important as the body is our precious vessel here and the tones of cherishment and desire coming from a king really light up our queenly self worth and goodness and also help to heal Inner Punisher and critic energies inside of us that we've received from birth family and our 3D culture.

To be with a King man is to feel that he is holding his OWN emotional process and soul growth and physical health. Raphael holds space for himself firstly and primarily. He 'goes in' when he needs to in order to feel what needs to be felt or experienced. Yet, also, he is very respectful and responsive to my intuitions and sense of what might be going on for him and even to guidance that comes through me. He leads his OWN process though, so it isn't about me taking care of him, or being on his 'side' or making sure that he grows or about trying to change him. That movement is happening on its own inside of him and it overflows into our USness ground. This allows me to 'relax' and be with myself and my own process and to also respond to our USness too.

To be with a King man is to be called into our own growth and process as women. It invites us to open our own hearts wider to match the man's vulnerability in every moment. It invites us to feel the masculine Protector aspects of us as women that guard our sexuality, our vulnerability, our femininity and to negotiate with these energies to be more available for ourselves and for the union. It invites us to KEEP waking up and to keep growing. It invites us into the conscious duality dance and all its richness of experience that flows from within us and then into union WITH him! It invites us to experience in a visceral way, a

real and grounded way, our expression as Infinite Love as reflected to us through the heart and soul of our King man mate!
~

Heart, Soul, And Body Transaction Grounds During Sacred Sexuality

> I return to you,
> like the sea to the shore,
> pulled in by our connection
> pushed out again by growth
> over and over, I tumble with you
> only to ease back out again
> each splash and crash
> a reflection of me to me
> each calm and balm
> an offering of me to me.
> There is no better way
> for me to see my heart
> yet through yours
> as our union beats
> to the cadence
> of a Divine drum. ~

My heart, soul and body are lit up and warm after making love with my beloved mate Raphael....I feel as if all dimensions of me have been ignited, enlivened, and yet a deep stillness and calm floods my BEing. My heart is held and claimed by our union...My body is adored and cherished by myself and by him...my soul is met and matched and welcomed in communion with his. We fly to other dimensions and yet we dwell in the most physical of places too.

And, over the years, this experience of polarized yet somehow perfectly fitted sacred sexuality is deepening and widening....not dissipating or going 'flat.'

Sacred sexuality...two words that stir the heart and ignite our imaginations. It can feel conceptual, this 'idea' of sacred sexuality, yet, in my experience, it is a frequency that is much beyond the mind. It is a frequency that arises in purer and purer forms related to the degree of depth and healthiness in the grounds of connection that are transacting in the relationship – heart, soul, and body grounds of relationality.

As the heart grounds of transaction in the partners deepen through consciously purifying through emotional work (particularly healing and integrating shadow aspects), the intimacy anchors the frequencies in the fourth or heart chakra. Without this grounding, the exchange may become too transcendent and there can be parts of us that are not really letting in the love that is flowing. We also advocate for a monogamous connection, a real claim by a King for his Queen and vice versa, in which to explore these frequencies as it offers the most safe space for the heart to be deeply involved. What affects our capacity to open our hearts is a radical self love and healing process, such as what we offer with our SoulFullHeart path.

As the soul grounds of transaction in the partners deepen through consciously awakening through soul healing work (especially integration of other lifetimes and soul legacy/Metasoul themes), the soul context enlivens and energizes the frequencies in the upper chakras. Kundalini and other tantric energies can move and weave between all the chakras of the partners. I have experienced recently that I can 'see' and feel us as the golden white filaments of energy that we actually are beyond the body-mind during love making with Raphael. This makes all of the body part on body part exchanges very interesting and beautiful! Without this opening up of soul frequencies, the sexuality remains limited to the physical and body dimension.

As the body grounds of transaction in the partners deepen through conscious health through body healing work (especially embodiment processes such as healthy lifestyle and food choices), the body connection grounds the frequencies in the physical plane and to the Earth. Without this opening up of healthy body frequencies, the transaction may become too floaty or transcendent.

I want to add that a key aspect of this capacity to transact in heart, body, and soul frequencies within Sacred Union for women is the healing and reclaiming of our feminine inside.....working with, loving, and healing the masculine aspects and masculine templates that we have received from our family, social and cultural (even collective unconscious!) conditioning! This applies to men as well as claiming and being with feminine aspects and energies inside themselves creates a transaction ground of more vulnerability and openness.

Even without a partner, these three grounds of relationality can be greatly healed and awakened as a single person. In fact, it is the inner ground that then overflows to the outer Sacred Union and leads to such nourishing experience of sacred sexuality and connection in heart, body, mind, and soul within a committed and mutual Sacred Union bond!

~

Sacred Union Codes Inviting You Into Union With Self, Getting Ready If Single, Completing Scared Unions And Relationships

The sacred love, the love of SELF ultimately that overflows into the love WITH another that creates a union. We are being invited into this sacred love WITH union of inner and outer, to begin with the unionizing of aspects of SELF....from the shadow to the light, to those from the Stars to those from childhood, those aspects that we have embraced and have BEcome our persona and unaware ego and those that arise from our soul and Higher Self.

Gathering together the pieces of SELF, inviting them into the light of our heart love, bringing them 'home' in our heart, letting them feel that an awakening version of US, an embodiment of our Higher Self is THERE for them. The most loving parental energy arises in us to hold the edges, the pains, the wounds, the doubts, the hiding, the compensating....to love and accept it ALL and then invite these aspects to transmute with love.

The codes for Sacred Unions are being downloaded now and you feel them if you are meant to feel them. If single, and especially if you are being fast tracked in ascension related to being a Leader/Teacher/WaySHOWer, you feel these Sacred Union codes as a renewed desire and need to BE with yourself and to be revealed to yourself, and to see what has been previously hard to see. It is a desire to 'clean out and get ready', similar to a pregnant mom's urges to get the nest ready before the baby. A key aspect of getting the nest ready is feeling the Inner Protector and what energies still guard your heart and soul and WHY.

If single, the codes are inviting you to be MORE OPEN than maybe you ever have been before to seeing and feeling your Sacred Union mate. You may even already know them, yet your Inner Protector may be filtering them out, judging them, or dismissing them or evaluating them from a certain perspective. Your Sacred Union mate is often NOT what you expect in terms of a physical package or even 'ideal geography' or even age difference....yet the grounds of HOT body talk, ALIVE mental talk, DEEP soul talk, VULNERABLE heart talk are undeniable once opened out to and let in. The codes are inviting you to PURSUE too, even women, with your vulnerability and openness and willingness to be hurt yet also willingness to experience a deeper love than you have ever known. To bring what you want and what you desire to the soul who has drawn your attention and interest. To move out of safety and comfort, to take the risk of being rejected (there is no REAL rejection at the soul level since all of it has been agreed to already).

If you are in a relationship, you may feel these Sacred Union codes as creating a rumble in yourself, in clarities around what you want and don't want, what you have been 'living with' versus what you really want. Being able to settle or shrink is running out of ground, you can no longer hide the truth from yourself or your deeper desires for a union that is based in ALL grounds of mind, body, heart, and soul. These SCARED unions, or those based in more codependent frequencies than health, are getting shaken up as the grounds that used to allow them to continue (safety, comfort, Inner Parent and Child hookups) are flooded with PURE love from the Sacred Union templates and Guides, Divine Source, and those of us in Human form exploring and embodying this Sacred Union ground. Again, we can support you in SoulFullHeart to walk out the completion of the scared union, to claim your SELF, to deepen the process of healing SELF, to overflow self love.

These completions of scared unions can happen rapidly right now where the inertia of the previous years is dissolved away in the frequencies of PURE love. A soul that has been awakening and a heart that has been healing just vibrates too high to remain in the stuck, lower frequency ground anymore of a relationship where their partner is not coming with them into awakening and healing. This higher vibration (Often sought out alone by the awakening mate or 'outside' the relationship) starts to flood the relationship and either transforms it into something new, or collapses it.

These Sacred Union codes are an invitation to move into a 'next place' of evolution for our species, where we experience moving from a wounded "I" to a healthy "I" to more and more a "We". Sacred Union offers the remembrance of this ground, of the unity consciousness we know as higher selves and our soul fractals/Guides know too. It is a remembrance AND it is a new discovery too, as we heal our emotional bodies in NEW ways in this modern age that allow for a deeper and healthier transaction ground within union. Inviting into MORE love, with self and with other and where other becomes self and yet IS separate too in a delicious dance of conscious duality.

~

Sacred Union Codes Coming In: BEing In A Sacred Union, Not A Scared one

This writing is by Raphael and me:

"Sacred Union Codes Coming In!" We felt these words coming from our Guides today as we lay out in the sun together. These vibrational codes that are coming in via the sun are really an invitation, as well as the event that the invitation heralds. They invite us into deeper union with masculine and feminine energies in relationship expression with a mate (although there is a 'with yourself' invitation of course here too that is critical to embrace and embody the Inner Feminine and masculine.) We have been Sacred Union mates for nine years and what we call 'Counterpart Souls' here to serve love together.

These codes from Divine Source/Universe invite us into this experience of Sacred Union from a higher vibrational frequency of HEALTHINESS that hasn't been possible before. This healthiness aspect of Sacred Union differentiates itself significantly from what is commonly called 'twin flame' relationships where couples and individuals have too often suffered in a bond that lacked boundaries and self care, and used the idealized twin flame picture as a way to loop in a shadow playout of codependent suffering. We both have felt this differentiation is an important one, and we intend to write about it more in the near future. Sacred Union, along with the picture of what we are calling 'Counterpart Souls', welcomes us to explore into our deeply held fantasies about what an idealized romance could look and feel like, but it also offers clear guidelines about alive personal boundaries and awakenings that are necessary to ground that, make that possible, and keep it emotionally healthy.

This invitation to Sacred Union seems to be a critical aspect of the ascension process that will fast track many of us in ways not possible before, especially those of us called to be WaySHOWers and path layers ('bush whackers', as we have affectionately called it).

The desire for Sacred Union runs deep in our collective consciousness. Romantic movies, songs, stories....it all activates our passions, our desire for union with an 'other', joining together to experience both the exquisiteness of union and the powerful mirror that it offers of both our shadow and our light. We have experienced personally and in space holding with others for many years that a TRUE Sacred Union is one where there are ACTIVE and ALIVE grounds of transactability in heart, soul, body, and mind PLUS a larger container of good will, respect, and love that holds the exploration for the relationship.

In a TRUE Sacred Union, there is a commitment by BOTH individual partners toward their personal healing and growth and awakening. It is this personal and conscious commitment of both partners that opens out the mutual growth and intimacy possibilities. The personal precedes and fills the mutual, and this is a big part of what makes it a SACRED Union and not a SCARED one. In a Sacred Union, each partner's sense of growing self worth and soul embodiment floods into the 'USness' ground, which is what we call the third energy created when two people come together in relationship.

Sacred Union is evident in the 'transactability' in the 'USness ground' on many levels. The key pieces are hot sexual desire (that goes FAR BEYOND lust or just body chemistry); sharing deepest vulnerabilities of the heart; expansive connection between the souls (telepathy, remembrance of other lifetimes together that are happening NOW, clarity and service of love mission together); mental resonance of values and vibrant idea exchange; and a deep and easy compatibility in everyday, practical living.

People can get confused by the capacity or the potential of a relationship to become a Sacred Union, when really, it only qualifies as one if it is actually currently transacting in these grounds in a way that is ultimately nourishing for both partners MOST of the time. All too often one partner in a relationship will speak to their relationships' potential or their partners' potential as a reason to remain in a relationship that has little healthy nourishment. The harder truth to feel here is that remaining in a romantic relationship that has potential to one day, but doesn't presently, meet your deepest healthy needs and fulfill your wildest dreams serves to diminish the likelihood that the potential will be realized, unless it is being consciously worked by both partners.

A scared union, FAR more common, is based in codependence and the sticky grounds of the relationship that seems to be mostly hookups between different parts of people: the most common hookups being between the Inner Child in one partner and a Father or Mother Aspect in the other; or between two Inner Children; or two Inner Punishers or the Inner Punisher of one hooked up to the Shame part in the other; or an Inner Narcissist with the Inner Empath in the other; etc. The scared union is still a sacred one, in the sense that it is necessary for a phase and can offer a deep crucible of healing for souls who sign up to awaken within it.

Often times in a scared union, one of the partners 'wakes up' to what isn't working in the relationship and consciously wants more. He or she may engage in 'affairs' of different kinds, or they may admit they want to complete the relationship while the other 'doesn't get it'. Often it is the woman in the relationship who 'wakes up' before the man, who may be more hooked in to 'taking care of mom' and not conscious of how he is actually not happy in his experience of the union.

If only one partner is awakening and the other is not, this is NOT a Sacred Union as the souls are not aligning in mutual desire and illumination, inspiring each other to grow and remember. This is a painful crucible to go through for both partners, especially the one who is awakening with possible guilt and shame that can come up from the emotional body around any obligation and loyalty ideals. Inner negotiation can be helpful to navigate the completion and also healing the karma between the two partners. If one partner feels very committed to the relationship and the other does not and keeps 'running', which is justified in the twin flame paradigm, this is NOT a Sacred Union either as Sacred Union ground thrives on the sense of mutual dedication and devotion to the USness and being in it together.

For those who are ready and have been on the awakening, self healing, and ascension path, SACRED Union offers the end of 'shrinking to fit' to ANY relationship or settling for less than what your soul most deeply wants and desires. The codes coming now seem to be supporting that for those who are ready, their Higher Self and Guides will set up synchronicities for them to meet their Sacred Union Counterpart Mate (or to finally 'see' them if you already know each other). This meeting of your counterpart may even happen for those souls currently IN relationship together, which will certainly cause some major upheaval and emotional processing.

For those ALREADY in a relationship, these codes seem to be creating quite a SHAKE UP to the grounds of the relationship, amplifying and illuminating the deepest heart and soul desires AND the shadow aspects that may be hanging out there. Even Sacred Unions may be feeling this rumble and be called to recommit to the union in ALL domains and connect even deeper to the ultimate REASON why these Sacred Unions are coming together and being supported: to serve love. The service of love is the reason for it, which is a bigger context that provides a foundational energy of resonance for those souls experiencing it. The personal growth that Sacred Unions provide is, ultimately, for the service of love WITH others. This is the call that we feel is contained in these codes too….those who let them in and hear and feel this call will find that their previous form of service may collapse, reshape, go through a death or Dark Night, and arise again from the ashes in a NEW form that is deeply connected to their Sacred Union mate in co-creation and co-offering.

This invitation to Sacred Union is an ongoing one….certainly an ongoing process that offers such aliveness, goodness, magic, growth, and opportunity to serve love. The Universe seems to be hugely supporting and needing this dualistic experiment to move more consciously and healthily into these domains for those who join together and join their intentions together to serve love. The partners are then able to offer and serve love in an exponential way to those ready to receive it! It's a tall order, but the rewards are out of this world!

~

Sacred Union Is Calling And Inviting Us To Respond With Love

It is lying in bed with him, my head on his chest...the perfect fleshy pillow seemingly shaped just for me. It is sharing, always sharing, what is moving in my heart and my soul for it to land in his accepting embrace. It is so many early mornings of this, where I land in self AS I land in him AS I land in our USness.

It is THIS Sacred Union that brings me into self, introduces me to self over and over as it CALLS me into a higher self version to serve love from the overflow. It is THIS calling that my heart responds to with vulnerability. It is this calling that my soul responds to with awakening. It is this calling that my body responds to with longing. It is this calling that my mind responds to with inspiration.

It is the feminine form of me leaning into the masculine form of him. The polarity and duality dance of our gender-based edges merging and BEcoming and touching and entwining. The dance that creates and alchemizes a NEW energy that wouldn't be possible without each of us as the partners and creators. My side and his side and then in the middle where our energies meet is this union.....two "I's" coming together to create a "We" without losing our sense of self.

It is the letting go of the conditioned IDEAS of relationship, romance, and union....letting go of the templating and modeling that we received. Letting go of what doesn't serve the love to move between us and LETTING IN the essence of us that BEcomes the love more and more. The Inner Father and the Inner Mother held and identified and felt so that we can arise beyond these roles into the frequencies of TRUE King and Queen BEloveds.

It is THIS Queen inside of you that is waiting, ready, growing, choosing. She is getting her inner nest ready to receive these tones of Sacred Union into her world. She is responding to what FEELS like she most deeply wants and letting go of ALL that IS not, even as it can be so painful to do so. She is inviting Sacred Union of self into her life to overflow this energy of invitation OUT to her mate, as her inner frequencies of self love increase so does the strength of HER beacon.

It is THIS King inside of you that is pursuing, activating, growing, choosing. He is getting his inner kingdom ready to hold these tones of Sacred Union in his world. He is activating around what FEELS like what he most deeply wants and letting go of ALL that IS not, leading the necessary completions or explorations. He is inviting Sacred Union of self into his life to overflow this energy of invitation OUT to his mate…..as his inner frequencies of self love empowerment increase so does the strength of HIS beacon.

It is this Sacred Union for which we are ALL being invited to explore, to join, to feel, and to experience. The explorations of our inner unions of feminine and masculine and the OUTER expression of it from one awakening heart, body, mind, soul WITH another in the service of love with love and BY love.

~

Meditation To Connect With Sacred Union Frequencies From Within; With Sacred Union Guides Christiel And Magdalena; and With The Higher Self Of Your Sacred Union Mate

Close your eyes, go within, concentrate on your natural breathing in and out.

Imagine yourself in a space of pure white light. The light is surrounding you, holding you, and guiding you. The light is inviting you to vibrate higher, to move your frequency UP to a higher one. Feel this pure white light moving through you and through each of your chakras and through every cell of your body. Allow this light to move through and activate and clean each of your chakras, from your highest one, your stellar gateway, to your root. To your earth chakra below your feet. Feel the grounding from your feet down into Gaia and the connection that is there. Move out any lower frequency energies through you with the pure white light.

See yourself in a clearing in the woods surrounded by the pure white light. There is a stream running through and into many pools of water that are naturally formed out of rocks. These pools are emitting steam of a high vibrational and soothing frequency.

You take in the five elements of fire through the warmth of the sun to ignite your passions; water through the pools of water to purify your desires; air through the soft breezes to bring in movement and courage to change; Earth through the grasses and trees that surround you to ground you in goodness; and Spirit through the sense of your own soul and your connection to Divine Source and other Ethereal Guides, Angels, Spirit Animals you may be working with in the moment. Feel them joining you now, witnessing you now.

In this moment, we will call on Magdalena who is the ascended form of Mary Magdalene, offering us Sacred Feminine frequencies at a high vibrational rate. She has bright red hair, long and curly. Her energy is passionate and creative and sexual, offering you a reflection of your Sacred Feminine Queen (whether you are in a relationship or not). Magdalena comes forward toward you and takes your left hand. You feel infusions of Sacred Feminine, connection to your Inner Feminine, the possibilities of healing soul woundings held in other lifetimes around persecution and expression of your soul gifts and suppression of your femininity. If you are a woman this life, She infuses you with energies of your Queen. If you are man, she infuses you with the energies of YOUR Queen, your counterpart soul in feminine form, your mate of Sacred Union.

We will now call on Christiel, who is the ascended form of Yeshua or Jesus, offering us Sacred Masculine frequencies at a high vibration. He is passionate, provocative, truth telling... offering you a reflection of your Sacred Masculine King (whether you are in a relationship or not). He comes forward toward you and takes your right hand. You feel infusions of Sacred Masculine, connection to your Inner Masculine, the possibilities of healing soul woundings held in other lifetimes around patriarchy and expression of your soul gifts and suppression of your healthy masculine and over expression of your wounded masculine. If you are a man, he infuses you with energies of your King. If you are woman, he infuses you with the energies of YOUR king, your Counterpart Soul in masculine form, your mate of Sacred Union.

Christiel and Magdalena help you into the nearest pool and you get in...soaking in the warming and purifying waters. You feel the Sacred Feminine and Masculine energies come in from these two Divine Guides, moving through you and igniting your Inner Feminine and Masculine energies. Feel the twine of their energy, their wrapped in each other energy moving through you. Notice what comes up as this energy moves through. What do you feel inside? Do you feel resistance? Do you feel fear? Do you feel joy? Do you feel a sense of reunion? Do you feel a sense of sadness? Be with whatever feelings come up and hold space for them to just BE.

Feel the waters of Sacred Union hold you, invite you to go deeper inside of yourself, to accept and love ALL that you are and all that you feel. Invite you to feel and heal the templating and conditioning that you received from your birth parents and family around WHAT relationship is. Feel some of that templating letting go so you can let in the NEW possibilities of Sacred Union.

Christiel and Magdalena help you out of the water and you feel lit up and warm from the waters and their Sacred Union energies.

Now, we are going to call in the Higher Self of your Sacred Union mate, your mate of deepest union in the grounds of body, heart, mind, and soul. Feel the energy of this mate come into your field. They come to stand in front of you and you take each other in. You may already know them. They may be your current mate. OR they may be someone new or unknown to you. Take in their energy and notice how you FEEL when you connect with them. Notice how your heart feels. How your body feels. How your soul feels. How your mind feels.

Ask them to speak with you and if they have anything to say to you. Listen with an open heart. Say anything to them in this moment that you want to say, letting it come from your heart and soul. Again notice how you feel being around them.

They begin to fade away now, with the promise of connection in the future with you. Christiel and Magdalena give you a big embrace and also begin to fade away. You come back into the NOW moment again, while continuing to feel the high frequencies of Sacred Feminine and Masculine that have been activated inside of you.

~

PHYSICAL AREA

The Physical area of life includes your relationship to your physical body, your health, your nutrition, your sexuality desirability and expression.

3D: Your 3D Self has been conditioned to believe that it IS the physical body. The five senses are the main way of filtering reality and everything is related to in a physical way with only the physical being 'real'. The 3D Self is often disconnected from deeper embodiment of the body in terms of physical health and nutrition due mostly to unfelt emotional congestion in the pain body. This disconnection can lead to poor nutritional choices, lack of physical activity, suffering loops around weight and poor body image, and sense of not being physically and sexually desirable. Sexual desire may be low along with orgasmic capacity. As a woman, your physical energy may be mostly masculine in nature as there can be a deep fusion with a masculine protection energy related to your physicality and sexuality.

Your 3D Self may use food as a drug to numb painful emotions or as 'comfort food' (along with other comforts to soothe emotions, such as cigarette smoking for anxiety and alcohol for depression). You may also become obsessed with nutrition and part of you can become hyper vigilant about diet and exercise, stuck in suffering loops of self punishment and self criticism related to your body image. The way you feel about your body is hugely influenced by family and social conditioning. Often the way you feel about your physical appearance can be linked to your same gender parent and the templating you received there. Your 3D Self is conditioned to allopathic or mainstream medicine with trust in pharmaceutical solutions. It is the emotional pain body in your 3D self that draws disease, injuries, and illness.

4D: Your 4D Self is awakening to life beyond the body and experiences beyond the five senses. You are becoming more sensitive and attuned to energy and the sense that you ARE energy, not actually physical at all. You are also perhaps becoming aware or seeing the light or crystalline body or even experiencing symptoms from the process of ascension from a carbon-based to a crystalline body. You are connecting your physical health to your emotional, spiritual, and energetic (aural and chakral) health. Even as you are separating from the body only picture, you are devoted to keeping the ascension vessel that your body IS in good health, good nutrition, and healthy body weight (whatever that is for you.) As you are healing deeper layers of core unworthiness, you are feeling more sense of your desirability, sexuality, and what we call your 'love body' arises. You form a connection and communication with your love body in the sense of a deeper intuitive understanding of what foods your body most wants and needs and the emotional and spiritual reasons why you might draw illness, injury or disease.

Your 4D Self seeks out holistic, homeopathic, and alternative resources to help you with body health and nutrition, body healing work, energy work, etc. and if you experience an injury or illness. You may use yoga or chi gong or other body-based processes to connect to your spirituality and soul aspects. Your sexuality is expanding from a body-based, genital-based experience into one with more frequencies of chakra connection, energy movements (such as Kundalini), and other lifetime connection- Metasoul frequencies.

5D: Your 5D Self is embodied within your love body frequencies with a strong sense of self worth, self care, and self desirability related to your physicality. Your body is shifting from carbon-based to crystalline-based light body or has completed this process. Your crystalline-based body is sensitive to the foods and activities that you engage in and you may go through periods of fasting, cleansing, being vegetarian/vegan, mostly raw diet, etc. You can feel the life force energies of the foods that you eat in addition to the energy of those that prepare food for you, so you are particular about what you eat and where. You follow mostly your inner authority around your physical health and well being and are vibrating at a high enough level that lower density disease, injury, and illness is not drawn to you. Your body is a vessel for your experience of yourself as Infinite Love: beloved, cared for, inhabited, and expanded.

Questions For You:

How did you locate yourself related to the physical area of life – as primarily a 3D, 4D or 5D consciousness and why?

What are your frustrations in the physical area?

What are your desires in the physical area?

~

The Importance Of Sacred Space For Self Love And Care

I am emerging now, out of a sacred space. A space of self love and self care. A space where my primary focus was on my own needs. A space I have been in for almost a week, altered from the usual and brought into something new.

I found this space not from deep meditation practice, but rather through body illness, body detoxification, and body realignment. It might seem strange to offer that being ill provided a sacred space, but it did, as I surrendered to what it was bringing to me. Even as I certainly had moments of discomfort and pain, I could feel a trust that it was all part of a bigger process. It was preparing me for what is coming next both in my own life, in SoulFullHeart, and in the world.

As I sip on a potent concoction of herbal extracts given to me by our new herbalist, I feel the love of the plants that are moving through my bloodstream, bringing vitality, immunity.....life. I am newly focused now again on my nutritional health, taking it to an even higher level of self care and love....without self judgment or regiment or vigilance. Just tuning into what feels good, what is good, what is alive. That has been another gift of not being well as I could listen to what my body was telling me about eating foods (such as wheat and sugar) that lower my vibrational frequency.

This was a minor illness, easily cured, yet it brought the gifts of a need for a self containment after months of time spent in serving love to others, sharing my energy and writings, etc. My desire now is to continue this self care containment space without the need for illness. I feel a sense of increasing my practices of meditation, multidimensional travel, creativity through projects and to hold a protective container around my energy and what energies I take in.

My experience brings up for me a reminder of how important self care and self love are for all of us. Sometimes it takes an illness or emergency for us to actually go in and be in stillness, to rest, to breathe, to turn inward. Life can bring us this, yet, also, we can bring ourselves to life with an intention to give ourselves the love that we have been giving others and to connect with ourselves and parts of us in much deeper and more meaningful ways.

~

"I Want To Come Along": Moving From 3D Body To 5D Light Body

I am connecting with THE BODY, my ascending body and the collective 'body' of those of us who have chosen ascension as our path and process. I am connecting with this universal experience of body, this Human body vessel and temple, this fleshy form, that we've all agreed is the vehicle of our walking around life. Yet, this body is changing. It is growing. It is calibrating higher, vibrating higher. It is shifting from carbon to crystalline. It is transforming from being anchored in 3D to transitional and awakening 4D (integration of the astral body) and into 5D.

This is a HUGE process, a big deal as a marker in the evolutionary cycles of our species. Our souls can fly with our

Astral Self (as I am now calling our dream self, or self beyond the body in one aspect or layer of fourth dimensional consciousness), yet our bodies have not been able to come along. Our souls can soar into 5D consciousness, especially during Near Death Experiences (NDEs) and taking of peyote, ayahuasca, etc. Yet, again, the body is 'left behind' because its frequency has been too dense, too connected to Mother Gaia in a primordial way to 'come along' with the soul's vibration.

Yet now……NOW the body is ascending TOO. It is coming along, doesn't want to get left behind. This is what THE BODY is telling me in the moment, "Don't leave me behind! I want to come with you!" Dimensional shifts are about shifts in consciousness yet, also, there IS a shift in what you experience as your outer reality as well…..as what is inside is what you experience as the outside. Experiencing 4D conscious states and higher INSIDE of the body is a new experience and seems to mostly be bridged through meditation and going on multidimensional journeys for which the body comes along and 'holds' the awakening experiences.

In our 3D relationships with our bodies, we BECOME our bodies. Our 3D selves 'fuse' to our bodies and so every symptom, every experience, every emotion, every thought, seems to become trapped INSIDE of them. All of this trapping and fixation on the physical level creates dis-ease, illness, injury, unhealthiness, toxicity, being overweight, sexuality issues, addictions. All this trapping of consciousness inside of the body doesn't allow any breathing, any release, any energetic movement to happen, any cleansing, any POSSIBILITIES beyond the body.

THE BODY says, "I'm exhausted of this approach. I can BE SO MUCH more. I want to soar with your soul too. I want to be as crystalline as your chakras are becoming. I want to be as healthy, vibrant, and non-toxic as your healing heart is becoming. I want to experience the multi-dimensions. I want to travel to the stars. I want to flow in sexual and creative energies that come from Divine Source and spiritual inspiration."

Yes, this ascending body WANTS a lot. If we can feel this wanting and desire of the body to ascend WITH us, then we can respond to bodies from this higher frequency with self love and self care. This means that our ascending bodies will cycle through sleep differently than we are 'used to' and sleep 'patterns' will be interrupted. Sometimes our bodies will be needing A LOT of it for the calibration and crystallizing process. Sometimes they will be needing VERY LITTLE for so much new energy is moving through, becoming light, feeling like a caffeine buzz moving through our veins and through our bones. Sometimes our bodies will need 'crash naps' to reboot the consciousness, turn the conscious mind off, and implement a new frequency. The more flexibility we have in our days and in our nights to allow these fluxes and changes; the more we can flow and move with them letting our mind relax and surrender into them.

The ascending body is shifting around food needs too. The 3D body sought out comfort because so much was trapped INSIDE of it that it was looking for any kind of relief. Comfort often meant foods that weren't good for it, that weren't healthy, that actually made digestion harder and the body feeling not as vital. The 3D body, run by our 3D Selves, then made 'choices' that caused dis-ease and illness and that were out of alignment with our soul frequencies. Because the 3D body was cut off from the soul (not completely but enough), it was 'alone' in a 3D conditioned world that pushes toxic food, that keeps our body vibrational energetic frequency low.

The 4D body is awakening as the 4D Self is transitioning and learning, educating itself about what is healthy and what is not, about what is conscious eating and what is not. It is usually the 4D Self that chooses not to eat sentient BEings/animals anymore as the soul can't reconcile the killing frequencies of it anymore. Food as necessary fuel is the 3D body's mantra. And the 3D self 'uses' food as a numbing drug. The 4D and 5D body will probably need less food as it will run more and more on energy of higher vibrational love frequencies.

THE BODY doesn't want to numb out or be drugged anymore. "NO more chemicals please. NO more processed foods. No more drugs and things produced in a laboratory please," I can hear it pleading to us. It seems to understand if we are in transition around this and it is patient. Yet, also, it is eager to feel vital fuel running through all of its systems that run so brilliantly on their own day after day and year after year. THE BODY especially wants us to awaken to our soul's ability to use gifts from Mother Gaia and from our accesses to energy in order to heal it. We can help our bodies, especially in 4D transition and conscious integration of some astral frequencies into the body, by remembering our energy gifts and connecting with our chakras, cleaning them, making them as real as our physical body, caring intensely about their health and well being. And, of course, seeking out resources for health that are provided by Mother Gaia through herbals and supplements.

Oh, none of what is offered by THE BODY is an absolute. There are not 'rules' that you need to follow. The main thing the ascending body seems to want is communication and connection WITH you, to not be ignored, to not be resisted, to not be battled. Unhealed unworthiness in the 3D pain body creates a self punishing frequency related to the body. Healing this core unworthiness through inner work frees up frequencies of worth to CHOOSE better things for the body and to create a relationship with it that is based in self love. Also, connecting with and healing the aspect of you that holds self punishment and self critical frequencies can hugely shift this process into worthiness-based grounds as well.

Connecting with your ascending body puts you in emotional resonance with it and so what 'happens' to it (all the symptoms of ascension that everyone talks about) are felt and negotiated and navigated with deep self love, care, and awareness

AND with trust in the overall process as a gift from the Universe. THE BODY wants to be held with love and to come along into the frequencies of Infinite Love for which your soul knows and IS. And it seems as if we get to experiment with this process. We get to have all the gifts that can come along with it as offered by our newly glowing, shining, and loved up bodies as the vessel for experiencing it.

~

You Have A Body, You Are NOT Your Body With Kuan Yin

I have taken a certain pride in being embodied and 'grounded' in my body. My weight has been at a healthy place for a many years now and regular physical activity is just part of my lifestyle. I also experience great pleasure from making love with Raphael, which is grounded in our bodies, connected in our hearts, and expanding more and more into our souls.

So, I haven't been interested in being 'out of the body'....until recently I have been. Well, what I am more interested in is a balance where I can healthfully and vibrantly be in my body and also deepen my experience of out of body realities such as astral travel, Samadhi and other enlightened states, Kundalini energies, etc. I do believe a balance can be made and that's what it feels like some people are seeking through the Hatha yoga path.

Physical ailments usually accompany my major spiritual or emotional movements as toxicity moves out. I take note when this happens because I rarely get sick and have never broken a bone or had any kind of major injury or illness. So, the physical issues I do have are small and move quickly, but they can often be connected to my process.

As I am meditating with Kuan Yin today, I am feeling a particular ailment in my body that is minor but still irritating me. As I start with the "Ma Om" mantra (described here), Kuan Yin can feel my attention and focus moving to my body.

"I'm sorry," I quickly apologize. "I'm getting distracted by discomfort in my body."

"You HAVE a body. You are NOT your body," is Her immediate response.

Ok, I take that in and let it be a kind of repeated mantra.

I have a body. I am not my body.

Eventually, I have to ask her to clarify what She means.

"Your mind thinks that you ARE your body. It thinks you are a body shell and it fuses to that reality. This is very limiting. You are NOT your body. And, you are not your mind either."

"Then, what am I?"

She seems to light up then. "Now THAT is an interesting question. Also, interesting is the question: Who am I?"

"Yes, what and who am I, then?"

The image of a lotus flower blooms in front of me. I can feel immediately that She has sent it to me. I take its beauty in.

"This flower knows more of its essence than you do because it doesn't know anything. It just is," She replies.

I meditate on this and feel how right she is. I have spent over ten years in a pretty radical and intense self healing path that has led to the diving into the depths of my previously subconscious emotional and soul wounding. I have been asking the question, "Which part of me is feeling this?" in a dedicated way over the last decade. I have been through a series of subpersonalities over the years and through this incredibly effective process which allows for separation and objectivity from reactions through feeling them deeply, I have had more and more experience of the authentic expression of my being. What you can experience of your authentic being, that is, since it is very difficult to pinpoint since it isn't related to a role or self image. But, I can feel how even what I have attached to as my 'authentic self' or 'Higher Self' still has a dualistic filter around it.

"I just am," I respond, trying it on to see how it feels.

"It's ok you do so much defining and sorting of yourself, J bird. You've needed to do it and it was good. You are in a new phase now where you want to dissolve the "I" more so you can experience reality without separation."

I feel a slight wave of panic come over me at the thought of 'dissolving' myself, especially as I have spent so much work and energy to uncover my seemingly most authentic expression! My previous Spiritual Teacher used to say about the ego maturation process that happens through parts work and then the ego obliteration process that happens in sagehood practice is like having a Maserati sports car that you work very hard to get and then proceed to drive it off a cliff!

Kuan Yin feels this hesitation in me and a wave of compassion from Her washes over me.

"Your mind resists this. Your body resists it too. Even your 'authentic self', as you say, resists it. But that's OK because you still are what you are and aren't what you aren't," She says, smiling.

"Buddha taught that it is our sense of 'I' and our sense of separation that causes suffering. I have healed a lot of my suffering through the path I've been on but I am still curious about deepening what I have experienced beyond the mind and beyond the body. And, I guess, even beyond the 'I'."

"Who is saying that?"

I reflect for a moment. I immediately want to go to my usual mode of scanning for a part of myself that might be speaking but I know that isn't what she is looking for. Finally I settle for, "I don't know."

She nods and smiles at me. That feeling of not knowing who I am because I just am is a strange one and vibrates through me, loosening my mind and I can feel, jarring a little bit of my attachment to my body. A surge of energy moves from my crown chakra at the top of my head and down to the base of my spine and eventually out my root chakra.

Another lotus flower appears before me.

This time all I can do is laugh out loud, although I couldn't have told you why.

And Kuan Yin laughs with me and says, "That's better!"

~

Do The Foods You Eat Bring You Good Life Force Energy Or Do They Take It Away During 5D Ascension?

The physical body is our vessel for experiencing life here. It now seems to be possible to take our physical body 'with us' as we ascend into higher consciousness dimensions that were previously only accessible through our astral or etheric bodies. We don't actually go to a different physical location when our consciousness rises and 'dimensions' are not physical places, but rather states of awareness and how we filter and experience reality. The fifth dimension, or what we also call Golden Earth, is one of less sense of separation, peace, and opening out of our 'clair' gifts of clairvoyance, clairaudience, clairsentience, etc., and embodiment of our light body or crystalline body.

As our bodies shift from carbon-based to crystalline-based, our appetites and cravings will probably change. Foods that we could previously eat are no longer as digestible or desired. As we become more intuitive, we become more sensitive to sounds, light sources, temperature, and this heightened sensitivity includes food. Because we are wanting to stay in our bodies while we raise our vibrational frequency, what we put into our bodies in terms of food and water becomes increasingly important. The vibrational frequency of our food impacts us as every food has an energy.

There are many great resources around this topic and I am not an expert in it at all. What I share here is based on my own experience and that of others that I have served as clients over the years in their awakening and healing processes along with their desires (and my own) to be in vibrant and healthy bodies. I also hold that the biggest sense of what you need to eat comes from your own intuition and your body's guidance. Writing a letter to your body asking it what is best for it can be very illuminating. And, you can also write a letter and exchange a dialogue with any illness, disease, or injury that has manifested in your body and it can often be quite interesting and offer you a helpful sense of the emotional and spiritual root causes of what is happening.

The foods that raise your vibrational frequency the most are also the ones considered the most healthy in terms of nutritional value. Raw fruits and vegetables, especially organic ones, have a strong aura and radiate good energy. This is especially true for foods that been labeled as 'super foods' because of their nutritional value but also because of their high energy level. Herbs also have a very high life force and are often extremely medicinal and beneficial to your health. Taking herbal supplements every day can help you feel a baseline of health that will offset some of the other denser foods you might be eating. All this life force energy goes into you and complements the other things you are doing to raise your vibrational frequency such as meditation, yoga or natural exercise, cleaning/protecting/activating your chakras, listening to solfeggio tones in music, choosing to respond with love, making space for yourself and your feelings, etc.

This is a good way to think about which foods to eat or not: Do they compliment and bring you good life force energy or do they take it away? Processed foods, refined sugar, and vegetable oils strip away energy and can actually block the cells from letting in the new energy you are bringing in from the Universe with your Ethereal Guides and from within. To integrate your Higher Self into your physical body (which is ultimately the 'goal' of ascension), you need to be vibrating at a higher frequency. Your Higher Self waits in your etheric field in the meantime, at higher frequency dimensions, until you are 'ready'. Processed foods and refined sugar can actually densify your vibration and can delay the process of higher self embodiment.

Wheat products can be densifying as well, especially the GMO-based and hybrid stuff that passes for wheat and white flour these days. The 'wheat belly' phenomenon is well known and documented as the body slowly stores the extra carbohydrates as fat, especially in the stomach area. Sometimes extra body weight is the body's response to increased vibrational frequency as it works to ground and center you. Your natural body weight can be more revealed through a 'love body' that vibrates at a higher frequency with less weighing it down as your tones of self love and self worth increase.

I have been vegetarian and/or vegan for several years and it works well for my body and my awakening process. I felt a huge surge of energy when I stopped eating meat and that has continued to this day. I feel lighter and more in tune with all the sentient life on the planet. I originally stopped eating meat because of the way that animals are treated in the concentration camp settings of mass produced meat. I tried buying only organic meat for awhile and yet, eventually, lost a taste even for that. The more Divine Feminine energy I brought into my field, the less I could digest anything that had been 'killed.'

Beyond the health benefits, not eating anything that has been killed and limiting the amount of cooked food that you eat allows for more alive energy to move through your body and energy field. There are many wonderful resources that offer the benefits (emotionally, physically, spiritually) of following a predominantly plant-based, raw diet as more and more souls are waking up to this choice. Again, as you become more sensitive, it may even become difficult to eat in restaurants as you will be ingesting the energy of whoever served you and cooked your food. Whatever moods the cooks were in, whatever energy they were feeling and off gassing, goes into the food they serve you. After awhile, you can feel this quite acutely. I do a quick energy cleansing of restaurant food before I eat it by visualizing a white energy swirl moving through it when I eat out, which is pretty rare these days.

All that I offer here about nutrition related to 5D ascension is for you to take in and feel for yourself. Bringing awareness of how foods impact your energy level and if they serve your awakening and ascension process or not is ultimately an opportunity for self love and self care. Wherever the journey takes you, hold it with love for yourself and for the parts of you that just might need some denser foods at times. It is not about extremes here or being hyper vigilant. Holding the process with love and balance allows for the love flow that you ARE to expand and grow, which can be just that much more supported by the foods that you eat.

~

Embodying Our Higher Self Light Body During Ascension

My body still feels fragile from many days of re-alignment, recalibration, and detoxing as the ascension flu moves through. The energies of the detox are somewhat surprising feelings of 'being dense' and just not my usual joyful, creative, high energy, and connected self. This self I currently am, this version, feels like a transitional one.

I get this sense of knobs and dials being turned or maybe wires being restrung is more accurate. While this adjustment is going on, I feel like I am here but not quite here...in transition or the broadcast frequency is still fuzzy and not quite clear. I got an image during meditation this morning of a bright light body that is waiting for me, very close to my current auric field. I can feel the energy of its warmth and the vibration of its lightness and it feels like a beacon of elevated experience.

This 'suit of crystal light and heart warm frequencies' is waiting for me. I think I slip into it in moments, especially during the pass outs that happen frequently during meditation where I slip into a consciousness state that is not quite deep sleep and is not aware either. I travel to other dimensions in this space, float in worlds that are much more porous than this one. I visit with and connect with my star family and Ethereal BEings such as Archangel Metatron. This is happening during dreams as well and I often wake up feeling like I have travelled a lot during sleep.

    This connection with higher dimensions is possible when I am conscious. I have offered myself as a bridge for this kind of connection inside of myself which then extends to others through sharing messages primarily through writing. Right now, receiving messages for others is a bit dimmer than usual as I recalibrate in such a personal way. Yet, I feel moved to share my current process as often I think people's souls and Higher selves can relate to what I am sharing as a phase that they will too someday experience if they are not already. I can feel the Higher Selves that are reading this nodding their heads.....it does feel like the deeper embodiment of my Higher Self's body that I am seeing as coming to me and for me.

    The message, if I feel into one and listen in the moment, is that this is a sacred process and a sacred time. The new horizon of Higher Self embodiment aka ascension invites all of us to embrace where we really are in the moment, to honestly assess what is our trailing edge of being and what is our leading edge. Emotional healing of the 3D pain body frees up our frequencies and is not to be bypassed, as much as parts of you might want to do that out of fear of what you might uncover.

    It feels like with the accelerated energies available to all of us from the sun, from Gaia, from Star BEings, from Ethereal BEings, from the Divine. All of these sources are offering that now is the time to do something and try something brand new. To move your awakening process into a more public space if you have been private. To commit to a path of radical self intimacy and awakening with limitless possibilities to experience love with self, others, and the Divine. To claim your higher self and your light body as you claim your next venture of your journey back home.

    ~

Body Changes, Sleep Pattern Changes, HUM Energies

Mega interrupted sleep 'patterns' for the last few nights for me. I can sleep for about three or four hours, then I am awake for several hours, crash nap, and then repeat again. I can connect this to a late afternoon tea or some chocolate, yet, it feels deeper than that and more about connecting to something BIGGER that is happening in both the COSMOS and personally. Before I knew the ascension vocabulary of 'jumping or dissolving timelines', I would have called what I am feeling, 'anticipating change', feeling changes coming on an intuitive level, and feeling the 'rumbles' of change coming for me personally, my beloveds, SoulFullHeart, and the world at large.

Yet, this isn't anything NEW as change is the ONLY constant and we've been in transition for many years, both personally and globally. There is a HUM though, a feeling of something pulsing and alive, that wants to MOVE us on to the NEXT and the NEXT. Energies that want to move us on to whatever other place we are meant to be both inside of ourselves and what we experience as outer reality.

I can feel the sleep changes (crash naps for a few hours in the 'middle of the day' are newish too) as an aspect of the ascension process and actually a welcome disorientation comes where the mind can't 'track' the days and nights as well and it ALL starts to merge together, which is kind of the goal of ascension after all. The light body, the crystalline 5D body for which we are transitioning into more and more, doesn't probably need the same amount of sleep as our carbon-based denser body did.

I already feel that our relationship to food will change significantly too with much less solid food needed and mostly vegetables and fruits when we do eat. Many of us can and will 'live on light energy' most of the time and go days without eating. This is not that radical as we ARE energy and made up of energy, so all we really need - in another way - is energy, although preparing and eating food can be a wonderful experience. It feels like we will get to choose when we want to eat. Our body weights will be natural and healthy with no extra fat as fat is needed only as an anchoring into 3D reality. A very necessary one at times, yet also, one that densifies us ultimately.

Back to the HUM....I've been asked what it means to experience a 'collapsing timeline'....and today, as I was digesting wonderful openings and changes for some of us in the SoulFullHeart community, I had this sense of these changes feeling 'surreal yet natural.' This is a good way to describe a timeline collapsing...it feels surreal as in 'better than my known reality before' yet 'natural' in the sense of just fitting with essence and soul or Higher Self. Being open to timelines collapsing and shifting is really about being open to that 'anything CAN HAPPEN in ANY MOMENT'...this is tapping into the realm of Infinite Possibilities for which we ARE in our essence as a fractal from Divine Source.

So then, of course, with all this exciting anything can happen-ness, sleep doesn't seem as important even as it CAN BE critical to allow for the conscious mind to rest, the Astral Self to go explore, the integration of other lifetimes, the body to go into calibration and integration mode. I feel a trust in the moment in my body kNOWing what it needs for itself, rest and sleep will arise WHEN they are needed, and it is my mind that fixates on 'missing sleep' or 'not getting enough' or 'interrupted anything'. The mind tracks life through segments and counting down of moments where the soul and higher self just flow in the moment by the moment for the moment. Why does being awake at 3am feel any different than being awake at 4pm, since both of these 'markers' are illusionary and made up anyway? To the soul, these distinctions don't matter because they aren't even REAL.

The HUM is also in the cosmos. It is the waves of PURE love raining and washing over us from the great central sun, center of the Universe, and radiating out of our sun in the form of light codes in the sun rays, which I've been taking in a lot of lately. It's like the Universe is on a caffeine buzz, which feels both surreal AND natural. Momentum is the texture of the HUM too, a beat that is both relentless AND patient as it invites us to come along and also to keep UP with it. It invites us to 'come along' inside of ourselves, surrendering to the bigger picture and our Higher Selves, as we become more and more THAT surrender and THAT HUM in Human form.

Love to you and our sleepless and crashing nap states both…..and feeling the HUM together….

~

Sleep Pattern Interruptions, Astral Integration, Light Body Wisdoms Coming Forward

Sleepy today…..here yet NOT here, somewhere else still. Maybe still in the higher dimensions as I went there earlier to some 'frontlines' to offer love and ambassadorship, met up with some INTERESTING souls/Higher Selves in an intense environment. When I go this high dimensionally, it is all my conscious mind can do to hold the thread inside my body. It is time to astral project soon feels like to really claim a presence in these other places as I am being called more and more to ambassadorship WHILE also opening to serve individual women and groups of women.

It just feels like sleep is calling most of us in order to integrate, to journey and travel out of this body, and to visit with some soul aspects from other lifetimes. I am feeling the astral space opening up more for all of us and TO all of us…….dreams don't feel just like dreams anymore or like an off-gassing of subconscious content…they feel like travels to parallel realities, other lifetimes, visits..so real, so visceral, I am so THERE and it is possible that this is happening for you too.

Sleep is integration and sleeping when you want and as long as you want is SO good if you can…part of you, a 3D part probably, may not like the shift in 'routine' yet THAT is structure put on something that is completely fluid in the NOW anyway. This is where rigid work schedules are NOT easy to navigate.

The body's higher wisdoms are being released and woken up. Wisdoms related to how long to sleep and when. Wisdoms related to what to eat and how much. Wisdoms related to how many light codes to let in and when. Mine has guided me now to eat some grains (whole wheat baked by me preferably, brown rice) after none for a week. And, guidance has been to take in the light codes during sunset mostly instead of during the day….less intense that way and more soothing, more feminine, more heart opening and less activating (which is GOOD for a phase too.)

I tried on a bathing suit the other day and stood in front of a full length mirror for the first time in awhile. We don't own one and they aren't really that common here in Mexico (other than storefront windows.) And, I've defused from an over focus on looking at and analyzing my appearance (Lots of emotional healing to clear THAT one with my Inner Punisher and critic.) So, I was sort of amazed to see the changes in my body and how it just looked and felt different to me since the beginning of the year…..much leaner, more muscular (although I don't DO any exercise really, other than walking around and climbing stairs every day), and just shinier somehow, vibrant, younger. The light body glowing somehow more…it was neat!

Forces beyond our minds are leading all of this, it feels like. We just get clues and bits and pieces of guidance to keep us on track mostly. We get bread crumbs thrown on the trail to navigate slowly our way home. People who come from kNOwing around the ascension process or the body symptoms or what will happen next may be coming from a part of them that is not comfortable with not knowing as I don't think we CAN actually know much beyond what our intuitions offer at times.

LOVE to you on this journey to integrate the stars and our hearts and our souls in this vessel called Human body turning to crystalline.

~

Releasing Body Traumas At The Cellular Level During Ascension

I spent the first days (maybe weeks) of my life inside of a incubator. I was six weeks premature and had underdeveloped lungs or specifically small air sacs. The incubator provided the controlled environment I had left early in order to begin an incarnation during one of the potentially most tumultuous times in Human history. The fact of my early birth and time in the incubator are aspects of my life story, yet, I had previously re-lived the emotional reactions I felt during that time during a process group many years ago: fear, powerlessness, and a strong desire to go back 'home'.

This last week, with my lungs in an agitated state and a deep cough, my body took me back to this time when I was newly born with fragile lungs. I heard the whoosh of the machines near me and the muffled sound of the nurses' voices. Occasional hands would come in through the openings and sooth me or take me out of the incubator for feeding and cleaning. What I had not previously remembered were the Light BEings around me, brightness outlining angel wings. I had not realized before that I came close to death (maybe my mother never told me or didn't know). The Ethereal BEings were there to offer that I needed to stay to live out my purpose on Earth....I had 'a lot to do'.

I could feel the memory of this newborn experience living in the cells of my body, in my DNA, which as it is upgrading in the ascension process is letting go of the memories stored within from my lifetime as a carbon-based Human BEing. I also felt this week the memories stored at a cellular level from fifteen years of cigarette smoking. I started when I was 17 and quit nearly 13 years ago now, yet the damage from so many inhalations of nicotine and other chemicals seems to live inside of my cells: in their memory. Over the years, I felt the emotional pain that drew me to smoking and, also, the biggest motivation of all, which was a means to escape daily life for a few minutes and have peace to myself. This week, I am experiencing the cells purging the memories of this repeated damage.

I'm sharing these experiences because they illuminate for me an interesting aspect to the physical phases of the ascension process. This process is about raising our vibrational frequency to experience a higher consciousness and filtering of reality that is more in alignment with our essence as Infinite Love and from a Divine source. What does it actually mean for a body to become a crystalline body or Christ Consciousness/fifth dimensional (and higher) body? None of us actually know, although many are experiencing the transition to it.

We are experiencing food craving changes and appetite shifts. This is leading to more and more people choose being vegetarian or vegan, eat more organic vegetables, no longer eating processed foods, as they connect eating certain foods with a raised or lowered vibrational frequency. We are getting headaches that are beyond just some pressure in the head and that feel like things are actually getting rearranged inside of our skulls which, in a way, they are. The pituitary and pineal glands especially are getting rewired and expanded. You can almost hear them crackling with new energetic strands being wired up. I have seen mine forming new crystal structures that look like snowflakes. They become the new processing center for the new Crystalline Human, along with the heart chakra.

There are the ascension flu symptoms that I've been experiencing lately which I now feel, as I shared, is actually the cells letting go of memories of illness and damage. We can't take these denser frequencies 'with us' and so they need to be moved out of the vessel to continue the rise in vibrational frequency upward. I recommend thinking about what might be stored in your body's cells, what memories of 3D life might you need to heal and release? There doesn't seem to be 'time' when it comes to cellular memory, so even the earliest childhood experiences of physical trauma are stored.

The sense that I have about all this, and what I have been offered many times by my Guides, is that this is all part of a sacred process. This sacred process has been given to us as a gift by Gaia herself who is ascending already and our hostess is inviting us to come along. It's a process provided to us by Star BEings who want to exist with us in a collaborative world on a Golden Earth. The discomfort of purging, releasing what no longer serves, moving beyond the old to embrace the new....it is all worth it in the dawning of a new beginning, new reality, with new bodies in a new world made of love.

~

Ascension Flu Offers Opportunity To Go Within

Ascension flu has been making its way through our home. Not surprising considering how much upgrading, shifting, and transformation is going on for both Raphael and I. Every day in the last month is seeming to bring new clarities, altered states, awakenings, intense connections with Ethereal BEings....big shifts both personally and in our relationship. This is what it feels like the increasing electromagnetic energy fluctuations of 2017 are offering ALL of us.

On one level, it's the typical flu with runny nose, congestion, cough, fever, overall tired feeling. Yet, felt from the perspective of ascension, you can get a sense of the sloughing off that is going on....letting go of old frequencies, congested frequencies, to continue to rise up into higher dimensional spaces. The cells of our bodies are changing at the DNA level and with that a flushing out of toxins that have been stored for life.

Always, when the body doesn't feel well, is there an even deeper invitation to go within, hold space for yourself, feel what is going on inside. My creative output of the last month has been a lot, the words just come and come with the next project and piece arising before the last one is complete. Always from joy, not obligation, does this creativity arise and is just fueled by the recently more robust response from those of you who have taken in my writing with such resonance and love.

I can feel in my heart chakra, in my chest, that I have taken in some heart cries and aches of the 'world'...maybe because I've been posting about sacred romance and the longing runs so deep in our collective consciousness AND unconsciousness. Also, fourth chakra congestion is about letting in more love. This I can feel for myself and I hear Metatron offering, "Yes, Jelelle, you serve love and you give and you share AND also you let in and receive too. It is a flow, a circle, a reciprocal opportunity."

I feel like I have been letting in this new reality of response and yet, of course, there is the adjustment that is at a deeper level, a tendril here and there of unworthiness or just a sense of surreality about what it feels like is coming for me personally and for SoulFullHeart.....a phase of growth and goodness, of new involvement and drawing more souls to engage and co-create with us.

So, with this FLU (Filaments Lighting Up!) I am going within, creating a little cocoon inside and letting in self love and care (plus the wonderful love of my beloved) and Metatron, who is a bit impatient to keep creating with me and yet, he seems OK to wait, letting this one ride out. He has about four books that he wants me to start reading anyway!

There is certainly nothing glamorous about this aspect of the ascension process, yet it feels sacred nonetheless and an important adjustment and realignment to the new consciousness and body upgrades coming in!

~

Following The Clues That Your Soul Is Offering You Related To Everything In Your Life, Including Ascension Body Symptoms

"Everything is data"....this I like to offer about the awakening and ascending and growing process. Everything that we are drawn to, every movie, every piece of music, every relationship, etc. Everything that we resist. Everything that we resonate with. Everything that we let go of. Everything that we experience in our emotional, spiritual, mental, social, and physical bodies. ALL of it offers us data and information about ourselves, our souls, our emotional bodies, our physical bodies, our healing process, our growth…… if we are willing to LOOK at it and FEEL it from this perspective with curiosity and self love.

There are so many clues and hints and signs that we are given by our Higher Self and Guides/Soul Aspects. These are like breadcrumbs for us to notice, to pick up, and to follow on our journey to remembering who we ARE as SOULS here. These are like pieces to put together of our puzzle for remembering our essence as multidimensional BEings. None of what we experience is 'just coincidence' as we have been conditioned to believe in 3D reality. ALL of it is part of the BIG picture of the WHO, and the WHY, and the WHAT, and the HOW of our essence expressing here.

Because we chose amnesia and soul forgetting in order to really lean into and inhabit the 3D experiment, we have to become a love detective of sorts for ourselves in order to put the pieces of our soul picture back together again, in order to facilitate our own remembering process again. The love detective energy inside of us is curious……SO CURIOUS about it all and is also WILLING to question everything that we have in our lives from a soul perspective with an openness to let it go if it doesn't serve our expression AS LOVE.

This love detective energy helps us move out of victimhood because it accepts that we have CHOSEN what we experience as a soul and it ALL serves our growth (no matter how hard or painful it is.) This love detective is building a case for our expression of our soul and is tracking down the clues that SHOW how our souls are peeking out at us ALL THE TIME (sometimes SHOUTING at us actually)....we just need to listen, to feel, and to take in.

Let me offer an example of this that has come up a few times lately in sessions with women. You may feel that your current job or career or business is not really a reflection of your soul. You may consciously feel that it is 'dense' or more '3D' and very much feel a desire to leave it. However, I invite you to take a moment to feel what your choice of livelihood is reflecting about your expression of soul gifts as it always seems to be, in one way or another, to one degree or another. For example, let's say you are a salesperson and you have come up with a new way to offer sales....really feeling what the deeper needs of the customers are and they even acknowledge and thank you for this. Your co-workers notice how your approach is different and maybe you are even being invited to become a manager to train others.

This example shows how your soul gifts of being a Healer, being empathic and feeling other people's feelings, being a Teacher and Trainer of souls, is all expressing in this job. Is this job the long-term one for you in terms of serving love from a 5D energy? Probably not, but being curious about it from a love detective place offers you clues about WHAT your soul purpose is here and how you might express it. And it gives you a new way to hold it and think about it as you transition to more of that soul purpose expression.

Another example comes up around the body symptoms that so many are experiencing related to ascension. There seems to be a collective and universal experience of these body symptoms as our carbon-based bodies transmute to crystalline, 5D light bodies. Many people express and comment and share about these symptoms. Yet, rarely, do they ASK their bodies what the specific symptoms MEAN for them. They often just write it off as 'part of the ascension process.' Yet, the deeper (and more interesting) ground comes up when you ask: What are these symptoms trying to tell you and have you FEEL about your body and also your emotional body and perhaps your chakras too?

Rather than just 'asking for guidance' to your Ethereal Guides (which you may relate to as being 'outside' of you), try asking your BODY itself about what is going on. This can be done during meditation through visualization or through written journaling or both. Rather than looking outside for a read out on what is going on with your body or just commiserating about it, feel it for yourself and let some of the clues of your own process come to life for you. Also, listening to and taking in what your body is trying to tell you often greatly relieves, reduces, or cures the symptoms that are occurring.

Most of what I offer is a reflection of self permission for people to become their own love detectives by modeling and templating that for them during sessions, group calls, writings, videos. I am immensely and authentically curious about them and come from this place, often asking more questions than giving reflections (although sometimes that comes through if it is needed.) I offer an example of this because I LIVE this.

Everything is data for me about me in my life…offering a next piece of illumination or possibility for me in my process. A recent example is how I've related to sinus congestion and allergy reactions that come and go for me, leaving me feeling 'flu-like'. Rather than just saying, "I have allergies" (which is the mainstream 3D way to look at the body), I ask myself, "What are these allergies and nasal congestion connected to? What are they trying to tell me?" And then I go into ALL of my bodies (physical, emotional, mental, spiritual, social, chakral) to feel the answers. Sometimes I get more questions (new places to go) than answers, but always I can connect what is manifesting with something related to my process.

In this example of the flu/congestion symptoms, I have been feeling how I am still moving out previous congestions from my emotional body of not being seen or heard related to my soul gifts for the last several years except for with a small group of people. The recent GOOD watering of resonance and support and being seen (and read) from a growing number of souls is flushing these congestions/these oils out. I am 'catching up with myself' is the feeling, or rather my personality (whatever lingers there of 3D and 4D Self) is catching up with my Higher Self/5D Self embodiment that is happening more and more just naturally for me. Another layer of this is connected to activation of my causal chakra, which is an ascension chakra located at the back of the head.

I have been stepping into my gifts as a Galactic Love Ambassador and into energies of battlegrounds offering love as possibility, with the Reptilians especially. The causal chakra seems to hold our abduction woundings (one of the key ways that access to our memory of being Star Seeds is blocked) along with the emotional body. BOTH bodies need our love and healing to allow more openings to our Star BEings aspects/Guides. At least this is what I have discovered in my process of remembering my star origins and merging consciousness more with my Star BEing aspects.

And yet ANOTHER level of this congestion manifestation for me has to do with clearing out congested energy for others (women that I hold space for) and, more and more, for the collective. I don't seem to get any personal body reactions when I do this UNLESS I have something to feel personally about it…..if I do, then it will show up for me to feel into. The other layer here too that we ask ourselves in SoulFullHeart with just about everything is, "What part of me is connected to this and why?" As you are usually connecting with one specific part at a time in the process, you would check in with that part of you to see if the body symptoms are connected to them (they usually seem to be the part's way of 'getting your attention'. This especially happens in the beginning of the process as you access energies in your emotional body and they 'burp' up for the first time.)

This may seem a bit overwhelming to you in this moment to feel into something as simple as nasal congestion from so many different perspectives, yet, with practice, it becomes quite natural AND so empowering. AND it helps with getting to the root cause of WHY the symptoms are happening at an emotional body level, which is key to the alleviation of them. Rather than just fusing to the reality as it presents itself, you feel through the deeper meanings to it. This offers so much more magic, healing and love possibilities to your life. And, your love detective gets to respond and discover MORE and MORE, contributing to your arising embodiment of your Sacred Humanity here with Gaia at this time of great change and transformation.

~

FINANCIAL AREA

The Financial area of life includes your relationship to money, material wealth, abundance, livelihood, soul purpose expression and purpose.

3D: The conditioning that your 3D Self receives around money is a materialistic, capitalistic worldview where accumulation of wealth is valued, often over all else. Money is seen as the primary motivation for work exchange. Emphasis is placed on finding a 'good career that pays well' and the educational system can support this conditioning as well. How your 3D Self feels about money is connected to the templating you received from your birth family. High anxiety frequencies can connect to the perceived sense of lack or scarcity around money and money flow, even if it is abundant. Money subconsciously represents love to the 3D Self so the perception of abundance or scarcity is connected to the deeper emotional woundings of the 3D Self. As a 3D Self, you are likely to be doing a job or career that you do not like or that 'pays the bills' but is not connected to your deeper soul passion. This decision usually connects back to unhealed unworthiness in the 3D pain body.

4D: Your 4D Self is awakening to the illusion of money that 3D conditioning offered to you. You are feeling how money is an energy flow, an 'idea' that is actually neutral once the emotional projections have been healed around it. You become attracted to and engaged in gift exchange with others, choosing not to use actual currency when you can with others in resonance with you. As a 4D Self, you are transitioning to earning your livelihood from sharing your soul gifts and serving love. If you do need to do something else to 'earn money', it is usually connected to your soul gifts in some way as you are not drawn to suffering as you move into upper 4D consciousness. You are shifting from focus on material gain to spiritual gain, even as you have desires and needs associated with a personal 'bounty' that reflects the increasing goodness you are feeling about yourself and about life. You may go through some ups and downs, completions and endings related to money during your lower 4D journey, such as needing to declare personal bankruptcy, being audited, losing a business or dissolving a business partnership, seeking new opportunities, and greatly reducing your personal income as you shift to your soul purpose work providing your livelihood.

5D: Your 5D Self feels the illusion of money and has separated from the need for material gain as the primary goal of life. Your 5D Self relates to abundance as an energy that originates from within, rather than something 'gifted' from the external world. Your definition of abundance is not about material wealth, although wealth is welcomed if that serves your soul purpose and capacity to serve love to others. True wealth comes from a visceral sense of your innate goodness and intimate union with others and the Divine.

You no longer feel entitled to money or material wealth and are deeply grateful for the blessings and synchronicities that come your way as you share more and more of your soul gifts. You give within exchanges based on good will and resonant ground and you receive with and from the same energy back. You don't have anxiety about if your needs will be taken care of as you trust the Universe that lives within you and outside of you to provide for you. As you vibrate more and more with the frequency of Infinite Love, you feel every moment for the Infinite Possibilities that it offers related to receiving and giving abundance that goes much beyond material wealth.

Questions For You:
How did you locate yourself related to the financial area of life – as primarily a 3D, 4D or 5D consciousness and why?
What are your frustrations in the financial area?
What are your desires in the financial area?
~

Money As An Exchange Of Energy: Conversations With Archangel Metatron

"Money is energy. It is an exchange of energy and, in another way, it does not exist and is only as real as the perception that you project upon it and the way that you relate with it. It is not the root of all evil as fear of love is what roots in evil or darker frequencies ," says Archangel Metatron in response to a question I asked him about the higher consciousness definition of money.

"Yes, that has been my sense of money for many years," I answer, smiling at him.

He smiles back at me and continues, "Third dimensional reality – with its dualistic frequencies of separation and lack – has projected these feeling tones onto money. To the 3D Self, the perceived lack or abundance of money directly relates to the often subconscious sense of this inside of themselves."

"When we feel 'tight' or 'lacking' about money, it represents feelings of scarcity about love in our lives…."

"Yes, Jelelle. When there is an inner sense of abundant flow of love with yourself, with Divine Source, with others….then money is felt to be abundant, no matter how much of it there actually IS in the bank account."

I digest this as a deeper truth in the moment even though this has been a process ground of expansion for me over the years and in serving others, including coaching small business clients on how to think about the financial area of their businesses.

"In my experience and experience guiding others, the 3D Self especially uses the 'earning of money' to stay in suffering loops, especially around putting their energy and focus into jobs that aren't connected to their passion purpose or soul purpose work," I say. "This can be a transitional phase for people…to move out of doing a job just for the money to receiving their livelihood from the expression of their deepest soul passion. It has been a transition for my mate Raphael and I that has taken many years. Should I tell that story?"

"Yes, please, Jelelle, I feel it would be helpful," says Metatron, sending a wave of golden love my way. I take his love into my heart, feeling it infuse my 'story' with new frequencies of relevance and gratitude.

"I worked an 'office job' for many years to support my daughter and myself. There was usually some connection to my passion purpose in these jobs: as a medical assistant in a cancer center, as an editor and reporter for a small business journal, as a coach and manager for small business clients. Each job seemed to bring me a step closer to the embracement of my soul gift expression. As I started really focusing on my emotional healing and spiritual awakening process, I eventually became a facilitator of others, holding space for their exploration, while earning money to do this. I left the office job and 'steady paycheck' environment ten years ago and have not returned to it."

"Raphael ran a painting contracting business in the Vancouver area for thirty years and we both lived off of the income from that until a few years ago when we left our client base there to move to Mexico. Raphael went through many transitions around the business, yet there was always an open and conscious question for us about if our deepest soul purpose work could provide the means of our livelihood rather than the painting business. We were serving others through SoulFullHeart, earning money through space holding and selling our books, yet, also we made sometimes difficult choices in our lifestyle to support this transition. We moved into an RV, sold almost everything we owned twice, declared bankruptcy, and left Canada for Mexico where the cost of living is much less and you can grow your own food year-round."

Metatron nods at me to continue, knowing that I am not one prone to 'telling my story' as it often doesn't feel real to me anymore and may not have the juice that the present moment does.

"We have lived very simply since being here in Mexico. We lived off of the last of the painting money savings (including using it to buy a piece of land on an off-grid ranch where we can retreat to if needed) until it ran out. Then, Gabriel and Kalayna began to earn money teaching English online. Their earnings, in addition to what we bring in through sessions, books, and donations into SoulFullHeart, is what currently provides the livelihood for all four of us."

"One of the biggest shifts in how I related to money came from sharing money as a community, pooling all of it from what we earn as individuals to be shared together, for the last few years. The amazing thing about this is that because of our ground of transparency and the SoulFullHeart process itself, which is our mutual way of relating, we have been able to bring reactions and triggers to each other around this without any conflicts arising because of it. There has been very little tension about sharing the money with each other and the sense of gratitude around it flows freely between us all."

"This IS wonderful, Jelelle! This is more the way that money and alchemy flows in fifth dimensional consciousness. The energy exchanges with others are based in good will, gratitude, and a personal sense of inner abundance. Coming from this place of open abundant heart tones, sharing is natural and there is a deep trust that whatever you give will come back to you and the Universe will provide for you."

"Yes, and somehow, from this place, all the needs of each individual person get met through this exchange, Metatron. The deeper phase for us in this transition to fifth dimensional consciousness around money is for ALL of our money and alchemy flow to be coming from SoulFullHeart and its offerings. And to experience a deeper abundance of goodness and beauty related to our living spaces. We also feel that gift exchange with others, including others coming to live with us here in Mexico and sharing in and contributing to the community pool of money, is a key aspect to the fulfillment of our vision and our desires. We are all visualizing this during meditation, connecting with our Guides like you around it, and continuing to focus on inner healing and expanded heart and soul consciousness. It is a journey in process for sure."

"Your story invites others to feel what their journey is related to this transition from 3D consciousness around money to 4D awakening to 5D," Metatron says. "And I invite them, in this moment, to feel where they may be associating lack of love or abundance in their lives with how they are experiencing their money flow. I invite them to feel how the ways they earn their livelihood is connected to their soul purpose gift expression and ways that it is not. I invite them to feel their deepest desires related to money flow, abundance, and external (and internal) experience of it. I invite them to feel how much trust they feel that the Universe will provide all that they need."

"This is a powerful invitation, Metatron. It is one that we offer as well in exploration of this ground from a higher consciousness perspective while holding the space inside to feel all the reactions that come up in response to it!"

"That is a magical thing indeed and I look forward to supporting others in this journey too!"

"Me too, Metatron….me too!"

~

Life Transitions, Trust And Surrender

Raphael and I were just digesting how much has changed for us since coming into Puerto Vallarta exactly five months ago in June, 2016. We had about $40 on us with just enough money coming in to live very cheaply for he and I, plus Gabriel and Kalayna. Prior to that, we had been living for 19 months in a remote setting, off-grid, limited to no internet connection and our nest egg that we brought with us from Canada to buy land, etc. had been spent six months earlier.

Thanks to the efforts of Kalayna and Gabriel teaching English online, we were able to move to Puerto Vallarta so that all of us could be together in community. For a month, we lived in a space with three rooms, with Kalayna and Gabriel sharing a bedroom with two twin beds. We got our three bedroom apartment after the first month and at least could all have our own bedrooms. We felt grateful for everything that we had even though it was very little. Living on our ranch, eating what came from our gardens and very simple food, not going to restaurants or movies or shopping…it had taught us to appreciate the very simple things in life and that which matters the most: love and connection.

Eventually, people began to become drawn to SoulFullHeart and having sessions with us, mostly through connecting on Facebook. We had only been on Facebook for about three months prior to that, so it was all very new to us. We didn't and don't have a 'marketing or sales strategy', we are just ourselves as much as possible – offering a way of life and process that we live as our daily reality within community. I was shocked and stunned in a very good way to begin serving women in session space after letting all of it go in terms of being a 'teacher' or 'facilitator' and surrendering it to the Divine while I was at the ranch.

Just this last month, through a freelance opportunity for a tech startup, we are earning quite good money (especially for Mexico) plus with facilitation donations and Kalayna's and Gabriel's pay as teachers. We are now able to afford eating in restaurants, to buy new clothing (after two years of wearing the same things all the time), and for Kalayna and Gabriel to rent their own separate studio apartments that happen to be in the same building as us! This living arrangement more fits our vision of sharing community space for meals and group circles when desired and for everyone to have their own individual living spaces otherwise.

The Divine has given us so much since coming to the city….abundance in the form of people and, yes, in the form of money. Our desires that had been suppressed somewhat on the ranch are now coming forward for higher quality things that will last over time, not fall apart, and are truly worth the money.

So much trust and surrender has been needed over the last few years....willingness to live with very little, 'give up' so much of what we thought mattered, only to be shown over and over that when we are not expectant or entitled so much love can come to us and in so many forms! Now that we are going to visit the ranch again for a few days starting tomorrow, we can check in with who we are now, who we were then, and maybe get some sense of who we will become....although that, of course, is in Divine hands!

~

Money As A Mirror Of Our Relationship To Love

This writing is by Raphael:

Let's get real for a moment about money...not 'brutally' real, but lovingly and honestly real with ourselves about money and its role in our lives.

While we're at it, let's break the cultural silence around money. Let's feel money's all too real, larger-than-life role in our lives, its limitation in our choices, and also, its potential for deep rebirth inside of us.

Let's begin this worthy quest with some 'quest'ions. What role does money play in your sense of whether you get to lead the life you really want to or not? How much space does anxiety about money take up in your life and dictate the options you feel you have or don't have? How do you imagine your life would look and feel different if money were no object? What current relationships in your life would be different were it not for financial necessity? Do you love the country and location where you live, or is it also more about financial necessity? What about how you earn money in the world? Is it in alignment with your deepest sense of calling and purpose, or is it more about holding down a job that you dislike or even detest? How could these tough and sensitive money questions, and the truth-telling mirror that money is, be used to either set us free or keep us small indefinitely?

So many are finding the issue of money to be one of the strongest tethers or anchors keeping them stuck in a 3D reality while they are wanting and even aching to inhabit a deep ascension process of being in tune with their Higher Self, their Guides, and their deeper gift expression in the world. So how do we enter a new timeline where money is concerned? How can we transmute this issue of money from one of the biggest hindrances to our ascension/awakening process, into one of our greatest means of awakening?

I'd like to share with you my own personal bigger-picture lens through which I've come to see money. See what resonates for you as your truth, and of course, as always, pass on the rest, or shelve it for further inquiry if you're not sure.

My truth is that we are not victims in any way to money, or to the powers that be around money, or to debt, etc, All perception of ourselves as victims of a money system gone awry is in large part, in service of a part of us wanting and needing to stay small and secure in what it knows and feels as familiar. (I'm not saying that we don't have a corrupt money system. I'm saying that we don't have to be subject to a corrupt money system.)

Money itself and its role in our lives is a mirror that doesn't lie and what it so effectively mirrors is our relationship to money and ultimately our relationship to love, which is ultimately what money is – simply a carrier of energy. Finding the courage to open out this truth alone can begin a whole new wave in your world around money. If this is true, then money and its role in your life is something in your direct control. I am responsible for the current circumstances in my life around money. I am not a victim in any way around money. Not all of me may feel this is true all of the time, but this too is in my circle of influence to change.

A key piece in beginning a significant shift here is seeing that money itself is not the issue, but instead it is our relationship to money that is the issue. It's not the thing, but our relationship to the thing that determines what is healthy or unhealthy.

Let's shift now to weave in some practicalities around money in light of this bigger picture.

If you feel stuck in a job you don't like, feel into how a part of you must feel something desirable about this job from its point of view, or obviously you wouldn't be there. In getting to know this part of you, what negotiations could you come to with this part of you that would either make the job more bearable for the time being or allow you to take steps to chart a new course for yourself?

Which leads to the next piece…what is it that you really love? What is it that you would do for no money just simply for the fun of it? And what if that expression of your gift could also be your means of earning a living? What is it that expands you out as you engage in it, rather than contracts you inward? What is it that you feel called to? The word 'career' comes from the latin 'vocarre' which means 'to call'. None of us are without a calling, some of us just haven't consciously heart it yet. So what steps could you take to engage in this calling expression more and more in your life? My truth is that there is always a beginning place that one is aware of, yet beginning there is a negotiation with the part of us who isn't quite ready to begin there.

Getting started there at this beginning is being on the path of sacred calling that opens out the next pieces in terms of direction, courage, and recognition by others in the world. Why would we think that offering something less in the world than our deepest gifts would be a good idea where our wellbeing is concerned? Value always flows to need and back again in a continual loop. What are you giving in the world that others need? Giving yourself to the deepest needs are what provides a deep security where material needs are concerned regardless of what's happening 'economically'. Seek to start your own independent economy where what you supply in the world is in high demand! This could be as simple a beginning as cleaning up trash in your neighbourhood, and gifting yourself to Gaia in this way, and adding waves of love and beauty to the world around you as you do. Starting there will lead you to your next piece as you feel into your deeper guidance around calling and purpose. You will not be without remuneration for your contribution.

Another piece is to let go of the idea of ever 'retiring.' You will be ever in gift exchange and contribution in the world as long as you are here. Life, if anything is a symbiosis of life exchanging with life. Here, it's actually impossible for life not to look after you. Life begets life. Retiring, in the normal way it's related to is to take yourself out of the contribution picture which is really taking yourself out of the life picture. You may change roles and let go of a career path, but see yourself as a deep and profound contributor as long as you have breath.

If you are living on a so called 'fixed income' (or from a saved nest egg), you are going to want to 'unfix' it. The ways you can do that are all about changing your relationship to money. Some of the most anxious people financially are people with significant savings, where the amount of anxiety actually INCREASES with the more money they have, and the longer they have it. Money itself only does good as it is transacted. Money in stasis is dead money, like fresh fruit going bad, losing value and causing anxiety as it sits there. Money in motion on the other hand is a love machine. What gifts of love could you give yourself with that money that will actually increase your trust in a benevolent universe?

And what about debt? Why on Earth would you stay in commitment to old debts that you have little hope of ever paying off? This is a big way that people stay stuck using a self image picture of 'doing the right thing' and commit themselves to a drudgery of debt. What deeper gifts are you justifying withholding from the world as you do this so called 'right thing'? The only debtors' prison is the one you willingly remain in while the door is unlocked awaiting your courage and choice to leave. Bankruptcy is way easier than most imagine. For many, even simpler will be Debt Repudiation – just walking away from accumulated debts. The blocks to seeing and feeling this are all emotional in my truth. What gifts could you give the world after you have given yourself permission to break an unhealthy commitment to debt? Again, I ask 'how could any strategy for financial security be valid if it's about giving something less than your best gifts in the world?' Symbiosis simply doesn't work inside of a withhold!

Another big piece you can feel into is to gift money-as-love into places that align with your soul purpose and path. Giving money is a powerful way to plant seeds into the soil you desire to rebase your life direction and growth into. Money is only energy and all energy is sourced ultimately in love. I would love to be in a love-gift money exchange place with you if my work is a gift to you. You can do that on our Patreon page here:https://www.patreon.com/soulfullheart. Maybe fully receiving the gift I have for you can't occur for you until you enter into a deeper reciprocity with me, and vice-versa. Again, it's the flow of love and the flow of money in a seedtime-and-harvest reality that moves our worlds, both internally and externally.

Another big way to move your relationship to money is to see every expense you have as a 'gift of you' instead of a bill to pay or an obligation. You are now gifting the power company money in exchange for the gift they gave you of electricity piped into your home. Wow! You are gifting the grocery store with love-money for their love gifts to you that nourish your body. What could be more sacred? You just got all this benefit, just by giving them some digits from a computer screen or some magical pieces of paper! If you can't give this gift with joy, you are corrupting the gift, along with your own alchemy.

Maybe you should more consider refusing their gift and setting up your own solar system or growing your own food if that feels more in alignment with your deepest love expression in the world. Can you feel how big this is to stop 'paying for' anything, to be instead in a love gift and deep gratitude exchange with everything you acquire in the world for your wellbeing? Talk about entering Golden Earth Now...! And doing it all from a change in heart.

I'm curious how this is landing in you. Can you feel a 'New World Order' wanting to arise inside of you personally?

The old ways of relating to money may still have some inertia as they continue to move through your life, but the very big difference is that these movements are diminishing, as new ways are arising. You are entering a new world at a rate and pace that is in alignment with feeling all there is to feel along the way. It's in feeling this 'all there is to feel' as blossoming Sacred Humans that change happens. It is here that our inner and outer worlds are transformed.

~

Feeling Your Relationship To Money

This is written by Raphael:

Our relationship to money (which is ultimately an illusion) can either be a source of suffering or freedom. First up, money itself isn't your and my problem. The challenge with money is in our relationship to money. There's a big difference there and a ton of freedom for you right there if you're open to it.

Money is an external. Your relationship to money is an internal. The same can of course be said about so many things in life, and a heap of freedom can be found by exploring this same principle in all these areas. It's not the thing itself that makes something helpful or a hindrance in your life, but your relationship to the thing that makes all the difference. And, I might add, how parts of you relate to money is where the exploration about money gets very interesting and illuminating.

If we are here to learn and grow as souls in this ongoing discovery of Infinite Love in an Infinite Universe of Infinite

Possibilities, then money is surely going to be one of our biggest classrooms. Most of us use and need money to buy the things we want and need. It's as central to our lives as breakfast.

But, money isn't real. Well, it's real enough, okay, I'll give you that. I'll accept it if you give me some and all that. But essentially, on a deeper meta level, money isn't real at all, as we think of it, and it's important to feel this if we are going to shift our relationship to money. We Humans made up money as simply a means of exchange. Then we all agreed to recognize it as such and voila, 'We're in the Money' as the song goes.

But now we see why money holds us so spellbound, whether in its abundance or absence. Money is something we can't live without, right? Well, yes and no. I'm physically not going to die tomorrow if I run out of money, but in all likelihood, I'm going to need to find some before too long to buy the things I need for life sustenance. If the love of money is the root of all evil, then I'm one evil guy because my mind is on money a lot. And so is yours, right?

But what is money then if it ultimately isn't real? Well, we can say and pretty easily so, that money is energy. Everything in the universe is energy, even what we call matter and physical objects are all energy. And the ultimate source energy of the universe is love.

What money really is……..is simply love.

Now, we can see why we are collectively so crazy about it. None of us can or want to live without love. And we also have all kinds of scarcity and abundance reactions around love too that get projected onto our ideas about money. And now, we can begin to see why it's all about our relationship to money that makes all the difference rather than money itself.

In November 2014, Jelelle and I left behind and retired from our primary source of income in my painting contracting business and decided to move to Mexico. Our combined net worth nest egg and available credit gave us enough to live modestly for a bit more than a year. I have earned about the equivalent in the last two years of what I earned in an average few days of painting. Needless to say, there's been a ton to feel and process around our relationship to money! And I wouldn't trade it for anything.

As that year of living off of a dwindling nest egg went by with no awareness of how we were going to get any more money, there was plenty of anxiety to feel. It wasn't crippling anxiety because of the work we had done previously in our relationship with money, but there was still anxiety. What I learned as I was spending this painting nest egg money that I earned in Canada was that the energy in that money itself had a lot of 'fossilized' anxiety in it. I was coming into more and more trust, and the anxiety was actually associated with the energy in the money itself and where and when and how it was earned.

When we reached the end of that money, life opened out magically in the form of Kalayna and then Gabriel finding teaching English gigs online, and we are beginning to receive money donations for SoulFullHeart sessions. I've never been more 'broke' in my life and I'm the happiest I've ever been in relationship to money!

I have desires for more, even plenty more, but I feel so much trust that whatever the Universe brings me, it's what I need for my growth. Last month a man who was interested in SoulFullHeart wanted to meet us and took us out to dinner at what was pretty much the fanciest restaurant I've ever been to. Sitting there in my falling apart sandals after living off of the monthly budget of what I used to spend at Starbucks in a month was an almost overwhelming experience. I did go to tears at one point letting it in.

But what's your story around money? Does it feel like a source of suffering or freedom in your life? What 'you do for dollars' or pesos, wants to be transmuted more and more by feeling all there is to feel around your relationship to money, which ties into your deepest existential need for love. All of this shifts into less suffering and more freedom from the tyranny of money as you feel and heal your relationship to money.

If you give your greatest gifts into the world and you die because you couldn't live off of it, would there be any better way to go? Really, I feel that is what we are all being invited to live into, to change more and more into living in a gift economy.

"All you need is love, love….love is all you need!"

ENVIRONMENTAL AREA

Through your heart, you feel the pulse of all life, the love for which all is made.....the portal to compassion.

Through your soul, you remember the stars, your star family, your star seed origins.....the gateway to reunion.

Through your heart, you become self loving and self accepting, love overflowing.....the flow of goodness.

Through your soul, you awaken to your mission and purpose in being with Gaia, sharing your gifts.....the service of love.

Through your love, you heal the karmic binds within and with others, the patterns of learning and lessons.....the cycle for growing.

Through your love, you reclaim your Sacred Humanity, your origins as an aspect of Divine source.....the reason for existence.

~

The environmental area of life includes your physical surroundings, geography, global and galactic environment, the natural world, minerals and crystals, and animals.

3D: It has been necessary for your 3D Self to have certain denser frequencies in order to fit in and survive third dimensional reality. These densities can lead to a screening out or filtering or numbing down of the impact of the environment around you or awareness about what is happening in the larger global environment. Your 3D Self has learned to adapt in environments that may be toxic in different ways or at least lower your vibrational frequency rather than raise it. You may be consciously suffering over or dislike your current geography, yet are 'living with it' somehow.

You are less impacted and sensitive to sounds, smells, energies in your environment and less aware of how you impact others around you. You may have some intellectual awareness about what is happening with Gaia's environment and your personal impact on the Earth, yet may feel not much motivation to change your lifestyle around it or advocate for change. You may feel connected to animals yet may not yet be aware of the telepathic and visual communication that is possible with animals or how sensitive they are to energy. Your 3D Self can find solace in nature, glimpses of soul tones, yet it may still feel like nature is 'outside' of you and something to visit as a physical space.

4D: As you are raising your frequencies into 4D, your 4D Self becomes much more aware of the impact of the environment around you. You are becoming more and more sensitive to sounds, smells, and energies around you. You are sensitive to the energy of places and geographies and are transitioning to choices that are more in alignment with the vibrational frequency that you feel within you. You are drawn to be around nature or near the ocean or mountains, wherever you can connect with your soul.

You are aware of your impact on the Earth and are becoming aware of environmental issues and causes. You may go through a phase of becoming very concerned about collapse of the 3D world and of climate change and other environmental issues. And your 4D Self can become self righteous and angry too, needing to protest against the 3D conditioning you received. You have a deepening relationship with animals and feel them to be conscious BEings who can be communicated with telepathically and you may align your soul purpose with healing and communicating with animals. You may also decide, based on this communion with animals, to become a vegetarian or vegan (and to raise your vibrational frequency). You use crystals and stones to add in your healing and increase your frequency, becoming personally connected to their energy.

5D: Your 5D Self is connected deeply to animals, nature, and Gaia as a consciousness. Mother Gaia is a living, feminine consciousness that you can also feel inside of you, along with the entire Universe. You can connect with Gaia through many ways and need time with and in nature to feel the bigger context of life.

You realize that Gaia doesn't need saving as She is a creator goddess and has chosen the 3D experiment too.

Your environment supports your vibrational frequency and is as beautiful as you are and feel. You choose to be in areas of high energy, near ley lines or vortexes, or bodies of water or mountains. You prefer to be in communities with people that are resonant in soul frequencies with you and the same vibrational frequencies as yours. Your connection to animals brings you much joy and healing and you feel how you can not 'own' a 'pet' but rather experience the deeper connection and communion that occurs when an animal agrees to be your companion. You are connected to minerals and stones, using them regularly and with reverence. Your inner environment is very expansive and you have access to multi dimensions, parallel universes, galaxies, heavens, the Akashic Records, and many other 'places'.

Questions For You:

How did you locate yourself related to the environmental area of life – as primarily a 3D, 4D or 5D consciousness and why?

What are your frustrations in the environmental area?

What are your desires in the environmental area?

~

Mutual Reverence With Mother Gaia:

Look at any beautiful image of nature. Take it in. This beauty is you. This beauty you see in this image is as beautiful as you are. I show you my beauty so that you may see your own. Always, I have been here to provide this for you. Always, I have wanted you to see that you ARE beautiful too.

You come to me, you take me in, you pause to let me in. You swim in my waves. You sit on my sand. You lay on my beaches. In this place, you find reverence. You feel reverence toward me. You pay much of your 'money' to live near this expression of me.

Yet, I want to tell you, as I am a mother to you as my embrace holds you and supports you. I want to tell you that the reverence you feel toward me is but a re-minder of the reverence that YOU are. And this I reflect back to you. I reflect reverence FOR you in my waves, in my trees, in my mountains, in my breezes, in my landscapes. I offer this beauty of me so that you might finally SEE and FEEL your own.

You who are reading this, taking in these words, you feel the exchange of beauty, the exchange of reverence between us. You pause, you reflect, you walk mindfully, you do not destroy. You are the keeper souls of my energy, my stewards. You are the hope and possibility that burns bright and shines and beacons to others.

It matters, your reverence for me, and it matters even more your reverence for yourself. It matters, it makes a difference, it propels changes forward. It propels our ascension together forward as reverence is the stuff of grace, appreciation, acknowledgement of worth.

I offer you many gifts of rejuvenation, nourishment, connection to ALL, connection to cosmos, connection to No-Thing-Ness, connection to my animal children. I offer these with reverence for you and all I ask as you accept these gifts is to feel yours in response. I offer you these gifts so that you might see that you have access to all of these frequencies already, that they live inside of you, that they ARE you, that I AM YOU too.

I am raising myself UP because it is time for me to do and be so. It is my phase of UPness. I invite you to come along, those of you in reverence and appreciation and goodness. I invite you to come along with me into this exploration of your Sacred Humanity and the expression of the best of what your hearts and souls can express in those Human bodies. I invite you to come along on the next phase of this journey together to experience the expression of New Earth Or Golden Earth Or Golden Gaia. I invite you to come along with the deepest feeling of appreciation and love, from the depths of my inner groundings to the heights of my orbit crowded with Star BEing friends.

I invite you to come with reverence for the beauty expressed by me and that lives inside of you already, just waiting for the water of more love!

Much much love to you my beloveds,
Mother Gaia

~

No Need To 'Save' The Earth: BEing Creator Gods/Goddesses With Creator Consciousness Goddess Gaia

It is a time to let go again of what comes from fear in order to let in MORE LOVE. ALL Of us are being invited into this it feels like. This is the invitation of the Universal energies that keep just WAVING into Gaia's atmosphere and She is taking these waves in and broadcasting them out to help US shift too. She'd like us to come along with Her.

To 'come along with Gaia' means trusting the process of awakening and remembering, of letting go…..how it unfolds without markers or clear directions most times. How it is only a sense in the heart of desire or a pull in the soul of resonance. How it is offered in signs and synchronicities and connections…..ALL beyond the 3D Self and its control. It can be negotiated with the 3D Self yet it is beyond the scope of the conditioned mind. How it is a ping or a ring or cling of something that feels faint at first and then becomes clearer, the draw becoming stronger, the way becoming revealed, the destiny aligning…..

Mother Gaia is SO FINE by the way. I checked in with Gaia on 'Earth day', and She was reassuring, at least in the timeline I'm in She was reassuring. Even with the timeline playing out in 3D of pollution, environmental damage, overcrowding, toxicity, deforestation, devastation in so many natural settings…..SHE is fine and more than fine……She is arising into pristine RADIANCE.

How? Because Her 3D condition has been possible through collaboration WITH us. The playouts of the destruction and pollution have been HER choice too….an experiment. She is choosing something ELSE now, a new Earth, a Golden Earth experiment. She is inviting us to come along with Her yet She is NOT victim to us. Do you see? Do you see how so many people make Her a victim to Humanity and project that she needs 'saving'? This is also how they feel about themselves and parts of them feel that they need saving too.

She IS SO powerful, this is what I felt with Her yesterday. And, she is in awe and reverence of OUR power too. Not in the power OVER expression that some souls are in as a playout of the wounded masculine, 3D reality timeline….but in Humanity's power WITH capacities and our Creator-Source Infinite Love and Infinite Awareness expressions for which we ARE already embodying more and more. SHE wants to reflect this to us and wants to be reflected back AS JUST AS POWERFUL. Creator Gods and Goddesses in Human form living WITH a planetary consciousness Creator Goddess Gaia……beautiful and expansive picture, isn't it?

No need to "Save the Earth"…..trust that She is exactly where she is choosing to be as a consciousness and something maybe rests inside of you then. Maybe a part of you that has wanted to go to battle for Her, yet is tired from battling, can rest more? The going to battle phase can be an important and sacred one during the awakening process as you become more aware and conscious about the conditionings in the 3D timeline. As you awaken to choosing love over fear in how you relate with the Earth and as it transitions to feeling more and more like a feminine consciousness Gaia expression WITH you.

I feel Mother Gaia inviting you into trusting that YOU are exactly where you need to be too, even as you are invited to choose love and your soul bigness expression in every moment.

No need to save you either. You are WAY too big for that energy.

If we are not 'saving' each other or Gaia or anything, then we can truly BE in reverence WITH each other. Saving each other only happens when we feel separate, when we are in codependence, getting unfelt needs met, projecting unconscious things. We may choose to serve love WITH each other in a specific way (as like what happens in our SoulFullHeart session space) BUT it is a mutual choice made by souls, Higher Self, and EVEN the 3D Self based in reverence, a temporary phase as the soul being guided remembers more and more their SOUL and embodies these frequencies more and more to open up more mutual grounds.

Also, speaking of letting go with the support of Mother Gaia……Raphael and I were swinging in a hammock last night under the tropical trees with a squirrel RIGHT over our heads in the branches, munching on seeds and showering them down on us. The squirrel seemed to represent Gaia too in a fur suit as the energy was so playfully intrusive! In this seed shower, it felt like WE WERE seeding too….new possibilities and new timelines. I felt Mother Gaia holding the space for these possibilities too as Raphael and I felt them through in a way together that I am SO grateful for as it is the deep trust ground of love and respect between us that has made so much change and transition possible!

It feels like this MIGHT BE geography for us, shiftings, travel, all connected to serving love……and yet this isn't something to kNOw right now, but to be open and trusting in the process and in the kNOW. To let the desires move through and see where they take us. Just like Gaia actually, who seems to BE Being the same. It is comforting to be in union with such a powerful, catalytic, BIG creator GODDESS yet also able to be SO gentle and SO playful in energy!

~

Mutual Reverence With Gaia

In the moment, a great question asked of me in the comments on Facebook that I responded to and thought I would share the exchange:

Question: "What about the part of Gaia that is being poisoned, paved and cut? How do we nurture that part?"

My response: It feels to me like Gaia will actually ascend that damage by continuing to move into the healing that will come when a lot of that activity stops as She moves into more 4D and beyond. The activity stops as the souls awaken, as disclosure brings gifts from Star BEings that greatly change our transportation needs and energy needs AND repair the damage too, as those souls who DON'T change either leave the body or experience a timeline running where things stay the same or get worse. I can only share what is in my heart around this yet many are offering the same picture.

Oh and how we nurture Gaia is the same as how we nurture ourselves…making the inner connections, healing the pains and wounds (especially in the 3D pain body), choose to serve love in every moment, take risks that serve our soul, connect with soul family, etc.…all these serve Her too as our consciousness shifts and She benefits too with that shift.

And I like to connect with Mother Gaia as a consciousness directly and she is very warm and very forgiving of it ALL….very much like Mother Mary actually! I asked her forgiveness for all the damage we have done and she embraced me SO deeply and forgave me right away and asked me to forgive myself and ALL Humans. She was so gracious and understanding and she helped me shift my consciousness around it. She also offered that just giving our energy and attention to nature and in nature helps Her to heal, even if it is just taking care of houseplants!

~

Experiencing Oneness At A Busy Beach

It is the busy season here where I live in the resort town of Puerto Vallarta, Mexico. It is my first season here experiencing this as I spent the last two winters in Mexico at a remote ranch about three hours from here. I haven't been to the ocean to swim in awhile as my focus has been very inward, lengthy periods of meditation, and then expressing and serving SoulFullHeart outwardly mostly through writing. Today, Raphael and I both felt a desire to take in the detoxifying ocean waters, float on our boogie boards while meditating, soak in vitamin D in the form of sunlight.

I was amazed as we walked along the main beach in town, Los Muertos Beach, how many people there were located in such a small space, clustered tightly together in beach chairs in front of Oceanside restaurants and beach clubs where you spend a certain minimum amount of pesos in exchange to sit at the ocean, have food and drink delivered to you while vendors come along every few seconds to offer you items to buy.

The intensity of the energy of all these people about blew me over. Every person I made eye contact with felt as if they were suddenly inside of my skin. Not only could I feel them (which as an empathic Healer is the norm) I felt like I WAS them. I admit that it scared part of me because it was intense. I could feel their emotional reality, like I was looking out of their eyes at the world. I could feel their pain, I could feel their desires. Oh, and they seemed to be so full of both! They are here on vacation, so much desire for goodness and wanting to experience the best things in life for them: ocean, fun, sun, food, drink.

I pulled my aura in as tightly as I could to my body, which can help when feeling a lot of intense energies around you. I turned my focus to the aerating energy of the negative ions in the air and the rumble sound of the waves crashing on the shore. I sent as much love and light as I could to every person that I became joined with.

We walked to the very end of the beach which is our favorite spot as it is cut off by hills on two sides and the energy is good there, the water is clear, and the waves are sometimes mellower. Plus, there were about 95% less people there and only a few vendors. My heart opened up as I had some space to breathe, go in the water with Raphael, soak in the sun, watch and feel people from more of a distance on the shore.

It was amazing to me to see how many people felt comfortable in high density frequencies, literally crammed in with so many other people. It seemed to be more comforting to be externally focused and surrounded by distractions. This, to me, is a good, relatable example of third dimensional or 3D consciousness. It is the sense that going along feels better than being different. It is more comfortable to go outward then go within. It is reassuring to be in crowds of people. The energies that were very overwhelming to me were acceptable to their 3D selves and even comforting.

Fourth or fifth dimensional consciousness (4D and 5D) is represented in the desire for physical and energetic space. Being drawn to spaces that offer some 'breathing room' where you can be with your own energy and check in with yourself. The choice of where to sit on the beach seems so simple in one way but it also can be telling. I have sat in the beach chairs by the restaurants before and I probably will again, just not when it is so busy and also when I am less sensitive and opened up as I am right now during this time of intensifying energies that are integrating and vibrational frequency upgrades into deeper 5D realities. Or maybe when more of these energies integrate and I can beam out love without feeling overwhelmed.

I am not judging without love any of this or the people as I offer this example to illustrate the difference in the vibrational frequencies of 3D, 4D, and 5D. I wanted to weep at both their desire AND their pain. I wanted to weep with compassion for them and for myself and even as I felt different from them I also felt deeply connected to them and KNOW that we are all ONE. I am not an elitist about ascension. I want the entire Human race to all raise up together our frequency to compassion, peace, love, non-violence, embracement of our soul gifts, etc. I often feel as if we cannot if even one of us is not and yet, also, I feel at the same time, how it just isn't what some souls will choose or are meant to choose. And, their journey and choices are as sacred as mine or anyone else's.

Being inside of others and them inside of me like I experienced today is an aspect of the awakenings into Oneness that are happening for me more and more. I admit that it is going to take time to get used to some of this even as it has been many years of this process. I also feel, as many others do, that the energetic frequencies of Gaia, the sun, and even the solar system are amplifying everything immensely, which has an impact on our sensitivity and capacity to feel others too. Overall, I feel grateful for the experience as it allowed me the opportunity to truly feel how connected we all are even with our individuality and the opportunity to teach on the dimensional frequencies from a relatable place. I'm left with a sense of the connection that all of us have to each other even as we can seem so separate in other ways.

~

Messages Of Love, Warmth, Light From The Sun Through Light Codes:

Powerful light codes today downloading from the sun….I'm getting that it's not about the warmth of the rays so much as the vibrational frequencies coming through them. It could be just as strong and effective at boosting your auric field in a cold climate as a warm one (although it's more likely to be sunny obviously in a warm one.) It seems so genius to me really….to boost the consciousness of ALL of us through one of the few universal things that we experience…sunlight.

It really does feel like an aspect of the overall 'plan' for Gaia's ascension to transmit codes this way that could lead to our suppressed DNA strands reactivating, our pineal gland being energized and activated (third eye center), Vitamin D levels going up. The crystalline body likes and needs the sunshine. I see it all the time here in Puerto Vallarta, Mexico…people coming from cold, rainy, overcast climates and seeming to just about be dying for the sun (and the warmth too) when they get here. They lay under it for hours, looking like Human solar panels, recharging what they've been missing.

This seems basic to be offering to get in direct sunlight as much as feels comfortable for you, yet we've received so much conditioning about the dangers of UV rays. Conditioning meant to suppress our desire for it, our need for it, and our activation underneath it. Getting regular direct sunlight and ideally meditating while receiving it into your body provides this immediate sense of higher frequency, relaxation, expansion…this is why I feel that people crave to lay out in it.

If you do undertake some sun therapy, do track and feel how much you are taking in. It is strong right now in the sense of what is coming through and I've been guided a few times that it's not 'really for me'…meaning, the blasts are for those who are on the tipping point of awakening and need the boost rather than those of us who are pretty firmly on our way. So, we are more sensitive to it and smaller doses are probably very effective because our auric field and chakras are less congested. Most people will not be conscious of what they are taking in through the sun and this too means it will not go in as deeply.

Also, taking pictures of the sun is amazing right now as it shifts and changes in so many different forms and frequencies. It has looked like a tetrahedron a few times now and also a portal many times in photographs with many different colored orbs or Ethereal BEing 'tracks' showing up.

~

I lay down at the sun's altar of sand and sea, receiving its gifts of coded energies and language in the light. I feel its warmth beaming down on me in varying degrees with subtle shifts in heat, intensity, and frequency from day to day. I take in the messages through my hungry skin, through my purifying pineal gland, through the stones I place near me, through my crystallizing and transforming cells, through my opening and healing heart, through my expanding and waking UP soul. I feel much gratitude to the sun (and the cosmic sun too) for what it GIVES and GIVES of life, of light, and of love.

    This is what I hear when I listen and receive as I lay in the sun and I wanted to share with those of you on this fast track of ascension and awakening for which the SUN seems to be a primary source of collective support, Universal activation, and galactic connection to create changes both inside and outside….

    The sun's warmth says to us, "Trust that life is GOOD. Trust that life is based in LOVE. Trust that life is WARM. Trust that life will return to warmth, goodness, and love even when it FEELS (and may need to be) temporarily cold or hard. Trust that THIS warmth is the essence of YOUR heart and soul too."

    The sun's catalytic energy says to us, "You can GROW. And you don't HAVE to suffer anymore. Feel ANY aspect of your life that is leading to suffering. Feel the deeper reasons WHY. Feel the power that you have to change whatever it is from INSIDE of you. To Feel and heal. To be with the aspect of you that is attached, that is scared, that is settling, that is suffering. BE with this inside and the OUTSIDE will change. You will BECOME this change as more and more SELF love overflows moving you from suffering and into love."

    The sun's NOW presence says to us, "NOW is the TIME. NOW is the time to change the INNER to experience the GOLDEN EARTH, 5D REALITY, that you most WANT and desire. It IS now. Your inner grids are preparing to support this new experience of reality. Your DNA is arising to recode you to this new frequency. You inner matrix is dropping so you can see more clearly your bigness. Your inner veil is lifting so you can remember your soul legacy and connect with your other lifetimes. NOW you can BE all of this."

The sun's light says to us, "You are meant to SHINE. You are meant to TURN ON your beacon. You can turn it from inside of yourself with self love that then SHINES it out to others. You become like a lighthouse for yourself and others, your beaming heart helping to navigate the rocky waters and the sudden storms. You become a way shower, shining the light in the darkness for yourself and others to find your way back again to the light."

The sun's love says to us, "PURE Love is the ONLY constant. You can return to it over and over. You can lay in it, soak it in, feel it FILL you up again. You can use it to raise your frequency to a higher rate and pitch and tone. You can experience it with your Guides, which you BEcome more and more over time. You can experience PURE love more and more in relationship as you draw those that reflect this to you AS you. You can experience the PURE love that you ARE and have ALWAYS been.....infinite and constant as I am."

~

Feeling Wonder During Ascension Shifts, Shifts in Nature Too

Shifting realities, shifting timelines....sometimes in the same afternoon and even, same hour! Shifting in the clouds too, the ocean, the sun.....today I was at the beach with Gabriel and we drifted into a zone together of theta waves and no mind, yet not quite asleep. When we first got to the beach, there were quite dense clouds in the sky and when we 'woke' up it was clear and bright with very wispy clouds only. I don't know how much 'time' passed but it could not have been long. And the water was glistening, shining, crystalline when we 'woke up'...my sense (beyond what the mind could 'know') is that we collapsed a timeline and went into another one. The weather patterns helped us track it but it feels like this is happening ALL the time and more and more as the photonic waves come rolling in and the solar winds too.

So many things like this are happening too during dream states which feel more like 'working things out on the astral level'…..clearing karma from other lifetimes AND, I got the sense the other day, actual cellular memory of EVERY movie, tv show, song, etc. that we have taken in coming up during sleep to be released. The energy of all these things we have taken in is stored in our cells and has to clear out. I have watched, listened to, taken in A LOT of intense things in my past, so even though I no longer do and am very careful about the energetic frequencies of what I take in….so many years of denser frequencies now need to come out.

You might find this too and probably why we've been guided to be very sensitive to websites, tv shows (haven't watched any in a long time), movies (only porous or good energy), music (solfeggios and meditation music mostly, high frequency)….THIS does feel important as we already have so much to clear out, why add more to it?

There are some powerful energy waves available 'out there', yet I'm not feeling to subscribe to the sense some others have shared that things are going 'crazy' and that many spiritual people, lightworkers, etc. are having a difficult time or falling under the influence of negative entities, lowering their vibrations, etc. I guess I just don't follow that timeline anymore. I feel SO MUCH love in all this activity….Venus in retrograde, solar winds, equinox coming soon….these are shiftings which offer MORE love as support to hold and feel what needs to be felt. Responded to with love (and not anxiety or fear or judgement) does so much to help in the acclimation to it. Sort of like…if you THINK all of these things 'out there' will cause you extreme difficulties emotionally, spiritually, and physically, then they WILL.

There is much to feel that is in shadow, stored in the 3D pain body, has been numbed out, for many people and within the collective consciousness and unconsciousness. Yet, held with love, at a rate and pace that you can bear, woven with goodness moments and gratitude, it can be navigated with grace, even if you need to 'hold space' for difficult things that come up. The willingness and practice to go within, to create a safe and self loving space to feel, will help HUGELY with this process of feeling and healing.

     I just took you into my timeline with me with this writing. Sometimes I wonder how I can even write one word after another when I am not in linear reality. Wish I could go on a 'wonder walk' with you, as I call it, where 5D (and probably beyond) consciousness is the lens for which we wonder experience everything we see and feel. Not to bypass feeling but to serve and fill the container that holds the reactions and feelings. You can take yourself on wonder walks though by being in the moment, slowing down, letting your Inner Child lead, letting your Star BEing aspects come in to 'visit', letting Angelic frequencies soar inside, letting time not exist.

     Also, what is happening 'outside' and 'in the cosmos' offers a wonder walk too. It invites a wonder walk on the inside mostly and THEN this shifts and changes what you experience on the outside as the lens is of wonder and Infinite Possibilities. The shifts in the cosmos are then taken in from this wonder lens too. The timeline of wonder is a WONDERFULL one…I highly recommend it.

~

Intense Energies During This Time Of Transition From 3D to 5D

     It is a time of intense energies. Waves of light washing over Gaia from the sun, from Star BEing friends, from portals and star gates both within and with-out. These waves of light are calibrators to raise our frequency, to boost the vibration of Gaia as She continues to move from the denser vibrations of 3D to 4D and 5D and beyond. Lightworkers, Grid Workers, Psychics, Healers, Teachers are feeling this as an intense time of energy surges and calibrations and I join them in feeling this as a particularly intense time of energy shifts. For those of you who are sensitive and awake to energy, you can probably feel it quite intensely and acutely.

Experiencing body symptoms is common as our bodies vibrate faster and faster, turning from carbon-based to crystalline. DNA strands are activating and repairing without us having to do anything for this to happen. The light that is available is doing it for us although if you ask for it and want it, this accelerates the process. DNA getting switched on feels tingly at times in the scalp and at times is downright painful with surges of pain around the crown chakra and down the neck and spine. A throbbing forehead or third eye is common too, which I have experienced several times now.

Sleeping well and hard feels so important as the mind and the 3D Self shut down to let the 4D Transitional Self and the 5D Higher Self step in. Wanting and needing a lot of sleep is a good thing as everything recharges. Not being able to sleep or interrupted sleep patterns is also common. The awakening 4D Self has dark and light, the contrasts and polarities and dualities are being pushed up to be felt. It mostly exists in the astral or etheric realm although for those of you who have been consciously bringing it forward through connecting with aspects of yourselves, you ARE it most of the time. And the Higher Self is becoming embodied as well, more and more higher frequencies of light living in the body, walking around as the higher self and integrating Guides from the 'outside' to the inside.

Holding space for yourself includes checking in with aspects of yourself and how they are feeling and digesting these changes.

Starting a journaling dialogue with your 3D, 4D and Higher Self can be very illuminating. You can start by writing a letter to each of them (based on your experience of each) and then listen for a response back, writing down whatever you hear. You can then engage in a question and answer type dialogue written down or out loud. Stay in your heart as you engage with these aspects of yourself, maintaining a curious and loving energy toward them. Let the feelings of these aspects (especially the 3D and 4D Selves) come back to be felt and held by you. You will be amazed how much this can help with the transition.

Shadow is coming to light. Shadow is oozing out at times, bursting out in emotional upheavals. It is a time of unveiling which it feels like will continue hugely in 2017. It is a time of decision making and changing life circumstances, feeling deeper desires and soul claims bubbling up to be integrated. There is a sense of there being 'no time to lose' and more sense that time is an illusion and very urgent at the same 'time'. Our bodies are changing, our hearts are opening up, our souls are embodying and ALL of it is held within Infinite Love.

These transitional times are held with so much support and love from our Star BEing friends and family. They are watching and feeling and helping in any way that they can. The lower vibrational 'negative' Star BEings are finding it harder to be here and it feels like eventually they just won't be able to hang out around Gaia as the frequencies change too much. It reminds me of when Dorothy poured water on the wicked witch in Wizard of Oz…the witch just dissolved into nothing, screaming her head off. It feels like this is how it will be for these lower vibration Star BEings, running away from the light and love to lurk in the shadows again somewhere else. It feels as if many of them are gone already with their Human puppets soon to be exposed to the masses.

Many animal species are ascending already, seeming to 'go extinct' in our 3D reality but actually being preserved by our Star BEing friends in arks in Golden Earth-5D Gaia, waiting for Gaia's consciousness and Human consciousness to ascend to a place of communion and cooperation again. This is the aspect that makes my heart most happy and my Inner Child smile.

As I'm writing this, I'm feeling my energy continuing to shift to one of holding excitement and a big sense of Infinite Possibilities for the future. In my transition from 3D to 4D, I went fully into the collapse of 3D life scenario, including living off grid, and felt very deeply the collapse of industrial life as it has been and what that would mean for me personally and for the world. Now, I am feeling it is still a possibility, yet I don't feel the hopelessness or despair that part of me once did. Old will need to make way for the new...in both galactic and personal ways.

Yet, all these changes and transitions are held by and orchestrated by and made BY LOVE FOR LOVE WITH LOVE. You are being invited to feel increasing trust in this through the visceral experience of these changes in the deepest cells of your ever changing body, in the opening of your healing heart and ache for intimacy and authenticity, and in the expansion of your soul and the embodiment of your Higher Self through integration of soul fragments existing in many dimensions and eras.

~

Offering Love During An Etheric Visit To Standing Rock

During meditation, I etherically visit Standing Rock, North Dakota - the scene of much protesting against the development of a pipeline for oil through Native American lands. I see and feel a village, a town, that is coming together, forming together through passion, purpose, and awakening. The foundations of this village are about protecting that which brings life, the waters that have long been polluted, long been corrupted, long been taken for granted. The foundations of this village are about a sense of spontaneous community where the heart of Sacred Humanity beats like the drums to unify, serve, and witness.

The smoke from campfires is thick, crowding the air. The noise is the thickest of all but it is not destructive noise. It is drumming from many different groups clustered together in undulating circles of bodies, soft limbs beating on hard surfaces, trying to beat away the hardness of fear. It is chanting, the range of feminine to masculine, joining together in old words that have little meaning in modern language. It is talking, communicating to put together meals to feed many people food that is donated from all over the world.

I offer an energetic touch of love to those that I pass over, desiring to provide even for a moment a boost for them to keep going, a sense of support and union. It feels like some of this goes in and some are starving for it, their heart chakras strained from so much output. The rivers that are the reason for it all feel like lazy witnesses, neutral in comparison to the charged energy around them.

The most intense energies are in an area that they call the 'frontlines', war lingo, and here I feel more of the darker entities that are feeding off the intensity of the stand, the fear of love pulsing against love itself......I touch the hearts of these entities too and the police that stand with blank faces and plastic shields that cover over a cascade of conflicting emotions inside of them. Their inner conflict is a desire to just go or to join in with the protectors, but the duty, the money, the uniform...it binds parts of them to stay, to use water itself as a weapon against those there to protect it.

Floating above the camp are many Ethereal BEings polarized to love, offering showers of pure energy to those below....to raise the vibration, to soothe the parts of people that are in trauma and in rage. Joining them are others like me, traveling in the way that suits them without body. These others are offering love too in the form of energy and we acknowledge each other with a gentle nod. Native ancestral spirits hover here too, connected to the lineage and history of this land and this stand.

Time is not linear here, but layered, this standoff is already in the grids and has already happened....it is an unhealed wound in the collective unconscious, it is an unhealed wound in the third dimension known as the 'United States'. There is only love to offer here and only love to heal the fear and the wounds caused by it.

~

Living Your Dream Life In A Dream Setting As Your Dream Self

I live in a city of dreams. People travel here to Puerto Vallarta, Mexico from around the world to come on vacation or to spend half the year or to live here. They come with their dreams of sun, of fun, of connection with others and with themselves. They come with dreams of escape and a sense of freedom from routine. They come with a wish for MORE than what they experience everyday: more enjoyment, more warmth, more fun, more quiet time, more peace, more LOVE.

I feel them here on the beaches, on the Malecon oceanside walk, on the cobblestone streets, right across the street in the vacation rental apartment building…I feel them walking around here and they are dreaming. They are shedding their outer skins of coats and heavy clothes for sandals and bathing suits and they are wondering if and how they could somehow move here or come here more? They are dreaming of leaving their jobs or businesses behind and starting over , a new life by the sea. They are dreaming of a new version of them that could do and BE this, that could 'give it all up' and start over.

This feeling of 'living a dream' is an apt way to describe what it feels like to live in fifth dimensional consciousness more and more. Your LIFE feels like a dream. Your LIFE feels like a vacation. Your LIFE feels more and more like YOU as you feel in your 'best moments'. You no longer experience compromises in what you are putting your energy into and what is getting your attention. You don't have a life you dread or worry about or experience suffering over to 'go back to.' You may still experience moments of pain that come up, especially from integration of soul aspects and soul legacy themes. Yet, this temporary pain is held as sacred and the joy you feel in your heart holds it and responds to it.

This feeling of living a dream as 5D reality is not dependent on geography BUT the geography you choose and the relationship that you have with it IS important. If you are experiencing suffering over where you live because its weather patterns do not fit you (too cold, too hot, not near the ocean, not near the mountains, too many people, not enough people, no resonant community, etc.), if it does not make your SOUL sing to be THERE, it is impacting your deeper embodiment of your Higher Self. And, you need that environmental lack of resonance until you don't any more and the desire flows for more matching of internal and external.

When people come here, they are close to their dreams. They can feel what their dream life might look and feel like but, most importantly, they can feel what THEY might feel like living it. This is when the Higher Self is getting closer. This is when fifth dimensional consciousness is peeking in. I feel the Angel BEing inside of everyone walking around here, no matter where their current consciousness level is at, because it GLOWS here as they give themselves more self permission to glow more here. But, this is inside of ALL of us, this glow of our 5th dimensional Self, and we'll remember and return to it eventually as that is our journey here, feels like.

Awakening happens when the dreams that come up (like the feelings that are triggered on vacation) are then internalized and explored. Going within, the dreams can come alive INSIDE.

They can rumble from the inside, moving and flowing, to push up places that are in resistance and fear to inhabiting the dream self of love and the dream of a life of love. With this awakening comes the questioning and the evaluating, the process of transitioning out of one way of experiencing life at a third dimensional frequency and on UP into more goodness, more love, more walking around dream life that starts from INSIDE, which then shows up on the outside. With this awakening comes the eventual changes and choice points that move life forward in surprisingly unknown and beautiful directions.

What are your dreams? What are they inviting you to feel INSIDE? What are they inviting you to feel about your dream self? What are the next steps to feel in embodying that dream self? Your dream self and dream life are waiting for you to claim them as you go within, as you explore, as you claim the love that you ARE.

~

SACRED FEMININE

      She is blooming, fertilized by a rich inner world of self discovery

      She is inviting, inspired by the Divine to be a beacon of light for herself and others

      She is discerning, guided to hold boundaries with love and take space when needed

      She is beautifying, attuned to the exquisite possibilities around her

      She is serving, called by love to share her heart and soul gifts with others

      She is holding, created from a container space inside to bake on what needs to be felt

      She is expanding, integrated with her multidimensional, cosmic self and star seed origins

      She is arising, drawn to embody her authentic and vulnerable expression

      She is BEing, energized beyond busy mind to experience life from stillness

      She is the Inner Feminine (for both women and men)….feeling her with open heart, open mind, open soul invites her forward to play, to dance, and to LOVE….more and more, to Become

    ~

What Is Sacred Femininity And SoulFullHeart Woman?

      What is Sacred Femininity? As I feel into the answer to this question, I connect to my heart, soul, and body……listening for a response:

      My heart says, "Sacred Femininity invites the hearts of others out to dance, out to play, and out to be in love. It transacts with openness and vulnerability, eager for every moment to be real and meaningful, whether it is light or it is deep. It is willing to feel what needs to be felt and accepts that which is both in light and in shadow. It aches for union, to be connected, and to see itself through love transacting in resonant relationships."

My soul says, "Sacred Femininity is unknown. It is arising. It is mysterious. It can wait to be noticed and it can draw. It can be so deeply still and it can be beautifully active. It is contrasts and paradoxes. It lets love lead, trusting that the rest will follow. It is open to being watered by the frequencies of the Divine Feminine and the Divine Mother, in whatever forms that She comes. It is healing that from the soul's history which blocks the current flow of love in relationships with others, self, and the Divine."

My body says, "Sacred Femininity is desire, the rush of orgasm and the joy of afterglow that comes from heart open sexuality with self or with a beloved mate. It is expressed in the physical with a softness that is visible in body, audible in voice, and in touch – gentle at times and passionate at other times. It is natural and real, beyond the images of physical perfection and is not found in the chemicals and products that cover and make over. It is beautiful in all its expressions, in all its ages, and all its packages."

As I connect to these answers inside of myself related to this question of Sacred Femininity, it feels like the answers are the same to the question, "What is a SoulFullHeart woman?" The specifics of what it means to be a SoulFullHeart are offered in depth on our website. Essentially, it is about being in a place of awakening consciousness in the heart and soul through engaging in the SoulFullHeart healing process. This leads to an increasing sense of individuation or healthy ego maturation with more experience of union with yourself, others, and the Divine as an expression of Infinite Love.

A critical aspect of this exploration into 'what is sacred femininity' in the future is to feel what is NOT femininity but is actually an expression of masculinity or comes from our birth mother (or other primary feminine caregiver) templating or is a product of our cultural conditioning.

It can be quite an illuminating journey to feel the way that masculinity expresses inside of us and how it can 'live inside' as masculine aspects of us or what we call, subpersonalities. These masculine aspects form a strong protective energy for which many frequencies of sacred femininity are buried beneath. As we get to know and love them, they can begin to rest and trust us more and allow our femininity to start flooding into our field with often quite transformational results in our physical, emotional, and spiritual experiences of life.

Our relationships with our birth mothers is another key ground of exploration related to our sacred femininity expression. Individuation is a process of feeling through how we are impacted by the template that our mothers offered to us about femininity and feeling into how parts of us relate to that template now. Also, we can be deeply influenced by social and cultural conditioning, especially when it 'rewards' the development of a persona aspect of us to 'fit in' and seek acceptance around our gender expression.

The frequencies of Sacred Femininity that we explore as SoulFullHeart women are ones that I am honored to share with women in my life in the form of sister, friend, student, healer, and teacher.

I offer this humbly and yet with a sense of worth that is based on my own experiences of increasing sense of this inside of myself over the last decade of being dedicated to my own deepening sacred femininity embodiment process. Life has provided many teachers for me in this journey, primarily in the form of relationships such as with my Raphael, my adult daughter, sacred friendships with other women and men, women that I am honored to serve and hold space for, and both Human and Ethereal Guides.

Please join me on this journey into the unknown dimensions of Sacred Femininity and may we both grow, learn, transform and experience much love along the way!

~

Divine Feminine Energies Coming In To Balance Out Masculine Activations:

Solar geostorms, sunspot flare ups, photonic light waves beaming down through sun rays…..all this outside activity of stirring and churning, blaring and flaring. It is a fiery picture, isn't it? A rather masculine energy. Many souls are tuning into this activation energy that ignites and wakes UP as it stimulates our light bodies, our emotional bodies, our mental bodies, our social bodies (social bodies……...new one for me to name, yet feels SO TRUE). All these bodies are like planets in our inner galaxy rotating around the orbit of our soul and the sun of our heart and the moon of our unconscious. All this stimulation can bring up symptoms and unease and detox in all of these bodies too as the 3D Self and unaware ego resist, release, and ultimately let go at a rate and pace negotiated by the Higher Self.

In the physical body as it transitions to 5D light body UP can come the residues of what we have chosen and lived on a cellular level. The toxicities and energies we have taken in of eating BEings that have been killed; the frequencies of chemicals and foods made in laboratories; the exchanges during sexuality that weren't based in love but something less; the habits and patterns that lead to less vital experience of body, INdigestion. And again, the 3D Self can amplify these symptoms, make them worse, grab onto them, suffer or linger in them and the love of the growing Higher Self embodied YOU invites a moving on, holding space, yet, keep moving on into love.

The emotional body is releasing pain as the Higher Self YOU is activating love codes, PURE love messages, NEW messages of love to hold space for the movement of what has previously been subconsciously stored to move into the light of your consciousness. Suffering is a tone that maybe you (and parts of you) have gotten USED to, yet it is NOT the tone of Golden Earth, 5D frequency. It is not the tone of the higher self-embodied Sacred Human. It is not the tone that Gaia emotionally wants to feel anymore. BIG changes may be necessary to move suffering out of your life, to say 'no more' to suffering in the emotional body, in the mental body, and in the social body. BIG changes navigated with those PURE love messages coming in, creating a NEW reality where big changes are navigable at a rate and pace that you can BE with.

  I feel a Divine Feminine ray, a softness, is beaming down TOO....to balance the masculine activation frequencies, stronger than I have felt Her before as more clearing has happened in the outer grids and in the collective and in souls to allow Her to come through more. It felt foggy to offer Her for all these years even as it was bright inside of me and in my soul. She seemed to be shrouded in veils and mysteries in terms of outside perception of Her. Yet, more and more, is Her brightness coming through to be seen and felt and remembered.

  The four energies of the Divine Feminine that I was awakened to in 2010 after remembering Reiki energy still feel relevant to me as a way to connect with Her as you also embody them more and more AS YOU....this can be for both men and women. The four energies are the Mary ray of pink and blue energies offering purity, innocence, compassion and forgiveness. The Magdalene ray of ruby red, offering sisterhood, Queen mate, sacred sexuality (with partner or with self). The Kuan Yin PURE white ray offering nondual frequencies, beyond the mind, beyond the body, stillness, and BEing in the Now. The dark, black as night ray of the Dark Mother offering death as a form of rebirth, inviting embracement of the shadow, the necessary dark to go with the light.

  You can physically see these energies of the Divine Feminine (and Divine Masculine) in photographs when you place yourself in front of the sun and take pictures with a digital camera. What is in your auric field will then be revealed to you. The orbs or rays of energy show up in different tones and colors and you can connect with them to feel what they are trying to tell you.

Take a moment to feel, hear, and see what these energies are offering to you, what She is offering to you....write down the messages, speak the conversations out loud, bring Her energy into your meditation space. Ask to connect with one of the faces of the Divine Feminine I have mentioned above during meditation and one of them will show up for you...the one you are most needing and wanting in the moment. Or maybe MORE than one...

These energies of four seem to infuse and offer a balance of our femininity within (again, yes, men too). Each one of the 'faces' of the Divine Feminine is a reflection of our faces. Each one of their energies offering a mirror to our energies. Like the seasonal shifts, I have felt each one connected to a specific season too even as they are ALL of them. Mary has felt like autumn or fall; Kuan Yin like winter; Dark Mother like spring; and Magdalene like summer. This has worked for me in activating and connecting with them....use what works for you.

The Divine Feminine is HERE to balance out the masculine, is needed, and while in more polarity sense now in the mostly still 3D collective consciousness....She moves more toward subtlety as your frequencies raise up. Bring Her into your heart to remember and to bring love into the wounded from birth mother places in the 3D emotional body. Bring Her into your soul to remember and to bring love into the wounded soul frequencies from patriarchal dominance and other lifetime experiences of persecution, hiding soul gifts, suppression of the Divine Feminine. Bring Her in and experience Her reflection of the love that you ARE...

~
~

Embodying Sacred Feminine Frequencies

The Sacred Feminine, the Divine Feminine, the woman living more and more from the place of fifth dimensional (and higher) consciousness....She can be a mystery, an arising question to live into more than about clear definitions or set answers. There is a sense that her energy invites and draws others as she serves love WITH in all areas of her life and in most moments. She lives from a sense of personal integrity and authenticity, having embraced her inner shadow with love and courage, and inspires others to BE the same. She leads with vulnerability, her strength coming from bringing what is real in her heart and soul. She invites others into a possible resonant ground that reflects a mutual truth possibility rather than contending or trying to prove that she is right. She is able to take action on what is necessary to be done in order to serve love as an expression of her soul purpose and connection to Divine Source.

The sense of what it IS to be an ascending Human in female form seems to be a deepening, spiraling, nonlinear process. There are curves and turns, offering the next layer of discovery or another 'round' of experiencing a pattern or loop repeating itself and offering another piece of our puzzle. As we awaken, and especially in the 4D transition phase, we may become less polarized in our gender expression as we burn away and let go of what is not who we really ARE in feminine expression but rather what we have been conditioned to be. We are invited to feel what is NOT actually authentic femininity, what seems to come instead from a wounded masculine expression or place of being or aspect inside of us.

Holding space for women and my own process around embodying my sacred femininity, healing the emotional body, awakening the soul, integrating karmic aspects from other lifetimes has offered me a higher perspective on the patterns and themes that often play out in this process. The word 'sacred' is important as a key marker of movement in this process is from being SCARED of the Inner Feminine to being SACRED with it….. holding it with an increasing sense of reverence and curiosity.

A key differentiation place in this process is to become conscious about the template we received from our birth mothers, other significant female caregivers, and birth sister(s) relationships. It can be very illuminating to ask the questions: What was the templating I received from my mother around what it means to be a woman? What templating did I receive from other female caregivers and from my sister(s) around what it means to be a woman? How does the energy and messages of this templating impact me now in all areas of my life? How does this energy express in my relationships?

Connecting with your 'inner birth mother' can lead to great healing and separation. A simple way to do this is to write a letter (and out loud during meditation too if you want) to your inner mother telling her how you experience her energy in your life and invite her to write back. You then begin a written dialogue together with you asking her questions about herself and discovering more about this energy that lives inside of you as you 'took it in' like a sponge your whole life. As you connect with your inner mother, you will begin to 'defuse' or separate from this energy, allowing for more objectivity about it and with more arising of your authentic essence. It may not be possible for you to embody your authentic or genuine frequency of femininity while in relationship with your mother and a phase of taking space from the relationship may be necessary to experience more clarity, perspective, and growth.

Another key aspect to the Sacred Feminine embodiment process can be connecting with wounded masculine energies that you have taken in and embodied. This can especially present itself in an Inner Protector aspect, a usually masculine feeling and looking energy that expresses as a guardedness and uses weapons of protection such as energetic shields, swords to jab and pierce (internally and toward others), etc. Negotiation with the Inner

Protector allows for more authentic gender expression of femininity as this aspect often guards the Inner Feminine and conscious negotiation with it can lead to deeper embodiment and access.

Connecting with energies of the Divine Feminine in different frequencies as Ethereal Guides provides a new templating to replace the ones you are letting go of. I have mainly experienced connection with Divine Feminine Guides showing up in the energies and forms of Mother Mary, Magdalene, Kuan Yin, and Kali/Dark Mother. Experiencing these Guides (and however She shows up for you) during meditation allows for an infusion of multidimensional yin frequencies of comfort, nurturing, creative alchemy, sisterhood, stillness, healthy sexuality, passion, desire, and much more. These frequencies serve as healing balm to the places inside that experienced the wounded feminine and still suffer around it.

Another aspect of embodying the Inner Feminine is connecting with and healing karmic and archetypal wounded feminine soul themes such as non-vulnerable priestess, pious nun, matriarch/Queen, warrior, medicine woman, witch, and more. Karmic playouts can express in persecution wounding experiences (both as the persecuted and the persecutor) that greatly suppress or impact your ability to express your soul gifts as a woman teacher, WaySHOWer, and Healer, for example. Or another example is feeling how sisterhood wounding or traumatic experiences from other lifetimes may influence your relationships with women now. The push away from or the surrender to patriarchy is a big one for most of us with ways that it energizes and plays out in the now and impacts our gender expression.

Embodying the Sacred Feminine is holding space for the emotional reactions and previously undigested emotional frequencies that come up from the emotional body during the awakening and ascending process. It is also making space for and surrendering to the 'rumble' of death and rebirth of the feminine that wants to move through your life and clear out what no longer serves you or serves love. Rebirth can only happen with death or with letting go. Letting go of frequencies that don't match you anymore in all areas of your life, making changes at a rate and pace that is self loving WITH negotiation with parts of you if possible allows for the blooming of your Inner Feminine from a small seed to full, ever arising expression of your BEing in female form.

~

An Ache For Feminine Stillness

I feel an ache for stillness. There is a space inside that misses its imprint; where there would be stillness is, instead, vibration.

I inherited this vibration from my mother, who inherited it from her mother and so on. The vibration wants what it can't have; it is frustrated by life; it is impatient and yearns for control. In my whole lifetime experience of my mother, I can never remember her being truly still inside or outside.

Is it fair to expect this templating from any woman when our society has so suppressed its expression? Our got-to-go, keep busy and stay busy culture is the opposite of still. It buzzes with drugs like caffeine, refined sugar, antidepressants, and hyper entertainment. It pulses with florescent lighting, electromagnetic and microwaves, and artificial environments. It rings with blasting music, traffic noises, and cell phones.

Where is a woman to learn of her core; that place inside of her that is vastly and deeply at rest? The masculine expression inside of a woman activates early on and he takes over the show; moving and shaking us forward; engaging with learning institutions and career ambitions that support overachievement and 'doing over being'. This male side of us is given the juice he needs to move; there is no countering force offering support for NOT moving.

I have tasted of my stillness in moments; it is soft, so soft, and yet powerful in its depth and breadth. It contains and holds all of life, even its active expressions. I have received some sense of it not from my mother or from other women, but from the Divine Mother and Spirit Guides and women from parallel dimensions. Because our dimension has become so dominated by the rational, the masculine, the active…I have needed to expand my quest for experience of Sacred Feminine stillness beyond the limits of our five sense reality.

I have found this place that is missing in our culture in the parallel dimensions of Golden Earth and Avalon. Avalon, the isle of apples, a temple to the Goddess, lives as an archetype and can be traveled to through meditative visits called Immramma (a Celtic method of astral travel.) Golden Earth is the fabled land of 'milk and honey' where disconnect and violence don't exist and the best of Humanity reigns forth. These places are magical in their own right, yet it has been my connection with two of my Metasoul Sisters that has brought the most nourishment. I share about my journeys and awakenings to Avalon and beyond in my book *Keep Waking Up!*

I don't know if true feminine stillness *can be* embodied in our modern times on this Earth dimension. My desire is to take the frequencies that I experience in these parallel places and integrate them here, as much as is possible. This integration process becomes like an oven, baking the legacy of stillness inside of all women – until it is warm enough to overcome the charged vibrations of our modern world.

~

To Be With Mother Mary And The Divine Feminine

She waits for me by a pool of water, surrounded by a soft pink light, the rose quartz light of soft heart energy. Her 'typical' heavy robes and cloak around her head have been replaced with crystalline folds of light and she feels both naked and fully clothed. She has arisen above "Mother Mary", certainly above the religious picture of her….yet, she is OK with being called

Mother Mary for now and for me to call Her this as I have been for many years now.

To be with Mary is to be with comfort, with nurturing, with tender possibilities of healing. She feels both our Humanity, our very Human heart, AND our soul and transcendent aspects. To be with Mary is to feel the innocence of our BEing as it lives in the heart of our Inner Child who heals from wounded, 3D expression to magical 4D to crystalline 5D integrating in with our adult expression more and more. To be with Mary is to feel instantly and completely forgiven for our shadow and for our fears.

Today, by the pool, Mary cups her hands together and offers me a drink of the glowing water. I sip from it, feeling the energies of rejuvenation, purification, and stillness too somehow move through me. I feel the energies soothing and inviting me into my feminine capacities and expressions that Mary represents, that Mary IS, and that I AM too.

In this flow of Divine Feminine energy, I can feel the places in me that have been energized by a good kind of activated masculine energy (by taking in sun codes, by connecting with Archangel Metatron and merging with his energies AS he activates my Angelic aspects more and more). I am soaking in the restfulness AND the stillness. It is like they are wrapping around each other from within, as they do in the dance with my beloved Raphael. Moving into my passion expression and serving love has brought in a necessary masculine energy of activation balancing with the feminine.

I also feel Mary inviting me to feel 'the cries of women' as I am feeling the 'cries of the world' without suffering over the suffering that is felt.

This feeling of connecting with the 'cries of women' is an aspect of the activation of the higher heart and higher frequency, more crystalline cosmic heart. Since I have a specific purpose to serve love with women in the exploration and expression of Sacred Humanity in the form of the feminine, it is important that

I am connected to the cries of women even if I am in a different place emotionally from what most women probably experience of life.

The cries of women are moving through me and I feel the frustrated sadness at the heart of the 'cries'…so many desires for MORE, so much sadness when it doesn't come. It feels like a vast swirl of energy and Mary holds me while I dip a consciousness toe into it, offering that we will feel more together as we go in response to women and also whatever I need to have illuminated for myself for which there is still something left to heal and feel.

To be with Mother offers a new template of nurturing mother…without stickiness, without grab, without codependence, without HER needs dominating the space. She offers healing for our birth mother woundings (which we ALL have) that were passed on to us through the unhealed emotional bodies of our mothers. She brings in a new frequency of mother, offering women especially a clearing out and purifying of their mother experience and their own capacities of motherhood toward themselves and others.

This is to be with Mary….being open to feeling and healing, both on a personal level and for those drawn to serve love with others to also feel the cries of the world and the cries of those for whom you are drawn to serve. Feeling the cries, hearing them and yet not becoming them allows you to offer a way and BE a guide to activate the remembrance of the soul and Higher Self.

Many years ago, Mary offered me an updated prayer, 'Hail Mary' to do with Her….a more esoteric prayer/invocation freed of religious tones to connect with Her energies. I found it very comforting and it helped me to connect with Her energy as I recited it during meditation:

"Hail Mary, Full of Grace
The Divine is with Thee;
Blessed art thou amongst sacred women,

And, blessed is the fruit of thy womb, Jesus.
Holy Mary, Mother God
Pray for all of us lovers
At the hour of our death and rebirth
Amen"

~

Meditation To Meet Your Inner Protector And Your Inner Feminine

Close your eyes, go within, concentrate on your natural breathing in and out.

Imagine yourself in a space of pure white light. The light is surrounding you, holding you, and guiding you. The light is inviting you to vibrate higher, to move your frequency UP to a higher one.

Feel this pure white light moving through you and through each of your chakras and through every cell of your body. Allow this light to move through and activate and clean each of your chakras, from your highest one, your stellar gateway, to your root. To your Earth chakra below your feet. Feel the grounding from your feet down into Gaia and the connection that is there.

See yourself in a forest surrounded by the pure white light. The forest is beautiful and vast. It offers the sense of exploration and journey, a sense of adventure to unknown places. There is a stream nearby, running through and weaving through the trees. You can hear it babbling at you.

Take in the five elements of fire through the warmth of the sun; water through the running stream; air through the soft breezes; Earth through the grasses and trees that surround you; and Spirit through the sense of your own soul and your connection to Divine Source and other Ethereal Guides, Angels, Spirit Animals you may be working with in the moment. Feel them joining you now, witnessing you now.

In this moment, we will call on Mother Mary, who has frequencies of both light pink and blue in her energies. She is comforting and nurturing, offering you a reflection of your innocence. Mary comes forward into the woods and stands on your left side, holding your hand. You feel infusions of nurturing, unconditional love coming from her, a sense of your purity and that you can do no wrong in your essence. You feel forgiven for what part of you feels you have 'done wrong' in the light of her love from other lifetimes.

We will now call on Magdalena, a divine feminine guide and ascended teacher. Magdalena's energy is deep red, like a rose. She is passionate and creative and sexual, offering you a reflection of your Sacred Feminine Queen (whether you are in a relationship or not). Magdalena comes forward and stands behind you, lovingly throwing her arms around your shoulders. You feel infusions of pure sisterhood, connection to all women, the possibilities of healing soul woundings held in other lifetimes around persecution and expression of your soul gifts and suppression of your femininity.

We will now call on Kuan Yin, a Divine Feminine guide and bodhisattva. Her energies are pure white like winter's snow. She offers us the energies of stillness, restfulness, moving beyond our busy minds, healthy self protection. Kuan Yin comes forward and stands on your right side, holding your hand. You feel Her template of stillness and nondual frequencies offering you a place beyond your mind and an experience of your core.

We will now call on the Dark Mother, who we can also feel as Kali. You can feel her rumbling energy around and through the ground as it shakes beneath your feet for a moment. Rather than a deeply personal connection with her, Dark Mother reminds us of the necessity of the death and rebirth cycles of life, the chaos that can lead to growth, and to be open to change.

With Mary on your left, Kuan Yin on your right, and Magdalena walking behind, they lead you down the path in the woods that you see before you. You may feel excitement as they lead you on this path into the unknown, you may feel some fear, embrace all that you feel as it comes up.

The path winds through the woods and ends at a clearing. In the middle of the clearing is a large castle. Picture this castle however you would like to, see it in front of you. Notice too how it FEELS to you as you approach the castle. Begin to open up to the sense that inside of this castle is your essence…..is your most Authentic Self, is the embodiment of your Higher Self. Inside of this castle is your most precious treasure of Sacred Humanity, and your inner femininity. Let this into your heart and begin to connect to this energy.

(Follow the meditation for meeting your Inner Protector that is included in the Spiritual Area section of this book.)

You walk back through the woods with Mary and the others. Eventually they too fade away yet their template of feminine stays with you. Infusing and offering you a sense of balance. Open your eyes and come back to the present moment.

~

Forgiveness Of Self And Others: With Mother Mary

Forgive them their busyness,
They know not how to be.
Forgive them their violence,
They know not how to act.
Forgive them their blindness,
They know not how to see.
Forgive them their lack of conscience
They know not how to feel remorse.
Forgive them their judgment,
They know not how to discern.
Forgive them their numbness,
They know not how to feel.
Forgive them their hatred
They know not how to love.

Forgive them their greed,
They know not how to receive.
Forgive them their destruction,
They know not how to create.

~

This message came to me through ascended teacher Mother Mary in 2010 after I was attuned to remember Reiki energy or Christ consciousness energy. I was struggling at the time, in recovery in many ways from leaving a spiritual group, soul family, that I was deeply connected with and felt was my soul work. I chose to leave, yet the very sudden loss of connection with the group pushed up deep feelings of rejection, hurt, frustration, and rage. Such an important process, such an important crucible for me to have experienced.

During this time, I was struggling with forgiving my soul family in the group who would no longer be in relationship with me. I was especially conflicted about forgiving the leader of the group, my former Spiritual Teacher, and surrogate father who had 'kicked' me out with very harsh energies. These edges in my emotional body and in the aspects that held them needed soothing, comfort, and love.

Mother Mary visited me and offered waves of soft blue and pink light. She embraced me, reflecting to me my purity and innocence. She offered me these words of forgiveness to extend toward those who I perceived had hurt me, an extension of the words spoken by Yeshua as he died. And, more than anything, she encouraged me to embrace them toward myself and the parts of me that had been so drawn to the group, had done harm to others, parts of me that were like the formerly beloved Spiritual Teacher. I was also awakening to the difficult realities of the 3D world and the abuses on so many levels going on related to the planet, animals, toward other Human BEings. She was offering forgiveness energy toward all the 'perpetrators' of these abusive frequencies too.

She offered that while they are in a sleep-walking state and in fusions to shadow aspects, people do not 'know' how to create, how to be, how to love, how to feel, how to see...yet they CAN remember. Their essence, their soul CAN remember when responded to with love, invited into love, felt with love. In this loving energy response, held both INSIDE and toward 'outside', possibilities of love exist and arise. In this loving energy, we can REMEMBER the love that we ARE again.

With Mother Mary's love and embrace, I came to forgive myself and others. I came to see that I had needed the experience of my Dark Night Of The Soul, this experience that was so painful, in order to purify my heart and soul of shadows that I could not have seen and felt any other way. It had to be dramatic. It had to hurt. It had to burn away the edges and places that were there due to karmic patterns and soul legacy playouts. To be a teacher truly offering a compassion-based response, I had to feel that compassion for myself and also for others who parts of me felt had deeply hurt me.

This forgiveness ground is offered to you to as modeled and templated by the Divine Feminine. The Divine Feminine can come in many forms of Ascended Masters, Archangels, Spirit Guides, Spirit Animals, Teachers, Healers, Space Holders. She offers the frequencies of forgiveness of self and of others, a compassionate ground that feels the pain that others are coming from, and so understands why they are as they are. She offers a remembrance of how the heart CAN forgive and then arise into a new ground where love becomes a possibility again.

She offers a way to digest with love ALL that is happening during this transition from 3D to 4D to 5D consciousness, the death and rebirth cycles, and the shadows that are coming out to heal. "The rose is burning yet in its essence it is still a rose," she says now about the current circumstances playing out in politics, government, military, etc. Feeling compassion for the burning, sending it love, yet NOT burning yourself is the balm that is offered by forgiveness frequencies.

Embracing forgiveness makes space inside and soothes the edges. Letting it in makes space for the possibilities that love wants to bring and is inviting us into every moment.

~

When Your Mate And Other Relationships Aren't Awakening With You: Sacred Feminine

She is expanding, growing, learning. Each drop of remembered kNOWledge waters the seed of her Sacred Human Self and she so WANTS to grow now. Looking and searching for resonance to mirror her growing sense of soul, she needs the NEW reflection to transform into the NEW her that is waiting, spring loaded to become WHO she REALLY is.

She aches for MORE….more love, more light, more growth, more newness, more connection, more intimacy, more joy, more passion, more realness, more authenticity, more health. She feels this desire for MORE most of her moments and the ways and means to suppress it with distractions are not working as well as they used to. The part of her that wants to protect her from pain and keep her safe TRIES to suppress the wanting and the growing, yet THAT doesn't seem to be working in the ways that it used to anymore.

Her friends, her family, her mate…they are watching this transformation as witnesses who, on a soul level 'signed up' to witness it. Maybe they are uneasy about it. Maybe they are resistant about it. Maybe they are inspired by it. Maybe they are coming along. Maybe they are not.

Oh, and her mate….if he is not feeling the same stirrings and call of healing the heart and awakening the soul, her heart aches to share this WITH him. Staying on her side in moments (let it arise in him through him) and then venturing over onto HIS side again (please come with me!) and back and forth. This is an uneasy dance, with no easy answers, with neither partner doing anything wrong nor BEing wrong.

As the dance plays out, she may reach a place where she can no longer 'shrink' to the old dynamic ground in the relationship to be with him. The place where they used to 'meet' each other has literally collapsed through her own growth and this has CHANGED the ground of their 'USness'. The USness has shifted from wherever it was when they agreed to BE together as it is based on energy and NOT an actual contract at all.

She may reach this place of not being able to allow the dynamic anymore in a dramatic sweep of realization that leads to immediate changes and transitions and completions. She may reach this in small increments and through negotiations with self and with him along the way. Through this negotiation maybe he WILL come along because it is his time and his desire to be and do so. OR he cannot and yet…..on she moves because now her growth cannot be contained without staying in suffering or in a lower frequency EVEN as love remains.

This is written for and inspired by women I have connected with through SoulFullHeart recently in this situation, finding (and ultimately choosing on the soul level) themselves HERE….in this place of awakening while their mate doesn't seem to be coming along with them. I feel how this situation can be reversed too, with the man awakening and the woman choosing to remain in the same consciousness frequency….yet it feels to me that most often it happens in this way as yin has tended to lead in these grounds.

Drawing this situation is a reflection of the woman to look into herself. It is an invitation to feel how her mate's (and those in other relationships) lack of resonance reflects a shadow aspect of herself that is ALSO not in resonance with her growth, a part of her that may resist awakening, or is very afraid of it. If she is deciding to stay within the relationship even without the deeper soul resonance and even perhaps outward resistance and maybe even abusive frequencies, then there IS a part(s) of her that feels the same way for which his lack of resonance represents. Without access to these parts of herself, she will make it about the outside, about him, about others RATHER than about herself for which they are just a reflection. Focusing on the outside in this way leads to disempowerment feelings and more sense of suffering and impotence.

She is not a victim but rather willing participant in this dance until she no longer chooses to be. Going within to find the parts of her that are represented here is the way to access her inner power, to feel possible next steps and choices, to navigate from HER side.

Living within a relationship with mutual resonance of body, heart, and soul with Raphael for close to nine years has filled my woman's heart with loved UPness, compassion and I can template a NEW way for women to experience themselves within a Sacred Union ground. And a new way to relate to themselves for which ALL aspects of themselves (even those in shadow) are held and explored with a loving curiosity and tenderness WITH internal boundary setting also happening when it is needed.

There is a NEW way of 5D relationship in which their mate is inspiring them to grow, supporting ALL of their movements which support their soul, and which love becomes more and more pure between the two partners as they dedicate themselves to their inner healing and soul awakening. Often what people feel is 'love' in romantic relationship is actually a sticky, codependent frequency of need from one part of them to another part in their mate (example, Inner Child in the woman hooked up with the Patriarch in the man, the Matriarch in the woman hooked up with the Inner Child in the man, Inner Punishers in both hooked up together.)

It is a complicated dynamic and yet love will steer through it if there is willingness to feel, to heal, to grow, and to be REAL with what the emotional reality actually IS and the degree of suffering over suffering that exists from inside. No more suffering becomes the motivation for change until love leads the way more and more with suffering becoming a rarer occurrence. It IS possible to experience this PURE love ground in relationships to the degree it is happening from within, from inside, from one aspect to another.

~

THIS AND THAT ABOUT LOVE

Light wants to illuminate, shining on places in the shadows, bringing in illumination to the far reaches and deepest corners.

Love wants to sooth the edges, bring balm to the places that bristle and burn and churn and yearn.

Light wants to unify, exposing that all comes from the same source, divided temporarily until gathered together again.

Love wants to initiate, inviting you into trust in yourself, in love with yourself, in connection with yourself, in discovery of yourself.

Light wants to embrace darkness, making it safe to go there when you need to even with quaking knees and shaky heart.

Love wants to transmute darkness, turning the gifts and gems that are lying in dusk and bring them into the shine of the heart's sun.

The light of love has the power to move anything from feared into loved, from distrusted into surrendered into, from wounded into healed, from resisted into accepted, from separated to unified, from pushed away to embraced.

The light of love invites you to feel it ALL, not transcend or avoid what is difficult, yet shine the light on it ALL with your heart and it becomes not foreign but then familiar. You remember then that you ARE this light, that you ARE this love, that you have chosen to be in different frequencies for growth yet you can return and embody these higher frequencies whenever you want and more and more as you want and need to.

~
Life Speaks To Us Of Love

Life speaks to us of love, over and over, as we become more receptive to listen, our hearts more open to receive, and our souls more embodied to remember.

This language of love is a Universal signal, broadcast by our Beloved home Gaia, amplified by the hearts and souls of every awakening being in their expression of essence. To listen, to tune in to this signal begins from Within, from INSIDE, to adjust our inside experience to experience something different on the outside.

More and more souls are hearing the language of love, responding to the signals, being awoken by the higher frequency broadcasts. Becoming in resonance with these love frequencies pushes up ALL that needs responding to from inside, ALL the places and aspects that need love and care and healing. Not all at once does this occur, as it is offered at a rate and pace that you bear as directed by your Higher Self and Ethereal and Star BEing aspects.

Yet, up it comes…..the oil pushed up by the water. This oil that was hidden or stuck can gush through at times in your 3D pain body and 4D Awakening Self can cause disruptions of sleeping cycles, eating patterns, physical illness. And especially emotional churning, as that which has been stuck in your emotional body loosens and flows. Many people are expressing this as their reality right now…intense emotions coming up that feel 'old' or from previous experiences that they thought they had healed beyond. Yet, the quality of the love water coming now from the Universe, the higher frequency of it, pushes up another layer of emotional oil to be felt and healed.

Life speaks to us of love…even in the oil and especially in the emotional reactions that are offering such a visceral sense of what needs your attention. Your pains, your difficulties, your feelings that aspects of you have about being lost or being disconnected or wanting to just 'give up and go home'…these are pushed up to receive the water of your love (first and foremost) and then receiving love with others in the forms of soul mates, soul friends, teachers and space holders, Ethereal Beings and Guides. MORE water of love to respond to the oil, over and over until the oil is washed out and the flow of life can move through your healing heart and soul.

SO much love to you during this experience of transitional and transformational times…

~

Being At The Saturation Point Of Love

Are you at your saturation point? This is the point at which love has saturated your heart and your soul enough that you tip over into a brand NEW life and experience of life. This kind of love is beyond lust and beyond duty. This love is risky and catalytic. This kind of love comes from the purity of a healing heart, from the liberating frequencies of a healing soul, from the groundedness of a healing body.

You have taken this love in from resources outside of yourself that you have drawn to you. You have dipped into the pool of THIS LOVE inside of your own heart by going within during your inner journeys. You have experienced THIS LOVE with Angels, Spirit Guides, Divine representatives, Star BEings. You have received THIS LOVE from others in relationships that are formed from resonant soul grounds of transaction. You have immersed yourself often in the waters of THIS LOVE in whatever forms you could find and draw to you.

Before the saturation point, what has previously NOT been from this love has still been able to be digested by you somehow. It has been familiar and comfortable to parts of you, your 3D Self, and allowed to still exist in your life. You can trust that it has needed to be there…..whatever it is….relationships, jobs, food choices, lifestyle choices, geography, etc. It has needed to be there until your heart saturation point is too high and then that which is lower in vibrational frequency can no longer be digested by you.

This indigestion phase, this time of feeling what no longer works and CAN no longer be in your life, can be difficult and, at times, painful. The parts of you that are attached can bring up protest and resistance and fear. You may feel like you want to 'go back' to how you used to be and maybe, in some ways, you do and for moments you 'fuse' to the lower frequencies. You become the lower frequencies again.

Yet, at the saturation point, you are now more motivated by love than you are by suffering. You want more love. You feel if love is in the ground of each person you relate with and if they are saturated too, then love can flow. Often, a person from your 'old' life wants you to stay as you were. You may make the difficult choice of needing space from them while you still love them, while your higher selves can still have a transaction ground together. Taking space is a mercy for them too as your tugging on them in the past to 'get it' or 'come along' relaxes and they can arise and claim their sovereign path.

At the saturation point, you can no longer 'shrink to fit' any of the relationships in your life, the roles in your life, the duties in your life, the energies or frequencies that are NOT you in your soul and heart essence. Shrinking offers you only crumbs when you want MORE of the full meal that love offers.

The saturation point invites you to make CHANGES….changes in your exterior world to support the love that you feel inside and want more of. It invites you to be bold, to JUMP IN, to Let Go and Let GOD…..what you may be clinging to out of security becomes an anchor and you release it to free up your energy.

If you are still filling up, needing more love to get there to the saturation point and be there…..find this love, let this love in INside of yourself, draw the relationships and community and people who will transact this love with you. Fill up until you reach the saturation point for which love overcomes fear and re-union with your essence is YOU more and more.

The saturation point invites you into the unknown, trusting that whatever comes next is from love. Daring to risk, daring to share, daring to be vulnerable, daring to be uncomfortable, and daring to love. Are you at or close to the saturation point? If you are, the moment to be and claim and feel Love is NOW.

~

PURE Love Wants You AS You

PURE love wants to fill the vacancies made by your awakening, your claiming, your ascending, your arising into your essence.

PURE love wants to claim the spaces created by your letting go of what didn't resonate or feel like the NEW you or reflect your soul.

PURE love wants to create bonds from the places left from the heart chord binds that you so courageously are cutting, the karmic binds that you are so boldly feeling and letting go.

PURE love wants to act as a balm to the healing wounds that you so tenderly love, allowing healing at the root cause and therefore release of the causal energy.

PURE love wants to remind you of your birthright to experience it as it is YOUR essence and your expression as a fractal from Divine Source.

PURE love wants to invite you into a world of magical experience of multidimensional experience, arising wonder and goodness, both inside and outside.

PURE love wants to come to you in the form of nourishing relationships with souls who are resonant, who support you, who share their soul gifts with you and you with them, who form a commUNITY through mutual embracement and values resonance.

PURE love wants to embrace you in the form of Archangels, Angels, Spirit Guides, Ascended Teachers, Unicorns, Dragons, Elementals, star family, to bring in the higher dimensional frequencies of your soul and provide a container for your arising.

PURE love wants you AS you, in your uniqueness, your sensitivity, your emotionality, your soul bigness, your essence, your arising, and your becoming…..

~

The Inner Space Program: Mission To Infinite Love!

Love wants to open up the universes of unexplored territories that exist inside of you…every time you go within, you'll discover MORE. And you feel more and more your essence AS Infinite Love. The most interesting exploratory space program is the inner space one!

When led by your curiosity and self love, infinite journeys await you as you experience the universes that exist inside of your soul and heart.

Going Within, taking the space, being alone, closing the eyes, discovering the music that opens your heart and soul out (or not). Be in bed, be in nature, be on the couch, be on the floor….just BE. Connect with Guides to help you navigate the sometimes foreign terrain.

Find resources to serve your explorations, open you up, and help you negotiate with the parts of you that are afraid or anxious.

Feel with your heart, let your tears flow, let your smiles come, talk out loud, emit some tones, move your body around, invite pure energy in.

Your soul knows what to do and your Higher Self is waiting to help. Your inner space program is waiting for you, sign up now!

~

Holding Space For The Blocks To PURE Love To Heal

The Universal flow and glow of life inviting you to let go into it….to ride the waves of PURE love that are surrounding you at all times. Feeling, being with, holding space for the blocks and the layers that act as a 'suit' around your field to resist and repel these love frequencies at times and in certain ways. These blocks and layers have energy, they have story, they have feelings. They can be directly connected with and embraced with love and curiosity. They fall away and dissolve and heal AND integrate into the WHOLE you, Higher Self you, fractal of Divine Source YOU.

Direct connection with these defenses, these protections and projections, these wounds and bruises is what allows them to move and heal. These karmic playouts and results of so much energy building up without release inside of your soul and your soul group in all its expressions happening NOW as there are no past lives in that way…..These karmic playouts and unhealed emotional frequencies cycle over and over and build up in intensity influencing you in so many ways that the conscious mind cannot track yet the heart and soul feel the impact of them.

The symptoms of these playouts show up in so many ways – in dysfunctional and sticky relationships, in ill physical health, in emotional reactivity, in inability to manifest, in blocking of PURE love, in repeated patterns of suffering, in unworthiness, in shame, in anxiety, in SO MUCH suffering.

Yet, in your tears are the answers for the healing as to feel them, to allow them, to be with flow from your heart and your soul is a washing away and a release of the built up energies. Your tears are the language of your heart that are telling you where your love is needed next. Your tears are the language of your soul sharing the story of your bigness and what you are missing in connecting with it and ALSO releasing reunion grief when the remembering and reconnection HAPPENS in response to your tears.

The light and the PURE love from the Divine, from Angels, from star family, from soul family connections….this love is water for your growing Sacred Human Self, your becoming embodied 5D Self, who holds the space for this exploration into the shadow, who allows the tears to flow, who offers a possibility end to the suffering cycles.

Make room and space for this transitional pain to move through, for the tears to offer you the story of your heart and soul, and love will be the response every time.

~

Love Invites You In

Love invites you in, to hold, to feel, to BE. It takes the form of your beloved. Your beloved self, your beloved mate, your beloved friends, your beloved children, your beloved family, your beloved Guides…..your BE-LOVED by your love and you by theirs.

Love invites you to remember, to embrace, to awaken. It takes the form of your returning. The return to Divine Source, Divine Love, Divine Mother, Divine Father, Divine No-Thing-Ness, Divine Light, Divine Warmth, Divine Embrace.

Love invites you to change, to risk, to lead, to serve. It takes the form of your desires. The desires of your heart and your soul that move into a flow that releases the stuck places…. the desires that bring a spark to your heart and to your life.

Love invites you to become and to arise. It takes the form of your essence as Infinite Love expressing as a Sacred Human ascending, growing, learning, shifting always and in ALL WAYS.

~

What We Experience As Given by Love For Love With Love

I was guided to higher frequencies, beyond five senses, today where all is made of white filaments with rainbow auras. I was just overcome by the brightness and beauty of it all, especially Human BEings in their essence as Infinite Love, too bright to even look in the eyes.

Hours (no time really) I floated here, dimensional traveling, Angels and Guides surrounding me…..and yet also feeling the core of my heart beating strong even as my body became lighter and lighter. Feels like it was an energetic boost to allow more overflow to others, more love, stillness, and less reactivity. What a gift!

My body reacted initially with some pain last night as a portal of some sort opened, a vortex, and yet it is moving now...birth pains held with Infinite Love and seemed to serve a purpose. Shook off some negative entities that had attached along the way, like being dipped in bright love and all the dark falling off.

I would not be able to let this in without also going to the tears (and there were those too), saying goodbye and letting go to what I thought was my purpose and my place to serve it, allowing the part of me that was so invested to feel sad....tears even with a smile as I realized that it is all given in Love held by Love for Love....

Much Love is moving from my heart to those who read these words, may you feel the energy of it and let it in whatever way you feel to...

You are much bigger and brighter than you can even imagine!

~

Moment By Moment Choosing Love

Moment by moment....this is the way for ascension, for awakening, for remembering. In the moment feeling what is raising your frequency, feeling what is not. Choosing to continue, choosing to stop. This is the way, choosing your consciousness. Awareness is the choice of what you are putting your energy into, what you are participating in and if you want to continue or not. Awareness is realizing the impact of the energy you have taken in, the 3D conditioning you have chosen, the conditioning you have experienced by often NOT being aware.

Moment by moment....the dedication of this practice is what brings the transcendent experiences, the sublime, the refined, the blissful, the reunions with aspects of your Multidimensional Selves. The embodiment of your Higher Self comes from this dedication, this focus, this willingness and openness to shift, to change, to rebel at times, to go against the grain. It BECOMES your life as it feels more ALIVE than anything else and so this choice of dedication becomes easier and more natural.

Moment by moment….you experience what makes it worth it, you experience more and more love. The experience of choosing consciously love in every moment, to rise up into love again if you fall into fear. Even loving the fear that still lives inside. Loving the conditioning, the many, many layers of it, like cobwebs over you, as you untangle and loving THAT too. Love makes the HARD worth it and holds the feelings of being lost, being estranged, being isolated, being different. Love makes the HARD worth it when you are being vigilant when others are not, being conscious when others are not, being aware when others are not, being love when others are not.

Moment by moment…..claiming of your mission, your purpose, the REASON you came here and left the higher frequencies behind voluntarily. Bringing in those higher dimensions, connecting with star family frequencies, Angelic realms, Divine source, going within to bring them in reminds you of your purpose. Going within reminds you that you ARE them. Your SOUL's purpose is in the moment claiming, over and over, reflected in the choices that you make (or don't make), reflected in the relationships that you put energy into to reflect to you what you need to see of you. In the moment claiming and remembering what you came here to BE and DO. Re-energizing with that reminder and bigger picture in the moment.

Moment by moment…..the invitation is choosing your soul, choosing the bigger picture, choosing the higher energy, choosing the self loving, choosing the resonant ground, choosing to serve love above all else, choosing to hold space for your feelings, choosing to go within, choosing to claim your soul purpose. In every moment, the invitation is choosing LOVE.

~

Love Finding Its Way AS YOU

Love opens up vistas of possibilities in every moment, each new curve and turn offering the Infinite Unknown....

The stumbling, crawling, fighting and purging...it is WORTH it as love's embrace helps you find your way to your inner home.

The filters gone, the blinders off, the light shone on the dark...you can feel the miracle in the Now.

Completions and endings bring new beginnings, letting go allowing for more letting in....

This enlovenment, enlightenment, awakening of SELF, claiming of YOU creates a life filled with magical inner landscapes....

This ascending, growing, changing creates a life filled with not what you have known, but what you are BECOMING, more and more, as love finds its way AS YOU....

I love you...keep going! Keep being! Keep loving!
Jelelle ~